D1268156

The Order
of the Synoptics

Why Three Synoptic Gospels?

"Fundamental changes in scholarship
are the result of anomalies or tensions
between a prevailing paradigm and empirical observations."[1]

"The discoveries of historical criticism are too often
simply a commentary on a misconception."[2]

---

[1]Douglas Sturm, "The Learned Society and Scholarly Research," *Bulletin of the Council on the Study of Religion* 12:2 (April 1981): 1.

[2]Étienne Gilson, *Héloise and Abelard* (London, 1953) 153.

BERNARD ORCHARD
HAROLD RILEY

The Order
of the Synoptics

Why Three Synoptic Gospels?

PEETERS

MERCER

ISBN 0-86554-222-8

The Order of the Synoptics
Copyright © 1987
Mercer University Press, Macon, Georgia 31207
All rights reserved
Printed in the United States of America

Library of Congress Cataloging-in-Publication Data
Orchard, J. Bernard, 1910–
The order of the Synoptics

    Bibliography: p. 281
    Includes indexes.
    1. Bible, N.T. Gospels—Criticism, interpretation, etc.
2. Synoptic problem. I. Riley, Harold. II. Title.
BS2555.2.O74   1987   226'.066   87-5593
ISBN 0-86554-222-8

Contents

Part Two
THE HISTORICAL TRADITION
Bernard Orchard

Part Three
HOW THE SYNOPTIC GOSPELS
CAME INTO EXISTENCE
(A tentative reconstruction of the history of their composition
by means of a synthesis of the evidence drawn from parts one and two)
Bernard Orchard

Foreword

This study is the first attempt to coordinate, within the compass of a single volume, the three separate lines of argument necessary to solve the Synoptic Problem, namely the historical and patristic evidence, the internal critical evidence for mutual literary dependence, and the "scenario" necessary to show how the tensions between the first and the second lines of argument can be satisfactorily resolved. It is the work of two scholar priests, Harold Riley, an Anglican, and Bernard Orchard, a Benedictine monk, and forms a further link in a series of studies of the Synoptic Problem, initiated by John Chapman, Christopher Butler, and later developed by William R. Farmer, David L. Dungan H.-H. Stoldt, T. R. W. Longstaff, and many others who have over the past fifty years helped to expose the weaknesses of the various Markan-Priority hypotheses, and have now built up a strong case for the contrary hypothesis known as the Two-Gospel Hypothesis, a recent development of the old Griesbach Hypothesis.

This volume is the third and final element of a trilogy on the Synoptic Problem; the first volume, *Matthew, Luke and Mark* (Koinonia Press) was published by Orchard in 1976 and restated the argument for Luke's dependence on Matthew and prepared the way for his second volume, *A Synopsis of the Four Gospels in Greek* (T. & T. Clark, 1983), which offers a visual presentation of the literary dependence of Luke on Matthew and of Mark on both Matthew and Luke. The present work completes the series and the case for the Two-Gospel Hypothesis, and consists of three parts: part one ("The Internal Evidence") is the work of Riley, while part two ("The External Evidence") and part three ("How the Gospels Came into Existence") are by Dom Bernard.

An adequate solution demands adequate reasons not only for the fact that Mark's pericopes are almost always longer and fuller than Matthew's or Luke's, not only for Mark's "zigzagging" between Matthew and Luke, not only for the virtual unanimity of the patristic evidence in favor of the priority of Matthew, but also to explain why there are *just three* Synoptic Gospels, no fewer and no more. And since all theories of Markan Priority rely either on hypothetical sources or questionable conjectures, which all have the effect of dating the gospels later than the Apostolic Age, there is now warrant for a study that places them a generation earlier, and thus firmly in the historical context of that very age.

Part one does not attempt to deal with the usual flaws in the argument for Markan Priority, for these have been adequately dealt with by other writers. Instead, Riley works out an original argument in which he shows how the thematic order of Matthew cannot be derived from Mark, nor can that of Luke; and he is then able to show that Mark is in fact derived mostly from our Matthew and our Luke. His section concludes with a refutation of G. M. Styler's "key-passages" in favor of Markan Priority.

In part two the historical testimonies are approached scientifically, that is to say, in chronological order according to the dates of the documents in which the evidence has come down to us. Thus the vital Papias testimony is dealt with only when the discussion reaches the fourth century witnesses. In the course of this part the following points become clear: (1) that the evidence for the apostolic origin of the Gospels is in reality both consistent and cogent, despite the two or three minor discrepancies, for which adequate explanations are available; (2) that the late appearance (in mid-second century) of the first direct written attestation of the authorship of the Gospels is in itself no argument for disregarding its value; and (3) that the "John the Presbyter" legend is a fabrication of Eusebius on the basis of a single comment of Dionysius of Alexandria. Thus the conclusions of part two support those of part one.

Part three, however, will probably be the principal object of critical concern, and understandably, in view of the revolutionary yet conservative nature of the thesis proposed. For here there is a great problem, since scholarly integrity requires that a serious effort be made to see if the data of the patristic tradition, now shown to be compatible with the critical evidence, actually slot into the historical development of the Primitive Church as portrayed in the Acts of the Apostles. In fact they do, and part three shows that it makes excellent sense, historically speaking, for our Greek Matthew to be the first gospel and for our Luke to be the second, with Mark chronologically in the third place. In fact, if Acts was written and completed before Paul's release from his Roman confinement, it makes good sense to see Matthew as composed for the primitive Jewish Christian Church described in Acts 1-12, and Luke to have been written for Paul's converts of Acts 13-28. In other words, each Gospel reflects a well-defined stage in the development of the Church, seen against the background of the struggle between the Circumcision and the Non-Circumcision parties, Peter and Paul being the two key figures.

This hypothesis faces two practical obstacles, however, namely, (1) lack of evidence for a date for Matthew before A.D. 50, and (2) the problem of the date and importance of Galatians in the Primitive Church's development. The former objection is in part met by the recognition of Paul's use of the Greek text of Matthew in 1 and 2 Thessalonians in A.D. 51-52 (cf. Orchard, "Thessalonians and the Synoptic Gospels," *Biblica,* 1938). The latter objection is met by F. F. Bruce (see his *Commentary on Galatians,* in loc.) who shows that the seeming conflict between the two visits of Paul to Jerusalem mentioned in Galatians and the three visits mentioned in Acts can be satisfactorily resolved; and this enables us to see the "Conference between the 'Three Pillars' and Paul" in its proper perspective, and to perceive its lasting importance for the church. These obstacles removed, it becomes clear that the role of the Gospel of Mark, the interpreter of Peter, is to act as a bridge between the parallel traditions represented respectively by the Gospels of Matthew and Luke. Its success in doing so helps to explain why it disappeared from view for a long time, as it had fulfilled its immediate purpose.

We are happy to acknowledge that the ground for the reception of this particular version of the Two-Gospel Hypothesis has been prepared over the past ten years by a whole series of international conferences (notably by the 1984 Jerusalem Gospel Symposium), which have succeeded in regaining scholarly respectability for theories that reject the priority of Mark and restore it to Matthew.

Ealing Abbey, London   *J. B. Orchard*
August 1986   *H. Riley*

Abbreviations

Works Quoted, or Consulted

BAG   Bauer-Arndt-Gingrich, *A Greek-English Lexicon of the New Testament* (Chicago, 1957)

BJRL   *Bulletin of the John Rylands University Library of Manchester*

CBQ   *Catholic Biblical Quarterly*

CCHS   *A Catholic Commentary on Holy Scripture* (Edinburgh, 1953)

CSCO   *Corpus scriptorum christianorum orientalium*

CSEL   *Corpus scriptorum ecclesiasticorum latinorum*

DB   *Dictionary of the Bible,* ed. John L. McKenzie (London, 1968)

DBS   *Dictionnaire de la Bible, Supplément*

DTC   *Dictionnaire de théologie catholique*

FP   *Florilegium patristicum,* Monumenta aevi apostolici I, ed. G. Rauschen (Bonn, 1904)

GCS   Griechischen-christlichen Schriftstellern des ersten Jahrhunderte

HTR   *Harvard Theological Review*

JBC   *Jerome Biblical Commentary* (London, 1968)

JBL   *Journal of Biblical Literature*

JETS   *Journal of the Evangelical Theological Society*

JRS   *Journal of Roman Studies*

JSNT   *Journal for the Study of the New Testament,* Sheffield

JTS   *Journal of Theological Studies*

MG   Moulton & Geden, *Concordance to the Greek Testament* (Edinburgh, [5]1978)

MLM   *Matthew, Luke, and Mark,* J. B. Orchard (Koinonia Press, 1976)

NCCHS   *A New Catholic Commentary on Holy Scripture* (London, 1969)

NTS   *New Testament Studies*

ODCC   *Oxford Dictionary of the Christian Church* (Oxford, [2]1974)

OSFGG   *A Synopsis of the Four Gospels in Greek,* J. B. Orchard (Edinburgh, 1983)

PCB   *Peake's Commentary on the Bible* (London, 1962)

PG   *Patrologia Graeca,* ed. J. P. Migne, 162 volumes (1857–1866)

PGL   *A Patristic Greek Lexicon,* G. W. H. Lampe (Oxford, 1961)

PL   *Patrologia Latina,* ed. J. P. Migne, 221 volumes (1844–1864)

Rev Ben *Revue bénédictine*
Rev Bib *Revue Biblique*
  SPAW   Sitzungsberichte der preussichen Akademie der Wissenschaften
         (Berlin, 1882-1921)
ThStud   *Theologische Studien und Kritiken*
   TRE   *Theologische Realenzyklopädie* (Berlin, 1976–)
    TS   *Theological Studies*
    TU   Texte und Untersuchungen zur Geschichte der altchristlichen Literatur
         (Leipzig, 1883–)
   WDB   *Westminster Dictionary of the Bible,* ed. H. S. Gehman
         (Philadelphia, 1976)

Other Abbreviations

  2DH   Two-Document Hypothesis
   EH   Eusebius's *Ecclesiastical History*
  EHS   *Einheitsübersetzung der Heiligen Schrift: Das Neue Testament*
        (Stuttgart, 1979)
   ET   English translation
   GH   Griesbach Hypothesis
  2GH   Two-Gospel Hypothesis
  ICC   International Critical Commentary
  NEB   New English Bible
  UBS   United Bible Societies

Part One
INTERNAL EVIDENCE
Harold Riley

The Significance of Order

1. The Problem of the Order of the Gospels

Which was the first of the Synoptic Gospels to be written? The external evidence is all in favor of its being St. Matthew's, but is this confirmed by the internal evidence? That it is not has been almost universally agreed through many years; that in fact Mark was the earliest Gospel, and indeed was used by Matthew and Luke, is still the most common view of biblical critics. It has been so now for a long time. When Sir John Hawkins published his classic book *Horae Synopticae,* he could write of Mark's priority as "a practically certain result of modern study of the 'Synoptic Problem.' "[1] At a later stage, E. Trocmé could say of the Griesbach Hypothesis (that Mark used Matthew and Luke) that "as a theory, it is not worth confuting."[2] Griesbach was defended however, by W. R. Farmer in *The Synoptic Problem* published in 1964, since when it cannot be so easily brushed aside. So, for example, in 1976 J. A. T. Robinson noted, "The consensus frozen by the success of 'the fundamental solution' propounded by B. H. Streeter has begun to show signs of cracking. Though it is still the dominant hypothesis, incapsulated in the textbooks, its conclusions can no longer be taken for granted as among the 'assured results' of biblical criticism."[3] It is because it is not only so incapsulated in textbooks,[4] but is also taken for granted in many studies of New Testament theology, that it is important that it should be critically examined, and the following chapters are a contribution to that examination.

To come to a conclusion about the relationship of the three Synoptics to one another, a major consideration must be that of the relative order of the

---

[1] *Horae Synopticae,* 2nd ed. (Oxford, 1909) 115.

[2] E. Trocmé, *Formation of the Gospel according to Mark* (ET: London, 1963) 10.

[3] J. A. T. Robinson, *Redating the New Testament* (London, 1976) 93.

[4] Cf. D. E. Nineham, *Saint Mark* (Penguin Books, 1963): "As most readers will know, when St. Matthew and St. Luke were writing they both had copies of Mark in front of them" (11).

contents of the Gospels of Matthew and Luke with that of Mark, and it is
this with which we shall be principally concerned here. It will therefore be
convenient first of all to set out a table of the order of Mark, with those
parallel passages in Matthew and Luke which are in the same sequence.
For the sake of simplicity, pericopes are grouped together under a common
title when there is a group in which all the members continue in the same
order in Mark and in one or other of the parallels.

2. The Order of Mark and Its Parallels

	MT	MK	LK
The Baptist and Jesus' Baptism	3:1-17	1:1-11	3:1-22
Temptation	4:1-11	1:12-13	4:1-13
Into Galilee	4:12-17	1:14-15	4:14-15
Call of Four Disciples	4:18-22	1:16-20	
Events at Capernaum		1:21-38	4:31-43
A preaching tour	4:23	1:39	4:44
The Leper		1:40-45	5:12-16
Five Occasions of Controversy		2:1-3:6	5:17-6:11
Healing of Multitudes	4:24-25	3:7-12	(6:17-19)
Calling of the Twelve		3:13-19	(6:12-16)
Sermon on the Mount (Matthew)	5:1-7:27		
Sermon on the Plain (Luke)			6:20-49
Matthew's narrative continued	7:28-8:34		
Luke's Narrative continued			7:1-17
The Apostolic Commission (Matthew)	9:35-10:42		
Matthew's narrative continued	11:1-12:21		
Luke's narrative continued			7:18-8:3
"He is beside himself"		3:20-21	
On Collusion with Satan	12:22-30	3:22-27	
Sin against the Holy Spirit	12:31-37	3:28-30	
Jesus' True Kindred	12:46-50	3:31-35	
The Parable Collection			
Parable of the Sower and comments	13:1-23	4:1-20	8:4-15
Lamp under Bushel/Bed		4:21-25	8:16-18
Parable of Seed Growing Secretly		4:26-29	
Parable of Mustard Seed	13:31-32	4:30-32	
Use of parables	13:34-35	4:33-34	
The Parable Collection continued (Matthew)	13:36-52		
Across the Sea and back		4:35-5:43	8:22-56
Jesus Rejected at Nazareth	13:53-58	6:1-6a	
Commissioning the Twelve		6:6b-13	9:1-6
Opinions concerning Jesus	14:1-2	6:14-16	9:7-9
Death of the Baptist	14:3-12	6:17-29	
Return of the Apostles		6:30-31	9:10a

The Five Thousand	14:13-21	6:32-44	9:10b-17
Walking on the Water, and Healings	14:22-36	6:45-56	
Defilement, Traditional and Real	15:1-20	7:1-23	
Syro-Phoenician (Canaanite) Woman	15:21-28	7:21-30	
The Deaf-Mute (Matt. Healings)	(15:29-31)	7:31-37	
The Four Thousand	15:32-39	8:1-10	
Pharisees: Sign and Leaven	16:1-12	8:11-21	
The Blind Man		8:22-26	
Peter's Confession	16:13-20	8:27-30	9:18-21
First Prediction of the Passion	16:21-23	8:31-33	9:22
"If any man will come after me"	16:24-28	8:34-9:1	9:23-27
The Transfiguration	17:1-9	9:2-10	9:28-36
The Coming of Elijah	17:10-13	9:11-13	
The Epileptic Boy	17:14-21	9:14-29	9:37-43a
Second Prediction of the Passion	17:22-23	9:30-32	9:43b-45
True Greatness	18:1-5	9:33-37	9:46-48
The Strange Exorcist		9:38-41	9:49-50
Warnings against Temptation	18:6-9	9:42-50	
Discourse on True Greatness (continued)	18:10-35		
Departure in Judea	19:1-2	10:1-2	9:51
Luke's Central Section			9:52-18:14
On Divorce and Adultery	19:3-12	10:2-12	
Jesus blesses the Children	19:13-15	19:13-16	18:15-17
On Riches and Discipleship	19:16-29	10:17-31	18:18-30
Third Prediction of the Passion	20:17-19	10:32-34	18:31-34
The Sons of Zebedee	20:20-28	10:35-45	
The Blind Bartimaeus	20:29-34	10:46-52	18:35-43
The Triumphal Entry	21:1-9	11:1-10	18:28-40
Jesus in Jerusalem	21:10-11	11:11	
Cursing of the Fig Tree	21:18-19a	11:12-14	
Cleansing of the Temple		11:15-17	19:45-46
Conspiracy against Jesus		11:18-19	19:47-48
The Fig Tree Withered	21:19b-22	11:20-26	
The Question about Authority	21:23-27	11:27-33	20:1-8
Parable of the Wicked Husbandmen	21:33-46	12:1-12	20:9-19
Questions on Tribute and Resurrection	22:13-33	12:13-27	20:20-40
The Great Commandment	22:34-40	12:28-34	
Question about David's Son	22:41-46	12:35-37a	20:41-44
Woes to Scribes and Pharisees	23:1-36	12:37b-40	20:45-47
The Widow's Mite		12:41-44	21:1-4
The Eschatological Discourse			
Prediction about the Temple etc.	24:1-22	13:1-20	21:5-24
False Christs and False Prophets	24:23-28	13:21-23	
The Coming of the Son of Man	24:29-36	13:24-32	21:25-33
Conclusion: "Take Heed, Watch"		13:33-37	

Discourse continued (Matt.)	24:37-25:46		21:34-36
Conclusion (Luke)			21:37-38
Jesus' Death Predicted	26:1-5	14:1-2	22:1-2
Anointing at Bethany	26:6-13	14:3-9	
Betrayal by Judas	26:14-16	14:10-11	22:3-6
Preparation for the Passover	26:17-20	14:12-17	22:7-14
Jesus Foretells his Betrayal	26:21-25	14:18-21	
The Last Supper	26:26-35	14:22-31	22:15-34
Gethsemane	26:36-56	14:32-50	22:39-53
The Young Man who Fled		14:51-52	
Jesus before the Sanhedrin	26:57-68	14:53-65	22:54-55
Peter's Denials	26:69-75	14:66-72	22:56-62
Jesus Delivered to Pilate	27:1-2	15:1	23:1
Trial before Pilate	27:11-14	15:2-5	23:2-5
Jesus Condemned to Death	27:15-26	15:6-15	23:17-25
Jesus Mocked by Soldiers	27:27-31a	15:16-20a	
The Road to Golgotha	27:31b-32	15:20b-21	23:26-32
Crucifixion	27:33-43	15:22-32a	23:33-38
The Two Thieves	27:44	15:32b	23:39-43
Death of Jesus	27:45-54	15:33-39	23:44-48
Witnesses to the Crucifixion	27:55-56	15:40-41	23:49
Burial of Jesus	27:57-61	15:42-47	23:50-56
Women at the Tomb	28:1-8	16:1-8	24:1-9
"The Longer Ending" (disputed)		16:9-20	

There is clearly a relationship between the order of Mark and of the other Synoptics that demands explanation. Was the order of Mark built up from that of the others, or is the order of Matthew and Luke derived from that of Mark? The answer to this question is vital for a proper understanding of the Gospels.

3. The Rationale of Order If Mark Is First

If Matthew and Luke are dependent on Mark, how did their authors proceed? Both followed the same sequence as Mark as far as Mk 1:15, and Matthew, by including the Call of Four Disciples, as far as Mk 1:20. But at this point, Matthew ceases to continue in Mark's order, and Luke takes over from Mk 1:21 to 3:19. That brings Luke to the same point as that at which Matthew and Mark parted company, the Sermon on the Mount (or "on the Plain") which they insert into Mark's text. But then the reverse process takes place: Luke no longer follows Mark's order, but Matthew begins to do so, with the group of episodes from Mk 3:22-35, until at the Parable of the Sower all three Synoptists come together (in the Huck and Aland synopses). Then Matthew gives way to Luke at Mk 4:21-25, but when they have both omitted the Parable of the Seed Growing Secretly (Mk 4:26-29), it is Matthew who is again parallel to Mark to Mk 4:34. Mark's group of parables is complete, but Matthew continues with other parabolic material to complete the second of his formal discourses.

Mark now continues with a group of stories about Jesus crossing the Sea of Galilee and returning (Stilling the Storm, the Gerasene Demoniac, and Jairus's Daughter, 4:35-5:43), but now it is Luke that follows Mark's sequence, before Matthew can continue with the Rejection at Nazareth (Mk 6:1-6a; Mt 13:53-58); then Luke, but not Matthew, has the Commissioning of the Twelve, before all come together for Mk 6:14-16 and parallels, with the reference to the Baptist, after which Mark and Matthew record the Baptist's Death; but it is Luke that with Mark relates the Return of the Apostles, before all three are together again with the story of the Feeding of the Five Thousand.

It is at this point that Luke's "Great Omission" occurs, and Matthew and Mark are in parallel, except that Mark has one of his two miracles peculiar to himself, where Matthew has a more general statement of healings (Mk 7:31-37; Mt 15:29-31), and Mark also adds the second of his two miracles, the Healing of the Blind Man (8:22-26). Then all three Synoptics come together with Peter's Confession, and continue from Mk 8:27 to 9:50, except that Luke omits Mk 9:11-13 and 9:42-50, and Matthew omits Mk 9:38-41.

So we come to a point where again Matthew continues with the rest of one of his formal discourses, and Luke parts company with Mark to insert his long central section of teaching. It is after that that we enter the period of approach to Jerusalem, and to the story of the Passion. From this point on, the three Synoptists are in parallel, except that sometimes Matthew, and sometimes Luke, has omitted items of Mark's narrative. Except for 14:51-52, they never omit the same one. The disputed "Longer Ending" of Mark (16:9-20) raises other questions, and need not be considered here.

There is one outstanding fact that emerges here: at every point where Matthew ceases to follow Mark's order, whether for a short or longer period, Luke continues in it; and wherever Luke ceases to follow Mark's order, Matthew in his turn continues in it. There is surely an inescapable conclusion to be drawn from this. If Matthew and Luke were dependent on Mark for the order of events, they must have agreed together that they would do this. Without constant collaboration, the result would be quite impossible. That they followed such a course is incredible, and therefore the conclusion cannot be avoided that the hypothesis that they were dependent on Mark cannot be sustained. No one can justifiably maintain the hypothesis of Markan priority as an "assured result of modern criticism" without producing a convincing, or at least plausible, explanation of the facts of order; it has yet to be produced. The alternative is that Mark made use of both Matthew and Luke, with apparently a greater dependence on the former.[5] If so, how did he proceed?

4. The Rationale of Order on the Two-Gospel Hypothesis

If Mark made use of both of the other Synoptics, he began with a précis of material found in both (Mt 3:1-4:11; Lk 3:1-4:13), and continued in parallel with both, with Jesus going into Galilee, and still with Matthew for the Call of Four Disciples (Mk 1:16-20; Mt 4:18-22). At this point, Matthew prepares, with a summary statement about preaching and healing, for the inclusion of the Sermon on the Mount, which, with a great deal of other teaching material, Mark does not purpose to include. It is a point at which he has to decide whether he prefers the way in which Luke has described Jesus' activities at greater length before coming to his version of the great Sermon. It is Luke's order for which Mark opts; so he follows Luke, from 1:21-3:19 (= Lk 4:31-6:19), with the solitary excision of Luke's Call of Peter (Lk 5:1-11) already covered by the inclusion of Matthew's Call of Four Disciples; and with the slight inversion of Luke's last two pericopes (that is, a summary, and the Appointment of the Twelve, Lk 6:12-19 = Mk 3:7-19) which are Luke's own preparation for the inclusion of the Sermon. That Mark is aware of the inclusion of the Sermon in both Matthew and Luke is suggested by his recording the names of the Twelve in 3:13-19 (as Luke has them before the Sermon), and by the similarity of his wording in 3:13, ἀναβαίνει εἰς τὸ ὄρος, to Matthew's ἀνέβη εἰς τὸ ὄρος, closer than Luke's ἐξελθεῖν αὐτὸν εἰς τὸ ὄρος. .

Having departed from Matthew's order, what then is Mark to do next?[6] The last episodes he has copied from Luke are those of the Plucking of Grain on the Sabbath and the Man with the Withered Hand, which have a dif-

---

[5]When J. J. Griesbach in his *Commentatio* (1789, 1790), and more recently W. R. Farmer in *The Synoptic Problem* (1964), argued for the dependence of Mark on Matthew and Luke, this was not only from the evidence of relative order; but this is a fundamental question, with which the present study is primarily concerned. At the end of the last century, F. J. Bleek singled out "in particular, the selection, order and connection of the various sections" as a matter for special consideration (*Einleitung in das N.T.*, 1869). Griesbach's *Commentatio* is reprinted, and also translated into English, in B. Orchard and T. R. Longstaff, *J. J. Griesbach: Synoptic and Text-critical Studies, 1776-1976* (Cambridge, 1979).

[6]Griesbach, *Commentatio* section II: "The probable reason can generally be given why at a given time he [Mark] deserted Matthew (although he has set himself to use him as his chief guide) and attached himself to Luke, and why putting away Luke he once more attached himself to Matthew; and further, it can also be understood why, precisely in this passage of Matthew and not in another he again connects up the thread which he had previously broken by passing over to Luke" (translation as in Orchard and Longstaff, *J. J. Griesbach*, 108).

ferent place in Matthew (12:1-8, 9-14) where a summary similar to that followed from Lk 6:17-19 also follows (Mt 12:14-21). What Mark does is quite natural: he continues from where this material occurs in Matthew, with the accusations of Collusion with Satan (Mt 12:22), to which he prefixes a short addition of his own, "He is beside himself" (Mk 3:20-21). So he continues with Matthew into his chapter of parables (Mt 13).

With the parable of the Sower, and the added material about parables, Mark (4:1-20) finds himself again in parallel with Luke, and he continues with a further item from Luke (Lk 8:16-18), the reference to the lamp which no one puts under a bed (to which with a recollection of Mt 5:15 Mark adds for good measure "under a bushel"); a section from Luke which has also conveniently picked up a saying included in Mt 13:12. The parable of the Sower, which might perhaps be more appropriately called the Parable of the Seed Sown, is clearly regarded as valuable for Mark's general purpose, for he adds to it a parable, peculiar to his Gospel, of the Seed Growing Secretly (4:26-29), and one other parable from Matthew, also about Seed Sown—the parable of the Mustard Seed (Mt 13:31-32; Mk 4:30-32). Mark then closes his section about parables, by continuing to follow Matthew, with the pericope on the Use of Parables (Mt 13:34-35; Mk 4:33-34).

Like the Sermon, Matthew's Parable Discourse has brought Mark to the point where he has to decide how to continue. One obvious answer is to continue with Luke, and thereby to fill up some of the gaps from Matthew's narrative. The episodes of the Stilling of the Storm, the Gerasene Demoniac (Matthew's two Gadarene Demoniacs) and Jairus's Daughter therefore follow (Mk 4:35-5:43). Having made this insertion, Mark then resumes where he had left off at the end of Matthew's parabolic chapter, with the story of Jesus Rejected at Nazareth, presumably because, as is the case with the Call of the Fisherman, he makes Matthew rather than Luke his authority when they have different but allied stories. Then with the Commissioning of the Twelve, from Luke, he comes to the section on Opinions about Jesus, where Matthew and Luke come together again (Mt 14:1-2; Lk 9:7-9), and so can follow Matthew with the story of the Baptist's death, in a natural sequence. Having inserted this, Mark can return to Luke, to record the Return of the Apostles, and so come, with Matthew and Luke together, to the Feeding of the Five Thousand.

After the Feeding, Mark's course is simple: Luke has nothing to correspond to Mt 14:22-16:12, and Mark simply has to follow Matthew's order. His only variation is that when Matthew has a general statement of healing at 15:29-31, Mark replaces this with a particular Healing of a Deaf-Mute, and at the end of this material adds the Healing of a Blind Man. The two episodes are related in a remarkably similar style, which marks them out from all other healings in Mark or in the other Synoptics; we will look at them more closely at a later stage.

From the Confession of Peter (Mk 8:27-30), right through to 16:8, Mark follows Matthew closely, with occasional additions from Luke. There is one short addition by Mark, the episode of the Young Man Who Fled (14:51-52). Apart from that, Mark is simply following Matthew's order, with an eye on Luke.

The conclusion of all this seems inevitable; it seems unrealistic to regard this arrangement of the three Gospels as a result of Matthew and Luke's having used Mark; it is easy to see how Mark could have made use of Matthew and Luke. This conclusion is supported by the following consideration.

5. Markan Priority Possible Only on the Assumption That Matthew and Luke Had Worked Together

With a few exceptions, such as the Healing of the Deaf-Mute and the Blind Man at Bethsaida, and the Parable of the Seed Growing Secretly, the whole of Mark's Gospel has its parallels in Matthew or Luke or in both. The existence of the exceptions proves nothing (although on the hypothesis of Markan priority their omission by Matthew and Luke would call for explanation), for none of the Evangelists lived in a vacuum in which he could never have heard anything relevant to add to his main written sources. What is remarkable is that, as the table printed above shows, the whole of Mark's material (apart from these minor exceptions) is not only included in the other two Gospels, but that between them these preserve it completely in its own order. For, if Matthew and Luke used Mark, it is clear that each of them was willing to move Markan material into different contexts. So, for example, Matthew has moved Mk 1:40-45 (the healing of a leper) to a later point (giving it a chronological context—"When he came down from the mountain"—absent from Mark); and Luke has moved the material of Mk 3:22-30 to a much later point (Lk 11:15). The natural result of such willingness on the part of both to rearrange material would be to make it impossible to restore Mark's order by the mere process of alternating between parallels in Matthew and Luke. But the table shows that this is possible.[7] We therefore come to a conclusion similar to that already

---

[7]It is instructive to compare with the table in ch. 1 the treatment of the list of 29 passages drawn up by E. P. Sanders and discussed by F. Neirynck (*The Argument from Order and St. Luke's Transpositions*) in the appendix to his *Minor Agreements of Matthew and Luke against Mark* (Leuven, 1974) 391ff. They are divided into four categories: (a) seven passages in which "Matthew and Luke agree against Mark's order"; (b) five passages "dif-

reached: if Mark is prior to Matthew and Luke, they must have agreed that whenever the one was to desert Mark's order, the other must preserve it. It is hard to believe.

6. The Clue of the Roll Format

When we draw the inevitable conclusion that Mark used Matthew and Luke, there is an illuminating corollary. In choosing the episodes with which he continues his narrative, Mark never turns back; he always goes forward with the text either of Matthew or of Luke. Incidentally, this accounts for his omission of the stories of the Centurion's Servant and of the Messengers of the Baptist; to find them, he would have had to wind back one of his scrolls. The idea that if Mark used the other two gospels, his order could only have been achieved by a "scissors and paste" method is as false as it is anachronistic.[8] Mark did not have before him neatly printed books with numbered pages with which he could easily turn backwards and forwards for reference. With two scrolls of continuous text, one of Matthew and one of Luke, he unrolled them forward steadily to find the appropriate place in each. The effect of his procedure is to be seen in the closer dependence of narrative on Matthew when following Matthew's order, and on that of Luke when he is following Luke's.[9] An apparent exception is

---

ferently placed by each of the three evangelists''; (c) four passages where "either Matthew or Luke has a different order from that of Mark''; and (d) seventeen passages where "Matthew and Luke agree in the same common (Q) material at the same place relative to the Marcan outline.'' Neirynck comments "The author does not seem to have a high esteem for the argument from order dealing only with full pericopes. . . . The relative order of individual phrases is one thing, but no less important is the phenomenon of the order of pericopes (*Perikopenfolge, Ordo narrationum*).'' This is a valid comment, and it is noticeable that if we subtract from the lists the examples that are (in Neirynck's words) "replacements of a single sentence'' (or part of a sentence), and "inversions within the same section,'' which are not difficult to explain, all the other Markan passages are accounted for, in their relation to Matthew or Luke in the table in chapter 1 as falling in blocks of material that are in the same sequence. Since, as Neirynck says, we should study "the relative order of the gospel sections as a literary phenomenon,'' a comparison of these lists with that table confirms its significance, with its implications for the dependence of Mark on Matthew and Luke.

[8]Cf. E. P. Sanders: *The Tendencies of Synoptic Criticism* (Cambridge, 1969) 270: "If Mark had conflated Matthew and Luke, he would not have had to analyze their common matter and labor to include it. He would simply have copied first one and then the other, thereby automatically including what was common to them, excluding any chance that they would agree against him, and also creating agreements with each of them against the other.''

[9]We have no certain evidence that the prototypes of our four Gospels as they came from the pens of the respective Evangelists were written on papyrus or parchment rolls, which were, however, the invariable form in which all pre-Christian documents were written. E.

Mk 13:9-14, which follows Luke's order, while the text is closer to Matthew; but Mark is so familiar with Matthew's Gospel that it is not surprising that here he recalls some of Matthew's phrases.

7. Mark's Use of the Scrolls of Matthew and Luke

a. Mark 1:1–6:6a

If Mark unwound his scrolls in the way suggested by the order of his selections, it would seem that for his first five chapters and as far as 6:6a (after which point he only needed to turn aside from Luke for the insertion of Mk 6:45–8:26, and omit Luke's Central Section, Lk 9:51–18:14, to keep both scrolls open at the same point) he would be dependent on his familiarity, and consequently his memory, of the one not open before him for any contributions he might take from it. And of the two, he would seem to be more familiar with the wording of Matthew, and more influenced by it.[10] He has also some additions, or amplifications, of his own, which of course he could use if he had previous knowledge of the episodes narrated, though not all of them need such an explanation.

At two points in these early chapters there are narratives common to Mark and Luke without parallel in Matthew. At Mk 1:21, Lk 4:31, Jesus goes to the synagogue at Capernaum: the account of his teaching there in Mk 1:21-22 is identical in substance with that of Luke, apart from the addition of the words "not as the scribes" (1:22). The words are part of the wording of Mt 7:28-29, at the end of the Sermon on the Mount, which Mark has just passed over, and his whole phrase might either be due to reminiscence

---

G. Turner (*Greek Papyri: An Introduction,* paperback ed. rev. [Oxford, 1980] 10-11) quotes C. H. Roberts that no early text of the Greek New Testament known to us was written on the *recto* of a roll, viz., "When the Christian Bible (to use a slightly anachronistic term) first makes its appearance in history, the books of which it is composed are always written on papyrus and in codex form." But B. M. Metzger (*The Text of the New Testament,* 2nd ed. [Oxford, 1968] 5-8) has no doubt whatever that the original prototype of the Gospels and other books of the N.T. canon were inscribed on rolls, of no greater length than 31 or 32 feet. It seems that rolls prepared for commercial use were normally of this length, and Luke-Acts would in fact fit well onto two such rolls. It seems that the Christians began to transcribe the Gospels into codices, perhaps even in the first century A.D., for convenience of use in the Christian liturgy. See also below, part 2, ch. 3, §8.

[10]Cf. Griesbach, *Commentatio,* section III: "And in the same way, Mark too could surely have consulted the writings of Matthew and Luke without being obliged to copy out their narratives *word for word.* Undoubtedly, after reading any given pericope of Matthew or Luke or both, he set about writing and recorded what he has read in them, just as he retained it in his memory. . . . Sometimes, while he was writing, he may have taken perhaps a further look at the writings of Matthew and Luke; nevertheless, he need not have always thought that necessary" (p. 123 of translation as cited in n. 5 above).

or to his having just unrolled his copy of Matthew past the Sermon.

Mark, like Luke, passes on without interruption to the healing of the demoniac in the synagogue (1:21-28; Lk 4:35-37). The only significant change from Luke's narrative is the alteration of Luke's "when the demon had thrown him down in the midst" to Mark's demon "convulsing him and crying out with a loud voice," a phrase closely similar to Mk 9:26, in the story of the epileptic boy after the Transfiguration, and to the words of Mk 9:20, Lk 9:39, describing the symptoms of his epileptic before his healing. In both cases Mark's additions are likely to be his own interpretation of how a demon acted. He adds the same detail ("he was always crying out") to his narrative of the Gerasene demoniac, Mk 5:5.

The second section common to Mark and Luke only, is that of Jesus' departure from Capernaum (Mk 1:35-38; Lk 4:42-43). Mark is again substantially the same as Luke, except that he adds "and there he prayed" to the statement that Jesus "went to a lonely place," a sufficiently natural interpretation; and that for Luke's "crowds" (οἱ ὄχλοι), who were seeking Jesus, Mark specifies "Simon and those who were with him," though Luke's "crowds" reappear in the statement "everyone (πάντες) is searching for you." Mark may have independent information, but he may be merely making a deduction from the fact that Jesus had been staying at Simon's house, and, as he has said, with "Andrew, with James and John" (1:29).

Mark's preference for Matthew is to be seen in his choice of Matthew's narrative for episodes for which Luke provides different but comparable stories. These include the Rejection at Nazareth, the Call of Peter, and the Anointing of Jesus by a woman (Lk 4:16-30; 5:1-11; 7:36-50). But when Mark is following Luke's order and finds a fuller account of the same story as in Matthew, he acts differently.

An example of this is the story of the Healing of the Paralytic (Mk 2:1-12; Mt 9:1-8; Lk 5:17-26). Mark and Luke are in the same sequence, and they are much closer to each other than either is to Matthew. With one possible exception, all the details of Mark's account are included in Luke, but not in Matthew. Mark and Luke write in different styles: Luke, the man of letters, has his own methods; his word for the paralytic's bed is, as in Mt 9:2, 7, κλίνη, varied to κλινίδιον in 5:24 and to "that on which he lay" in 5:25; whereas Mark consistently uses κράβαττος; but no point that Mark makes is absent from Luke. For instance, Mark's "not even about the door" is implied in Luke's "finding no way to bring him in." The one apparent exception is the phrase "carried by four," but this is so natural and almost inevitable an understanding of how the pallet could be let down, that it is probably due to no more than Mark's picturing of the scene. Matthew's account is much shorter, and has provided some of Mark's wording, as when Jesus calls the paralytic "son" (τέκνον) as against Luke's "man," and in Mark's phrase "some of the scribes" in 2:6. But the whole account is that of Luke, and in the sequence of Luke, though with reminiscences of Matthew.

A second instance is that of the Gerasene Demoniac (Mk 5:1-20; Lk 8:26-39; Mt 8:28-34). Matthew's account is quite succinct; Mark's and Luke's narratives are more detailed. In spite of the confusion of the manuscripts, they seem to agree in the form "Gerasene" against Matthew's "Gadarene"; and they agree in speaking of one demoniac, as against Matthew's two. Mark has some details peculiar to himself. In 5:5 the words "night and day" and "bruising himself with stones" are peculiar to him; but the reference to tombs and hills (ὄρεσιν) may simply reflect Luke's reference to tombs (Lk 8:22) and "on the hill" (ἐν τῷ ὄρει) in Lk 8:32. For Luke's final comment that the man proclaimed what Jesus had done "throughout the whole city," Mark has "in the Decapolis." The outstanding item in Mark which is absent from Luke is the figure 2,000 for the number of the swine. It is an extraordinary, and surely unmanageable, number for a herd of swine; it would seem probable that Mark supposed this to be the number of men in a legion and so had inferred it from the demoniac's answer to his name. It has the marks of a secondary feature added to the story. One feature that betrays Mark's dependence on Luke is his statement in 5:15 that the man was clothed, when he has not previously recorded, as Luke 8:27 had, that "he had worn no clothes."

Again it appears that Mark, when following Luke's order, was primarily dependent on Luke, with some recollections of Matthew (e.g., 5:1, "to the other side"; Mt 8:29, "to the other side of the sea"). In a further instance Mark and Luke continue with the story of Jairus's daughter and the woman with the hemorrhage (Mk 5:21-43; Lk 8:40-56), told in rather greater length in Mark, but in both much more fully than in Mt 9:18-26. Only Mark and Luke have the name Jairus, and call him "a ruler of the synagogue." Most of Mark's details are found in Luke, though not always at the same points. Luke, for instance, records the age of Jairus's daughter at the beginning (8:42), Mark at the end (5:42); Mark's "the father and mother and those who were with him" (5:40) is equivalent to Luke's "Peter and John and James, and the father and mother of the child" (8:51). Mark however, has some special features: for Luke's brief statement that the woman with the hemorrhage "could not be healed by any one" (8:41) Mark has a much longer statement of her sufferings "under many physicians" and that she "had spent all that she had, and was no better, but rather grew worse" (5:26). The words of Peter to Jesus in Lk 8:45 are in Mk 5:31 ascribed to "his disciples." And only Mark gives the Aramaic phrase

"Talitha cumi." There are therefore some special elements in a text that is otherwise verbally very close to Luke, with some verbal parallels with Matthew (e.g., Mk 5:23, Mt 9:18, "come and lay your hands on her"; Mk 5:28, "If I touch even his garment"; cf. Mt 9:21). Two details in Matthew that surely reflect an earlier form of the story than Mark's are "the fringe of his garment" (Mt 9:20; Lk 8:44), where Mark only has "his garment"; and "the flute-players" of Mt 9:24, absent from both Mark and Luke.

As before, we find Mark's narrative best accounted for by his having rewritten Luke, with some recollections of Matthew's text; and in this instance with a few special additions of his own.

It is not only in these longer narratives, however, but throughout the whole of Mk 1:21–3:19, for which Mark and Luke are in the same sequence, that Mark is closer to Luke than to Matthew.[11] The story of the demoniac in the synagogue (Mk 1:23-28) and that of the departure from Capernaum (Mk 1:35-38) are without any parallel in Matthew. When there is a parallel in Matthew in a different sequence, Mark and Luke still show a greater affinity, which can be seen at many points in substance and in wording. One example will suffice: the healing of Peter's mother-in-law as recorded in Mk 1:29-31; Lk 4:38-39; Mt 8:14-16. Mark and Luke agree as against Matthew in noting that Jesus left the synagogue, in speaking of "Simon" and not of "Peter," and of "Simon's mother-in-law" where Matthew has "his mother-in-law"; and Mark's "they told him of her" corresponds to Luke's "they besought him for her." The only significant element in the story common to Mark and Matthew but not Luke, is the statement that Jesus "took her by the hand" (Mk 1:31), or "touched her hand" (Mt 8:15). The pattern is the same as in the longer stories.

If any one of the narratives of Mk 1:21–3:19 is considered in isolation, it can be argued that Luke is dependent on Mark, not Mark on Luke; but what calls for explanation is the fact that the closeness of their narratives is associated with their being in the same sequence. Markan priority gives no answer to this; it is Mark's dependence on Luke and Matthew that is confirmed.

After a short insertion of his own (3:20-21), Mark is in the same order as Matthew from 3:22-35; similar material in Luke is in a different context. It is sufficient to note that there is no point of wording or of substance that suggests Lukan influence. This is in marked contrast with what has preceded, when the common sequence was between Mark and Luke.

---

[11]Cf. Farmer, *The Synoptic Problem*, 211: Mark "tends to agree more closely with Matthew when they follow an order different from Luke, and with Luke when they follow an order different from Matthew."

With the Parable of the Sower, Mark comes at last (in the Huck and Aland synopses) into the same sequence of both Matthew and Luke (Mk 4:1-9; Mt 13:1-9; Lk 8:4-8). The text of Mark is close to that of Matthew, but Mark and Luke agree in speaking of "seed" in the singular as against Matthew's plural. Then in the interpretation of the parable (Mk 4:13-20; Mt 13:18-23; Lk 8:11-15) where there is some confusion in all three Gospels between the equation of the seed with "the word" and with those who receive the word, it is Matthew who has the singular for "any one who hears the word," and Mark and Luke who use the plural. Before the interpretation there is the short section on the reason for parables (Mk 4:10-12; Mt 13:10-11; Lk 8:9-10), closer to Luke than to Matthew. And at 4:21-25 Mark adds further comment, parallel to Lk 8:16-18; but the influence of Matthew is seen in Mark's adding "under a bushel" before "under a bed," and in his insertion of the saying about "the measure you give," both additions coming from other contexts in Matthew.

After his insertion of the Parable of the Seed Growing Secretly, which is peculiar to his Gospel, Mark includes that of the Mustard Seed, in line with Matthew. There are, however, similarities with the version in Lk 13:18-19, in that Luke introduces the parable with a question, "What is the kingdom of God like?," and Mark has a double question (duplications being a common feature of his Gospel) to the same effect. Both Mark and Luke speak of "the kingdom of God," whereas Matthew has "the kingdom of heaven."

Finally in 4:33-34 Mark is parallel to Matthew, with nothing corresponding in Luke.

Throughout the whole parable section, Mark's narrative is just of the kind we should expect, when he has both Matthew and Luke available as sources.

From this point, Mark continues with Luke's order, with the Stilling of the Storm, and the stories of the Gerasene Demoniac and of Jairus's daughter; the latter two stories we have already considered; that of the Stilling of the Storm is told in a form closer to Luke than to Matthew, but there are some connections with Matthew's wording, which betray a knowledge of his version. There are also some details that are peculiar to Mark: "and other boats were with him" (4:36) and "in the stern asleep on the cushion" (4:38), which have impressed some as signs of Markan originality and therefore of priority; they may show that he was familiar with the story before he was writing his Gospel, but they do not contradict his literary dependence on Matthew and Luke. We shall consider the significance of such Markan additions to his written sources at a later stage.

Having used Luke's continuation after the parables, Mark now does the same with Matthew's, and in the narrative of the Rejection at Nazareth there is no indication of influence from Luke's very different account, which Mark has already passed over.

b. Mark 6:6b–16:8

From 6:6b onwards, Mark is closely in sequence with both Matthew and Luke. At three points there are additional Markan incidents: the Healing of the Deaf-Mute (7:31-37, when Matthew has a summary of healings), and of the Blind Man (8:22-26) and the Flight of the Young Man at Gethsemane (14:51-52). At two points there are gaps in the parallelism with Luke: from Mk 6:45 to 8:26, Luke's "Great Omission," and between Mk 9:50 and 10:1, where Luke's central section of teaching (9:51-18:14) is passed over. There are similar omissions from Matthew's discourses (Mt 18:10-35 and 24:37–25:46). It was clearly not Mark's intention to include so much teaching material; allowing for this, the three Gospels are for the rest of the story in very close parallel.

There are places where Matthew or Luke provides material lacking in the other, and where we can see how Mark made the desired insertions. At 6:6b-13, he is in parallel with Luke only, and then at 6:14-16 with Matthew also. His wording betrays an amalgamation of Luke and Matthew. (With Luke, Mark records that "some said" that John had risen; with Matthew he also says that Herod said this.) Then Mark, like Matthew, narrates the Death of the Baptist, but after this returns to Luke's reference to the Return of the Apostles (Mk 6:30) and so, with both Luke and Matthew, to the Feeding of the Five Thousand. From this point onwards Mark is close to Matthew, some of whose episodes have no parallel in Luke.

There are, however, some Lukan insertions. At 9:38-41 Mark like Luke has the Episode of the Strange Exorcist; he adds to it a logion found elsewhere in Mt 10:42, but Matthew's words "because he is a disciple" are represented by "because you bear the name of Christ"—the language of the Christian Mission, and a clear indication of Mark's secondary character.

After the Triumphal Entry into Jerusalem, Matthew (21:10-11) passes immediately to the Cleansing of the Temple, and then to the story of the cursing of the barren fig tree. His narrative seems to mean that the fig tree withered in the sight of the disciples, though this does not necessarily follow from the next words: "When the disciples saw it, they marvelled and said, How did the fig tree wither at once?" (If Matthew has compressed a story told in a more extended way in a tradition reflected in Mark's version, this may be a parallel to the story of Jairus's daughter, where in Luke and Mark the girl is first spoken of as dying, and only afterwards as dead, but in Matthew's more concise version the girl is spoken of as dead from the beginning.) Mark makes his own understanding of what happened to the fig tree clear, by relating the Cursing before the Cleansing of the Temple, passing over Matthew's account of the latter event. Then in dealing with the Cleansing, Mark gives the same sort of details as Matthew, except for Mt 21:14-16, and adds one of his own: "and he did not allow any one to carry anything through the temple." But it is noticeable that Mark's first words, "and he entered the temple and began to drive out those who sold" are identical with those of Luke and that the episode is followed, as in Luke but not in Matthew, by the notice of the conspiracy of the chief priests and scribes (Mk 11:18-19; Lk 19:47-48). It is after this Lukan insertion that Mark returns to Matthew's record of the reaction of the disciples to what had happened to the fig tree, and so to Matthew's order.

There is one further notable point at which it is Mark and Luke who are in parallel without Matthew. Matthew's long condemnation of the scribes and Pharisees (Mt 23:1-36) has already been covered in Luke at 11:37-54. Luke does not now cover the same ground, but gives a short excerpt and includes two sentences, whether copying Matthew if the text of Mt 23:14 is authentic, or making his own insertion: "who devour widows' houses and for a pretense made long prayers. They will receive the greater condemnation" (Lk 20:45-47). The words lead naturally to the inclusion of the story of the Widow's Mite. Matthew's long discourse can hardly have been built up on the foundation of the words in Mark; Luke, followed by Mark, whose wording is practically identical with Luke's, could easily have used Matthew.

The story of the Widow's Mite is typically Lukan. Mark's only reference to widows is in this connection (12:40,42,43); whereas Luke shows a great interest in widows and their welfare, and has a number of references both in the Gospel (2:37; 4:25, 26; 7:12; 18:3,5) and in Acts (6:1; 9:39, 41). Mark's only significant addition to the story is in the words "which make a quadrans" after "two lepta," which itself suggests the secondary character of his narrative. It is in line with other explanations such as Mk 7:3-4, which were unnecessary for the readers of his sources, but became necessary at the time and for the people for whom he wrote. The story and its absence from Matthew have been an obvious embarrassment to many critics who have accepted Markan priority; no difficulties arise when it is recognized that Mark is subsequent to Matthew and Luke.

2

The Thematic Order of Matthew

If we cease to assume that Matthew had Mark as a source (and also that the order of Matthew results from his expansion of Mark), the question arises whether that assumption has meant that we have been missing the significance of the development of Matthew's thought as it is to be seen in the order in which he has presented his material. It is to a consideration of this that the conclusions of the previous chapter lead us. We need to look afresh at Matthew, as we should have done had it been the only Gospel which had come down to us. So in the investigation of Matthew's order that follows, no reference of any kind will be made to the Gospels of either Mark or Luke. Only after that shall we consider the implications for the Synoptic Problem.

1. Indications of Order

Order can be of two kinds, either chronological or thematic. And since Matthew's Gospel deals with the birth, life, and death of Jesus, and the birth must come at the beginning and the death at the end, there is bound to be a broadly chronological order. The information about Jesus' ministry that lies between can have been arranged in more than one way, and even in the final chapters, which treat of the events at Jerusalem, there are elements such as some of the parables of 24:45–25:46 that may have been inserted in their present place for other than chronological reasons. Above all, in the chapters on the ministry we need to look carefully to see how things are arranged.

It has often been suggested that the five discourses of the Gospel of Matthew (5:1–7:27; 9:35–10:42; 13:1-52; 18:1-35; 24:3–25:46), which are followed by a variant of the rubric "Now it came to pass when Jesus had finished these words," are a major clue to the structure of the Gospel. "The division of St. Matthew's book by the five great discourses," wrote Austin Farrer, "is perhaps the most widely recognized structural characteristic of this Gospel as a whole."[1] The number five has suggested to some that

---

[1] Austin Farrer, *St Matthew and St. Mark* (Westminster, 1954) 40.

Matthew was making a parallel with the five books of the Pentateuch, but it is only by a forced interpretation that the Gospel can be given a fivefold structure. What is significant is the point in the Gospel at which each of these discourses is inserted.

At the beginning of the Galilean Ministry we are told of the great crowds that followed Jesus (4:25), and that "seeing the crowds" Jesus went up the hill, followed by "his disciples." The Sermon is then a collection of Jesus' teachings, inserted before the story of the ministry is continued. At 9:35 a new section begins: again there is a summary of Jesus' work, and again it is when "seeing the crowds" (9:36), that the discourse follows, this time to prepare laborers for the harvest. The third occasion, also after a reference to "great crowds" (13:1), is when the parabolic teaching to the people is illustrated. It does not begin a new section of the Gospel, but on the contrary is included here to clear the way for an entirely new development that begins with the record of the Baptist's death, to the significance of which we shall have to return.

The fourth and fifth discourses are different. In each case we are told that the disciples came to Jesus (18:1, 24:3), and in response to their question there follows an account of his teaching, not all necessarily spoken on the same occasion. The former of these comes at the point where Jesus is about to leave Galilee, the latter immediately before the Passion Narrative begins. All five discourses fit neatly into the structure of Matthew's Gospel; the structure itself does not depend upon them.

To appreciate that structure, we have to look at three contemporary events to which Matthew refers as affecting the course of Jesus' life. They are all concerned with John the Baptist. The first is the coming of John "preaching in the wilderness of Judea" (3:1); it brought Jesus "to the Jordan, to John, to be baptized by him" (3:13). Jesus' baptism, and the subsequent temptation are the only items of information about the life of Jesus at this period that Matthew records. The second event was John's imprisonment; it led to Jesus' Mission to Galilee: "Now when he heard that John had been arrested, he withdrew into Galilee" (4:12); and "From that time Jesus began to preach" (4:17). The third was John's death, an event which Matthew would not have recorded had it not been significant for its influence on the career of Jesus. "Now when Jesus heard this, he withdrew from there in a boat to a lonely place apart" (14:13); the subsequent events, as we shall see later, result in some delay before we come to the second significant phrase in the text: "From that time Jesus began to show his disciples that he must go to Jerusalem" (16:21).

We have then a basic structure[2] discernible in the Gospel:

(1) Introductory: The Coming of Jesus (1:1-4:11);
(2) The Ministry (4:12-16:20);
(3) To Jerusalem (16:21-28:20).

Can we distinguish within this framework a more detailed pattern? Some events may clearly be connected in chronological sequence, but Matthew, who has collected allied teaching material together, as with the parabolic material of chapter 13, may also have found it useful to connect narrative elements for other than chronological reasons. So far as chronological sequence is concerned, it would seem at first sight that he has himself supplied links to indicate the order of events, but they need to be treated with caution. Some are imprecise. A number of episodes are introduced by the words "at that time," as at 11:25; 12:1; 14:1; and the words "at that hour" at 18:1 may be no more than a variant of the same phrase, which may mean no more than "in those days," like the *in illo tempore* with which the gospel lections of the old Roman missal were introduced. The phrases may indeed reflect Semitic usage, as in Gen 39:11 and 1 Sam 3:2, where "on that day" only means "on a certain day."

There is a similar imprecision when episodes begin with the word "then" (τότε), as at 9:14; 11:20; 12:22; 13:36; 15:1; 19:13. It probably indicates temporal sequence in the story of the Passion (26:14,31, 36; 27:3, 27), but it is at least vaguer in the earlier chapters. Some episodes are introduced by a phrase with a participle (as at 8:1, 5, 14, 18) specifying the locality of the incident recorded: "coming down from the mountain," "entering Capernaum," "entering Peter's house," or "seeing the crowd." In such instances it is the whole context that has to be taken into account.[3] Thus the whole series of incidents beginning respectively at 8:18, 23, 28 and 9:1 clearly belongs together, but in other cases no specific sequence is implied and other reasons may account for the order of the narrative. It is the function of exegesis to identify them.

---

[2]Cf. the discussion by J. D. Kingsbury in *Matthew, Structure, Christology, Kingdom* (London, 1976).

[3]Cf. C. H. Dodd's note in *Historical Tradition in the Fourth Gospel* (Cambridge, 1963) 63, that "in Luke 9:57 πορευομένων αὐτῶν ἐν τῇ ὁδῷ, means 'once when they were on a journey,' Luke 17:12 εἰσερχομένου αὐτοῦ εἴς τινα κώμην 'once when he was entering a village' (cf. Luke 11:29, Matt. 17:24 etc.)." What Dodd notes about Luke applies also to Matthew.

2. The Coming of Jesus, Mt 1:1-4:11

After the initial genealogy, the introductory section of the Gospel is obviously arranged in chronological order, from the Birth of Jesus to the Temptation. There is however, in the narrative a feature that should alert us to a concern that pervades the Gospel: the fulfillment of Old Testament prophecies.

The account of Jesus' Birth concentrates on one point, his virginal conception. There is no attempt at a circumstantial account,

but this was done
that there might be fulfilled what was spoken
by the Lord through the prophet, saying
Behold, a virgin shall conceive and bear a son,
and his name shall be called Emmanuel. (1:22-23)

The story of the Magi follows, and the significance of the fact that "Jesus was born in Bethlehem of Judea" is emphasized by the quotation

for thus it is written by the prophet,
And you, Bethlehem in the land of Judah,
are by no means least among the rulers of Judah,
for from you shall come a ruler
who shall govern my people Israel. (2:6)

The significance is the same, whether the words are meant to be part of what the chief priests and scribes said, or are the Evangelist's explanation of their answer "In Bethlehem of Judea."

The same pattern is seen in the narrative of the Flight into Egypt, with the quotation "a voice was heard in Ramah" (2:18), and at the return from Egypt with the obscure reference to what was spoken by the prophets, "He shall be called a Nazarene" (2:23).

A new phase begins with the coming of the Baptist, and again there is a formal quotation: "For this is he who was spoken of by the prophet Isaiah, saying":

The voice of one crying in the wilderness,
Prepare the way of the Lord,
Make his paths straight. (3:3)

If in the account of the Baptism of Jesus there is no formal quotation, it remains true that the words "This is my beloved son, with whom I am well pleased" (3:17) are so close to those of 12:18, "my beloved with whom my soul is well pleased" (quoted as "spoken by the prophet Isaiah," though the word "beloved" [ἀγαπητός] is not Isaianic) as to hold for Matthew an implicit reference to those of Isaiah.

For the story of the Temptation there is no occasion for editorial additions, since Old Testament quotations are part of the story.

3. Galilee of the Gentiles, Mt 4:12–9:34

At 4:12 we start the first of the two long divisions of the Gospel that deal with the public activity of Jesus. It continues to 16:20, culminating in the confession of Peter. It begins, as we have seen, at the arrest of John: "Now when he (Jesus) knew that John had been arrested, he withdrew into Galilee" (4:12). It consists of six sections of connected material, the first extending from 4:12 to 9:34.

Matthew could have begun at this point with the bare historical statement that when Jesus "heard that John had been arrested, he withdrew into Galilee, and leaving Nazareth he went and dwelt in Capernaum" (4:12). In fact he makes two additions: he calls the new center "Capernaum-by-the-sea" (Καφαρναοὺμ τὴν παραθαλασσίαν), and he describes Galilee as "the territory of Zebulun and Naphthali." Both additions reveal his concern with the words of the quotation that is to follow, which speaks of the "way of the sea," and uses the same tribal names. When Matthew wrote those words they were an anachronistic term for what was currently spoken of as Galilee. Already at 2:1 Matthew, before quoting the words of Isaiah, "Bethlehem in the land of Judah," has used the current phrase "Bethlehem of Judea"; but now, with his mind directed to a prophecy of special significance for him, he inserts its own phrase. He is not concerned with the original meaning of the "way of the sea"; the sea he is concerned with is the lake of Galilee, and Capernaum is "by the sea."

So the quotation that is to be the "text" of Matthew's ensuing narrative follows (4:15-16):

The land of Zebulun and the land of Naphthali,
way of the sea, across the Jordan,
Galilee of the Gentiles;
the people who sat in darkness have seen a great light,
and to those who sat in the region and shadow of death light has dawned.

(Is 9:1-2)

It is after this quotation that the crucial words occur: "From that time Jesus began to preach" (4:17).

The quotation from Isaiah is included, not as an incidental if interesting reference to Galilee, but because Matthew writes within a rabbinic tradition that has its own methods of exegesis, and one that has taken on new life as Christians pored over the Old Testament scriptures to see what light they shone on the significance of Jesus' life. "Every scribe who has been trained for the kingdom of heaven is like a householder who brings out of his treasure what is new and what is old'' (13:52), and the treasure that the Evangelist draws on consists not only of traditions of what Jesus had done, but also the Scriptures he has fulfilled. Matthew therefore does not arrange his Gospel in strict chronology, either in recording all the events of Jesus' career, nor in putting all his sayings in a chronological context. At convenient places he starts with a quotation from the Scriptures, and makes this a text that is illustrated by the traditions of Jesus' life. The order of events recorded need not always be that in which they occurred, but in the order suggested by the text being expounded. Moreover, Matthew's interest is not historical in the sense that he was concerned to know just what the words quoted meant when they were first spoken or written; he was concerned with the deeper meaning they can be made to carry. ''A virgin shall conceive'' may not have been written as a prophecy of the Virgin Birth of Jesus, nor the voice ''heard in Ramah'' have been spoken with a foreknowledge of events at Bethlehem, but they have taken on a deeper meaning because of the coming of Jesus.[4]

So the relevance of the ''text'' is to be illustrated by incidents not necessarily recorded in the order in which they occurred, but by picking up its references. And first, taking up the phrase ''way of the sea,'' Matthew records that Jesus at Capernaum (τὴν παραθαλασσίαν) walked by the sea (παρὰ τὴν θάλασσαν) of Galilee, where he called four fishermen to follow him. It need not have been the first thing he did in his Ministry, and indeed is unlikely to have been so; that is not the point, what matters is that an episode is recorded that already sets the scene for the narratives and teaching that are to follow, in Galilee, with Capernaum-by-the-sea as its central place. After this Matthew can make the general statement that Jesus ''went about all Galilee'' teaching, preaching, and healing (4:23), and that the crowds began to follow him. They came from Galilee and Judea and the Decapolis. ''The Decapolis'' is an adequate description of one of the regions, but Matthew has not forgotten his text, and adds ''and across the Jordan'' (πέραν τοῦ Ἰορδάνου, 4:25, cf. 4:15), which means the same area. Having now set the scene, Matthew can proceed to an exposition of Jesus' teaching and preaching, through which a ''great light'' had indeed shone on those who ''sat in darkness.'' The Sermon on the Mount (5:1–7:27) therefore follows, with a short comment on the effects of that teaching on the hearers (7:28-29). The cleansing of the leper that follows, the first example of healing to be given, is recorded as occurring when Je-

---

[4]This is very different from describing Matthew's text as a midrashic expansion of Mark, as in M. D. Goulder, *Midrash and Lection in Matthew* (London, 1974). J. Drury (*Tradition and Design in Luke's Gospel* [London, 1976]) treats the Third Gospel in the same way: ''Over all, Matthew could be seen as a *midrash* on Mark, Luke on both of them,'' 44.

sus "came down from the mountain" (8:1-4); its position is therefore presumably due to a tradition of this chronological connection.

The incident of the healing of the centurion's servant follows (8:5-13). The opening words, "As he entered Capernaum," may not imply that this episode followed on the previous one in immediate historical succession; tradition sometimes preserves the recollection of the locality of events better than that of their temporal sequence. Matthew has taken us back to Capernaum-by-the-sea in "Galilee of the Gentiles," and appropriately tells the story of the Gentile centurion. Its significance is emphasized by the words of Jesus "Not even in Israel have I found such faith" (8:10), and by the insertion into the story of the apparently separate logion "I tell you, many will come from east and west, and sit at table with Abraham, Isaac, and Jacob in the kingdom of heaven" (8:11-12). The healing of Peter's mother-in-law and of sick people on the same evening (8:14-17) complete the Capernaum narrative. This has illustrated the original text, but Matthew also sees another fulfillment of prophecy: "He took our infirmities and bore our diseases" (8:17).

Matthew now turns again to his guiding text, this time to the words "the way of the sea, across the Jordan"; and a series of episodes, which *do have* a chronological connection, follows. Jesus is to go "to the other side (εἰς τὸ πέραν), when a scribe offers to go with him but is warned of the cost of discipleship (8:18-20). Then, because of its similarity, another example is added (8:21-22), an insertion into the chronological sequence, but conveniently added here. Then there follow the stories of what happened when Jesus was crossing the sea, the stilling of the storm (8:23-27), and when he came "to the other side," the meeting with the Gadarene demoniacs (8:28-34), and when he returned "to his own city," the healing of the paralytic (9:1-8). Matthew has so far taken up a number of hints from his original text—"the way of the sea, across the Jordan, Galilee of the Gentiles." It has been in that context that he has shown how "the people who sat in darkness have seen a great light, and for those who sat in the region and shadow of death light has dawned" (4:16). He brings this part of his Gospel to a close with illustrations of how the light has shone for some of those who in different ways "sat in darkness." The cure of the paralytic took place at Capernaum, and it was "as Jesus passed from there" that he called Matthew the tax collector. The opportunity is therefore provided for showing that Jesus was ready to sit at table with tax collectors and sinners; it was the sick, those who were aware of their own weakness, who needed a physician. The quotation from Hosea 6:6, "I desire mercy, and not sacrifice" (which occurs again in Mt 12:7), points to his mission of compassion, which goes beyond the righteousness of the scribes and Pharisees. A pattern of Torah-observance, for which Hosea's word "sacrifice" can stand as a symbol, had developed, which, by keeping those who observed it from mingling with "sinners" and the unclean, was preventing the exercise of that mercy which God desired. It was like an old garment that could not be repaired just by adding a patch of new cloth, or like old wineskins that could not be used for new wine. So the claim to independence for Jesus and his disciples from the rules of an outworn piety is reinforced by the inclusion of the answers to John's disciples about the neglect of fasting (9:14-17).

Then Matthew recounts, very briefly, three occasions when Jesus showed compassion. First, the story of the ruler's daughter who had died, with that of the woman with an issue of blood encapsulated in it (9:18-26). To lay hands on the dead girl, and to be touched by the woman, would mean to incur "uncleanness," but mercy had to triumph over "sacrifice." The ruler and his daughter stood in literal fact "in the shadow of death." Secondly, the giving of sight to two blind men (9:27-31) made the light dawn on them when they had been in "the region of darkness." Matthew has not forgotten his "text." Finally, the exorcising of the dumb demoniac (9:32-34) included as happening "as they were going away," completes the list of different kinds of works of mercy since the Galilean ministry began.

4. The Cities of Israel, Mt 9:35–11:30

After his series of illustrations of Jesus' ministry in Galilee, Matthew begins a new section of his Gospel with a generalized statement: "And Jesus went about all the cities and villages, teaching in their synagogues and preaching the gospel of the Kingdom, and healing every disease and every infirmity" (9:35). There is no Old Testament quotation to provide a clue to the arrangement of what follows, nor are there any references to Galilee, apart from the references to Chorazin, Bethsaida, and Capernaum when Jesus upbraided "the cities where most of his mighty works had been done" (11:20-24). The section begins with the commission of the twelve disciples, and continues with the second of the discourses which is followed by the rubric "and it came to pass when Jesus had finished" (11:1). No particular event is on this occasion recorded as following the discourse; there is simply a repetition of the fact that Jesus went on "to teach and to preach in their cities." On the other hand, the introduction to this discourse has its similarities with that to the Sermon on the Mount: both record Jesus' healing ministry, in both it is "seeing the crowds" (5:1, 9:36) that occasions the discourse, and both discourses are given to his disciples, though it is only on the second occasion that having spoken to "his disciples" of the harvest and the need for laborers, Jesus is said to have called "his twelve disciples" and given them their charge. The resulting discourse is therefore concerned with their immediate task (10:5-16) but also includes material that relates to the continuing Christian mission, in which Matthew's readers are concerned.

Jesus "went about all the cities and villages"; there is no indication whether or not these were all in Galilee. There are hints later in the Gospel that he was familiar with the locality of Jerusalem and had contacts there (21:2; 23:37; 26:6, 18, 36, 55), but the concern of this part of the Gospel is of a more general character. The validity of Jesus' own mission is witnessed to by what he is doing, as is claimed in the answer to the question of the Baptist, who is still in prison (11:2-6); Jesus' witness to John is naturally attached to this episode (11:7-19). He has met with different reactions: cities that have seen the mighty works to which John's attention has been called were upbraided for their lack of response, but Jesus thanks his Father for the "babes" whose hearts have been open to his revelation (11:25-30).

It is because of this generalized concern with mission that the word "cities" keeps recurring. Before the commission to his disciples, Jesus "went about all the cities and villages"; at its close he went on "to teach and preach in their cities." The commission was to "the lost sheep of the house of Israel" (10:6), to "the cities of Israel" (10:23); the word "city" occurs in the discourse at 10:5, 11, 14, 15, 23 bis, and after it (besides 11:1) at 11:20. Matthew's habit of conflating different materials in his discourses is seen in references that go beyond the immediate mission of the disciples: "you will be dragged before governors and kings for my sake, to bear witness before them and the Gentiles" (10:18); and "brother will deliver up brother to death, and the father his child, and children will rise against parents, and have them put to death, and you will be hated by all for my name's sake" (10:21-22), but it is the theme of mission that holds the whole section of 9:35–11:30 together. The text is influenced by the Old Testament in two places: by Micah 7:6 at 10:21 and by Malachi 3:1, and perhaps Exodus 23:20, at 11:10; but this is not significant for the structure of the whole section.

5. The Chosen Servant, Mt 12:1-50

Having painted a picture of Jesus' work in Galilee, and followed this by a more general statement about the mission to the cities of Israel, Matthew passes in his next section to the significance of Jesus' own office. Matthew has already recorded that Jesus had proclaimed that mercy was above sacrifice (9:13), and this is now repeated (12:6) with the claim that "something greater than the temple," the place of sacrifice, had arrived. The words are to have an echo in the statements towards the end of the section, that "something greater than Jonah" (12:41) and "greater than Solomon" (12:42) had arrived.

So first of all, in the story of the plucking of ears of corn on the sabbath, "the Lord of the sabbath" (12:8) defends his disciples, and is then reported as healing a man with a withered hand on the sabbath day. When there was a plot to destroy him, Jesus "withdrew from there" (12:15), but crowds followed him; and when he had "healed them all" he "charged them not to make him known" (12:16).

Just as the words of 4:12, speaking of Jesus' withdrawal into Galilee, led at 4:14 into the quotation from Isaiah 9:1-2, and so to the illustration of its phrases in the mission to Galilee, so now the words "and he charged them not to make him known" trigger an even longer quotation from Isaiah, which is in its turn to be illustrated by what follows (Mt 12:17-21).

This was to fulfil what was spoken by the prophet Isaiah:
Behold, my servant whom I have chosen,
my beloved with whom my soul is well pleased.
I will put my Spirit upon him,
and he shall proclaim justice to the Gentiles,
he will not wrangle or cry aloud,
nor will anyone hear his voice in the streets;
he will not break a bruised reed,
or quench a smoldering wick,
but he brings justice to victory,
and in his name will the Gentiles hope. (Is 42:1-4)

It is the charge of Jesus "not to make him known" that leads to the inclusion of the prophecy that Jesus "will not wrangle or cry aloud in the streets"; the quotation itself will suggest other ways in which the prophecy has been fulfilled.[5]

The key words that control the selection of the following material are "servant" (παῖς), "Spirit" (πνεῦμα), "judgment" (κρίσις) and "Gentiles" (ἔθνη). First, Matthew takes up the reference to the Spirit. The healing of the blind and dumb demoniac (12:22-30) brings on the accusation that Jesus is in collusion with the prince of the demons, and leads to Jesus' response that "if it is by the Spirit of God that I cast out demons, then the Kingdom of God has come upon you." The warning about "blasphemy against the Spirit" is a natural continuation (12:31-32).

Then Matthew takes up the second-key word: "judgment" (κρίσις), which occurs twice in his quotation (κρίσιν τοῖς ἔθνησιν ἀπαγγελεῖ

---

[5]For a valuable study of Matthew's use of Old Testament quotations, see O. Lamar Cope, *Matthew, a Scribe Trained for the Kingdom of Heaven* (Washington DC, 1976).

. . . εἰς νῖκος τῆν κρίσιν), in both cases with a reference to Gentiles. In the continuing passage (12:33-37) comes the warning that "on the day of judgment men will render account for every careless word they utter." When some of the scribes and Pharisees demand a sign from heaven, it is said that the Gentile men of Nineveh and the Gentile queen of the south "will arise at the judgment with this generation and condemn it" (12:38-42). The reference to "this generation" provides a link for a further addition, on the Return of the Evil Spirit (12:43-45), which concludes with the saying "so will it be also to this evil generation."

The whole group of material closes with the pericope about mothers and sisters and brothers (12:46-50); a reference to fathers is conspicuous by its absence. It is not just those who "do the will of God," or even "the will of their Father," but "the will of my Father," who are described as Jesus' kindred. The quotation from Isaiah began with the words "Behold my Servant (παῖς) whom I have chosen, my beloved with whom I am well pleased." Matthew has added the word "beloved" (ἀγαπητός) to the text of Isaiah, thereby assimilating the words of the quotation to those of the Father's voice at Jesus' baptism, "This is my beloved Son (υἱός), with whom I am well pleased" (3:17). Although the word παῖς represents the "servant" of Isaiah's text, it could be understood or interpreted as meaning "son," and it seems clear that it is this meaning that Matthew attaches to it. It is therefore the Son of the Father in heaven who receives his disciples as his kindred; and the assertion of sonship provides an "inclusion" from the first words of the quotation.

6. Seeing, Hearing, Understanding, Mt 13:1-58

Matthew passes to his collection of parables in chapter 13, with what is possibly but not necessarily meant as a chronological link, with the words "On that day Jesus went out of the house and sat beside the sea." This is the first occasion on which Matthew records a parable, and it provides the opportunity for inserting others. The later phrase in 13:36, "Then he left the crowds and went into the house," cannot refer back to 13:1, for the coming of the disciples in 13:10 to ask about the meaning of parables itself implies a return of Jesus to privacy after speaking from the boat. The series of parables is therefore dependent on a thematic arrangement, but its place in the gospel is the result of Matthew's connecting the occasion of the Parable of the Sower with the events of 12:46-50. "The Kingdom of God is come upon you," and the parables speak of its proclamation and its nature.

If we have been right in interpreting Matthew's methods so far, we should be able to see how his mind is working in this collection of material, though the arrangement of the three pairs of parables after the Sower is peculiar, and may result from a process of addition to an earlier draft of the Gospel material. The collection starts straightforwardly enough: first comes the Parable of the Sower (13:3-9), ending with the significant words "He who has ears, let him hear." The question of the disciples—"Why do you speak to them in parables?"—follows with the answer—"because seeing they do not see, and hearing they do not hear, nor do they understand" (13:10-13). It is these three words—see, hear, understand—that lead into the question from Isaiah 6:9-10, and are followed up afterwards. The quotation (13:14-15) is probably intended as a commentary by Matthew, and not as part of Jesus' words, which (without this insertion) would continue quite smoothly from 13:13 to 13:16.

The quotation is again a lengthy one:

You shall indeed hear
but never understand,
and you shall indeed see (βλέψετε)
but never perceive (ἴδητε)
for this people's heart has grown dull,
and their ears are heavy of hearing,
and their eyes they have closed,
lest they should perceive with their eyes,
and hear with their ears,
and understand with their hearts,
and turn for me to heal them. (Is 6:9-10)

(The variation between the words translated "perceive" and "see" is insignificant: in 13:13 Matthew can write "seeing they do not see" without varying the verb.) The key words are immediately taken up: "Blessed are your eyes, for they see and your ears for they hear" (13:16); "Many prophets and righteous men longed to see what you see, and did not see it, and to hear what you hear, and did not hear it" (13:17); "Hear then the parable" (13:18). In the interpretation of the parable, we have "When any one hears the word of the Kingdom and does not understand it" (13:19); "he who hears the word" (13:20, 22); "he who hears the word and understands it" (13:23).

So far then, the sequence is straightforward. It could have concluded quite naturally by the words of 13:51-52, "Have you understood all this?" Before this, however, three pairs of twin parables have been inserted. Those of the Tares (13:24-30) with its interpretation (13:36-43) and of the Net with a similar but more concise interpretation (13:47-50) have been interrupted by the insertion at some stage in the development of this corpus, of the parables of the Mustard Seed and Leaven (13:31-33) and those of the Hidden Treasure and Pearl (13:44-46). The comment on the use of parables, with a different Old Testament quotation (13:35; Ps 78:2) seems to have been an introduction to the interpretation of the Tares before the whole parabolic discourse was organized by the Evangelist. (Compare 13:34, "All this Jesus said to the crowds"; 13:36, "Then he left the crowds.") Finally, the whole parabolic discourse is connected again to the events of the ministry by the characteristic phrase "And it came to pass when Jesus had finished these parables," and the episode of Jesus' rejection at Nazareth (13:53-58) points to the contrast between those who had understood and those who could only take offence at Jesus' words, for whom he could do little "because of their unbelief."

7. Jesus—Who Is He? Mt 14:1–16:20

From 3:1 to 13:58 Matthew has worked through a number of themes. Then from 14:1 to 16:20 there is an intermediate section, which from different points of view can be regarded as either the close of the first half of the Gospel with its culmination in the confession "You are the Christ, the Son of the living God," or in terms of the chronology as the beginning of the second half, marked by the death of the Baptist. It is on the latter event that the chronology depends, the three stages in the adult life of Jesus are all influenced by what happened to John:

(1) In those days came John the Baptist preaching in the wilderness of Judea (3:1);
Then came Jesus from Galilee to the Jordan to John, to be baptized by him (3:13);
(2) Now when he heard that John had been arrested, he withdrew into Galilee (4:12);
From that time Jesus began to preach (4:17);
(3) Now when Jesus heard this, he withdrew from there in a boat to a lonely place apart (14:13);
From that time Jesus began to show his disciples that he must go to Jerusalem (16:21).

The parallelism of Matthew's wording in (2) and (3) is significant:

(2) ἀκούσας δὲ ὅτι Ἰωάννης παρεδόθη ἀνεχώρησεν εἰς τὴν Γαλιλαίαν.
(3) ἀκούσας δὲ ὁ Ἰησοῦς ἀνεχώρησεν . . . εἰς ἔρημον τόπον.
(2) ἀπὸ τότε ἤρξατο ὁ Ἰησοῦς κηρύσσειν.
(3) ἀπὸ τότε ἤρξατο ὁ Ἰησοῦς δεικνύειν.

Between 14:13 to 16:21 there is of course a wide interval, which calls for explanation. The whole section begins with the subject of John's death (14:1-12). In recording it, Matthew is not straying from his subject which is the career of Jesus, into a bypath of interesting but extraneous information. Jesus has already made one major decision when he was informed of what had happened to John: he withdrew into Galilee, and began to preach. Now he is informed of the final act, John's execution; John's disciples "went and told Jesus" (14:12). Again Jesus "withdrew," but he was not yet ready to take his disciples into his confidence. So a series of events is recorded as taking place in chronological sequence: the Feeding of the Five Thousand (14:13-21), the Walking on the Sea (14:22-33), and the return to Gennesaret (14:34-38). The same consideration holds for the episode concerning the meaning of defilement, a section which Lamar Cope (see n. 5 above) regards as being a "very strong" example of material organized on the basis of an Old Testament quotation. What concerns us here, however, is its context: it is related as following on the arrival at Gennesaret and the coming of Pharisees and scribes from Jerusalem (15:1); and it is followed by the words "and Jesus went away from there, and withdrew (ἀνεχώρησεν) again to the district of Tyre and Sidon" (15:21)—out of the territory of Herod. It was there that the healing of the daughter of the Canaanite woman took place (15:21-28). If at this point the narrative had continued with the Confession of Peter (16:13-20), it would have appeared that Matthew was now following a strictly chronological order. The proximity of Caesarea Philippi to the territory of Tyre and Sidon would suggest a natural connection between the events at these places. In fact a group of passages, of which that of the Feeding of the Four Thousand is the core, intervenes between them. What is the explanation?

It is not necessary for our present purpose to decide whether the two stories of the multiplication of loaves refer to the same incident or to two separate ones. The editor of the Gospel clearly thought there were two. But it is beyond dispute that the similarities between the two stories are very great. Some may arise from the evangelist's own style: in both, for instance, Jesus is said to have had compassion on the crowds, but this has already been said at 9:36 on a different occasion. Others cannot be so accounted for: details like the repeated order to sit down on the grass or the ground (14:19; 15:35) or the references to men "besides women and children" (14:21; 15:38) add to the general similarity.

Before the first Feeding, the crowds came and Jesus "healed them" (14:14); before the second, "great crowds" came, many kinds of disablement being specified, "and he healed them" (15:30). Then in the accounts of the Feedings there are the obvious similarities, and of course notable differences, as in the numbers given. After the first Feeding "the disciples got into the boat" (14:22); at 15:39 Jesus "got into the boat." On arrival at the other side, at 15:1, "Pharisees and scribes came"; at 16:1, "the Pharisees and Sadducees came"; in each case a condemnation of their teaching follows, although in very different forms.

A common pattern is discernible; the editor of the Gospel has been aware of two traditions; he has regarded the two feedings as separate events, and to include both he has inserted 15:29-16:12 at an obvious place, so that like the previous narrative, it should precede the Confession of Peter.[6]

After this insertion, we come then to Peter's Confession of Jesus as the Christ (16:13-20), the climax of the whole narrative from 4:12 onwards. The revelation of Jesus as "the Christ, the Son of the living God" is followed by the promise of the building of the church on the rock which is Peter; the whole Gospel will close with the revelation of the risen Lord, followed by the commission to make disciples of all nations.[7]

8. "A ransom for many," Mt 16:21–28:20

The last major division of the Gospel is now about to begin. Matthew can now pick up the clue of 14:13, "Now when Jesus heard" of the Baptist's execution. All that has followed has led to the recognition by the disciples that Jesus was the Christ. This was not something for public proclamation (16:20); it was the disciples who were to begin to understand its implications. The new stage was being entered into: "From that time Jesus began to show to his disciples that he must go to Jerusalem and suffer" (16:21).

From this point the structure of the Gospel is basically a chronological, not merely a thematic one. Until chapter 26 begins the story of the Passion, there are indeed groups of teaching material, in discourses and parables, which do not necessarily imply a time sequence, but the structure into which they are fitted is that of the passage of events. After Jesus' declaration that "he must go to Jerusalem and suffer," there follows the warning, "If any man will come after me, let him deny himself, and take up his cross, and follow me" (16:24-28). Then after "six days" there comes the Transfiguration, a proclamation of the Father's approval before the narrative is resumed, comparable to that made at Jesus' baptism before the beginning of the Ministry. Identical words—"this is my beloved Son, with whom I am well pleased"—occur in both episodes and emphasize the correspondence between them. Jesus can now speak of the days when "the Son of man is

---

[6]It is noteworthy that Lagrange, who held that an Aramaic Matthew lay behind our Greek Matthew, considered it possible that the second multiplication of the loaves (at 15:32-39) had not belonged to the Aramaic original; M. J. Lagrange, *Évangile selon Saint Matthieu* (Paris, ³1928).

[7]Mt 16:20 is a conclusion formula, as is Mk 8:30. In Lk 9:21 similar words are used, but the narrative runs continuously into the prediction of the Passion. Matthew both concludes an episode at 16:20 and makes a new start at 16:21.

raised from the dead'' (17:9) as he gradually prepares his disciples for the future; almost immediately a similar reference occurs: ''the Son of man will suffer'' (17:12).

After the Transfiguration and the events following immediately upon it (17:1-21), the journey to Jerusalem is about to begin. The disciples are now together, or gathering together (συστρεφομένων) in Galilee, and to their distress are warned of what lies ahead (17:22-23); then for the last time they enter Capernaum, where the question of the payment of the temple tax is raised (17:24:27). The narrative is then interrupted by the insertion of the discourse of chapter 18. As in the other formal discourses, Matthew brings together a variety of material (in this case including two parables), without necessarily implying that all was spoken on the same occasion, but after the stereotyped phrase at its conclusion—''And it came to pass when Jesus had finished these sayings''—the chronological thread is taken up again: ''He went away from Galilee and entered the region of Judea beyond the Jordan'' (19:1-2). At 20:17, while Jesus and his disciples were ''on the way,'' he warned them again of what lay ahead, and the point is emphasized again in the following incident dealing with the request for the sons of Zebedee, that the Son of man came ''to give his life as a ransom for many'' (20:28). At 20:29 the little group has passed through Jericho; at 21:1 ''they drew near to Jerusalem, and came to Bethphage, to the mount of Olives''; and at 21:10 Jesus actually entered Jerusalem. It is in interpretation of the purpose of the journey that all the predictions of the Passion occur.

From 21:10, when Jesus enters Jerusalem, the basic structure is inevitably a chronological one. Matthew may have chosen convenient points at which to insert teaching material, such as the Parable of the Great Supper (22:1-14), the denunciation of the scribes and Pharisees (23:1-36), and in his last formal discourse (24:3-25:46) a series of parables (24:37-25:46); but the events of the Passion impose their own sequence on the narrative. There is an appropriateness in the words that follow the last of the great discourses: ''And it came to pass when Jesus had finished *all* these sayings'' (26:1); from that point it is the events that speak for themselves.

Matthew's treatment of the life of Jesus results from the interplay of different factors. There is first a basic appreciation of its historical order: the Infancy, the Baptism by John, the Galilean ministry which followed John's arrest, the withdrawal to the north after John's death, followed by the confession that he was the Christ and by his announcing of his decision ''that he must go to Jerusalem'' (16:21), the approach to the city, and the events of the Passion.

For the first Christians, and especially for the first Jewish Christians, the life of Jesus was a fulfillment of the purposes of God, to which the Scriptures (the Old Testament) bore witness, and what happened to him was "according to the Scriptures" which bore witness of him. Rabbinic exposition of the Scriptures provided a method that could be put to Christian use. There was no need to invent stories about Jesus on the basis of Scriptural texts; that would be literally preposterous—putting the cart before the horse. But scriptural texts could be used to organize the arrangement of episodes in his life, and to reveal fulfillments that need not have been in the minds of the ancient authors; and Matthew makes good use of this possibility. To him, that would be more important than giving the exact chronological order of every episode and pronouncement, even if he had been able to do so. Within the broad chronological arrangement, there was ample room for such a treatment. Within that framework, the teaching of Jesus has to be inserted and arranged in suitable groups or in organized discourses. Similar matter could be collected together, without any implication that it must have been spoken on the same occasion. Parables such as those of chapter 25 could for instance be attached to the discourse of chapter 24 as the most convenient place for them, and similar considerations would account for the arrangement of other teaching material, especially when scripture texts (as in 12:18-21 or 13:14-15) provided a suitable framework. We do not need to go outside St. Matthew's Gospel to account for the order of its contents. The Evangelist provides the evidence for himself.

3

Matthew and Mark

In the well-known words of Papias quoted by Eusebius,[1] Mark wrote accurately "but not, however, in order." Whether or not that is a true judgment, it is clear that *Matthew* did write "in order," an order that can be understood without reference to Mark. The question arises, could Matthew's order have been one imposed on material that he derived from Mark? We have seen that if it was Mark who made use of Matthew and Luke, the Markan order is easily and naturally explained. If, on the contrary, it was Matthew who used Mark, is there an equally plausible explanation that would account for Matthew achieving his result by his inclusion of excerpts from Mark? We must look at the facts this way round if we are to find the answer to that question.

1. The Coming of Jesus, Mt 1:1–4:11

It is of course clear that if Matthew used Mark the Infancy stories must be an addition to the Markan narrative. The account of the Baptist and of Jesus' baptism, which follows in Matthew (3:1-17), is sufficiently similar to that of Mark (1:1-11) for borrowing to have been in either direction, though Matthew has the fuller narrative. There is, however, one feature of Mark that points strongly to dependence on Luke: both Mk 1:4 and Lk 3:3 have the phrase "preaching a baptism of repentance for the forgiveness of sins." The comment of M.-E. Boismard is convincing: "This way of speaking is not Markan but Lukan: the word 'repentance' is nowhere else read in Mark, but eleven times in Lk/Acts; the expression 'baptism of repentance' is not read elsewhere in the N.T. except in Acts 13:24 and 19:4; if the formula 'for the forgiveness of sins' belongs to the primitive theology (Mt 26:28; Col 1:14; Eph 1:7), this remission of sins is only connected with 'repentance' in Lk 24:47; Acts 2:38; 3:19; 5:31; 8:22; 26:18, 20."[2] The evidence points to Mark's dependence on Matthew and Luke, not to their dependence on him.

---

[1] Eusebius, EH VI.39.15.

[2] In P. Benoit and M.-E. Boismard, *Synopse des Quatre Évangiles*, vol. 2 (Paris, 1972) 25.

After this, the Temptation of Jesus is treated by Mark (1:12-13) with a brevity that by itself leaves the reader with little understanding of its significance. Jesus is "tempted by Satan," but no indication is given of the character of that temptation; "the angels ministered to him," but why this was needed is left unexplained. Only by a knowledge of Matthew or Luke can the reader see the point of the episode. And Matthew and Luke could not have developed their own narratives out of Mark's suggestions.

2. Galilee of the Gentiles, Mt 4:12–9:34

At 1:14 Mark notes that "after John was arrested, Jesus came into Galilee." This bald statement misses the nuances of the corresponding words of Matthew: "when he (Jesus) *heard* that John had been arrested, he *withdrew* into Galilee"; for Matthew's "*from that time Jesus began* to preach," Mark has only the word "preaching." Matthew, with his quotation from Isaiah, has set the scene for what follows; while Mark has only provided a short introduction for the stories he is now to relate. Indeed it reads like a précis of Matthew and Luke, before he settles down to his main subject.

Mark's first story is the Call of Four Disciples (1:16-20). It is not the most obvious way to begin the narrative of the Ministry, and its opening words have called for comment. "The construction of the Greek (παράγειν παρά) is unusual, and commentators generally are agreed that the reference to the Sea of Galilee is an addition made by St. Mark—no doubt a deduction from the contents of the story."[3] The commentators so agreed have assumed Markan priority. But in Matthew the words "by the Sea of Galilee" arise immediately from his taking up the words of the Old Testament quotation and his reference to "Capernaum-by-the-sea." Matthew did not need Mark's reference; Mark's words are natural if he followed Matthew.

Mark continues with the story of Jesus in the synagogue at Capernaum (1:21-28), which is without parallel in Matthew; the parallel with Luke is very close. Again the opening is a little strange—"And they went into Capernaum"—since it would seem that that was the scene of the previous episode. The corresponding words in Luke are more appropriate: "And he went down to Capernaum" (4:31), for Luke has inserted the story of the preaching at Nazareth. Mark seems to have copied Luke's words, when he really did not need them. And if Matthew used Mark, he ignored the whole episode, for no very obvious reason. Nor does Matthew continue as Mark

---

[3]D. E. Nineham, *Saint Mark* (Penguin Books, 1963). But the construction is not untypical of Mark. It is in line with other examples of "duality." See F. Neirynck, *Duality in Mark* (Leuven, 1972).

and Luke do with the healing of Peter's mother-in-law and the sick at evening (Mk 1:29-34; Lk 4:38-41), although this material is appropriate to his interest in Capernaum and will still be used in the context of the Galilean Ministry (8:14-17). Mark's note on Jesus leaving Capernaum (1:35-38) also has no parallel in Matthew. It is followed in Mark (1:39) by a short note (as in Lk 4:44) announcing a preaching tour, for which there is a rather fuller parallel in Mt 4:23, after which Matthew speaks of the crowds who came to Jesus (4:24-25) and so leads into the Sermon on the Mount. The insertion of the Sermon at this point in Matthew does not in itself militate against the possibility of his use of Mark, but the continuation of the narrative at its close is significant. Matthew does not go back to the material that Mark has been using (Mk 1:21-38); with this omission both Matthew and Mark come to the healing of the leper (Mt 8:1-4; Mk 1:40-45; Lk 5:12-26). There is, however, a difference; in Matthew the story is in a definite context—"When Jesus came down from the mountain"—and provides a transition to the story of the centurion. Mark gives no precise context, either of time or place: he merely says "And a leper came." His story is at the same point as its parallel in Luke, who is almost equally vague: "While he was in one of the cities" (Lk 5:12). If Matthew depended on Mark, he invented the context; but it is out of character for him to have done so.

Matthew continues with the story of the centurion's request (8:5-13), which is also found in Luke (7:1-10) but not in Mark. If Mark is following Luke, there is no problem, for they both come to the first of a collection of five occasions of controversy (Mk 2:1-3:6; Lk 5:17-6:11).[4] Matthew is to use the first three of these in his Galilean section (9:1-17), but although the first of them is definitely placed by Mark in Capernaum (Mk 2:1) and they would have fitted here into Matthew's overall plan, he does not use them at this point. On the contrary, he has a definite context for the first, relating that it occurred after crossing the sea when Jesus had got into a boat and returned "to his own city" (9:1), whereas Mark merely says that Jesus "returned to Capernaum after some days" (Mk 2:1). This in itself is a little strange, following on the statement that Jesus "could no longer openly enter a town" (Mk 1:45). Mark's story of what happened at Capernaum, the healing of a paralytic, is closer to Luke's than to Matthew's, but Luke only gives the vague indication that it was "on one of those days"

---

[4]Cf. J. B. Tyson, "Parallelism in the Synoptic Gospels," NTS 22:3 (April 1976):292: "Perhaps the major problem which may be raised relates to Mark's failure to use 33-36 pericopes which he found in Matthew and Luke. The study of sequential parallelism suggests that he omitted them because they were in variant sequences in his sources. Mark used almost everything which exhibited sequential parallelism in his sources."

(Lk 5:17). The most natural explanation of Mark's reference to Capernaum is that it comes from a reminiscence of Matthew.

Mark has a collection of five stories of controversy, as Luke also does; in Matthew they are in two groups, although there is a link between them in the use of the same quotation (absent from both Luke and Mark), "I desire mercy and not sacrifice" (Mt 9:13; 12:7). In spite of this connection Matthew does not gather the five stories together as a unit; the first three of them—the healing of the paralytic, the call of Matthew the tax collector, and the question of fasting (9:1-17)—are given a particular context: at the beginning, it is when Jesus returned across the sea to Capernaum (9:1), and at the end the narrative is resumed in the words "while he was thus speaking" (9:18). The two groups, of three and two stories, are therefore for Matthew set in different contexts; it is only the second group that leads to the statement that the Pharisees "took counsel against him [Jesus] how to destroy him" (12:14).

Those who have accepted Markan priority have frequently suggested that Mark's group of five controversial episodes, which show marked differences of treatment from what precedes and follows it, had been gathered in a group before their incorporation into his Gospel.[5] What they have been precluded from seeing is that if Luke used Matthew, it was he who made the collection that Mark accepted, and that it fits easily and naturally into his own thematic arrangement.[6] There is no need to suppose that Matthew broke up the collection.

What Matthew had done, at the close of the Sermon on the Mount, is to bring Jesus back to Capernaum, where the centurion made his request, and then to complete the little group of Capernaum stories with the healing of Peter's mother-in-law and the sick at evening (8:1-17), ending with the quotation in comment: "He took our infirmities and bore our diseases." Mark has his own, and a different, Capernaum group, parallel to Luke, and containing his passages (Mk 1:23-28; Lk 4:33-37; Mk 1:35-38; Lk 4:42-43) which have no parallel in Matthew. If we accept that Mark used Luke, the problems disappear.

After the Capernaum group of stories, Matthew relates a series of events that are related to the crossing of the sea, "to the other side" (8:18-9:26). The corresponding section in Mark is from 4:35-5:43, but Mark has the three stories of controversy (Mt 9:1-17, Mk 2:1-22) in a different place, in his collection of five. In Matthew they are closely linked to the crossing of

---

[5]Cf. R. H. Lightfoot, *History and Interpretation in the Gospels* (London, 1935) 110.

[6]See below, ch. 4.

the sea: the healing of the paralytic came after "getting into a boat he [Jesus] crossed over and came to his own town" (9:1); the call of Matthew the tax collector was "as Jesus passed on from there" (9:9); the question of fasting is not only linked by "then" (τότε) to what precedes, but it is connected to the following story, that of the ruler's daughter, which begins "while he was thus speaking" (9:18). It is moreover significant that in the passages that Mark has dealt with in 2:1-22, the text is closer to that of Luke than to that of Matthew. The indications are all in favor of Matthew's arrangement being prior to that of Mark. Matthew concludes this part of his Gospel with the stories of the healing of two blind men and a dumb demoniac (9:27-34), which have "doublets" elsewhere in his Gospel (20:29-34; 12:22-24); it is with these later "doublets" that Mark is in close parallel.

3. The Cities of Israel, Mt 9:35–11:30

After an introductory paragraph (9:35-10:1) and the list of the twelve apostles (10:2-4), Matthew's next section, dealing in a more generalized way with the mission of Jesus and his disciples, opens with the second of Matthew's set discourses (10:4-42). What follows in this section (11:1-30) has no parallel in Mark though it has in Luke. This is also true of the latter part of the discourse (10:26-42) with the single exception of Mt 10:42, parallel to Mk 9:41; and it is noticeable that in this verse Matthew's "because he is a disciple" reveals a more primitive vocabulary than Mark's "because you bear the name of Christ"—one of the many occasions where Mark falls naturally into the language of the later Christian mission. It is therefore only between Mt 10:6 (after the list of the apostles) and 10:25 that there could be any question of Matthew having used Mark. First, Mt 10:8-12 has a parallel in Mk 6:8-11, where Mark's permission of staff and sandals, as against Matthew's prohibition, is best understood as applying to the missionaries of the Empire, not those of Galilee. The second parallel, of Mt 10:17-21, is in a different context in Mark (13:9-13); again it includes the words that point to the secondary character of Mark's wording: "and the gospel must first be preached to all nations." The case for Matthew having made use of Mark in this discourse is flimsy indeed.

4. The Chosen Servant, Mt 12:1-50

We have already seen that a common theme runs through Mt 12:1-50: two stories, that of plucking corn on the sabbath and the healing of the man with the withered hand, lead to the statement that there was a plot to destroy Jesus (12:14), so that "Jesus, aware of this, withdrew from there" and ordered those whom he healed "not to make him known." This leads into the quotation from Is 42:1-4, which controls the selection of what follows. If Mark is alternating in his dependence on Matthew and Luke, and has run up to the Sermon on the Plain in Luke's Gospel, it is natural enough that he should turn back to Matthew as his primary source at the point where, as in Luke, the story of the man with the withered hand is the last episode related. Is it equally plausible that Matthew could have used Mark, and still have achieved his existing text?

At 6:17-19 Luke is leading into his own form of the great Sermon, and speaks of the crowds who came to Jesus, "to hear him and to be healed." Mark (3:7-12) is closely parallel but he includes the points made by Matthew that "Jesus withdrew," and that he ordered those healed "not to make him known." Mark's words are a conflation of two texts that deal with different situations. By this it has become possible for Mark to revert to Matthew's order; Luke also has material parallel to Mt 12:22-50, but it is an entirely different context (Lk 11 and 12; 6:43-45; 8:19-21). What is also clear is that Lk 11 and Mt 12 are in much closer correspondence, and contain much common material which is absent from Mark. Neither of them can have achieved this result by being dependent on Mark; Mark's text is a shortened form of their common account. In consequence, when we come to the pericope of Jesus' True Kindred (Mt 12:46-50; Mk 3:31-35; Lk 8:19-21) we find what we should expect—a much closer relation of Mark's text to Matthew's than to Luke's.

5. Seeing, Hearing, Understanding, Mt 13:1-58

Mark, for whatever reason, has nothing to correspond with either the material about John the Baptist (Mt 11:2-19; Lk 7:18-35), or with that which follows in Matthew (11:20-30) or its parallels in Luke (10:12-15, 21-22). That would follow from his having changed his course at the junction provided by the story of the man with the withered hand. Nor does he include the accounts of Lk 7:36-8:3, which are particular to Luke. That is in line with his non-use of other material that is peculiar to Luke as against Matthew, such as Luke's account of the call of Peter (Lk 5:1-11). He is therefore at the same point in both Matthew's and Luke's Gospels, the Parable of the Sower.

Is there any indication of the direction of dependence between Matthew and Mark? The answer is that there is one very clear indication at Mk 4:12. Matthew has in effect repeated himself by including the words "this is why I speak to them in parables, because seeing they do not see, and hearing they do not hear, nor do they understand" (13:13), and also the quotation from Is 6:9 beginning "you shall indeed hear but never understand." We should not expect Mark to include such a quotation, but the similarity of the words in the two formulations has affected Mark's text, a combination of words from both of these; he has been aware of both the direct words of Matthew, and of his quotation. A little synopsis makes this clear:

MATT 13	MATT 13	MARK 4
13 ὅτι βλέποντες	14c καὶ βλέποντες βλέφετε	12a ἵνα βλέποντες βλέπωσιν
οὐ βλέπουσιν	καὶ οὐ μὴ ἴδητε . . .	καὶ μὴ ἴδωσιν
καὶ ἀκούουντες	14b ἀκοῇ	καὶ ἀκούουντες
οὐκ ἀκούουσιν	ἀκούσετε	ἀκούωσιν
οὐδὲ συνίουσιν.	καὶ οὐ μὴ συνῆτε, . . .	καὶ μὴ συνιῶσιν,
	15b μήποτε . . .	μήποτε
	ἐπιστρέψωσιν	ἐπιστρέψωσιν
	καὶ ἰάσομαι αὐτούς.	καὶ ἀφεθῇ αὐτοῖς.

MATT 13	MATT 13	MARK 4
13 that seeing	14c and seeing you shall see	12a that seeing they may see
they do not see	and not perceive	and not perceive,
and hearing	14b with hearing	and hearing
they do not hear	you shall hear	they shall hear
nor understand	and not understand	and not understand
	15b lest . . .	lest
	they should turn again	they should turn again
	and I should heal them	and be forgiven.

The order seeing-hearing is in Mt 13:13 and Mk 4:12; it is reversed in Mt 13:14. Mark's text is related to both parts of Matthew's. The quotation from Isaiah is integral to Matthew's Gospel; it is absent from Luke's, in which Lk 8:10b is only parallel to Mt 13:13; the reflection of it in Mk 4:12 is not in accordance with Mark's usual manner of writing; it is due to his dependence on Matthew.

In addition to the Parable of the Sower Matthew has three pairs of twin parables: the Tares and the Net, the Mustard Seed and the Leaven, and the Hidden Treasure and the Pearl. Mark has two Parables, those of the Seed Growing Secretly and the Mustard Seed, but they are not twin parables.

In twin parables, such as those in Matthew or the Lost Sheep and the Lost Coin in Lk 15:1-10, the meaning of the parable is what they have in common, the simile used is different. In Mark's two parables, it is the simile that is common to both—the image of "seed," but the meaning of the parables is different. Matthew, whose twin parables of the Mustard Seed and Leaven are also found in Lk 13:18-21, must have received them independently of Mark. It would therefore appear that Mark, while not wishing to include all of Matthew's collection of parables, has been attracted (doubtless for good reason in view of the use that he expected for his Gospel) by the theme of "Seed" in the Parable of the Sower to add two other parables, one not used by Matthew, which have the same illustration. His omission of the Parable of the Leaven would account for his note on the use of parables (Mk 4:33-34) following where it does, and characteristically he does not include Matthew's Old Testament quotation (Mt 13:35, compare Ps 78:2), although it was for the sake of showing this fulfillment of prophecy that Matthew had made the point of 13:34.

6. Jesus—Who Is He? Mt 14:1–16:20

At the beginning of chapter 14 Matthew records the interest that Herod was taking in the activities of Jesus (14:1-2), and proceeds to record the death of the Baptist. As we have seen, this is integral to the plan of Matthew's Gospel; just as the Baptist's arrest had occasioned Jesus' withdrawal into Galilee (4:12), so the death of John occasioned his withdrawal "to a lonely place apart" (14:13). And as, at the beginning, it was after John's arrest that Jesus began to preach in Galilee, so it was after the series of events that followed the Baptist's death that Jesus "began to show his disciples that he must go to Jerusalem" (16:21). The treatment of Mark is very different: the section on Herod's interest (Mk 6:14-16) is somewhat confused, in what appears to be a combination of phrases from Matthew and Luke. Matthew records that Herod said that John "has been raised from the dead"; Luke records that it was "said by some"; Mark records both. What is even more significant is that, while John's death was for Matthew a turning point in the career of Jesus, Mark inserts his account (with details that would not have added to the importance of the story for Matthew) as a sort of interlude, which allows for the passage of time between the sending out of the disciples and their return but has no subsequent effect on his story. Luke does not relate the Baptist's death. While Matthew reports that John's disciples "went and told Jesus" (Mt 14:12), and Luke reports that Jesus' disciples told him of the result of the mission he had given them, Mark leaves the story of the Baptist's death abruptly, and says the same thing as Luke. (Incidentally, when Mark has no parallel in Matthew, he calls John "the baptizer" (6:24); when Matthew has "the Baptist" so does Mark (6:25)—a further indication of Mark's use of Matthew.)[7]

At the Feeding of the Five Thousand, which follows, Mark is in parallel, and in sequence, with both Matthew and Luke (Mk 6:32-44; Mt 14:13-21; Lk 9:10b-17); but after that there is a long section (Mt 14:22-16:12; Mk 6:45–8:21) in which Matthew and Mark are closely in parallel with nothing in the same sequence in Luke, and indeed only a few odd verses have any relationship at all. In general it might appear that borrowing between Matthew and Mark might have been made in either direction. There are however some definite indications of the priority of Matthew. In dealing with traditions about defilement (Mt 15:1-20; Mk 7:1-23), Matthew as-

---

[7]See appendix 2, below.

sumes that his readers understand what the traditions of the elders were; Mark finds it necessary to include a long explanation (Mk 7:2-4); he introduces the technical word "Corban," but finds it necessary to explain— "that is, given to God" (7:11); he adds the note that thus Jesus "declared all foods clean" (7:19); and after the list of things that truly defile, which like Matthew he gives in the plural, he adds a further list, not found in Matthew for which he switches to the singular (Mk 7:21b). These are all indications of the secondary character of Mark as compared with Matthew. At a little further on (Mk 7:26) Mark again reveals the need of translating a term in Matthew into one better understood by the readers of his time and locality, when he substitutes for Matthew's "a Canaanite woman" the words "the woman was a Greek, a Syrophoenician by birth" (Mk 7:26).

It is also while Mark and Matthew are substantially in parallel, with nothing corresponding in Luke, that we get the revealing insertion by Mark of two miracle stories that are peculiar to him. Where Matthew at the end of the first Feeding cycle has a general statement of healings (Mt 15:29-31), Mark has the healing of a deaf man with an impediment in his speech (7:32-37), and after the second Feeding cycle, that of the healing of a blind man (8:22-26). These are the only miracle stories peculiar to Mark, and their characteristics merit attention. (In the following little synopsis the word "inarticulate" represents the Greek μογιλάλον, to avoid the usual periphrasis "with an impediment in his speech.")

MARK 7:32-36	MARK 8:22-26
32 καὶ φέρουσιν αὐτῷ κωφὸν καὶ μογιλάλον καὶ παρακαλοῦσιν αὐτὸν ἵνα ἐπιθῇ αὐτῷ τὴν χεῖρα.	22 καὶ φέρουσιν αὐτῷ τυφλὸν καὶ παρακαλοῦσιν αὐτὸν ἵνα αὐτοῦ ἅψηται.
33 καὶ ἀπολαβόμενος αὐτὸν ἀπὸ τοῦ ὄχλου κατ' ἰδίαν ἔβαλεν τοὺς δακτύλους αὐτοῦ εἰς τὰ ὦτα αὐτοῦ καὶ πτύσας ἥψατο τῆς γλώσσης αὐτοῦ	23 καὶ ἐπιλαβόμενος τῆς χειρὸς τοῦ τυφλοῦ ἐξήνεγκεν αὐτὸν ἔξω τῆς κώμης, καὶ πτύσας εἰς τὰ ὄμματα αὐτοῦ ἐπιθεὶς τὰς χεῖρας αὐτῷ ἐπηρώτα αὐτόν· Εἴ τι βλέπεις;
34 καὶ ἀναβλέψας εἰς τὸν οὐρανὸν ἐστέναξεν καὶ λέγει αὐτῷ· Εφφαθα, ὅ ἐστιν, Διανοίχθητι.	24 καὶ ἀναβλέψας ἔλεγεν· Βλέπω τοὺς ἀνθρώπους ὅτι ὡς δένδρα περιπατοῦντες·
	25 εἶτα πάλιν ἐπέθηκεν τὰς χεῖρας ἐπὶ τοὺς ὀφθαλμοὺς αὐτοῦ, καὶ διέβλεψεν καὶ ἀπεκατέστη καὶ ἐνέβλεψεν τηλαυγῶς ἅπαντα.
35 καὶ [εὐθέως] ἠνοίγησαν αὐτοῦ αἱ ἀκοαί, καὶ ἐλύθη ὁ δεσμὸς τῆς γλώσσης αὐτοῦ καὶ ἐλάλει ὀρθῶς 36 καὶ διεστείλατο αὐτοῖς ἵνα μηδενὶ λέγωσιν·	26 καὶ ἀπέστειλεν αὐτὸν εἰς οἶκον αὐτοῦ λέγων· Μηδὲ εἰς τὴν κώμην εἰσέλθῃς·
ὅσον δὲ αὐτοῖς διεστέλλετο, αὐτοὶ μᾶλλον περισσότερον ἐκήρυσσον.	

MARK 7:32-36	MARK 8:22-26
32 And they brought to him a deaf and inarticulate man, and besought him to lay his hand upon him.	22 And they brought to him a blind man, and besought him to touch him.
33 And taking him aside from the multitude privately he put his fingers into his ears, and he spat and touched his tongue,	23 And he took the blind man by the hand and led him out of the village, and when he had spit upon his eyes and laid his hands upon him, he asked him, "Do you see anything?"
34 and looking up to heaven he sighed, and said to him, "Ephphatha," that is, "Be opened."	24 and he looked up and said, "I see men, but they look like trees walking."
	25 Then again he put his fingers upon his eyes, and he looked intently and was restored
35 And his ears were opened his tongue was released and he spoke plainly.	and saw everything clearly.
36 And he charged them to tell no one	26 And he sent him away to his home saying, "Do not even enter the village."
but the more he charged them the more zealously they proclaimed it.	

There are two remarkable things about the form of this pair of miracles: the striking parallelism of structure between them, a parallelism that they do not share with any other miracle story; and the constellation of so many Markan usages in so short a space. The first of these is obvious from the two texts. The second calls for more comment. Mark uses φέρειν 14 times (4 times in each of Matthew and Luke), especially in the sense of "bringing" persons (7 times). The impersonal plural (as in "they brought" for "there was brought") occurs 22 times in Mark. The construction παρακαλεῖν ἵνα is found 5 times in Mark (Mt 1, Lk 2). The phrase "from the crowd" (7:33) also occurs in 7:17 in the same sense—"going away from the crowd"; the words "out of the village" in 8:23 have the same significance. The use of the Aramaic "Ephphatha" (εφφαθα = אתפתח), with its translation introduced by the words "that is," has its parallels in 3:17; 5:41; 7:11; 15:22; 15:34; the use of "Ephphatha" here is in line especially with the "Talitha coum" (Ταλιθα κουμ = טלתא קומ) of 5:41. The verb διαστέλλεσθαι, "to charge," occurs five times in Mark (once in Matthew, never in Luke).[8]

What then is the explanation of these facts? And why are the stories not recorded in Matthew or Luke? Many answers have been suggested to the latter question. It has been suggested that Matthew and Luke objected to

[8]For further examples, see Benoit and Boismard, *Synopse des Quatre Évangiles*, II:297.

the reference to spittle (an objection not felt by the author of Jn 9:6) that they "considered the manipulation of the affected organs and the use of material means like spittle to be unworthy of the Lord";[9] or again, that they disliked the thought that "the recovery of sight is gradual, and Christ asks a question εἴ τι βλέπεις; as though he were not sure how far recovery had taken place."[10] The multiplicity of such "reasons" is in itself an indication of the inadequacy of each of them, and to suppose that the two miracle stories were added to Mark's text at a stage later than when Matthew saw it would be a last desperate resort for the Markan priorist. Instead of asking why Matthew (and Luke) omitted these stories, it is more to the point to ask why so many of the features referred to are concentrated in these two stories, peculiar to Mark. And why is it that the two stories with so many parallels occur in this matter peculiar to him; why does it happen that no other miracle story in Mark has anything like the same correspondence?[11] The simplest, and surely the most convincing explanation is that the manner of telling them is just pure Mark, unaffected by the language of Matthew. If Mark used Matthew and Luke in constructing the Gospel, but added these stories in his own words, or even in the words he had received from another source, the problem disappears.

The question "Who is He?" receives its answer in the episode in the region of Caesarea Philippi. Like Luke, Mark simply gives in it the assertion that Jesus is the Christ (Mk 8:29), and indeed in the simplest form, "You are the Christ," when Luke has the fuller form "the Christ of God," and Matthew has "the Christ, the Son of the living God" (16:16). To Luke and to Mark it is the one point that needs to be made in the development of their themes. Matthew's addition of the blessing of Simon Bar-Jona (16:17-19), a unit with strong Aramaic characteristics, introduces matters that are outside the structure of the other Synoptics; its inclusion in Matthew in no way suggests that it is an addition to Mark, who like Luke would naturally enough omit it, having made his climactic point.[12]

---

[9]A. E. J. Rawlinson, *St Mark* (London, 1925) 102.

[10]So W. C. Allen, *Gospel according to St. Matthew*, ICC, 170. Allen lists other objections.

[11]There is a partial parallel in the distinctive Markan features of 5:41-48. In 5:41, λέγει αὐτῇ, Ταλιθα κουμ, ὅ ἐστιν is parallel to 7:34, λέγει αὐτῷ, Εφφαθα, ὅ ἐστιν, and both have καὶ διεστείλατο αὐτοῖς (5:43; 7:36).

[12]For Mt 16:17-19, see B. F. Meyer, *The Aims of Jesus* (London, 1979) 185ff.

7. "A ransom for many," Mt 16:21–28:20

From Peter's Confession onward, the three Synoptics are, so far as their common material is concerned, closely in parallel sequence.[13] At 18:21 Matthew picks up the thread of 4:17 ("from that time Jesus began to preach"), with the words "from that time Jesus began to show his disciples that he must go to Jerusalem." Mark, who missed the significance of Matthew's wording at 4:17, now simply has "and he began to teach them that the Son of Man must suffer many things" (Mk 8:31); the crucial word "Jerusalem," which reveals Jesus' decision and purpose, is absent, but the word "began" betrays Mark's dependence on Matthew, and the form of his sentence may well reflect his familiarity with the words of Mt 17:12, "the Son of man will suffer" (without parallel at that point).

At 17:24 Matthew has the pericope about the Temple Tax. It deals with a matter that would no longer be of concern for Mark's readers, if he wrote in Italy,[14] and its omission by Mark is wholly natural. It begins with the words "when he came to Capernaum," and Mark makes use of this phrase at the beginning of his next pericope (as he also does of Matthew's reference to "the house," Mt 17:25; Mk 9:33), where Matthew has the vague "in that hour" (Mt 18:1) and Luke gives no indication of context at all (Lk 9:46). In doing so, however, Mark betrays his knowledge of Matthew's story about the temple tax. Matthew has had a consistent sequence: "they were gathering in Galilee . . . they came to Capernaum . . . they came into the house." Mark has lost this consistency by saying at 9:30 "they passed through Galilee, and he [Jesus] would not have anyone know it." The words about secrecy are an editorial addition by Mark, and fit badly with the subsequent reference to Capernaum and "the house," where Jesus' presence would certainly be known. But the references are derived from Matthew's story about the temple tax, although this is omitted by Mark, to provide a setting for what follows.

We have a similar indication of Mark's awareness of material that he does not use, in his appending the words "and many that are first will be last, and the last first" at the end of the sayings about rewards for forsaking all (10:31) where they have no particular appropriateness. The words are used in Mt 19:30 to introduce a parable—"and many that are first will be last, and the last first, for the kingdom of heaven is like a householder"— and repeated at the end of the parable to provide an "inclusion": "so the

---

[13]Cf. the table in ch. 1, above, 4-6.

[14]For the significance of Mt 17:24-27 for the dating of Matthew, see J. A. T. Robinson, *Redating the New Testament* (London, 1976) 104-105.

last will be first and the first last.'' Mark has copied Matthew's opening,
but stopped short of the parable.

At 9:38-41 Mark has an episode (on the strange exorcist) in common
with Luke only. Then after the warnings against temptation (Mt 18:6-9;
Mk 9:42-50) there is a gap in the common synoptic sequence, due to Matthew's discourse continuing to the end of his chapter 18, and Luke's insertion of his central section (Lk 9:51-18:14). Mark picks up the thread
again when the narrative material is resumed (Mt 19:1; Mk 10:1), with the
departure to Judea. For the rest of the narrative of the Gospel, Mark is in
close sequence with Matthew and Luke, allowing for switching over from
one to the other when they have material peculiar to them.

To a large extent the narrative of the Passion imposes its own sequence,
and this accounts for much of the common order of the Synoptics for the
rest of the Gospel. There is one question of order, however, not the order
of pericopes, but of the events recorded, that calls for attention. It is commonly said that the dating of the Last Supper in the Synoptics (assumed to
be derived from Mark's narrative) is different from that of John. According to John (12:1) the Anointing at Bethany was six days before the Passover; the Supper took place ''before the feast of the Passover'' (13:2); Jesus
therefore died on the afternoon when the Passover lambs were sacrificed
(see Jn 18:28) and the Feast of Unleavened Bread fell on the next day, the
sabbath, which was therefore ''a high day'' (19:31), a sabbath for two different reasons. That is a clear and convincing chronology. How does Matthew compare with this?

As regards the Anointing at Bethany, Matthew inserts this between the
plot to kill Jesus and his betrayal by Judas. It is introduced by the words
''now when Jesus was at Bethany,'' and there is therefore no reason to
suppose that Matthew, having spoken of the plot two days before the Passover, has recorded, or has meant to record, the Anointing in its chronological order. So far there is no problem.

According to Matthew (and Mark) the chief priests and scribes decided
not to seek the death of Jesus ''during the feast'' (ἐν τῇ ἑορτῇ), an insertion in the narrative that would not have been made if Matthew meant
that Jesus actually did die on the day of the Feast of Unleavened Bread.
Luke omits the words ''not during the feast,'' but betrays his knowledge
of them by the words ''for they feared the people'' (22:2). Of all the Synoptics, Matthew is the one who is most at home in dealing with Jewish customs, and the least likely to make mistakes in recording them. There is,
however, one serious problem. At 26:17 Matthew puts the preparation for
the Passover by the disciples as on ''the first [day] of Unleavened Bread.''
If he were using words with technical accuracy, that would be the day fol-

lowing the sacrificing of the lambs, but in ordinary usage need mean no more than ''the first day of the festival.''[15] Luke, writing for a public less interested in what the Jews did day by day speaks of ''the day of Unleavened Bread, on which the Passover had to be sacrificed'' (22:7); and Mark follows him in this: ''when they sacrificed the Passover'' (14:12). Both are merely making a general statement about the whole complex of the festival. Where the problem lies is in Matthew's words ''on the first [day]'' (τῇ δὲ πρώτῃ), which Mark makes more specific by adding the word ''day'' (ἡμέρα), naturally enough. If an Aramaic original lay behind Matthew, his words might be due to a mistranslation, but since there is good reason to suppose his Gospel was first written in Greek, Matthew must have meant to write what he did. If he did not mean that Jesus was killed ''on the feast,'' it would appear that ''the first day'' was merely meant to refer to the first of the days during which the festival was kept, the day on which the necessary preparations were made for the unleavened bread to be ready for the Passover meal. The disciples' question would not be out of place on that day. Jesus' reply included the words ''My time is at hand'' (26:18), not found in either Mark or Luke, which are equivalent to saying ''My time is short'' with the implication that Jesus could not wait for the usual day for the Passover supper. The same implication would seem to underlie the words of Lk 22:15: ''With desire I have desired to eat this Passover with you before I suffer, for I tell you, I shall not eat it [or, I shall never eat it again] until it is fulfilled in the kingdom of God.'' There is no suggestion that the householder would be having the Passover meal on the same day as Jesus, who ''sat at table with the twelve disciples'' (Mt 26:20). The consciousness that the actual Feast of Unleavened Bread coincided with the sabbath may account for Matthew's describing it in 27:62 as ''the next day, that is the day after the Day of Preparation'' instead of simply as ''the sabbath.''

Luke and Mark are influenced by Matthew's text. If ''when it was evening'' in Mt 27:57; Mk 15:42, means after sundown, it was already the sabbath, and Mark's addition ''because it was the Day of Preparation'' means that he is thinking in terms of the Roman and not the Jewish day. He also adds for his non-Jewish readers one of his notes of explanation: ''that is, the day before the sabbath.''[16]

We can endorse the judgment of P. Bénoit on the dating of the Last Supper in the Synoptics: ''The only distortion in the Synoptic tradition was to

---

[15]Cf. Josephus, *Antiquities* II.317, ''a feast for eight days, called the feast of unleavened bread.''

[16]Cf. 3:17; 5:41; 7:3-4; 12:42; 15:22.

attribute a fully Passover character to what in reality can only have been an anticipation and evocation of the Passover that was to be celebrated on the following day, but included the institution of a new rite destined to replace it, a distortion which is easily explained by the liturgical origins of the narrative and comes back to the theological truth,''[17] with the caveat that it is not necessary to see this distortion in the Matthaean text. Luke has not taken into account the warning of Mt 26:5, ''not during the feast,'' and neither Luke nor Mark the significance of Mt 26:18, ''my time is at hand.''

As we go through the plan of Matthew's Gospel, there are clear indications that this plan has not been due to dependence on Mark, nor is it a pattern imposed on Markan material. On the contrary, the indications are that Mark has quarried material from Matthew and Luke.

---

[17]P. Benoit in *Rev Bib* (1958): 590-94; English translation: "The Death of Judas," in *Jesus and the Gospel,* vol. 1 (London, 1973).

4

The New Order of Luke

1. The Pattern of Luke

Alone of the Synoptics, Luke tells us that he is going to "write in order" (καθεξῆς, 1:3). In the broadest sense, Luke's order is the same as Matthew's—Introduction, Ministry, Passion; but in the second volume of the book in which he worked through the themes of the Christian kerygma Luke gives us a further note on his plan. Just as he indicates that the plan of the second volume is that of witness to the gospel "in Jerusalem, and in all Judea and Samaria, and unto the end of the earth" (Act 1:8), and then proceeds to illustrate this as he describes the progress of that witness in Jerusalem (1:1–8:3), then in Judea and Samaria (8:4–12:25), and finally to the capital of the known world, to Rome as representing "the end of the earth" (13:1–28:31), so in looking back to his first volume, Luke tells us that it was to deal with "all that Jesus began to do and to teach, until the day that he was taken up" (Ac 1:1). After his introduction, including the Infancy of Jesus (1:1–3:38), he therefore concentrates in the Gospel on "all that Jesus began to do" (4:1–9:50), then on what Jesus "began to teach" (9:51–18:30), and finally, in the narrative of the Passion, Resurrection and Ascension, on the events leading to "the day that he was taken up" (18:31–24:53).

Fortunately we can go further than that. Ever since the publication in 1936 of C. H. Dodd's *The Apostolic Preaching and its Developments,* it has been widely recognized that on the evidence of the speeches Luke records in Acts, he included these elements as constituting the kerygma:

(1) the proclamation of Jesus, the Son of David, as Christ and Lord;
(2) the Ministry of Jesus, "mighty in word and deed" (Lk 24:19);
(3) the Passion and Crucifixion;
(4) the Resurrection;
(5) the Ascension and Exaltation;
(6) the gift of the Holy Spirit;
(7) the witness of the apostles, with its call to repentance, and promise of forgiveness;
(8) the future coming of Jesus, and the consequent judgment.

It is this kerygma that provides the theme for Luke's two-volume work. The final element in it could not be treated in the historical framework Luke used, and it is therefore only introduced incidentally, and primarily in the words of Jesus. The first five elements are the subject of the Gospel, the Ascension making a link with the second volume, which continues the series. In the Gospel itself we therefore have this expanded form:

1:1–3:38 Introduction: Jesus comes, the Son of David, proclaimed as Christ the Lord;
4:1–9:50 The Ministry: Part I: What Jesus began to do;
9:51–18:30 The Ministry: Part II: What Jesus began to teach;
18:31–24:53 The Passion and Exaltation: "Until the day that he was taken up."

There is here a definite pattern, only partly dependent on that of Matthew, as indeed the material used will only in part be derived from him, for Luke has other material to use as well. The resulting pattern will therefore not be identical with that of Matthew, but Luke's claim to have written "in order" is fully justified. He uses that order to provide an appropriate framework for his own exposition of "the things fulfilled among us" (1:1).

2. The Introduction, Lk 1:1–3:38

Luke clearly has his own sources for the Infancy narratives, which are wholly independent of Matthew.[1] They appear to be three: that of the main narrative (1:5–2:52); that of the two songs—of Mary (1:46-56) and of Zechariah (1:68-80); and that of the genealogy. (The Song of Mary is inserted at the close of the story of the Annunciation and its endpiece, the Visitation; and the Song of Zechariah is inserted after the birth of the Baptist; each being added just before the final sentence of the narrative although the latter could very naturally have been fitted into the course of the narrative after 1:64.) With the narrative beginning with the announcement of the coming birth of the Baptist, Luke could not do what Matthew had done and make the genealogy the first thing in his Gospel; he therefore made it the last thing in his Introduction. These arrangements are of the same kind as Luke makes elsewhere, as for example in the place in which he records the Call of Peter (5:1-11), when he includes material from a source different from that of its context.

Coming to the period of John's preaching (3:1-22), Luke has Matthew's text available, but first he marks the new beginning with a six-fold dating, and connects what is to follow with what has already been related. So he passes on to repeat what he has found in Matthew, with two additions. In

---

[1]That Luke knew Matthew does not warrant the assumption that "Luke has woven the Matthean themes into his own tapestry: a tapestry made of Old Testament skeins" (J. Drury, *Tradition and Design in Luke's Gospel* [London, 1976] 126).

the first, he extends Matthew's quotation from Isaiah 40 to include the words "and all flesh shall see the salvation of God." Luke never forgets the end to which his story leads. The second addition, that of the practical application of John's message of repentance (3:10-14), coming from a different source, is kept back to add at the end of the Matthean text of John's preaching, before the words that contrast the baptism with water and that with the Holy Spirit and with fire lead on to the record of Jesus himself being baptized.

Apart from these two additions, Luke is following Matthew, and it is illuminating to observe his methods. There is a distinction between the way he treats the spoken words, and the narrative that enshrines them. In the spoken words, apart from small stylistic variants, he copies Matthew closely, but he clearly feels free to remodel the words of the narrative in his own style.

The introduction draws to its close, with the reference to John's imprisonment and the record of Jesus' own baptism. Here the reader reaches the first of the three peaks in the Gospel landscape: first, the Baptism, with the Father's voice saying "Thou art my beloved Son" as the seal of approval on Jesus' vocation; the second the Transfiguration, with the voice from heaven saying "This is my Son" as the seal on his Ministry; and finally the Ascension, the seal of his Passion. Now, before the story of the Ministry begins, Luke, as we have seen, appends the genealogy[2] to close the section.

3. "All that Jesus began to do," Lk 4:1-9:50

After the Baptism, Matthew continues, "Then was Jesus led up by the Spirit into the wilderness to be tempted by the devil" (Mt 4:1). Luke, to whom the Temptation was the beginning of the account of what Jesus did, extends this, with the significance of the Baptism in mind, to "And Jesus, full of the Holy Spirit, returned from the Jordan, and was led by the Spirit in the wilderness during forty days, being tempted by the devil." His phrase avoids the interpretation that could be put on Matthew's wording, that the Holy Spirit led Jesus into temptation (cf. Mt 3:13, "to be baptized"). Matthew and Luke differ in the order of the temptations. The ground of temptation was in the significance of the title "Son of God," and Luke may

---

[2]Luke seems to have had an Aramaic source for the genealogy, as is suggested by the misunderstanding of the word "Rhesa" ('Ρησά) in 3:27. J. Jeremias concludes that "we shall not hesitate to assume that Luke or his source may have preserved authentic material, at least for the last few generations before Joseph" (*Jerusalem in the Time of Jesus* [ET: London, 1969] 297).

have rearranged the order so as to end with an inclusion, the first and the last of the three tempations in his order beginning "If thou art the Son of God."

From the Temptation, Matthew moves rapidly to the Sermon on the Mount. He prepares for it by recording that Jesus left Nazareth for Capernaum and began to preach and heal in Galilee, and called his first disciples. He then passes immediately to his first compilation of Jesus' teaching. For Luke, the first thing to be done is to show "all that Jesus began to do," reserving the fuller treatment of all that he began to teach for later inclusion. Matthew himself at a later point (13:53-58) has a short narrative of Jesus "in his own country"; for Luke it is convenient to bring this forward, since he has a fuller tradition that supplies what he needs here, and enables him to begin where Jesus has lived hitherto, at Nazareth. It is significant that here, and here alone, he uses the form "Nazara," which he copies from Mt 4:13 (the only place where Matthew uses it), for he is still keeping his eye on where he has got to in Matthew's text.

Luke is therefore able to serve three purposes: he can set out a program for Jesus' Ministry; he can point out its character of fulfillment; and he can show the first signs of something he has already foreshadowed: "Behold, this child is set for the fall and rising up of many in Israel" (2:34). The theme of acceptance and rejection runs through all Luke's two-volume work: at Nazareth, in Galilee and at Jerusalem, and after, down to what are almost the final words of Acts: "By hearing ye shall hear; and shall in no wise understand, and seeing ye shall see, and shall in no wise perceive" (Ac 28:26).

At the point where Luke turned from Matthew's order (the point at which the reading "Nazara" appears, 4:16), Matthew was speaking of Jesus going to Capernaum, so to Capernaum Luke now turns. He has already had perforce to refer to it (4:23) as a place to which Jesus had already been, but this was incidental to his following a thematic rather than a chronological order. Omitting Matthew's Call of the First Disciples, for which Luke is to substitute a narrative from a different tradition, Luke merely adds Matthew's comment at the end of the Sermon (which he also leaves aside for the present) that Jesus spoke with authority (Mt 7:28-29; Lk 4:31-32). Luke is then ready to speak of Capernaum and the mission in Galilee, and having from another source the story of an exorcism in the synagogue at Capernaum, Luke inserts this here (4:33-37) before returning to Matthew.

Not having so far included the Call of Peter, it is convenient for Luke to resume, from Matthew's accounts of events at Capernaum, with the healing of Peter's wife's mother (4:38-39), to lead into the story of Peter's Call; just as the reference at Nazareth has led to the dealing with Capernaum. The story of healings at Capernaum therefore follows, as in Matthew (Mt 8:14-17; Lk 4:28-41); and Luke adds a note of his own, not taken from Matthew, of the departure from Capernaum (4:42-43), and so closes this group of narratives with the words suggested by Matthew's own conclusion before the Sermon on the Mount (Mt 4:22; Lk 4:44). Luke is fond of such summaries.

Having now covered the narrative material in Matthew as far as Mt 8:17, except for the Call of Peter and the two stories appended to the Sermon on the Mount, Luke now deals with the former (5:1-11). Having used the name of Simon previously, at 5:8 Luke speaks of "Simon Peter," making the identification clear.

Before beginning a fresh theme, Luke fills up another of the gaps in his use of Matthew. At Nazareth, Jesus had spoken of the widow to whom Elijah was sent, and of the leper cleansed by Elisha. Elisha had performed a miracle for a widow of whom God had said, "Behold, I have commanded a widow there to feed thee" (1 Kgs 17:9); Jesus had been sent from Nazareth (cf. Lk 4:43) (and no doubt there were many widows in Nazareth), and healed Peter's wife's mother, who "rose and served them." Elisha had healed a leper, and Luke seems to have been attracted to complete the widow-leper parallel (5:12-16). But in doing so he is careful not to invent a different context from that of Matthew; he gives a vague one instead: when Jesus "was in one of the cities."[3]

Luke has already recorded that Jesus met opposition even in his own city Nazareth. He now has to show that the opposition with which his readers were familiar in the growth of the Church was already manifest in an area broader than Nazareth. He therefore takes two separate groups of stories from Matthew (Mt 9:1-17; 12:1-14). It is the resultant group of five stories of conflict which was to reappear in Mark. For the first of these, the healing of a paralytic (Lk 5:17-26), Luke has a fuller version than Matthew's, but unlike Matthew, who has the story in a chronological order (Mt 9:1) and connects it with Capernaum, Luke only tells it for its lesson, and simply says it was "on one of those days." Then, because he is now following Matthew's sequence, he can add "after these things" in introducing the story of Levi and the tax collectors (Lk 5:27-32; Mt 9:9-13). It is not clear why he substitutes the name "Levi" for "Matthew."

Luke can still follow Matthew's sequence (Lk 5:33-39; Mt 9:14-17), for the next account in Matthew is of a controversy about fasting, since the disciples of Jesus did not conform to the practice of the Pharisees or of

---

[3] J. B. Orchard (*Matthew, Luke, and Mark* [Greater Manchester, 1976] 115n54) points out that this phrase of Luke's signifies an editorial transfer of a story to another location.

John's disciples. Controversy over fasting customs lasted into the period of the Church (cf. *Didache* 8; *Ep. of Barnabas* 3); to the Evangelist the matter was one that concerned the freedom of Christians from earlier traditions.

So far, in this part of the Gospel, Luke has been able to follow Matthew's order, but there are two other narratives in Matthew (12:1-14) that deal with related matters. Luke therefore, writing "in order," includes them here (6:1-11). Both are concerned with the keeping of the sabbath. As Luke has taken them out of their context in Matthew, he simply introduces the first story as "on a sabbath," and the second as "on another sabbath." Luke's text for the second story, the healing of the man with the withered hand, differs in some ways from Matthew's, and is perhaps modified by his having a different version also at his disposal. The story is of a pair with that of the healing of the man with the dropsy, recorded by Luke alone (14:1-6).

Luke has now been able to give a picture of Jesus' Ministry, and to speak of the opposition that he encountered. He can now begin to speak of Jesus' teaching to his disciples, and in effect to fill up the gap left by passing over Matthew's Sermon on the Mount. At its beginning, Matthew had said that "his disciples came," and only later, in parenthesis, gives the name of the Twelve (Mt 10:2-4). It was clearly convenient for Luke to name the Twelve here: "he called his disciples, and he chose from them twelve."

The difference between the two forms of the Sermon are obvious. That Luke shows some dependence on Matthew is suggested by his wording "But I say unto you" (Lk 6:27; Mt 5:44) when he had not included the earlier words "You have heard it said"; and by the words that follow the Sermon, "After he had ended all his sayings" (Lk 7:1; cf. Mt 7:28); and by the story of the centurion's servant following in sequence, Luke having already used that of the leper.[4] There is another remarkable fact: there is a great difference between the degree of identity between Matthew's text and Luke's in the passages which Luke has in the Sermon and those he includes elsewhere. The one exception is Mt 7:1-5; Lk 6:37-38, 41-42. Apart from it, if one takes Mt 5:3-12, 38-48, 7:12, 16-21, 24-27, all of which have parallels in Luke, only 30 per cent of Matthew's words are found identically in Luke's Sermon. On the other hand, in Mt 6:22–7:11 (omitting 7:5, "Pearls before swine," not in Luke), the percentage of words identical with Luke's in a different context is 69.5. One might have expected the opposite. Luke seems to have had two sources for the Sermon:

---

[4]See the comparative table of the two Great Sermons in J. B. Orchard, *Matthew, Luke, and Mark,* chart IIA, which shows that Luke follows Matthew's order in principle.

Matthew and a shorter version. He followed the non-Matthaean form in general in recording the Sermon, but used the additional matter in Matthew as a quarry for material for his teaching section. This gives a clear reason why the verbal correspondence between Matthew's text and that of Luke's Sermon is so loose, and that with Luke's later passages so close.

Having already included the healing of a leper (5:12-16), Luke continues with the next narrative in Matthew's sequence, the healing of a centurion's servant. Like Matthew, he begins by saying that Jesus entered Capernaum; then when Matthew's narrative uses a word (παῖς) which might mean either either a "child" or "servant," Luke avoids the ambiguity by using a different word (δοῦλος, "servant"), but at 7:6, when spoken words form the bulk of the text, he keeps closer to Matthew's wording, and uses παις where Matthew has it.[5]

In dealing with "all that Jesus began to do" Luke has therefore covered all the material in Matthew as far at Mt 8:17. He now passes on to Mt 11:2, and at first this looks like an abandonment of Matthew's order, but the matter calls for closer scrutiny. Luke has already used Mt 9:1-17. Mt 9:35–11:1 is the discourse on discipleship, the kind of material that Luke wants for the next part of the Gospel, "all that Jesus began to teach"; and Mt 8:18-22, on claimants to discipleship, can be used to introduce it. Mt 9:27-34, on healings of the blind and dumb is partly a general statement, and partly a doublet of Mt 12:22-24, which serves a more useful purpose, and will be used by Luke. This leaves only the stories of the Stilling of the Storm (Mt 8:23-27), the Gadarene demoniacs (Mt 8:28-34) and Jairus's Daughter (9:18-26), which Luke will include later, in that sequence. Apart from the one interruption caused by this transference, he is to follow Matthew's order of events up to the end of this part of the Gospel (9:50).

The omission of the material of Mt 8:18–11:1 enables Luke to come to the question of John from his prison, with the reply of Jesus pointing to the significance of his works. To justify the inclusion of the words "the dead are raised up," Luke, who unlike Matthew has not yet spoken of Jairus's daughter, inserts first the story of the widow's son at Nain.

---

[5]Cf. R. Bultmann, *From Tradition to Gospel* (ET: London, 1934) 33, who cites two passages (Mt 11:2-6 ‖ Lk 17:18-23 and Mt 7:8-10 ‖ Lk 7:4), the record of the messengers of the Baptist and the story of the centurion, where Matthew and Luke vary greatly in the wording of their introduction and conclusion, "but the kernel is handed down almost as a unity." The writers, Bultmann concludes, "clearly differentiated their responsibility towards the text of Jesus' words from their duty as narrators."

So, omitting the material that he wants for his teaching section, and two stories of controversy (Mt 12:1-14) which he has already used, but adding one story of his own, that of the woman with the ointment (7:36-50), Luke comes to Matthew's collection of parables (Mt 13:1-52). Just as in dealing with the Sermon on the Mount Luke recognized its place as a necessary element in describing Jesus' Ministry, but avoided making it the occasion for a lengthy collection of teaching, so now he limits his insertion to the Parable of the Sower and its interpretation. One pair of Matthew's other parables from the same collection he uses later in his teaching section— the Mustard Seed and Leaven. Here, having transferred the parable of the Sower to a new position, Luke, with his usual care, omits Matthew's precise setting in time and place ("on that day . . . by the sea side," Mt 13:1), and simply says "when a great crowd came together."

After this, Luke sets about filling in the gap left by the omission of narratives from Mt 8:23 onwards; again, having altered Matthew's order, he avoids Matthew's precise context (Mt 8:18). For the three miracle stories that follow (Stilling the Storm, the Gerasene Demoniac, and Jairus's Daughter, Mt 8:23-56) Luke has a fuller account than Matthew, and it may well be that it is his having another source as well as Matthew available that has influenced him in moving the material to this point.

In Matthew the three miracle stories are followed by two (Mt 9:27-34), which are doublets of, or at least very similar to Mt 20:29-34 and 12:22-24. It is natural for Luke to omit them here; so at Mt 9:35-38 Luke finds another of Matthew's long discourses (10:1-42), beginning with the sending out of the Twelve. Luke treats this as he has done the previous discourses: he takes account of it as showing what Jesus has been doing (9:1-6), but still leaves over the fuller exposition of Jesus' teaching for inclusion in his central section.

Luke can now skip a long section of Matthew (11:1–13:58) which, with the same reservation, he has already used. This brings him to the note in Mt 14:1-2 concerning Herod's opinion of Jesus. To Matthew, this is a useful introduction to the account of the Baptist's death, but this latter is irrelevant to Luke's main theme and is therefore omitted. What Luke does, by extending Matthew's note with the words "Who is this about whom I hear such things? And he sought to see him," is to foreshadow the part that he tells us Herod was to play in the Passion drama.

Omitting the story of John's death, Luke adds a note (9:10) of the return of the Twelve, and passes on to Matthew's next narrative, the Feeding of the Five Thousand, and then on to the Confession of Peter. For Matthew and Mark the latter event follows the second feeding miracle, but it is at this point that Luke's "great omission" occurs. Streeter felt compelled, "to ask whether Luke's 'great omission' can be explained by any other hypothesis than the absence of the material from his source," and tentatively suggested that Luke used a multilated copy of Mark.[6] But the omission does not demand such a drastic hypothesis. Luke has not unlimited space, and Mt 14:22-16:12 is not needed to complete his theme. He can omit the Walking on the Water and the healings that followed (Mt 14:22-36) without serious loss; and the passage about the Tradition of the Elders (Mt 15:1-20) is irrelevant to his purpose; nor did he need to add to his list of healings what followed in Matthew (Mt 15:21-31); while the Feeding of the Four Thousand (Mt 15:32-39) only repeated a point that had already been made. The tradition clearly made a connection between a great Feeding and the Confession of Peter, whether that was the Feeding of the Five Thousand or the Four Thousand, and Luke makes the immediate transition.

The first part of Luke's account of Jesus' Ministry ("all that Jesus began to do") is drawing to its close. It began with Jesus' proclamation of what he had been anointed to do (4:16-21); the fulfillment of this was claimed in the response to the question of John's disciples (7:22-23)—Jesus had done the works of the Messiah; it is time for the conclusion to be drawn in the response to Jesus' question to his disciples: "Who do you say that I am?" Peter's answer, "the Christ of God," is the conclusion to which the readers have been led (9:18-21). Because the rest of the Gospel is to go further, to show that the Christ must suffer, Luke prepares for this by including Matthew's words predicting the Passion, though even here it is put in the form that "the Son of man must suffer"; it is only after the Resurrection that Luke puts this in the form that "the Christ" had to suffer (24:26, 45), just as "while he was still in Galilee" Jesus had said "that the Son of man must be delivered into the hands of sinful men" (24:6, 7).

So Luke, like Matthew, comes to the Transfiguration, the great climax of this half of the Gospel. With the words "This is my Son" (9:35) we reach the second of the three peaks of Christ's manifestation, after which the words "Listen to him" are a fitting preparation for the exposition of Jesus' teaching which is to follow. From the rest of Matthew's narrative Luke includes the healing of the epileptic boy, as following on the Transfiguration, and the second prediction of the Passion, but not the story of the Temple Tax (Mt 17:24-27), no longer important to his readers. He includes the note about true greatness (omitting "at that hour," Mt 18:11, since he has broken Matthew's context), and adds to Matthew's text the warning of Jesus, "He who is not against you is for you" (9:37-50).

---

[6]B. H. Streeter, *The Four Gospels* (London, 1924) 175.

4. "All that Jesus began to teach," Lk 9:51–18:30

At 9:51 Luke begins the next main divison of his Gospel, in which he sets out the teaching of Jesus more fully. The setting is that of a gradual approach to Jerusalem, with periodic reminders of this, but they are of a very general nature until the approach to Jericho at the end of the journey.[7] Before that, only two references are to a particular locality (9:52; 17:11), in both cases because the reference is necessary for the point of the story. Luke makes no attempt to plot the course of a journey, he is merely reminding his readers of where the work of Jesus is leading him, and putting the record of his teaching in this setting, since he has now abandoned the order of Matthew's record. The reader is to learn from Jesus' teaching, but not to forget that he was always on the way to a goal, to Jerusalem and to the Passion. Only when the goal was, as it were, in sight, are we brought back to topography (18:31).

The first of Matthew's great discourses was the Sermon on the Mount. Luke has already drawn upon some of this material, some of it falls outside the special interests of Luke's Gentile readers, and the rest deals with a variety of subjects. It is therefore natural that Luke should start this part of his Gospel with the second discourse, the commission to the apostles. This is in line with his own description of his Gospel; "All that Jesus began to do and to teach, until that day on which he was received up, after he had given commandments to the apostles whom he had chosen" (Ac 1:1-2). After a brief introduction (9:51-56), Luke prefaces to the commission the incidents of would-be disciples, adding a third to Matthew's pair. Having already mentioned the commissioning of the Twelve, Luke, while "covering" Matthew's material, now gives instructions as addressed to the Seventy, about whom he must have learned from a different tradition. His text is not a close, but only a lightly edited, version of Matthew's, but we can easily follow his use of Matthew.[8] Beginning from Mt 8:18-22 ("would-be disciples"), and omitting the material from which he has already taken all he needs, Luke comes to Mt 9:35–10:16, the commission to the apostles. He omits the names of the Twelve, which he has already given. At Mt 10:17 the theme changes to that of the persecution of Christians, and this is followed by the passage about the witness of John; Luke

---

[7] See ch. 2, n. 3, above.

[8] If, as C. F. Evans says of Luke's central section, "the commentators have been at a loss what to make of it" (*Studies in the Gospels,* ed. D. E. Nineham [Oxford, 1955] 40), that is surely because they have not appreciated Luke's own statement in Ac 1:1-2 and his use of Matthew. It is these, and not the order of Deuteronomy (as Evans suggested) that provide the necessary clue.

therefore passes over this, and resumes at Mt 11:20 with the Woes on the Unbelieving Cities and, after a short insertion to record the return of the Seventy, with Christ's Thanksgiving to the Father (10:21-24). Passing over the material in Matthew that follows this (Mt 12:1-21), which he has already used, and the entirely different subject matter of Mt 12:22-45, and then what he has already used as far as Mt 13:15, Luke adds, as appropriate here, the blessedness of disciples from Mt 13:16-17. While the account of the return of the Seventy must go back to Luke's special source, the rest of the material after the commission (Lk 10:13-16, 21-24) is not only in Matthew's sequence but is also a close copy of Matthew's wording.

From the subject of the apostolic commission Luke turns to that of love of God and of one's neighbor, using material from some non-Matthean source or sources. It begins, in a form different from Matthew's, with the lawyer's question "What shall I do to inherit eternal life?" (10:25-28); Luke is incidentally covering the material of Mt 22:34-40. Other non-Matthean material follows (10:29-42).[9]

There follows a new subject, that of prayer (11:1-13), including the Lord's Prayer in a setting and form different from Matthew's, but allowing Luke to have covered Mt 6:9-13. After the Parable of the Friend at Midnight, Luke reinforces the lesson by a quotation about prayer from the Sermon on the Mount (Mt 7:7-11; Lk 11:9-13), with some variation from Matthew's wording.

Luke now turns his attention back to Matthew's text. Leaving aside for later use what Matthew has recorded about coming persecution (Mt 10:16-42) and has attached to the apostolic commission in one discourse, Luke deals with all the material he has not already used, up to the point where Matthew's collection of parables begins (Mt 13:1). He therefore finds himself at Mt 12:22, where Matthew begins to deal with three allied subjects in this order: the Beelzebul controversy (12:22-37); the demand for signs (12:38-42); and the return of the evil spirit (12:43-45). Luke very understandably changes the order, to deal with the questions about evil spirits first, and the demand for signs later. But he still brackets the subjects together, by prefacing the words "But some of them said, 'By Beelzebul the prince of the demons he casts out demons,' and others tempting him sought a sign from heaven" (11:15).

---

[9]The story of Martha and Mary (10:38-42) is an incidental witness to the existence of traditions that Jesus' ministry was not confined to Galilee. Luke may not have known that, as John relates, they lived at Bethany, but "the characters of the two sisters as represented in John are true to the picture of the present story" (J. M. Creed, *St. Luke* [London, 1930] in loc.).

After this, Matthew adds the incident of the coming of Jesus' mother and brothers (Mt 12:46-50), which Luke has already used (8:19-21); instead of repeating it, Luke now replaces it with another reference to Jesus' mother (11:27-28), with the same point that he has made before. Luke here reflects Matthew's order, though he uses different material. He then appends two sayings from the Sermon on the Mount (Lk 11:33-36; Mt 5:15; 6:22-23), fitting these in, as he does with excerpts from it whenever it seems appropriate. The condemnation of the Pharisees (11:37-54) follows: it has a different context from the corresponding text of Matthew (23:1-36); it is less close to Matthew's wording than the preceding passages; and it varies in its order. Luke seems to have drawn on a different source.

With a fresh introduction (12:1), which seems to show knowledge of Mt 16:5-6, Luke proceeds to the exhortation to Fearless Confession (12:1-12), parallel, with some variations, to Mt 10:19-20, 26-33. Then, turning to concern with worldly things, Luke has the Parable of the Rich Fool (12:13-21), followed appropriately by the insertion of a long passage from the Sermon on the Mount (Lk 12:22-34), very close in wording to Mt 6:19-33, except for the omission of Mt 6:22-23, which has already been used, and Mt 6:24, to be used almost exactly at Lk 16:13. Because this is an insertion from a different context, and not a continuation of the words preceding it, it is introduced by a new rubric: ''And he said to his disciples'' (which looks back to Mt 5:1-2). After a further non-Matthean insertion on watchfulness, a passage from Matthew (24:43-51) on the same subject is used, almost word for word, before a short parable is added (12:47-48).

That a Lukan source existed sometimes overlapping with Matthew can be seen at Lk 12:49-53, Mt 10:34-36. So far as order is concerned, the resumption of Matthew's material, after the use made of Mt 10-26-33 (Lk 12: 2-9), is natural, but it is Luke's text that throws light on Matthew's peculiar wording. Matthew has the strange phrase "to cast peace on earth," "to cast a sword," where the use of the word "cast" (βαλεῖν) calls for explanation. Luke has "to give peace," but this follows the initial phrase, not found in Matthew, "came to cast fire on the earth" (12:49). It is a detail of the tradition, not derived from Matthew, that accounts for Matthew's wording.

From 13:1 to 18:14 Luke seems to be much less dependent on Matthew, both for material, and inevitably now that he has taken so much from Matthew's text, for order also. At 13:18-21 he inserts the parables of the Mustard Seed and the Leaven (Mt 13:31-36); it is not very obvious why they are put in this place.

The thought of Jerusalem, and the consequent reminder that the end of the Ministry would be the Passion there, is the link that binds the next three passages. The first, on exclusion from the Kingdom (13:22-30), is not very close in wording to the parallels scattered in Matthew (7:13-14; 25:10-12; 7:22-23; 8:11-12; 19:30) and is probably from a different source. The second, with the warning against Herod (13:31-33) runs on from what precedes it, in that Luke, who consistently does *not* create false contexts, begins it with the words "in that same hour." The third, the Lament over Jerusalem (13:34-35), is practically identical with Mt 23:37-39 and in a place at least as appropriate as that in Matthew where Luke found it.

From 14:1 to 17:21 Luke shows little dependence on Matthew. At 16:17-18 he works in the only bit of the Sermon on the Mount (apart from what he has omitted because of its Palestinian background) that he has not been able to fit in before, on the Law and Divorce. But while the separate sayings of 17:1-6 (on Offences, Forgiveness, and Faith) differ from Matthew's text, the parallels in Matthew (18:6-7; 18:21-22; 17:20) suggest that Luke is now looking again at Matthew's order, to which he is shortly to return (Lk 18:15; Mt 19:13). The discourse on the Day of the Son of Man (17:22-37) has similarities with Matthew, but there are indications, such as the inclusion of "the days of Lot" as parallel to "the days of Noah" and the corresponding reference to "the day of the Son of man" (as against Matthew's "parousia of the Son of man"), that suggest the use of a different source.

Finally, before returning from his exposition of Jesus' teaching to narrative, and consequently to Matthew's order, Luke adds three parables (18:1-14).

5. "Until the day that he was taken up," Lk 18:31–24:53

Luke is to pass on to the Exodus that Jesus was to accomplish at Jerusalem, "the days of his assumption" (9:51). In the transition, from 18:15-30, he keeps closely to Matthew's order, and from then on, from the third prediction of the Passion (18:31) to the burial of Jesus (23:56) every episode in Luke which has a parallel with Matthew is, with one exception, in Matthew's order.[10] The exception is the inversion of the order of the account of the institution of the Eucharist and the foretelling of the betrayal (22:15-20, 21-23), probably made in order to lead more naturally into the following pericope about precedence among the disciples. Luke has additions to make to Matthew's narrative, and omits items from it, and there are other indications that his narrative was not wholly dependent on Matthew, but the similarities point to Matthew as one,

---

[10]Luke's Parable of the Pounds (19:11-27) and Matthew's Parable of the Talents (25:14-30) are differently placed, but they are too different in other respects to invalidate the statement in the text about the order of incidents.

and perhaps the chief of his sources. At 20:45-47, where Luke omits much of Matthew's criticism of the scribes and Pharisees, he shows that he is aware of Matthew's text, and uses the occasion to lead into the story of the widow's mite (21:1-4).

Matthew and Luke are therefore close to one another in the account of the Passion and the Crucifixion;[11] it is in the post-Resurrection appearances that Luke is wholly independent of Matthew, and this precisely because of the working out of his own scheme for the Gospel. After the initial proclamation of the first three chapters, in which Jesus is declared to be Christ and Lord and Son of God, a new start was made, dealing with the gradual revelation to his disciples about the person of Jesus. At Nazareth, Jesus had proclaimed what he had come to do; later, the Baptist was told, through his messengers, of what Jesus was in fact doing, and invited to draw his own conclusion; and at last, after Jesus' question to his disciples, this part of the Gospel culminates in Peter's confession: "The Christ of God." Then, from 9:51 onwards, it has been part of Luke's purpose to go beyond this, and to show that "the Christ must suffer"; it is the declaration of this that runs through his narrative of appearances after the Resurrection, and decides their selection. First, in the account of the women at the tomb the words are spoken: "Remember how he told you, while he was still in Galilee, that the Son of man must be delivered into the hands of sinful men, and be crucified, and on the third day rise" (24:6-7). In the following story of the walk to Emmaus the same point is made, with the added precision in the phrase that "the Christ" had to suffer, and that this was in fulfillment of the Scriptures: "was it not necessary that the Christ should suffer these things, and enter into his glory?" (24:26). Finally, appearing to the disciples, Jesus is recorded as pressing home the same lesson: "Thus it is written, that the Christ should suffer and on the third day rise again from the dead" (24:46).

After this, having led his readers to the proclamation of Jesus as the Christ, and then to that of the necessity of his suffering, Luke brings his first volume to an end with a short statement of the Ascension, before continuing in his next volume to the proclamation of Jesus as "Lord." He has built up his ordered narrative, partly out of material taken from Matthew, whose text he sometimes copies practically verbatim (e.g., Mt 3:7-10, Lk 3:7-9; Mt 6:25-33, Lk 12:22-32), and sometimes partly rewrites in his own style, though more freely in narrative than in direct speech (e.g., Mt 8:1-

---

[11]There are points of agreement between Luke and John that suggest that there were elements of tradition that they had in common. Cf. V. Taylor, *The Formation of the Gospel Tradition* (London, 1933) 53 and 53n1.

13, Lk 5:12-16, 7:1-10; Mt 11:2-6, Lk 7:18-23). He has also used material from some other source or sources, which sometimes overlaps with Matthew (as in the Great Sermon), and sometimes he chooses different narratives which can replace those of Matthew (e.g., Lk 5:1-11) because of their intrinsic interest; and sometimes he can add material, such as his own distinctive parables, that has no counterpart in Matthew.

All this has been arranged with great skill in the framework of what Jesus has done, of what he has said, and of how he went through Passion to his Resurrection. In that framework Luke has worked through the pattern of the Christian kerygma, leading his readers from the demonstration of the works of the Christ to the confession that Jesus was indeed "the Christ of God," and to the revelation of what that meant. In doing so, Luke shows how Jesus himself met with both acceptance and rejection, in his own town, in the land as a whole, and finally at Jerusalem. It is a feature that is to be continued in the book of Acts, as Luke completes his kerygmatic theme, and in doing so shows the gospel also as both accepted and rejected, as it is borne witness to in its progress from Jerusalem, to Judea and Samaria, and to the uttermost parts of the earth—from the capital of the Jews to the capital of the Gentiles, from Jerusalem to Rome.

5

Luke and Mark

1. The Ministry in Luke and Mark

Luke's order is clear and logical. By making a special section for the exposition of Jesus' teaching, and setting this apart (9:51–18:14) he was able, in speaking of all that ''Jesus began to do,'' to develop the first great theme of his Gospel, that by his deeds Jesus has been shown to be the Christ. Luke's Introduction (1:1–3:38) shows Jesus as the Son of David, and makes the proclamation that he is the Christ, the Lord, the Son of God. But it is after this that Luke sets out to establish that Jesus, by his Ministry, has proved himself to be the Christ. So, after the story of the Temptation, Luke begins with Nazareth, in a logical, not a chronological order as he knows very well (4:23), in order to set out Jesus' own understanding of his Mission at the beginning of his ministry. The words of Isaiah, ''The Spirit of the Lord is upon me, because he has anointed me to preach the gospel to the poor,'' and the rest of the quotation (Lk 4:18-19; Is 61:1-2; 58:6), are the text for the exposition that follows. It culminates in Peter's Confession, ''The Christ of God'' (9:20), and the Father's confirmation at the Transfiguration, ''This is my Son, my Chosen'' (9:35), as the whole section draws to its close.

In developing his theme, Luke works through the sequence Nazareth-Galilee-Jerusalem; Nazareth and Galilee first, then in his Central Section makes a transition towards Jerusalem, and then in the final chapters deals with events there. The sequence is logical, and at each the proclamation of Jesus is met by a mixture of acceptance and rejection (cf. 2:34). So first, at the point where Matthew records that Jesus left Nazareth (Nazara, Mt 4:13; cf. Lk 4:16) for Capernaum, Luke inserts his story of the preaching at that place. He does not propose to arrange his material on the basis of Matthew's Old Testament quotations, and passes over that of Mt 4:14-16, and also Matthew's account of the call of four disciples, instead of which he has a different story to relate; he turns then to stories about Capernaum and Galilee. Mark has not the same reason for omitting the call of the four disciples, and includes this, but then when Matthew passes on to record the Great Sermon, Mark turns to Luke for the continuation of narrative episodes, remaining in Luke's order until he reaches Luke's own form of the Sermon. So, in correspondence with Luke, Mark records the day's events at Capernaum and the following summary statement (1:21-39). Luke's own story of the Call of Peter, which according to his regular practice he has left to the end of the Matthean material, is one that Mark can omit, as he has already included Matthew's alternative.

Luke now records the healing of a leper (5:12-16) and, as we have already noticed,[1] we can appreciate his reason for including it at this point. Mark follows Luke in this; if he were not doing so, it would be difficult to assign any reason for his putting the story at this point. On the assumption of Markan priority "it is not easy to say precisely what it was."[2]

We come then to the occasions of controversy (Lk 5:17–6:11; Mk 2:1–3:6), in narratives that Luke has collected in one place, to fit into his overall scheme. All but one are in much the same form in Luke as in Matthew,[3] the exception is the story of the healing of the paralytic (Lk 5:17-26; Mt 9:1-8), where Luke has a much fuller account; as Mark is following Luke as his primary source here, it is this fuller account that he himself gives.

Luke is leading on from the proclamation of Jesus at Nazareth, through a series of the works of the Christ, to the challenge about their significance in Jesus's message to the Baptist (7:22). Among these works is the gospel to the poor (4:18; 7:22); it is therefore time for him to include the Great Sermon, which indeed begins with the words "Blessed are you poor."

In the tradition common to Matthew and Luke, there was an occasion when Jesus went "to the mount" (εἰς τὸ ὄρος)[4] and preached to his disciples (Mt 5:1; Lk 6:20). Luke, who has only had incidental references to disciples, takes the opportunity to name the Twelve chosen from among them (Lk 6:13); and Mark, following Luke, also includes their names at this point (3:13-19), after saying that Jesus "went up to the mount." There

---

[1]See above, ch. 4, §3.

[2]D. E. Nineham, *St. Mark* (London, 1963) in loc.

[3]Following Luke, Mark has "Levi" in place of "Matthew."

[4]A more accurate translation might be "the hill" as in NEB or, in more idiomatic modern English, "a hill." The words of C. H. Dodd used in a different connection are appropriate: "In such cases an English speaker would more naturally use the indefinite article" (*Historical Tradition in the Fourth Gospel* [Cambridge, 1963] 380). H. Conzelmann builds far too much on the supposed symbolical character of such references to locality: "Even in Mark 'the mountain' is a place of revelation. The symbolical significance is increased still more in Luke. There is no question of locating 'the' mountain. It is a mythical place, to which 'the people' cannot come" (*The Theology of St. Luke* [ET: London, 1960] 44). But there is no good reason for doubting that there is a real historical reminiscence.

is no logical connection in Mark for the choice of the Twelve to be associated with a mount; it arises from the arrangement in Luke, for which there is a good reason. Although Mark passes over the Sermon, as he does with other lengthy discourses, his wording reveals his knowledge of it, and in particular his knowledge of Luke's text.

Having now, by using Luke's series of stories, come as far as the Sermon on the Mount in both Matthew and Luke, it is time for Mark to turn his attention back to Matthew. He needs a connecting link between his two sources. The last episode he has dealt with before the material connected with the Sermon (Mk 3:7-19) is the story of the man with the withered hand, and this is recorded in Mt 12:9-14; it is the sort of connection Mark needs. In Matthew, it is followed by the long quotation from Is 42:1-4, which Mark passes over, but has already indicated that Matthew's text is now in his mind, as he quoted the phrase that Jesus "ordered them not to make him known" (Mt 12:16; Mk 3:12), which leads into Matthew's quotation and the material that interprets it. It is therefore Matthew that Mark now follows, after a short link of his own (Mk 3:20-21), as far as Mk 3:35. So he comes to the second point where, at another of Matthew's discourses and the Parable of the Sower (Mt 13:1; Lk 8:4), he has the two Gospels side by side.

All three synoptists have the parable of the Sower, and after it continue with the Reason for Speaking in Parables (Mt 13:10-17; Lk 8:9-10; Mk 4:10-12); but Mark passes over Matthew's quotation from Isaiah, though he betrays a knowledge of it (Mk 4:12), and follows Luke's shorter text. The comments of Mk 4:21-25 are derived from Lk 8:16-18, a collection of logia from different contexts in Matthew. The recollection of one of these (Mt 5:15) has resulted in the addition in Mark of the phrase "under a bushel" to the words "under a bed," which Mark derives from Luke's text at this point.

Mark now turns aside from Luke until he has finished his own little collection of parables. At its close, he also passes over the next pericope in Luke (8:19-21), since he has already used Matthew's narrative of the same incident (Mt 12:46-50; Mk 3:31-35). But Luke now provides the opportunity to include episodes that have been recorded earlier in Matthew where Mark was not able to use them. So there now follow the story of the Stilling of the Storm (with added details in Mark); and those of the Gerasene demoniac and of Jesus going to the house of Jairus, both in the fuller form that Luke, in contrast to Matthew, has preserved (Lk 8:22-56; Mk 4:35-5:43). Matthew, however, has appended to his parable collection the short narrative of the rejection at Nazareth and, as Mark has passed over Luke's different story at an earlier stage (Lk 4:16-30), he now includes the Matthean one. Having done so, he can continue with Luke by dealing with the Commissioning of the Twelve (Lk 9:1-6; Mk 6:6b-13) and in recording Herod's concern over Jesus. As the latter pericope is also the next one in Matthew (Mt 14:1-2), it provides, as other episodes have, a link for turning aside from one Gospel to the other. In Matthew it leads into the story of the Baptist's death, and Mark follows Matthew's example, giving a more circumstantial account.[5] At its close, to round off the story of the Commissioning of the Twelve, Mark picks up the Lukan thread again (Mk 6:30-31; Lk 9:10), and as both Matthew and Luke have led on to the story of the Feeding of the Five Thousand, this once again gives Mark a convenient opportunity to turn back to Matthew. From Mk 6:45 to 8:26, he is wholly independent of Luke.

After Luke's "great omission"[6] of Mt 14:22–16:12, Matthew and Luke come together with the narrative of Peter's Confession (Mt 16:13-20; Lk 9:18-21), and from this point their common narrative material is much closer in sequence until the end of the Gospels. For Luke, Peter's confession that Jesus is "the Christ of God" is the point to which he has been leading from the beginning. The proclamation made by Jesus at Nazareth has been followed up in the challenge of Jesus' words to the Baptist's messengers; their implication is now made clear in Peter's words. Having reaching this climactic point, Luke does not continue as Matthew does with the words of Jesus to Peter (Mt 16:17-19), and Mark contents himself with following Luke in this. Perhaps just because Luke has not included them, he also omits the rebuke to Peter (Mt 16:22-23), but they reappear in Mark (8:32b-33). Luke is already preparing for the second theme that is to run through his Gospel, that the Christ must suffer, and his sequence of the First Prediction of the Passion, the pericope of Taking up the Cross and Self-denial, and the story of the Transfiguration, with the insertion about the exodus that Jesus was to accomplish at Jerusalem, fit neatly into his scheme. He includes the story of the epileptic boy (Lk 9:37-43a) as an appendix to that of the Transfiguration, but, unlike Matthew, he makes a transition from it to the Second Prediction of the Passion: "But while they were marveling at all the things that he was doing, he said to his disciples, 'Let these words sink into your ears' '' (Lk 9:43b-44).

---

[5]For the story of the Baptist's death, see appendix 1, below.

[6]The table in ch. 1 shows how little this detracts from the development of Luke's narrative scheme. The phrase "Luke's Great Omission" was coined to show an omission, not from Matthew's order, but from Mark's; various suggestions have been made to account for it on that understanding. Cf. B. H. Streeter, *The Four Gospels* (London, 1924) 172ff.

Throughout the section of Mk 8:27–9:50,[7] Mark has affinities with both
Matthew and Luke, including some material that is paralleled in only one
of them; he is not concentrating on one special theme, or perhaps appre-
ciating that Luke is doing so. He has also some contributions of his own
to make: he adds some circumstantial detail to the story of the epileptic
boy, and uses some sayings about salt (9:49-50), which are partially paralleled elsewhere in Matthew and Luke (Mt 5:13; Lk 14:34-35), to close
this part of his narrative, leaving aside most of Matthew's continuing discourse.

2. Luke's Central Section, Lk 9:51–18:14

Luke now pursues a very different course; from 9:51–18:14 he has gathered together a body of teaching, interspersing it with repeated reminders
that Jesus was on his way to Jerusalem, as "the days drew near for him to
be received up." This is not an arrangement, or the kind of material, that
lends itself to Mark's series of episodes, and it is only after resuming with
material found in Matthew (Lk 18:15) that Mark begins again to be able to
use Luke.

3. Luke's Narrative Resumed, Lk 18:15–24:53

From the point at which Matthew and Luke come together again, with
the story of Jesus blessing children (Mt 19:13; Lk 18:15), there could no
longer be much difficulty in conflating their narratives. We need only take
note here of the places where Mark makes special use of Luke. For the episode of the Rich Young Man (Mt 19:16-22; Lk 18:18-23; Mk 10:17-22)
Mark uses Luke's simpler story in preference to Matthew's.[8] In other episodes he produces a combination of features from both the other Gospels,
as for instance when in Mk 10:29, Matthew's phrase "for my name's sake"
and Luke's "for the sake of the kingdom of God" become Mark's "for
my sake and for the sake of the gospel."

In the episode of the blind man at Jericho, Mark follows Luke, where
Matthew speaks of two blind men; and Mark adds the name of the man and
other details. Luke puts the episode when Jesus "drew near to Jericho,"
and Matthew "as they went out of Jericho" (Lk 18:35; Mt 20:29). Luke
may have meant no more than that Jesus came to Jericho, avoiding Matthew's "as they went out" in order not to interrupt the Matthean account

---

[7]The development of Mark's Gospel in this group of narratives can be easily seen in J. B.
Orchard's *Synopsis of the Four Gospels* (Macon GA/Edinburgh, 1983) §§174-86.

[8]See appendix 1, below, for a fuller treatment of this passage.

with the Zacchaeus story (which Mark omits) and the following parable. That would be in line with his practice elsewhere.[9] In any case, Mark conflates the two apparent contradictions: "And they came to Jericho, and as he was leaving Jericho" (Mk 10:46).

At the entry into Jerusalem, Luke does not record the incident of the cursing of the fig tree. Mark does so, but then follows Luke's order from Mk 11:15-19 before recording that the fig tree was seen to be withered on the next day. Matthew's narrative gives the impression that the withering was instantaneous on Jesus' word. Mark, however, must be deliberately separating the two parts of the story, for he includes the statement that "Peter remembered." That Matthew himself did not mean an instantaneous withering is perhaps implied in the question in Mt 21:20: "How did the fig tree wither at once?" The tense seems to imply some interval between the mount of cursing and of this being observed, and the phrase "at once" (παραχρῆμα), would still be appropriate. Mark has been able to achieve his result by turning to Luke's order for the Cleansing of the Temple and for the conspiracy against Jesus (Lk 19:45-48) before finishing his story.[10]

The whole of Mt 23:1-36, is occupied with the denunciation of the scribes and Pharisees. Luke has already included similar material, and so in Lk 20:45-47 only gives a short excerpt (changing "they make their phylacteries broad and their fringes long" to "go about in long robes" to give Gentile readers the general sense), with a condemnation of those who "devour widows' houses," in order to lead onto the story of the Widow's Mite (Lk 21:1-4). Mark follows Luke closely in both pericopes. For the story of the Widow's Mite Mark's text is entirely dependent on Luke; his addition "which make a quadrans" is secondary. Luke's phrase in 21:4 "they cast into the gifts" (ἔβαλον εἰς τὰ δῶρα) is also the more "primitive"; it refers accurately to the kind of chest, κορβανᾶς (cf. Mt 27:6) into which money was put; "the treasury" was strictly a room, to which the widow would not have access.[11]

For the narrative of the Passion, Mark is closely parallel to Matthew, with little dependence on Luke. Luke's additions to Matthew, such as the reference to the two swords (22:35-38), the account of Jesus' trial before Herod (23:6-12), the reference to the women who lamented as Jesus went to Calvary (23:27-31), or to the penitent thief (23:40-43), find no place in

[9]Cf. I. Howard Marshall, *The Gospel of St. Luke* (Exeter, 1978) in loc.

[10]See also J. B. Orchard, *Matthew, Luke, and Mark* (Greater Manchester, 1976) 93ff.

[11]Cf. M.-E. Boismard, in P. Benoit and Boismard, *Synopse des Quatre Evangiles*, 2 vols. (Paris, 1972) in loc.

Mark. When Matthew and Luke deal with the same events, such as the Last Supper, in different ways, it is Matthew that Mark follows. Throughout the Passion narrative it is Matthew's account on which Mark relies.

Our survey shows indeed that throughout the Gospel, Mark is indebted both to Matthew and to Luke, but it is Matthew who is always his primary authority, as one would expect if Matthew's Gospel had already been accorded a status in the Church before Luke resolved to write his own orderly account (Lk 1:1-4).

6

The Making of Mark

1. Why Did Mark Compile His Book?

If Matthew preceded Mark, "it is hard to say why Mark was needed," wrote G. M. Styler.[1] When the first volume of this study of the Griesbach hypothesis appeared, an otherwise sympathetic reviewer ended his review with the words, "But at the end of the day, I suspect that it [that is, the Griesbach hypothesis] will continue to be hurt by what has been a traditional objection to it. What point would there really be in writing Mark's Gospel for a church which already possessed Matthew and Luke?"[2] It is the thesis of this present book that Matthew and Luke did indeed precede Mark, and that therefore an answer to the objection is possible. We ought not to assume, in face of the evidence, that Mark could not have written after them, on the calm assumption that we today cannot see any possible reason for his doing so. The objection depends in fact on an underlying, and no doubt unconscious assumption, that all the Gospels were written for the same purpose and to meet the same needs.

This is clearly not so. It may well be that St. Matthew's Gospel was written as a "church book," intended by its author to be a manual of Christian teaching, and one to be read in Christian assemblies. At any rate that is what it became. At a very early stage it seems to have been accepted as "the Gospel." There are allusions to Matthew in Clement of Rome, the Epistle of Barnabas (in which it is quoted as Scripture—ὡς γέγραπται, "as it is written"), St. Ignatius, and the Didache which refers to it as "the Gospel" (15:3, 4); so that after considering this evidence, Lagrange concluded, "When one reflects that Clement was writing at Rome, where according to all appearances Mark's Gospel was born, and that Ignatius in a Gentile milieu should have had a preference for Luke, one can only ex-

---

[1] G. M. Styler, "Excursus IV," in C. F. D. Moule, *The Birth of the New Testament* (London, 1962) 231.

[2] G. O'Collins, in *The Month* (September 1977) reviewing J. B. Orchard's *Matthew, Luke, and Mark.*

plain the privileged position of Matthew by the start he had had."[3] If Matthew was written to be an authoritative church manual, it was surely fulfilling its purpose.

St. Luke's work is in form markedly different. Not only does it cover a much wider field, but its literary setting is of a very different kind. Luke's first volume opens with a formal dedication to a particular person, and after the fashion of the day this is taken up again at the beginning of the second. Luke can hardly have expected his dedication (Lk 1:1-4), or the whole of his second volume, to be read in the Christian assemblies of his day. If we go back behind the use that the church has subsequently made of his work and consider Luke's own intention, it appears much more likely that he expected his book to be added to the libraries of men like Theophilus and to be used for reading in people's houses.

Why then did Mark in turn compile his book? In the nature of things we cannot fully know all that was in the mind of any writer or what were all the circumstances that influenced him to write as he did.[4] What we can do is to examine what he has written, and to come to an assessment of the needs he met and the use to which his work was most likely to be put. If he seems to have made use of Matthew and Luke, we should consider what he dispenses with in his selection of material, how he treated his subject, and what extra contributions he himself made. Only after that can we ask what his purpose seems to have been. It is to this task that we now turn, and first of all to consider Mark's omissions—what it did not serve his purpose to include.

2. Mark's Omissions

a. The Infancy Stories in Matthew and Luke

"Has not the scripture said that the Christ is descended from David, and comes from Bethlehem, the city where David was?" (Jn 7:42). The words quoted in St. John's Gospel represent a precondition in Jewish eyes for any claim to be the Messiah. When the gospel was first proclaimed among Jews, the fulfillment of this condition had to be maintained, and it is not surprising that Matthew in his very Jewish book should begin his own account of Jesus with two chapters devoted to this theme. At its opening, he sets out the genealogy of "Jesus Christ, the son of David" (1:1), divided into groups treating of the "generations from Abraham to David," "from David to the deportation to Babylon," and thence "from the deportation to

---

[3]M. J. Lagrange, *Evangile selon Saint Matthieu* (Paris, 1928) ix.

[4]For a new theory, see pt. 3, below, esp. ch. 2.

Babylon to the Christ" (1:17). In the narrative that follows, Joseph, through whom the genealogy is traced, is addressed as "son of David" (1:20). Then Jesus was born in Bethlehem, the city of David, "as it is written by the prophet" (2:4-6). That is the claim, and there are reminders of it throughout the Gospel. Thus, when two blind men followed Jesus, they cried aloud "Have mercy on us, Son of David" (9:27); after a further healing "all the people were amazed, and said 'Can this be the Son of David?' " (12:3). The appeal to Jesus as "Son of David" is repeated by the Canaanite woman (15:22), and twice by two blind men at Jericho (20:30-31). At the triumphal entry into Jerusalem the crowds shouted "Hosanna to the Son of David" (21:9), as did the children crying out in the temple (21:15). In the questioning during his days in Jerusalem Jesus himself asked, "What do you think of the Christ?" to receive the answer, "The Son of David," and to follow this with the question how David's son could be his Lord.

This concern with the Davidic descent of Jesus is what we should expect of Matthew. When we turn to Luke, we are dealing with a writer who is addressing a different sort of readership, and one to which the fulfillment of this condition for the Messiahship of Jesus would be of less significance. But Luke has set out, on a canvas broader than Matthew's, to depict all the lineaments of the Christian kerygma, and this, as he illustrates in speaking of the witness borne to it, includes the same element of Jesus' Davidic descent. He refers to it in the preaching of Peter (Ac 2:25-30) and in that of Paul (Ac 13:23), in both cases in a broader context concerning David. Its place in the kerygma is also evident in the creedal summaries of Rom 1:3 and 2 Tim 2:8. Apart from any other considerations leading to Luke's inclusion of his first three chapters, it was inevitable that this should be dealt with. So Luke also has a genealogy, carrying back the ancestry of Jesus "being the son (as was supposed) of Joseph" back to David and beyond. And whereas Matthew sets out to show how Jesus, born at Bethlemeh, came to live at Nazareth, Luke conversely sets out to show how the Son of Mary of Nazareth came to be born at Bethlehem. In doing so, he tells us that Mary was betrothed to "Joseph, of the house of David" (1:26); that she was told that her Son would be given "the throne of his father David" (1:32); that Zechariah spoke of "a horn of salvation for us in the house of his [God's] servant David" (1:69); that in due course Joseph took Mary "to the city of David, which is called Bethlehem, because he was of the house and lineage of David" (2:4); and that the shepherds were told that a Saviour was born "in the city of David" (2:11).

It is in Luke's first three chapters that the name David keeps recurring; after that Luke passes to other elements of the kerygma. For the rest of the Gospel there are references to David only at two places, and at each of them in close parallel with Matthew. At Jericho a blind man twice addresses Jesus as "Son of David" (Lk 18:38-39: Mt 20:30-31), and at Jerusalem Luke, like Matthew, has the question about David's Son (Lk 20:41-44; Mt 22:41-45). The story of the blind men in Mt 9:27-31, so close to that of Mt 20:29-34, has no place in Luke, nor that of the Canaanite woman. The overlapping of the narratives of Mt 9:32-34 and 12:22-30 also may account for Luke's omission of the question "Can this be the Son of David?" from his single account. At the entry into Jerusalem Luke has neither the word "Hosanna" nor "the Son of David"; he has "the king" in place of the latter and "Glory in the highest" for "Hosanna in the highest." Matthew's further reference (Mt 21:15) has no parallel in Luke. The net result is that while there is no reason for supposing that Luke avoided the use of the title "Son of David," it is less conspicuous in his account of the Ministry than it is in Matthew's.

What then is the situation in Mark? In parallel with both Matthew and Luke, he has the double appeal of the blind man (whom he names Bartimaeus) at 10:46-52, and the question about David's Son (12:35-37a). Mark's shorter account of the accusation of collusion with Satan (3:22-27) provides no parallel to Matthew's reference in Mt 9:27, and the story of the Syro-Phoenician (Matthew's Canaanite) woman at 7:24-30 is introduced differently from Matthew's, and the appeal to the "Son of David" does not appear. At the entry into Jerusalem (11:9-10) the greeting "Son of David" is omitted, though there is perhaps an implied reference in the words "Blessed is the kingdom of our father David that is coming." There is no other reference of the kind in Mark's Gospel, and no reference to Bethlehem at all. The result is that there is less said to indicate Jesus' Davidic descent than in either Matthew or Luke, and this becomes more significant when we take into account that Mark has nothing parallel to their Infancy narratives.

Whatever other reasons Mark may have had for starting his Gospel where he did, two things are clear: first, that Mark saw his book as having a much more limited purpose than that of Luke's grand design; and second, that for Mark, writing in a Gentile environment, the claim that Jesus must be a Son of David had ceased to have the importance that it had for Matthew. Mark wrote for people with a different background, for whom the claims made for Jesus had to rest on other foundations.

b. Teaching

If Mark followed Matthew and Luke, why did he omit much of the teaching material he found in them? He was certainly very aware of Jesus' teaching office. Indeed the regular word that he uses for the title with which Jesus was addressed (presumably representing an original "Rabbi" or

"Mari") is the word "Teacher" (διδάσκαλος). Apart from two instances in the disputed Longer Ending (16:19, 20) Jesus is only once referred to as "the Lord" (11:3, parallel to Mt 21:3; Lk 19:31) at the entry into Jerusalem, and is only once addressed as "Lord" (κύριε), and that on the lips of the Syro-Phoenician woman (7:28, parallel to Mt 15:27), although that is a common form of address to Jesus in both Matthew and Luke, the latter of whom also uses the address "Master" (ἐπιστάτα).

However, references to Jesus' teaching are also common, sometimes in parallel with Matthew or Luke, as in 1:21 (Lk 4:31); 6:2 (Mt 13:54); or 6:6 (Mt 9:35); but also sometimes in addition to, or in substitution for, their wording. At 2:13 Mark, without parallel, notes that crowds gathered and Jesus "taught them"; at 4:1, when Matthew (13:1) says Jesus "sat beside the sea," Mark has "he began to teach beside the sea," and immediately after, in place of Matthew's "He told them many things in parables, saying," Mark has "He taught them many things in parables, and in his teaching he said"; at 6:34, in addition to Matthew's text, and instead of Luke's "He spoke to them of the kingdom of God," Mark has "he began to teach them many things." There are other examples at 8:31; 9:31; 11:17 and 12:35; and at 10:1 where Mt 19:1-2 speaks of the crowds and says Jesus "healed them," Mark has "he taught them." Although there is much teaching in Matthew and Luke which he does not use, clearly Mark does not underestimate the place of teaching in Jesus' Ministry.

It is impossible to draw a hard and fast line between narrative and teaching material; narrative will frequently incorporate teaching, and narrative episodes will be recorded because of the teaching they convey; and teaching material frequently will require a narrative setting to show its significance. Thus St. Luke's Gospel is basically narrative up to 9:50, but includes much teaching; the Central Section is basically teaching, but it has some narrative features. There is nevertheless a broad distinction between the two types of writing, and it is into the narrative type that St. Mark's Gospel falls. Often the teaching is the point that the narrative has to make, but formally it is incidental to the telling of the story. So the question remains: Why, if Mark wrote with Matthew and Luke before him and knew of so much teaching material, did he not include more of it in his book?

According to Mark, Jesus taught the crowds "many things in parables" (4:2; cf. Mt 13:2); in the interpretation of the parable of the Sower he referred to "all the parables" (4:13), and after including that of the Mustard Seed Mark adds "with many such parables he [Jesus] spoke the word to them" (4:33). At 12:1 he says that Jesus "began to speak to them," that is, to people who gathered about him, "in parables," although only one parable follows. Now it is generally recognized that the word "parable" (παραβολή) has a much wider range of meaning than we have come commonly to associate with it. Like the Hebrew *māshāl* (מָשָׁל), for which it was used as a translation, it could cover not only the stories or comparisons that we have come to speak of as parables, but other enigmatic sayings, or even more straightforward aphorisms. So in Mk 3:23 we are told that Jesus "said to them in parables, 'How can Satan cast out Satan?' "—a straightforward question, though it is immediately followed by the comparison of a kingdom or a house (dynasty?) divided, and by that of the strong man's house being plundered. At 7:17, the disciples asked Jesus "about the parable" (as at Mt 15:15) after his criticism of the traditions of the elders.

Nevertheless, Mark has a special concern about parables in the narrower sense. At 4:1-34 he narrates three of them: the Sower, the Seed Growing Secretly, and the Mustard Seed. It is in introducing them that he says that Jesus "taught many things in parables," and sets them in the context of "his teaching" (4:2); at the close he adds "With many such parables he spoke the word to them, as they were able to hear it; he did not speak to them without a parable" (4:33-34). In between the parables Mark deals with the reason for them (4:10-12), the interpretation of the parable of the Sower (4:13-20) and adds a further comment about how they are to be heard (4:21-25). "St Mark's aim," wrote Nineham, "was not even to provide a typical set of parables, for all the parables given here, and the sayings about them, are concerned in some way or another with the question of the nature and purpose of parables themselves."[5] We may add that after the parable of the Sower, Mark's two other parables are also about seed sown, and are in the nature of further applications of the message of the longer parable.

We come then to the problem of Mark's comments about the wide use of parables. It was in Jesus' "teaching" that he used them; "he taught them many things in parables"; "how then will you understand all the parables?"; "with many such parables he spoke the word." It is clear that Mark regarded the teaching of Jesus as being frequently and commonly given in such parables and that he uses 4:1-34 to make the point. It must be that St. Mark himself was familiar with a number of other parables, and regarded them as important. How is it then that he does not use them in his Gospel? Apart from the special case of the three in chapter 4 included to show how parables matter, the only other clear examples are at 12:1-12 and 13:28-32. The former of these, that of the Wicked Husbandmen, is different from all the rest in the Gospels, in that it is less an element in the teaching of Jesus for his disciples than a warning about what was to happen in the immediate future. At its close "they tried to arrest him," where "they" must

---

[5]D. E. Nineham, *St. Mark* (London: Penguin, 1963) on 4:1-34.

refer "to the chief prests and the scribes and the elders" (11:27), for "they perceived that he had told this parable against them" (12:12). The other parable, that of the Fig Tree (13:28-32)—not called a parable in Mark, though Luke does so call it (Lk 21:29)—is no more than a simple illustration as part of the apocalyptic discourse. With these two exceptions, Mark has no other parables to which to apply the lessons of 4:1-34.

We can hardly avoid the conclusion that St. Mark was aware of many parables of Jesus which he did not include in his Gospel;[6] that he was not setting out, like Matthew or Luke, to include an exposition of the teaching of Jesus for the sake of Christian disciples, but writing with a more limited purpose, and confining himself to the presentation of Jesus as the Christ and Son of God (cf. 1:1 and 15:39). His matter was "kerygma," rather than "didache."

"There is nothing antecedently improbable," wrote B. H. Streeter, "in the idea that for certain purposes an abbreviated version of the Gospel might be desired." But then he continued, with an illogicality equal to its acerbity, "but only a lunatic would leave out Matthew's account of the Infancy, the Sermon on the Mount, and practically all the parables, in order to get room for purely verbal expansion of what was retained."[7] Mark may be characterized with "verbal expansion," but there is no reason to suppose that this was his purpose. He wrote as was natural for him to do, as no doubt Streeter did. As regards the Infancy, we have already seen that there was at least one reason why it was less important for Mark to record this than it was for Matthew. As regards the parables, even if Mark wrote before Matthew, he must have excluded many examples with which he was familiar. Mark certainly left out much of Jesus' teaching, and we should have to recognize the probability of this even if he wrote before Matthew. What we need to see is what kind of things Mark left out; only after this can we begin to assess what his purpose was.

Mark certainly was very aware of Jesus as a Teacher, and frequently refers to that fact. He speaks of Jesus teaching in the synagogues (1:21; 6:2), in the open air (10:1), beside the sea (2:13; 4:1), in the villages (6:6), and in the temple (11:17). On two occasions he uses the significant phrase "in his teaching he said," as though what follows is only an excerpt of what might have been given at greater length: once at 4:2, before the parable of the Sower, where Matthew is in fact to give more material; and once at 12:38, where the same thing is true. Before the Feeding of the Five Thousand, when Matthew says that Jesus was healing people (14:14) and Luke

---

[6]Mk 10:31 suggests a knowledge of one unused parable from Matthew (Mt 19:30–20:16).

[7]B. H. Streeter, *The Four Gospels* (London, 1924) 158.

adds that he spoke of the kingdom of God (9:11), Mark says that ''he began to teach them many things'' (6:34). Mark, whether Matthew and Luke had already written or not, must have known of ''many things'' that Jesus had taught on some of these occasions, and still did not include them.

Mark no doubt was unlikely to organize his work after Luke's pattern with a separate teaching section. But if he had Matthew as his principal guide, he found lengthy records of teaching, notably in the famous five discourses, and first, in the Sermon on the Mount. The words of Mk 3:13, ''And he went up on the mountain,'' followed by the list of the Twelve, point to awareness of both Matthew's and Luke's form of the Sermon; and the words of Mark 1:22, ''He taught them as one who had authority, and not as the scribes,'' suggest an acquaintance with Matthew 7:29, where almost identical words are part of Matthew's formal conclusion to his Sermon. But Mark does not include the Sermon itself, and the question arises whether this is because, like the parables, it is not to his particular purpose. Luke himself has a shorter form of the Sermon, and makes no use of the parts that have a specifically Jewish background. Mark also, writing in a Gentile milieu, was not likely to use these. But both Matthew and Luke speak of the Sermon as addressed to disciples (Mt 5:1; Lk 6:20), and therefore represent it as a guide to Christian conduct, the one in Jewish, the other in Gentile environments; it is part of the διδαχή that follows acceptance of the κήρυγμα. It looks as if, as in the case of the parables, it is just this character of διδαχή that has meant that it was not within the range of Mark's purpose—a tentative conclusion, to be tested by further evidence.

Matthew's second discourse (10:1-42) deals with the commissioning of the Twelve, and with the conditions of Christian discipleship. In the preceding pericope, by which he leads into his discourse (9:35-38), he notes that ''Jesus went about all the cities and villages, teaching in their synagogues,'' and Mark's own account of the commissioning has a similar note: ''And he went about all the villages teaching'' (6:6); but unlike Matthew he does not then need to include the names of the Twelve, which he has already given in Luke's sequence (Mk 6:6b-13, Lk 9:1-6), and in substance closer to Luke's short account than to Matthew's ''Go nowhere among the Gentiles, and enter no town on the Samaritans, but go rather to the lost sheep of the house of Israel'' (Mt 10:5-6); they wrote at a stage and in an environment that made the words no longer appropriate, or even encouraging.

Matthew's discourse, however, does not end with the commission of the Twelve. It continues with counsel for Christian disciples in the days that lie ahead. The first part of this, which now envisages a wider Christian mission that will bear testimony also to the Gentiles (Mt 10:18), has its parallel both in Luke and in Mark in the later Apocalyptic discourse (Lk 21:12-19; Mk 13:9-13), which we have yet to consider. The rest (Mt 10:26-42) has parallels to it in Luke's central section, but is absent from Mark, with the sole exception of one sentence that he uses at a later point (Mk 9:41).

We have therefore the same pattern that already has appeared. Mark includes the commission of the Twelve as part of his story. What he does not give is the kind of teaching that Matthew and Luke provide for instruction in Christian living.

The next of Matthew's compilations of teaching is the group of parabolic material in 13:1-52, of which we already have taken notice. The only thing that needs to be added here, is that Mark's three parables at the corresponding place are all concerned with seed sown; they are, as Mark sees them, parables of the gospel proclaimed. The uncomprehending hearers of Matthew and Luke (Mt 13:1; Lk 8:10) have become to Mark "those outside" (4:10).

At 17:24 Matthew records that Jesus and his disciples came to Capernaum, and after the incident of the Temple Tax, expands his narrative from their question "Who is the greatest in the kingdom of heaven?" into the discourse that continues until 18:35. Mark also writes "they came to Capernaum" (9:33), and, omitting the matter of the Temple Tax, deals with the same question about who was the greatest. His text is in some ways closer to Luke's, and like Luke Mark then inserts the story of the Strange Exorcist (9:38-41; Lk 9:49-50) before continuing in parallel with Matthew with warnings against putting stumbling blocks in the way of "these little ones who believe" Jesus. At 9:41, in transition from Luke to Matthew he has added a logion from Matthew 10:42, but Matthew's word "disciple" has become "you who bear the name of Christ" (ἐν ὀνόματι ὅτι χριστοῦ ἐστε); and at 9:47 "to enter into life" has become "to enter the kingdom of God"; Mark's language reflects his concern with the proclamation of the gospel and its call to acceptance. As with previous discourses in Matthew, Mark has started from the same point as Matthew, and in each case, except that of the Sermon on the Mount, has included some of Matthew's material; but as soon as the discourse develops into an exposition of more general teaching, as this one does at Matthew 18:10, Mark has nothing to correspond. We see the same pattern each time.

The pattern is repeated when Mark comes to the apocalyptic discourse (of Mt 24:1–25:46; Lk 21:5-36). Mark records the occasion of the discourse in much the same way as Matthew, and then continues, mostly in closer parallel with Matthew than with Luke, but inserting material from Luke at 13:9-13. Mark brings the discourse to a conclusion with much the same wording, epitomized in his words "Take heed, watch, for you do not know when the time will come" (Mk 13:33), as is expressed in a different form by Luke: "Take heed to yourselves, lest . . . that day come upon you suddenly. . . . But watch at all times" (Lk 21:34-36). It is a warning that reappears in the parabolic material added by Matthew: "Watch therefore for you do not know on what day the Lord is coming" (24:42); "Watch therefore, for you know neither the day nor the hour" (25:13); but while Luke has a good deal that is parallel or similar to this added material, he has previously included it in his teaching section. Mark makes no use of it; an extended exposition of such teaching is outside his purpose.

There is then a consistent pattern seen in Mark's practice whenever he comes to the discourses in Matthew. He has produced his book, as its initial words testify, to proclaim "the gospel of Jesus Christ" (1:1), the good news of which Jesus Christ is the subject, but not to draw out all its implications for his disciples.

3. Mark's Language

It is urged by G. M. Styler that the roughness of Mark's style "is one of the strongest arguments for his priority.[8] On this roughness of style there is a general agreement. So Rawlinson has written,[9] "The Greek of Mark in particular is essentially a non-literary Greek, full of roughness and semitisms—the kind of Greek which might be *spoken* by the lower classes at Rome, and especially by those of them whose original home had been Palestine or Syria, and to whom Aramaic was the mother tongue. . . . The writing all through is vulgar, colloquial, unpolished, and is characterized by a singular monotony of style. There are hardly any connecting particles: the sentences and paragraphs follow one another in rapid succession, linked in the majority of cases by a simple *and,* or by the curiously frequent *and immediately.*"[10] The facts are not in dispute, but the question remains whether a colloquial narrative constitutes "one of the strongest arguments" that Mark preceded Matthew and Luke, or whether Mark could have retold stories in this style, although more literary forms already existed.

The very first words of the Gospel suggest a warning that Mark may not preserve a more original form of wording than the other Synoptists, but

---

[8]Styler, in *The Birth of the New Testament,* 227.

[9]A. E. J. Rawlinson, *Gospel of St. Mark* (London, 1925) xxxi-xxxii.

[10]Mark frequently used the word εὐθύς, which is commonly translated as "immediately" or by a synonym for this, only in the sense "then." This is especially true when there is no parallel in Matthew or Luke.

may be telling his story in the language of his time and place. His book sets out to present "the gospel of Jesus Christ" (1:19), and the word "gospel" (εὐαγγέλιον) here should give us pause. In St. Matthew's Gospel, the word is used of the proclamation of the kingdom of heaven. Jesus, according to Matthew, went about "preaching the gospel of the kingdom" (4:23; 9:35); at 24:14 Matthew speaks of "this gospel of the kingdom"; and at 26:13 speaks of "this gospel." The subject of the gospel is therefore consistently the kingdom of heaven; the "good news" is what Jesus himself proclaimed. Luke on the other hand never uses the noun "gospel,"[11] but does make use of the cognate verb (εὐαγγελίζεσθαι). In his introductory chapters he uses it in the wider sense, to "bring good news" (1:19; 2:10), and afterwards of Jesus himself bringing good news to the people or to the poor (3:18; 4:18; 7:22; 9:6; 20:1). When the subject of the good news is referred to (4:43; 8:1; 16:16), it is, as in Matthew, the kingdom of God. In no case, either in Matthew or in Luke, is Jesus the *subject* of the good news.

Mark uses a later, post-Paschal terminology. He begins his book with the words "The beginning of the gospel of Jesus Christ," which must mean the gospel about Jesus, the gospel of which he is the subject. At 1:14, at the point where Matthew has "Jesus began to preach" (Mt 4:17), Mark does indeed have "preaching the gospel of God, and saying, The time is fulfilled, and the kingdom of God is at hand," relating the gospel to the kingdom, but he immediately continues, in the terminology of the Christian mission, "Repent and believe in the gospel." At 8:35, when Mt 16:25 and Lk 9:24 speak of losing one's life "for my sake," Mark has "for my sake and the gospel's." At 10:29, when Mt 19:29 has "for my name's sake" and Luke 18:29 "for the sake of the kingdom of God," Mark has the double phrase "for my sake and for the gospel." At 13:10, without parallel in either Matthew or Luke, Mark inserts "And the gospel must first be preached to all nations"; and at 14:9, in parallel with Matthew's "this gospel" (26:13), Mark simply has "the gospel." In the disputed longer ending the words "preach the gospel to the whole creation" (16:15) follow the same usage.

It also comes natural to Mark to use "the word" (ὁ λόγος) for "the gospel." The usage became common in the early Church, and Luke uses it freely in Acts (e.g., 4:4; 4:29; 6:4; 8:4); even more frequently in that book he uses either "the word of God" (e.g., 4:31; 6:2; 6:7; 8:14) or "the word of the Lord" (e.g., 8:25; 15:35; 15:36). In the Gospels, Matthew speaks of "the word of the kingdom" at the beginning of the interpretation

---

[11]Except in Ac 15:7; 20:24.

of the Parable of the Sower (13:19), after which, in the rest of the interpretation, instead of repeating the whole phrase, he refers "to the word"
(13:20, 21, 22 bis, 23). He never uses "the word" in this sense at any other
point in his Gospel. Luke in the Gospel does speak of "the word" without
qualification, but only in his dedication to Theophilus (1:2). He speaks of
"the word of God" at three points (5:1; 8:21; 11:28) besides the interpretation of the parable of the Sower, and in that interpretation he first speaks
of "the word of God" (8:11), and then, like Matthew, simply of "the
word" (8:12; 13:15). On the other hand, Mark's Gospel has "the word,"
without qualification, in this sense at 2:2 and 4:33;[12] it is also in Mark's
longer ending at 16:20. Mark never uses the longer phrases. In the interpretation of the Parable of the Sower, where Matthew has "the word of
God," Mark has simply "the word" (4:14); then, like the others, he continues with this for the rest of the interpretation (4:15 bis, 16, 17, 18, 19,
20).

Just as Matthew's "the gospel of the kingdom" represents a more primitive usage than Mark's "the gospel," so does Matthew's "the word of the
kingdom" a more primitive usage than Mark's "the word."

Mark's opening words "The beginning of the gospel of Jesus Christ,"
like Matthew's "The book of the genealogy (γενέσεως) of Jesus Christ,"
use "Christ" as a name. Matthew indeed explains this at the end of the
genealogy in the words "Jesus, who is called Christ" (1:16), but repeats
his phrase at 1:18 "the birth (γένεσις) of Jesus Christ."[13] After that,
Matthew never applies the word "Christ" to Jesus as a name, and it is never
so applied by Luke in his Gospel; it begins to appear in Luke's writings of
Acts at 2:38. That Mark should have used it in what is in effect the title of
his book might be expected, but Mark does use it again at a later point.
The parallel to Matthew 10:42, "because he is a disciple (εἰς ὄνομα
μαθητοῦ)." in Mk 9:41 is "because you bear the name of Christ (ἐν ὀνόματι ὅτι χριστοῦ ἐστε)." As with the word "gospel" the use of
"Christ" as a name here is an indication of Mark's secondary character.

4. Mark's Annotations

The same conclusion is suggested by another of Mark's characteristics,
his short annotations, corresponding to the footnotes that appear in modern
books. When Mark introduces Aramaic words, as he obviously likes to do,

---

[12]Mk 1:45 could be a further example if the verse refers to Jesus, but this is very doubtful.

[13]The parallel with Matthew is even more marked if the words "the son of God" are
authentic in Mk 1:1; they would correspond to Matthew's "the son of David, the son of
Abraham."

he supplies a translation. So we have "Boanerges, that is, sons of thunder" (3:17); "Talitha coumi, that is translated, Little girl, I say to you, Arise" (5:41); "Corban, that is Gift" (7:11); "Ephphatha, that is, Be opened" (7:34); "the son of Timaeus, Bartimaeus" (10:46); and "Eloi, Eloi, lema sabachthani, that is translated, My God, my God, why hast thou forsaken me?" (15:34). (In the last of these instances, Mark's use of the Aramaic "Eloi" (ἐλωΐ) for Matthew's "Eli" (᾿Ηλί) has had the unfortunate effect of obscuring the reason for the reaction of the bystanders, "He is calling for Elijah (᾿Ηλίας)."

The same group should probably include 15:42; "the Preparation, that is, the day before the sabbath." And if Mark used Matthew, he would be using the same technique in translating Matthew's "Canaanite woman" (Mt 15:22) as "the woman was a Greek, a Syro-Phoenician by birth" (7:26). Mark's "the woman was a Greek" (that is, Gentile) is equivalent to Matthew's "Canaanite woman," and this has then the note of the woman's nationality added—"a Syro-Phoenician by birth." Finally, at 15:22, Mark has "the place Golgotha, which is translated the place of a Skull," parallel to Matthew's unusual phrase "a place called Golgotha, which is called the place of a Skull" (27:33).

Mark's "footnotes" are not confined to translation. At 2:14 he adds to Luke's "Levi" the words "the son of Alphaeus"; at 2:26, he speaks of what David did "when Abiathar was a high priest," with a not unnatural lapse of memory, Abiathar being the son of Ahimelech, the priest in question (1 Sam. 21:1-9).

At 12:42 Mark adds "which make a *quadrans*" to the reference to two *lepta* in the story of the Widow's Mite. It is his only significant difference from Luke's story, added for the sake of those unfamiliar with the coins actually given.[14] At 15:21, Mark adds to the name of Simon of Cyrene the clarification "the father of Alexander and Rufus," which must mean that the two sons were well known in the circles for which Mark wrote. If this was at Rome, the probability that Rufus was the person mentioned in Romans 16:13 is considerable. Both Mark and Paul assume that the man referred to was well known.

The most revealing of Mark's annotations is that of 7:2-4, in the discourse on defilement. The inclusion of the discourse, with that of the sto-

---

[14]J. M. Creed refers to the absence of the story from Matthew by saying "Between the two great discourses, the story of the widow's mite has dropped out. It need not be doubted that it was contained in Matthew's version of Mark" (*The Gospel according to St. Luke* [London, 1930] in loc.). The Markan priority of a story so characteristic of Luke's interests might surely have at least been doubted!

ries in Mark 2:1-3:6, is explicable in view of continuing controversies of Christians in their relations with Jews, including forgiveness in the name of Christ, table fellowship, fasting, and sabbath observance. To the discourse as recorded by Matthew, Mark adds the significant note "Thus he declared all food clean" (καθαρίζων πάντα τὰ βρώματα, 7:19).[15] Matthew's account assumes in its readers an understanding of the practices of the Pharisees and scribes who had challenged Jesus. Mark adds explanations: he refers to "hands defiled," and then explains, "that is, unwashed"; he continues with a long description of how "the Pharisees and all the Jews" acted. It is a clear indication of the secondary character of Mark's text in relation to Matthew's. The words of 7:13, "And many such things they do," and the addition at the end of the discourse to the list of things that defile (an addition marked by a change from the plural to the singular for each of them) are a further confirmation of this.

Mark's annotations are most naturally explained as additions made by him; there is nothing to suggest that they are features that have been systematically removed from his text by the other Synoptists.

5. Mark's Secondary Characteristics

To trace all the secondary characteristics of Mark's language as compared with Matthew and Luke would require far more space than can be given here. It must suffice to take a sample, in a story common to all three Gospels. It already has been suggested that so far as factual information is concerned, there is very little, if anything, in Mark's account of the healing of the paralytic (Mk 2:1-12; Mt 9:1-8; Lk 5:17-26) that could not be derived from the other gospels. Our present concern is with Mark's wording.

When Mark has the same wording as either Matthew or Luke, or both, there is no indication of the direction in which borrowing has taken place. What then is of significance?

(1) There are minor agreements of Matthew and Luke as against Mark in the phrases they use:

Mt 9:2, Lk 5:18: καὶ ἰδοὺ . . . ἐπὶ κλίνης, "and behold . . . on a bed."

Mt 9:2, Lk 5:20: for "he said" both have εἶπεν; Mk 2:5 has λέγει.

Mt 9:4 has "Jesus knowing their thoughts (ἐνθυμήσεις)"; Lk 5:22 has "Jesus perceiving their questionings (διαλογισμούς)"; Mk 2:8 has "Jesus perceiving in his spirit that they thus questioned (διαλογίζονται)." Though Matthew and Luke use different words, Matthew using one that he also uses at 12:25 and Luke one that he uses elsewhere six times in the Gos-

---

[15]See Ac 10:15; Rom 14:14; 1 Cor 10:25-27; Tit 1:15.

pel, they both use a noun where Mark has a verb. Mark agrees with Luke in using the same verb immediately afterwards: "Why do you question (διαλογίζεσθε)?"

Mt 9:7 and Lk 5:25 have "he went away to his house" (ἀπῆλθεν εἰς τὸν οἶκον αὐτοῦ); Mk 2:12 simply has "he went out" (ἐξῆλθεν).

Mt 9:8 and Lk 5:26 agree in speaking of fear, not mentioned by Mark.

(2) There are minor agreements as against Mark by omission. Mark has
2:1 "it was reported that he was at home";
2:3 "carried by four";
2:6 "in their hearts";
2:8 "in his spirit";
2:9 "to the paralytic";
2:9 "and take up your bed."

Of these, the phrases "in their hearts" and "in his spirit" add to the original story the further suggestion that Jesus' knowledge was the result of super-natural insight. "In their hearts" may be due to reminiscence of "in your hearts" in Mt 9:4; Lk 5:22; Mk 2:8.

(3) Mark's narrative shows a number of dislocations.

Parallel with Mt 9:3, where "certain of the scribes" are, quite naturally, mentioned for the first time, since Matthew has not "set the scene" before, Mark has added "sitting." Mark, like Luke, did "set the scene," but did not then include any reference to scribes. Mark has added Luke's "sitting" to Matthew's phrase, at a point where it is no longer very appropriate.

Mt 9:2 and Lk 15:18 agree in using the word κλίνη for "bed," and Mat-thew repeats this at 9:6. Luke, who is given to stylistic variations,[16] changes this at 5:24 to κλινίδιον, a related word, and then at 5:25 to "that on which he lay."[17] Mark consistently uses the word κράβαττος. There is no reason to assume that Matthew and Luke have independently elected to avoid this word; Luke himself uses it in Ac 5:15, where he has also another variant for κλίνη (κλιναρίων καὶ κραβάττων), and in Ac 9:33, in the story of an-other paralytic. Luke follows Matthew in first using κλίνη, and then makes his characteristic variations. But there is one odd result, for Mark takes up the phrase "that on which he lay" and in 2:9 adds it tautologically to his word for "bed"—"the bed, on which the paralytic lay."

At Mt 9:5, Lk 5:23, the question of Jesus "Which is easier, to say Your sins are forgiven, or to say, Rise and walk" is clearly in the original form. Mark's insertion "take up your bed" detracts from its incisiveness. He has antici-pated the words of the later command, where they are in place, as Jesus tells the paralytic to do three things: "Rise, take your bed, go home" (Mt 9:7;

---

[16]Cf. H. J. Cadbury, "Four Features of Lucan Style," in *Studies in Luke-Acts,* ed. L. E. Keck and J. L. Martyn (London, 1966) 92.

[17]Cf. Lk 23:18, "Barabbas," with 23:25, "the man who had been cast into prison"; 19:18, "disciples," with 19:32, "those who were sent" (Mt 21:6 "the disciples").

Lk 5:24; Mk 2:11). Luke repeats this threefold order of things when he says what the man actually did (5:25); Matthew, in his more concise narrative, does not then repeat "he took up his bed"; Mark does include this, but instead of "he went home" only has "he went out"—and so to some extent obscures the perfect fulfillment of Jesus' word of authority. It is Luke's text that explains Mark's wording.

Lk 5:25 says that at Jesus' word the paralytic "immediately (παραχρῆμα) rose before them"; Mk 2:11-12 has "he rose and immediately (εὐθύς) took up his bed." Mark's "immediately" has slipped into the wrong place.[18] Finally, Luke's account understandably adds "before them" (ἐνώπιον αὐτῶν) to the words "he rose up"; the words show that the bystanders were witnesses to the miracle. Mark also has "before them all" (ἔμπροσθεν πάντων at 2:12), but he adds this after "he went out." He has missed the vital point.

Mark's account is in the same sequence as Luke's, and is closer to Luke's text than to Matthew's. All the indications both from substance and form are against Markan priority.

6. Mark's Independent Features

It has been said that "the freshness and circumstantial character" of Mark's narrative have been regarded as the strongest of all the arguments for Markan priority.[19] If indeed they have this implication, this would be running counter to so much that points in the opposite direction. It is therefore a matter that calls for investigation.[20]

Mark is written in a lively and colloquial style, but this in itself proves nothing about priority, and when we take into account the possibility that the author had both Matthew and Luke to draw on, much that seems to be circumstantial can easily be accounted for, without assuming Markan priority. Nevertheless, there is a residuum of material that is specifically Markan, which could not be derived from Matthew or Luke. The question must therefore arise, from what source or sources, did he obtain it?

Whatever else Mark was, he was a member of the Christian community, who must have been familiar with much that was related at its gatherings. It would be remarkable if in those circumstances he could never have let this affect his writings. He was not in the position of one whose mind was free from all acquaintance with his subject before he was presented with

---

[18]Cf. Mk 1:20 with Mt 4:22 (εὐθύς), and Mk 1:26 with Lk 4:33 (φωνῇ μεγάλῃ).

[19]See n. 1, above.

[20]The matter has been investigated by R. Mushat Frye, "The Synoptic Problem and Analogies in Other Literatures," in *Relationships among the Gospels* (San Antonio TX: Trinity University Press, 1978) 278-80.

the two written Gospels of Matthew and Luke. It is not therefore a question why he should add anything, but of what kind of things he did add. These are of different kinds.

First, there are some substantial additions to what is recorded by Matthew or Luke. They include one parable (4:26-29), which presents no special problem, and two miracle stories (7:32-37; 8:22-26), very similar to each other in their wording and presentation, and similar also in the place they occupy in the Gospel: the one after the series of events following on the Feeding of the Five Thousand, the other after those following on that of the Four Thousand. Incidentally, they are both characterized by circumstantial detail. To these may be added the account of the death of the Baptist, which has many features that could not have been derived from Matthew (Mk 6:17-29; Mt 14:3-12), and the account of the healing of the epileptic boy after the Transfiguration, which has a number of features not paralleled in either Matthew or Luke (Mk 9:14-29; Mt 17:14-21; Lk 9:37-43). There is also the little episode of the young man who fled naked at the time of Jesus' arrest (14:51-52), which some have thought to record an experience of Mark himself.

There are distinctive features in Mark's narrative, even when it is in general parallel to Matthew or Luke, and indeed it is these which often give added "freshness" to his text. Many of them, as in the following list fall into groups together:

(1) At Capernaum
Mk 1:20, in the boat with the hired servants;
Mk 1:29, and Andrew, with James and John;
Mk 1:32, and the whole city was gathered round the door;
Mk 1:35, and there he prayed;
Mk 1:36, Simon and those with him.

(2) Healing by the sea.
Mk 3:7, Jesus withdrew with his disciples to the sea;
Mk 3:9, And he told his disciples to have a boat ready for him because of the crowd, lest they should crush him;
Mk 3:10, all who had diseases pressed upon him to touch him.

(3) Stilling the Storm.
Mk 4:35, On that day, when evening had come;
Mk 4:36, they took him with them in the boat, just as he was;
Mk 4:36, and other boats were with them;
Mk 4:38, but he was in the stern, asleep on the cushion.

(4) The Five Thousand.
Mk 6:31, And he said to them, Come away by yourselves to a lonely place, and rest a while. For many were coming and going, and they had no leisure even to eat;

Mk 6:37, And they said to him, Shall we go and buy two hundred denarii worth of bread and give it them to eat? And he said to them, How many loaves have you? Go and see (cf. John 6:7);

Mk 6:39, the green grass.

(5) Healings at Gennesaret.

Mk 6:53, and moored to the shore;

Mk 6:55, on their pallets to any place where they heard he was;

Mk 6:56, And wherever he came, in villages, cities or country, they laid the sick in the market places.

(6) Jericho.

Mk 10:46, the son of Timaeus, Bartimaeus;

Mk 10:49, And Jesus stopped, and said, Call him. And they called the blind man, saying to him, Take heart; rise, he is calling you;

Mk 10:50, And throwing off his mantle, he sprang up and came to Jesus.

(7) At Bethany.

Mk 14:3, ointment of pure nard (cf. John 12:3);

Mk 14:5, three hundred denarii (cf. John 12:5).

There are other items of information embedded in Mark's narrative, some of which give the appearance of coming, whether directly or indirectly, from the testimony of someone who had been present. None of the following could have been derived from Matthew or Luke.

Mk 3:20, Then he went home; and the crowd came together again, so that they could not even eat. (21) And when his people heard it, they went out to seize him, for it was said, He is beside himself;

Mk 6:13, and anointed with oil many that were sick;

Mk 7:24, And he entered a house, and would not have anyone know it, but he could not be hid;

Mk 9:30, and he would not have anyone know it;

Mk 10:17, And as he was setting out on his journey, a man ran up and knelt before him;

Mk 10:32, Jesus was walking ahead of them;

Mk 11:4, and found a colt tied at the door, out in the open street;

Mk 11:16, and he would not allow anyone to carry anything through the temple;

Mk 14:72, the cock crew twice.

It is clear from the material peculiar to Mark that even if he used Matthew and Luke, he not only had information of some events, such as the healings of the blind men and the deaf-mute which they did not record, but also that stories they told had also come to his knowledge from some other sources with features that he was to reproduce in his Gospel. There would be nothing surprising about that, but the external evidence for Mark's connection with Peter has naturally suggested that Peter was at least one of his sources, and probably the only one. In the nature of things, it is impossible for the internal evidence to prove that Mark derived material from Peter, but the incidental items Mark adds to stories told by Matthew or Luke would certainly be consistent with Peter being their source.[21] The question that remains is whether, if Mark had learned from Peter, he could still have used Matthew and Luke, as on other grounds he seems to have done. We have therefore to turn aside for the moment from the internal evidence to look at the much discussed statement of Papias, which is dealt with in Part II of this book, and in particular to his words that Peter "formed his instructions πρός τὰς χρείας, but not as forming a connected account (σύνταξιν) of the Lord's oracles."[22] It has been well said by R. O. P. Taylor in his book *The Groundwork of the Gospels* that since Papias, in treating of the formation of the Gospels, is dealing with a literary question, we must take the word χρεια, not in its general sense of "need," but in its special literary sense."[23] In that sense it bears a technical meaning: "an ἀπομνημό-νευμα (i.e., memorandum) which is succinct, with reference to some person, told to his credit."[24] It is this meaning that clarifies the words of Papias. Those who have translated them as meaning that Peter "adapted his instructions to the needs" have commonly added in brackets some such interpretation as "of his hearers" or "of the moment,"[25] and by so doing have obscured the meaning of the following words "but not as forming a connected account." A parish priest "adapts his instructions to the needs of his hearers," a general congregation or children or some special group; he adapts them "to the moment" or "occasion," Christmas or Easter, or a wedding or a funeral or whatever it may be; but no one comments that he has not made a connected account of his teaching. It is the distinction between χρεια and συνταξις that is the point of Papias' statement: Peter teaching by means of χρειαι, which Mark committed to writing, even though it could not be said that he wrote "in order" (ταξει). Speaking of Matthew, Papias is also quoted as saying that he did make a σύνταξις (τὰ λόγια συνετάξατο).[26]

---

[21]In parts 2 and 3 below the evidence that Peter was regarded as the witness to the tradition behind Mark is considered.

[22]But see pt. 2, ch. 4, below.

[23]R. O. P. Taylor, *The Groundwork of the Gospels* (Oxford, 1946) 29.

[24]Quoted by Taylor (ibid., 82) from a papyrus fragment of a lesson on rhetoric.

[25]E.g., "of his hearers" (Streeter); "of the moment" (Rawlinson).

[26]Elsewhere Eusebius, to whom we owe the Papias quotation, refers to St. Luke's Gospel as a σύνταξις (EH III.25.15), and, quoting Origen, speaks of Matthew's Gospel as συντεταγμενον (EH VI.25.4).

We have to see the Gospels against the background of the life of the church, where the episodes (the χρειαι) with which we are familiar in the Gospels are a basis of Christian instruction, repeated in order that they might be remembered. They might be expressed in rather different words in different parts of the church, and it is this situation that can explain, not only differences between Mark and the other Synoptics, but differences between Matthew and Luke also.

If Peter based his own teaching on such *chreiai,* it is natural enough that their wording should sometimes reflect personal memories which were not included in the tradition of all the churches, and that when Mark made his collection, he should have preserved them.

There are indeed passages that fit in very well with this possibility. So C. H. Turner, who advanced "the general conclusion that Mark's Gospel reproduces Peter's teaching,[27] in commenting on Mark 1:29, "they came into the house of Simon and Andrew with James and John," described this as "an awkard phrase which only becomes really intelligible when we put it back into the mouth of Peter; 'we came into our house, with James and John.' " (Although there is conflicting manuscript evidence as to whether the phrase should be read as "they came" or "he came," this does not materially affect the point.) Similarly, Turner puts 1:16, "he saw Simon and Andrew the brother of Simon," back into the mouth of Peter: "he saw me and my brother."

Turner makes a further point concerning a common feature of Mark's wording: "Time and again a sentence commences with the plural, for it is an experience which is being related." In his view, such a phrase as that of 1:21 or 9:33, "they went into Capernaum," or that of 14:32, "they came to a place which was called Gethsemane," reflect Peter's wording, "we came." And, on 11:21, Turner says "none but Peter would have *remembered* and said." It appears, however, that the greatest concentration of such possibly Petrine echoes is in the passage 1:16-38, dealing with a day at Capernaum. At the end of that day, Luke 4:42 says that "the crowds sought" Jesus; it would fit in with Turner's view that Mark in 1:36 speaks instead of "Simon and those who were with him."

The exegesis of these texts cannot of itself prove that there is such a Petrine background to Mark's phrases; what can be said is that they are fully consistent with that possibility.

---

[27]C. H. Turner in *Commentary on the Gospel of St. Mark,* vol. 1 of *A New Commentary on Holy Scripture,* pt. 3, 48-49, 55. The question of the relationship between Mark, the Gospel of Mark, and Peter is examined again in pt. 3 below in the light of the historical evidence.

With Matthew probably already in use with a semiofficial status, and with Luke also being known to him, Mark had considerable guidance available in making his own collection; and if he wanted to record the kind of instruction that Peter had been used to give, it is not surprising that he did not extend his purpose to include in his work the more extended passages of teaching he found in Matthew and Luke, or their introductory material. An outstanding thing about Peter's teaching must have been that he spoke at first hand the things that he had known from the time of Jesus' Baptism (cf. Ac 1:22; 4:20; 10:39). A short introduction leading up to the first preaching of Jesus in Galilee (Mk 1:1-13) would be adequate for Mark's purpose, a less ambitious one than that of either Matthew or Luke. It does not seem that the evidence of Papias is inconsistent with the priority of Matthew, and with the use of Matthew and Luke by Mark.

7. The Ending of Mark's Gospel, Mk 16:9-20

Why does Mark's Gospel break off so awkwardly at 16:8, and who then completed it with what follows in the canonical text? Mark had followed the course of his story to the point of the Resurrection, and then, whatever is to be said of what follows in 16:9-20, the narrative breaks off at 16:8. At the announcement of the Resurrection, the women who had visited the tomb of Jesus are left trembling and astonished, in fear and silence. Clearly Mark did not think that the silence was never to be broken, or he could not have known anything about it. But at that point he stopped. No one can say with certainty why he did, but we can see that there may have been problems for him. Matthew and Luke had been running closely enough together; now their accounts (Mt 28:11ff; Lk 24:13ff) are very different; Mark could have chosen to follow Matthew, but there were other possibilities. The Gospel told the story of Jesus' life, but the Resurrection appearances are not part of the history of Jesus, as though we could ask, for instance, what he was doing between the early Easter morning and the afternoon or evening when Luke says he appeared at Emmaus. The Resurrection appearances are part of the experience of Jesus' followers, not an account of what was happening to their Lord. According to St. John, Jesus told Mary Magdalene on Easter morning, "I am ascending to my Father"; St. Luke tells us of the Ascension as part of the experience of the disciples forty days later. The two statements are not contradictory or irreconcilable.[28]

Not all of the experiences of the Resurrection have been recorded. According to St. Paul, Jesus appeared "to Cephas, then to the Twelve," then "to more than five hundred brethren," then "he appeared to James, then

---

[28]Cf. P. Benoit, "The Ascension," in *Jesus and the Gospel,* vol. 1 (London, 1973).

to all the apostles'' (1 Cor 15:5-6). Of the appearance to Cephas (Peter) we have only elsewhere the almost incidental reference in Luke 24:34; nowhere, except in St. Paul's summary, is there any record of the appearance to James. Matthew has his own selection of material, and Luke, while limiting himself in the Gospel to incidents with one special point, speaks in the Acts (1:3) of Jesus appearing ''during forty days'' without further explanation. The field seems to be quite open for whatever selection the writer of a Gospel might make out of a number of possible occasions.

Whether Mark did not care to choose between Matthew and Luke, or whether he first stopped writing, and then decided to leave the fact of the Resurrection as the climax of his book, or whether he was puzzled as to what he should do, or broke off for some other reason, no one will ever know. Streeter offered a different opinion, that either the writing of the Gospel was interrupted by the author's death, or that the roll on which it was written was mutilated. ''There is no difficulty,'' he wrote, ''in supposing that the original copy of Mark, especially if the Gospel was written for the Church of Rome about A.D. 65, almost immediately lost its conclusion.''[29] It is a view that could only be sustained if the appendix, the ''Longer Ending'' of 16:9-20, is by another hand, which is indeed the common view. But is that true? Did Mark himself, having broken off at 16:8, subsequently make this addition? To this question we now turn.

Both the external and the internal evidence bearing on the question of the authenticity of Mark 16:9-20 have been examined by W. R. Farmer, in his book *The Last Twelve Verses of Mark*.[30] With regard to the external evidence, he comes to the conclusion that ''we can only say with certainty (concerning Mk 16:9-20 in this period) that manuscripts including these verses were circulating in the second century. Whether there were also manuscripts ending with ἐφοβοῦντο γάρ circulating in this archaic period, we do not know. . . . The presumption that the autograph of Mark ended at ἐφοβοῦντο γάρ is dependent, at least in part, on a widespread belief that a careful study of the linguistic, stylistic, and conceptional character of Mark 16:9-20 indicates that these verses do not belong to the rest of the Gospel.''[31] With regard to this internal evidence, after a review of the verbal features of the text, he writes of the twelve verses: ''Evidence for non-Markan authorship seems to be preponderant in verse 10. Verses 12, 14, 16, 17, 18, and 19 seem to be either basically, or on balance, neutral. Evidence for Markan authorship seems to be preponderant in verses

---

[29]Streeter, *The Four Gospels*, 338.

[30]W. R. Farmer, *The Last Twelve Verses of Mark* (Cambridge, 1974).

[31]Ibid., 74, 75.

9, 11, 15, and 20.''[32] It is with the internal evidence that we are concerned here, and what follows is largely based on the research in Farmer's book.

Whether or not the appendix (if we may so call Mk 16:9-20 for convenience) is authentic, there is a certain appropriateness in the Gospel ending, as it began, with a short summary, providing a frame in which Mark's collection of material is set. Mark 1:1-13 deals with the coming of John and the Baptism and Temptation of Jesus in a short space comparable to that in which the appendix deals with the Resurrection appearances and the Ascension. In both passages there are some distinctive Markan features, and in both there is an indication of dependence on Matthew and Luke, both for substance and for wording. In the appendix a similar connection with St. John's Gospel is also indicated, as we shall see. To appreciate what is said in summary form both in the introduction and in the appendix to the Gospel, we have to look outside them. And as the introduction takes us speedily through the traditions of the coming of John and of Jesus' Baptism and Temptation, the appendix takes us speedily through those found elsewhere in the more extensive range of narratives of the Resurrection, that of Mary Magdalene, as in John 20 (Mk 16:9-11); of two going into the country, as in Luke 24 (Mk 16:12-14); and those of a final commission and the Ascension, as in Matthew 28 and Luke 24 (Mk 16:15-20).

Mk 16:1-8 tells of the women who went to the tomb of Jesus early on Easter morning. There, as in Matthew 28:1 and Luke 24:10, Mary Magdalene is named first among them, but only in the appendix and in St. John's Gospel is she singled out as the first person to have seen the risen Lord. The appendix does not relate very closely to the story in John, but there is a curious linguistic similarity in 16:10. The words "She went and told those who had been with him" (ἐκείνη πορευθεῖσα ἀπήγγειλεν τοῖς μετ' αὐτοῦ γενομένοις) are in form, though not in their first words in meaning, similar to those of Jn 20:15 and 18: "She supposed . . . told his disciples" (ἐκείνη δοκοῦσα . . . ἀγγέλουσα τοῖς μαθηταῖς), and Farmer, chiefly on the ground that "there is no comparable use of ἐκεῖνος in Mk," regards 16:10 as the verse that "supports the view that these verses are stylistically different from the rest of Mark."[33] This is however not the only place that raises a question about the relation of words in Mark and in John. Apart from the Passion narrative, there are only two passages where the same episodes are recorded in both these Gospels. The first covers the Feeding of the Five Thousand and the Walking on the Water; and it is only in these two Gospels that the reference to two hundred denarii is

---

[32]Ibid., 103.

[33]Ibid., 86.

found (Mk 6:37; Jn 6:7). The other is the Anointing at Bethany (Mk 14: 3-9; Jn 12:1-8). Mark's account is substantially the same as Matthew's, but there are features in which it is similar to John's. At 14:3, Mark, in place of Matthew's "ointment, very expensive" (μύρου βαρυτίμου) has "ointment of pure nard, very costly" (μύρου νάρδου πιστικῆς πολυτελοῦς) almost identical with John's words μύρου νάρδου πιστικῆς πολυτίμου. Both in Mark 14:5 and John 12:5 the statement is made that the ointment might have been sold for three hundred denarii, where Matthew has only "for much." Mark, like John, has "Let her alone" (Mk 14:6 ἄφετε αὐτήν, Jn 12:7 ἄφες αὐτήν) and both Mark 14:8 and John 12:7 have the noun ἐνταφιασμός for "burial," where Matthew has the verbal form ἐνταφιάσαι. The problem of the verbal similarities between Mark 16:10 and John 20 are paralleled by those between Mark 14 and Jn 12.

The answer cannot be the simple one that John copied Mark, for it is when Mark varies from Matthew that there is a correspondence with John, not when Matthew and Mark are in parallel (as in the reference to the house of Simon the leper, or the pouring of the ointment on the head, where John has "feet"). Both in Mark 14:3-9 and in 16:10 it is a question of Johannine features, and in view of this it cannot be said that 16:10 could not have been written by the author of 1:1–16:8.

Farmer judges the evidence for Markan authorship to be preponderant in five of the other verses of the appendix (9, 11, 13, 15, and 20), and in the remainder to be neutral. The detective who finds a set of fingerprints on parts of a windowpane is not disturbed by the existence of "neutral" areas in which they do not occur. In any passage of twelve verses of Mark there will be such neutral areas.

The verses 9-11, dealing with the appearances to Mary Magdalene, from whom Jesus "had cast out seven demons" (cf. Lk 8:2), end, as does the story of the appearance to the women in Luke, with the statement that it was met with unbelief (Mk 16:11 ἠπίστησαν; Lk 24:11 ἠπίστουν). The story of the two disciples (Mk 16:12 δυσὶν ἐξ αὐτῶν: cf. Lk 24:13 δύο ἐξ αὐτῶν) leads to a further statement of unbelief (Mk 16:13 οὐδὲ ἐκείνοις ἐπίστευσαν which is also recorded in Luke 24:41 (ἀπιστούντων) at the appearance to the Eleven, and in Mark 16:14 (ἀπιστίαν αὐτῶν . . . οὐκ ἐπίστευσαν). The final commission, corresponding to the conclusion of St. Matthew's Gospel, still suggests Lukan references: the words "they will pick up serpents, and if they drink any deadly thing it will not hurt them" put in a more dramatic form those of Lk 10:19, "to tread upon serpents . . . and nothing shall hurt you." Then, as in Luke 24:51, Mark 16:19 briefly records the Ascension, before a final comment (16:20; cf. Lk 24:52), though the content is different.

There is therefore good reason for believing that it was Mark, coming to a decision to close his book as he began it, with a brief summary, who made use of material that he found in Matthew and Luke, and indeed apart from them, for his purpose.

8. Conclusions

We can therefore sum up the conclusions to which our study has led us. The internal evidence is consistent with the tradition that Mark set out to make a collection of the kind of *chreiai* on which Peter had based his teaching. Since Peter had not arranged them in order, Mark made use of Matthew as his principal guide, but also used Luke, and in consequence followed an order that alternated with the sequences of those Gospels, adding some further material, notably two miracle stories and a parable, which they did not contain. There are incidental details which may reflect Mark's recollection of Peter's own words when he used his *chreiai*. When Mark was following Matthew's order, he naturally tended to follow Matthew's wording more closely; when following Luke's, to be closer to Luke's text.

Mark was well aware of Jesus' work as a teacher, but his purpose was a more limited one than that of giving lengthy accounts of Jesus' teaching. The *chreiai* themselves were directed to give teaching arising out of specific occasions. And since Peter's experience of Jesus began at the time of Jesus' Baptism, Mark, after a brief introduction, could begin his collection from that point. He continued it to the time of the Resurrection, and then perhaps was at first uncertain what else to include. In the event, he added a brief summary by way of a conclusion.

Mark wrote in a predominantly Gentile milieu, and therefore frequently added notes to his text to explain practices or institutions with which his readers would not be familiar. He liked to recall actual Aramaic words or phrases which had been stamped on his memory, but he was always careful to give a translation. Some of the practices to which he referred could still be matters on which there was controversy, either with Jews, or perhaps with judaizing Christians, and Mark had to show what the attitude of Jesus to them had been. One Jewish belief, that of the necessity of Davidic descent for the Messiah, had fallen comparatively into the background, and mattered less to those for whom Mark wrote than it had for those in a different milieu. The Infancy stories of Matthew and Luke, which did not fall within his plan, were therefore the less necessary.

Mark wrote in a colloquial style, without great literary nicety. He was telling the stories again in the way that came naturally to him. The result was the lively manner of the speaker, rather than the thought-out arrangement of the professional writer. He might have to interrupt his story to include a detail which a more polished writer would have worked in before. He could sometimes use words, like "gospel," "the word," "Christ," in the ways that were current at the time of writing, instead of more original forms. If the meaning was clear, that was what mattered.

What purpose then did Mark try to satisfy? It is not likely that he sought to displace Matthew or Luke. His intention was more modest. Without pretending that we can know for certain, it would seem likely that his Gospel was meant to be a handbook for the guidance and encouragement of converts, or perhaps prospective converts, in the hands of teachers who like himself were concerned in leading others to the Christian faith. We have spoken of Mark's readers, but it is probable that a more accurate term would be "hearers"; they would probably be people, not all literate, who had Mark's words read out to them as part of their instruction. There is no reason to suppose that his book would not have filled a place in the needs of the Christian community. There were those for whom the Gospel, the kerygma, had to be proclaimed, before they were ready to assimilate much of the teaching they could subsequently be given. The Gospel of Mark would have served such a purpose admirably.

We must attempt to assess the *Sitz im Leben* not only of particular elements of the Gospels, but of the books as a whole. If Mark was written, as the tradition suggests, in the period that included the death of Peter, the Christian missionary had a daunting task. He had to present the Christian Gospel as a call to a new way of life, and to a new revelation of truth: "Repent and believe the gospel" (Mk 1:14). But the new way of life could not be merely a turning from evil in one's personal life and the acceptance of forgiveness, nor could the truth of the gospel be a matter of personal enlightenment and comfort. The call to repent and believe the gospel was a call to follow Christ, and his way had been the way of the Cross. Jesus, who had to suffer many things, had issued the warning "If any man would come after me, let him deny himself and take up his cross and follow me" (Mk 8:34). One who responded might lose his life, but "whoever loses his life for my sake and the gospel's will save it." The call to discipleship was a call to live under the threat of persecution, the prospect of martyrdom.

The convert would be one who would "seek Jesus of Nazareth, who was crucified" but "has risen" (Mk 16:6). The cost of discipleship could be great, but the future was with the gospel. The seed which is God's word would not always fall on good soil, but those who heard the word and kept it would bear fruit, "thirtyfold and sixtyfold and a hundredfold" (Mk 4:20); the seed would sprout and grow (Mk 4:36), and like the smallest of seeds which becomes the "greatest of all shrubs" (Mk 4:31), so the gospel had a great future before it.

In such a situation, what would the Christian missionary find most useful in his approach to potential converts? If Mark had the Gospels of Matthew and Luke available, it would seem that he had been for some time familiar with the former, and more recently with the latter. Indeed St. Luke's Gospel could hardly have been available for very long when he made its acquaintance. Mark's inclination would certainly be to make use of Matthew. All the indications are of the prestige it had in the early days of the Church. Nevertheless, not all its contents would be of immediate appeal to the persons with whom Mark would be dealing. Much that reflected its Jewish background would seem foreign to their concerns. Luke's Gospel was different. It was much more a book of the Greco-Roman world and one that in many ways would correspond more to the needs of the Gentile convert. It would have a strong appeal for Mark.

It is not difficult to understand the comparative neglect of Mark's Gospel in the later years, in view of its limited purpose. But Mark's Gospel still not only has its appeal in its presentation of the story of Jesus; it bears its witness that while the presentation may vary according to the circumstances of its hearers, there is one *Gospel of Jesus Christ, the Son of God.*

Appendix 1
Styler's Key Passages

(See C. F. D. Moule, *The Birth of the New Testament*, 2nd ed., Cambridge, 1981.)

Example A
The Death of the Baptist
Mt 14:3-12 = Mk 6:17-29

Styler argues that two features of Matthew's version betray a knowledge of Mark. First, that Matthew's phrase that "the king was sorry" (14:9) is in plain contradiction with his statement that Herod *wanted* to kill John. This is, however, to oversimplify the facts of the situation. If Herod "feared the people" (Mt 14:5) there is no inconsistency between his desiring John's death and his sorrow that it should occur in these circumstances. Josephus also says that Herod feared the influence that John had over the people, and that he thought it best to put him to death.[1] What Matthew says is wholly in line with the historical probabilities. Mark picks up Matthew's word "feared," and says that Herod feared John and kept him "safe"; but, after all, that means "kept him in prison." Mark's comment that Herod heard John gladly is not unlike Luke's comment in 23:8 that "when Herod saw Jesus, he was very glad, for he had long desired to see him," although Luke has already recorded the warning that "Herod wants to kill you" (13:31).

Secondly, Styler thinks that Matthew "has made another blunder"; he has overlooked the fact that the story began as a "flashback" (p. 294). But for Matthew the story is not a "flashback" at all; Matthew leads quite naturally into it, speaking first of Herod's concern about the renown of Jesus (14:1-2), and the record of John's death is for him an integral part of his narrative, as we have seen. Like John's arrest, his death is for Matthew a turning point in the career of Jesus. St. Mark's Gospel would indeed show no lacuna if Mark 6:14-29 were dropped out of it; for him the story is indeed a "flashback," breaking in on the Lukan order which has influenced him. For Matthew, the story has to come just where it is.

Styler notes that Matthew uses the title "King" as well as the more accurate "Tetrarch," and says that "this may be, but need not be, due to the influence of Mark" (p. 293). He fails to see that it is Mark's change from the word "baptizer" in 6:24 when there is no parallel with Matthew, to "Baptist" in 6:25 when there is, that is a verbal indication of the direction of the borrowing.

---

[1] Josephus, *Antiquities*, XVIII.5.

Example B
The Young Man and Jesus
Mt 19:16-22 = Mk 10:17-22

The story as told by Matthew is logical and consistent, with its lesson wholly in line with what Matthew has recorded elsewhere. A young man asks what is the good he must do to have eternal life, and Jesus replies by himself asking why he needs to ask that question: "The good [masc.] is one," he says, and while the words are certainly somewhat cryptic, the continuation shows that they must have been understood to imply that to do good is to obey God, who has revealed his will in his commandments. The answer of the young man is that he has always done so, but finds something lacking. So Jesus challenges him, if he would be perfect (τέλ-ειος), to sell all and follow him. The whole passage is in effect an illustration of the teaching of the Sermon on the Mount (Mt 5:17-48), in which Jesus, coming to fulfill the law and the prophets, claims more than the literal keeping of the commandments, and leads to the conclusion "You [his disciples] must therefore be perfect (τέλειοι)."

The obvious difficulty is the phrase "The good is one." Not following the Jewish line of thought, Luke or his source has been led (with Mark copying him) to the transference of the word "good" to the address to Jesus, but this has only led to the question "Why do you call me good?"—which is irrelevant to the logic of the episode as a whole. It has been argued that "the good is one" means the good law (νόμος),[2] but whether this is so or not, the phrase in Matthew must be intended to point to God's good will, manifested in the commandments, but not to be interpreted in the limited way seen in the righteousness "of the scribes and Pharisees." And by omitting "if you would be perfect" Luke and Mark have failed to pick up the connection with the original question, "What must I do to have eternal life?"

It may be added that if Mark had been Matthew's source, it is unlikely that Matthew would have boggled at Mark's words as suggesting that Jesus should not be called good: no other Christian writer seems to have seen such a difficulty.

---

[2]See O. Lamar Cope, *Matthew, a Scribe Trained for the Kingdom of Heaven* (Washington DC, 1976) 114.

Example C
The Son of David
Mt 22:41-46 = Mk 12:35-37a

In this third example, Styler's objection is to Matthew's "awkward logic": Matthew's question, he suggests, has in mind the antithesis that Jesus is the son of God, not "son of David."[3] But this is impossible. Matthew is, more than any other of the Evangelists, concerned to show that Jesus is the son of David. Jesus' question "Whose son is he?" is necessary to provide the occasion for what follows: when the Pharisees say that the Christ is the son of David, the question arises (as in Luke and Mark), how then is David's Lord his son?

Mark's opening phrase, "And teaching in the temple, Jesus answering said," really assumes something like Matthew's introduction. Mark is fond of inserting "answering" (ἀποκριθείς) before "said," generally in response to a question or a statement, but on occasion (9:17; 10:51; 11:14) only in response to a recorded situation. But here, at the beginning of his pericope, there is nothing to respond to, except on the assumption that the statement has been made, as in Matthew, that the Christ is the son of David. It is Mark's formulation that is secondary.

Example D
The Disciples' Private Question
Mt 24:3 = Mk 13:3

Matthew has "the disciples came to him [Jesus] in private, saying," where Mark has "Peter and John and James asked him privately." It is difficult to see any validity in Styler's objection that "the phrase 'in private' has an obvious force in Mark; in Matthew it has much less force."[4] Matthew's use of the word "came" is merely a matter of style; he has just said that the "disciples came to point out to him [Jesus] the buildings" (24:1) when they were already obviously with him; now the words that they "came privately saying" are the same in meaning as Mark's "asked him privately." The conclusion that "it seems likely that Matthew has unwittingly retained a phrase from Mark" is not justified. The same difference in style is to be found at Matthew 17:19 ("the disciples came to Jesus privately and said") and its parallel in Mark 9:28 ("his disciples asked him privately").

---

[3]Styler, in C. F. D. Moule, *The Birth of the New Testament* (Cambridge, ²1981) 295.
[4]Ibid., 296.

Example E
Pilate's Offer to Release a Prisoner
Mt 27:15-18 = Mk 15:6-10

Styler finds Mark's sequence "comparatively clear and intelligible" but thinks that "Matthew blurs the picture badly." Mark says that Pilate offered to release "the king of the Jews," and then that Pilate knew that Jesus had been delivered up out of envy on the part of the chief priests. Matthew makes Pilate offer a choice between Jesus and Barabbas, but, says Styler, "nevertheless he continues with 'he knew that it was out of envy that they had delivered him up.' " The logic is however the same: Matthew has made it clear that when he says "they had delivered him up" the reference is to the "chief priests and elders" (Mt 27:1-2, 12), and he now adds that they had to persuade (ἔπεισαν) the people to go against Pilate's implied expectation of their preference for Jesus. Styler says that in his judgment "passages (A) and (E) are decisive" (p. 298) for Markan priority. It is a claim difficult to appreciate.

Example F
The Question about Fasting
Mt 9:14 = Mk 2:18

Mark has "John's disciples and the Pharisees were fasting and they [that is, 'people' RSV] came and said to him, 'Why do John's disciples and the disciples of the Pharisees fast, but your disciples do not fast?' " Matthew has "the disciples of John came to him, saying 'Why do we and the Pharisees fast, but your disciples do not fast?' " Markan priorists, Styler says, "will have no hesitation in asserting that Matthew has made a tidy but unjustified abbreviation of Mark" (p. 297). It is indeed only a committed Markan priorist who would have no such hesitation. Matthew's statement reflects the situation in which there could be tension between the disciples of John and those of Jesus (cf. Jn 3:22-30); when Mark wrote, this no longer concerned him.

Styler's examples of parallels between Matthew and Mark certainly do not prove decisive for Markan priority; in dealing with parallels between Luke and Mark he seems less assured. He gives three examples.

Example G
Jairus's Daughter
Lk 8:51 = Mk 5:37, 40

Styler objects to Luke's phrase that "when he [Jesus] came to the house, he permitted no one to enter with him, except Peter and John and James and the father and mother of the child," on the grounds that the mother was already in the house and the father did not need permission to go into his own home. He adds that there is an awkward impression in Luke 8:53 that it was those of this inner group who ridiculed Jesus. But Mark also says that Jesus "took the child's father and mother" as well as "those who were with him, and went in where the child was." Luke and Mark are naturally understood to mean that the disciples and parents went into the chamber where the child was, not merely into the house. And there is no reason to think that it was this inner group ("all"—including the three disciples?) who ridiculed Jesus. As to the position of 8:52 in Luke's narrative, it is more easily accounted for if it was Matthew, not Mark, that he was using.

Example H
The Scribes' Commendation of Jesus
Lk 20:39, compare Mk 12:28, 32

Styler objects that Luke speaks of "some of the scribes" when he has not mentioned scribes previously, and says Luke could have picked up the phrase from the reference to "one of the scribes" in the passage from Mark that follows this incident (namely, Mk 12:28, 32). But Luke's introduction of "some of the scribes" is not more surprising than Mark's "one of the scribes" (12:28), when he has not mentioned scribes since 11:27. Incidentally, both Luke 20:39 and Mark 12:32 imply approval, which, says Styler, "is inconsistent with the last mention of the scribes" (p. 306). What is sauce for the Lukan goose is sauce for the Markan gander. And not all scribes need have been tarred with the same brush (cf. Mt 13:52).

Example I
The Injunction to Secrecy
Lk 9:21 = Mk 8:30

Styler's third example deals with one word. Mark at 8:30, as on two other occasions (3:12, 10:48) on both of which the same word and construction is found in Matthew's parallel, uses the word ἐπετίμησεν ("rebuke") in the sense of "strictly command." Luke 9:21 has the same word as a participle, "rebuking, he charged them." Styler thinks that "Luke surely betrays knowledge of Mark, since he adds Mark's verb as a participle" (p. 307). But this can only be maintained if Markan priority is already assumed; Luke has a similar usage at 4:41, and if in fact Mark used Matthew and Luke, he could have copied Matthew at 3:12 and 10:48, and picked up Luke's word here. Either course is equally possible. The example proves nothing.

We conclude that none of Styler's examples can be seen to bear the weight he put on them.

Appendix 2
"The Baptist"

Matthew speaks of John by name twenty-three times, and on seven occasions, in different parts of his Gospel, adds "the Baptist." Luke, after his first two chapters, speaks of John by name twenty times; on the first occasion he adds "the Baptist." Mark uses John's name sixteen times; on two occasions (6:25; 8:28) he adds "the Baptist," and on three he adds "the baptizer" (ὁ βαπτίζων: 1:4; 6:14; 6:24).

A. John the Baptist, Mk 1:4

At Mark 1:4 "John the baptizer" corresponds to Matthew 3:1, "John the Baptist," and to Luke 3:2, "John the son of Zechariah." Mark's phrase is part of his summary prologue to his Gospel (1:1-13), which exhibits connections both with Matthew's and with Luke's wording.

If Mark is prior to Matthew and Luke, neither of them can be wholly dependent on him for their extended accounts of the Baptist and of the Temptation. Mark's "the baptizer" will be his own natural phrase, and if Matthew and Luke have made use of Mark at this point, Matthew will have substituted his own "the Baptist" in redaction, and Luke will have altered Mark, to connect his narrative with that of his first chapter, by identifying John as the previously mentioned son of Zechariah (cf. his naming Joseph in 4:22, when Mk 13:55 has "the carpenter"). "The baptizer" remains a specifically Markan phrase.

Alternatively, if Mark is not a source for Matthew or Luke, he shows, in his material, acquaintance with both, or with traditions behind them. His actual phrases point to a knowledge of both of them, but in this summary account he is comparatively independent of them, both in order and in wording. "There came John the baptizer in the desert" was about the shortest form in which he could record the common tradition, and "the baptizer" appears to be the phrase that he most naturally used.

B. Herod and the Baptist, Mk 6:14

The second example is at Mark 6:14, parallel to Matthew 14:2 ("John the Baptist") and Luke 9:7 ("John"). So far Mark has not used "the Baptist," nor been in parallel with this phrase since Matthew 3:1. As in the previous example, Matthew and Luke differ from each other.

If Mark is prior to Matthew and Luke, Matthew may have altered Mark's word, and Luke may have just omitted it. For Mark himself 6:14 follows naturally on the usage of 1:4.

If Mark has made use of Matthew and Luke, the passage Mark 6:14-16, appears to be a conflation of both: Mark 6:14 being parallel to Luke 9:7, for what "*some* said," and Mark 6:16 parallel to Matthew 14:11-12, for what *Herod* "said to his servants." "John the baptizer" is then an expansion of Luke's "John," not an alteration of Matthew's "John the Baptist." Mark is given to such expansions, and "the baptizer" would be his natural wording for such an expansion here.

C. The Death of the Baptist, Mk 6:17-29

The passage Mark 6:17-29 is parallel to Matthew 14:3-12; there is no parallel in Luke.

If Matthew is here dependent on Mark, it is remarkable that he happens not to be using Mark's text where "the baptizer" appears, but finds his own form "the Baptist" appearing for the first time in Mark when he does so.

If Mark has used Matthew, he has first used his own form "the baptizer" as on the previous occasions; there is no parallel in Matthew. At 6:25 there is such a parallel to Matthew 14:8, and the connection in wording is very close. As on the other, later, occasion when Mark is in parallel with Matthew's "John the Baptist" (Mk 8:28; Mt 16:14; Lk 9:19), he uses the form he finds in Matthew. At that later point Luke has the same phrase.

Altogether, there are seven instances of the form "the Baptist," in Matthew, two of them in common with Mark. The same redactional formula is also used in other parts of his narrative, in five different chapters, but Mark never uses it independently. The probability is that the use in Matthew is due to a preference on the part of the redactor, while its use in Mark may be readily accounted for by copying. It is difficult to believe that Matthew found it in Mark, and himself used it throughout his Gospel, just happening to avoid the need to do so at the points where Mark (at 6:14 and 6:24) used "the baptizer."

The facts are most satisfactorily accounted for by the hypothesis that Mark is not prior to Matthew and Luke, and that Mark only used the form "the Baptist" when influenced by one of them.

Appendix 3
Duality in Mark

In a recent study[1] C. M. Tuckett sets out to provide, as the subtitle of his book says, "an analysis and appraisal" of the hypothesis that Mark used Matthew and Luke. The first of the phenomena he considers is that of Mark's duplicate expressions, and he closes the chapter in which he does so with the judgment that "the phenomenon of Mark's duplicate expressions gives no positive support" to this hypothesis. As Mark's dual expressions are so significant a feature of his style, this judgment should not go unchallenged.

It is not very clear how Tuckett chose his examples. He says that "attention has been limited to the categories numbered 10-13 by Neirynck" in his book *Duality in Mark,* which, as Neirynck himself implies, form a significant group of categories, as he compares them with the lists of Weiss, Holtzmann, Hawkins, Allen, and Cadbury.[2] Tuckett, however, has included some examples not found in these lists, and has not included all the examples in them. His own total is 213, Neirynck's would be 271. To consider Tuckett's case, it is his total of 213 that is taken as a basis here.

There is a clear mistake in one conclusion that Tuckett draws. Of his 213 examples, his lists include fifty-six where both Matthew and Luke omit one-half of Mark's expression, seventeen in which the two halves are split between them, and thirty-nine in which they omit the same half. Tuckett concludes that if Matthew and Luke were independently reading Mark, the number seventeen out of fifty-six is lower than would be expected. "The expected number would be half the total, i.e., 28."[3] But this is not true, whether the borrowing has been made from Mark, or from Matthew and Luke. There are many of Mark's dualisms where the two halves are not of equal significance, and it is inevitable on any hypothesis that the number of examples where Matthew and Luke agree should exceed that in which they differ. It is not only verse numbers, but the words of the text which have to be taken into account.

Secondly, of the 213 of Mark's dualisms, Matthew has one or both halves 152 times—124 times when Matthew and Mark are in the same sequence, twenty-eight times when they are not. There is no obvious reason for this discrepancy on the theory of Markan priority; it is accounted for if Mark

---

[1]C. M. Tuckett, *The Revival of the Griesbach Hypothesis* (Cambridge, 1983) 21.

[2]F. Neirynck, *Duality in Mark* (Leuven, 1972) 35.

[3]Tuckett, *The Revival of the Griesbach Hypothesis,* 21.

copied Matthew when following Matthew's sequence, and sometimes, though less frequently, recalled Matthew's phrases when not doing so. Luke has one or both halves of a Markan dualism 116 times: 114 times when Luke and Mark are in the same sequence, and only twice when they are not. The two exceptions (Mk 4:30, Lk 13:18; and Mk 10:42, Lk 22:25) are both questioned by Howard Marshall (himself holding the theory of Markan priority) as dependent on Mark, in his commentary on *The Gospel of Luke*.[4] Apart from these two doubtful instances, Luke has a part or the whole of these Markan dualisms only when Mark is in the same sequence with him. The figures as regards both Matthew and Luke, are a strong indication that Mark followed them in alternate sequence or when they were in the same sequence as each other.

Thirdly, we should consider separately the instances where a Markan dualism is represented in Matthew and Luke by one-half only, whether they use the same half or have different halves. Of Tuckett's list of 213, fifty-six are of this kind. Neirynck's groups 10-13 have a total of 271, of which fifty-two are of this kind. If we add the examples in Tuckett not taken from Neirynck, the total of 284 has seventy of this kind. Of these, twenty-seven are examples where, if Matthew and Luke used Mark, they chose different halves, forty-three where they chose the same. There is, however, a clear distinction between the two groups. When Matthew and Luke use the same half of a Markan dualism it is regularly true that the half they use is the inevitable or at least the obvious one to choose. Whenever it is a matter of indifference which half should be used (as in the famous example of Mk 1:32), Matthew and Luke consistently choose differently. So we come to a question similar to that which arises from the alternating sequence of Mark between Matthew and Luke. Just as we must ask, why should Matthew always stop following Mark's sequence at the point where Luke would take it up, or Luke do so whenever Matthew was to resume it. So in the case of Mark's dual phrases, if Matthew and Luke used Mark, how did it come about that whenever a free choice between two phrases was possible, they always chose differently? If Mark used Matthew and Luke, there is no problem: he sometimes used a phrase from Matthew or Luke and added to it, and when they used different phrases he often combined them together.

---

[4] I. Howard Marshall, *The Gospel of Luke* (Exeter, 1978) in loc.

Part Two
THE HISTORICAL TRADITION

Bernard Orchard

The State of the Question

1. The Rejection of the Tradition

The tradition about the origin of the Gospels is that those of Matthew and John are the work of the Apostles with these names, and that those of Mark and Luke were sponsored by Peter and Paul respectively. As far back as the records can be traced this has always been understood to mean that the first two are the accounts of eyewitnesses who were personally trained and appointed by Christ himself, and that the authority of Mark and Luke stems from the personal authority of Peter and Paul; all four are in fact described in the earliest documents as the ''ἀπομνημονεύματα of the Apostles,'' that is, their personal memories. The written evidence for these statements goes back to the third quarter of the second century to such highly respected and authoritative figures as the martyrs Justin and Irenaeus, and to the Anti-Marcionite Prologues and to the Muratorian Canon. This tradition was confirmed by Jerome and Augustine in the fourth century and remained virtually unchallenged until the eighteenth century.[1]

The Enlightenment not only witnessed the rise of critical history, among the successes of which was the detection of pseudepigraphy and forgery in Christian tradition as well as in other spheres of the pre-Enlightenment past; it also signalled the triumph in the eighteenth century and subsequent European culture of rationalist ideals and antipathies, and the consequent divorce of Reason both from the tradition of faith and from tradition in principle, that is, from all tradition. The result was an era of wholesale ''prejudice against prejudice,'' which, as H.-G. Gadamer put it, entailed the emasculation of tradition. While some aspects of the Enlightenment[2]

---

[1]The reliability of the Unwritten Tradition has been well stated and documented by R. O. P. Taylor, *The Groundwork of the Gospels* (Oxford, 1946). For a modern appraisal of the historicity of the Gospels, see Franz Mussner, ''The Historical Jesus and the Christ of Faith,'' in *Dogmatic v. Biblical Theology,* ed. H. Vorgrimler (London, 1964) 197-239 (English translation of *Exegese und Dogmatik* [Mainz, 1962]).

[2]For a summary of the origins of the Enlightenment, to which further reference is made in the next paragraph, see ''The Enlightenment'' in ODCC.

have imposed themselves as indispensable acquisitions, others—including the repudiation of tradition as such—have recently met incisive critique among such seminal thinkers as Gadamer, Voegelin, and Lonergan. The present study, situated in the immediate context of the recent reopening of the Synoptic question, reflects this larger, and equally recent, context of the rehabilitation, on philosophical and theological grounds, of tradition in general.

In the heyday of rationalism, however, historical critique, having raised searching questions about the hundred-year gap between the Apostles and Evangelists and the first clear literary attestations bearing on the origins of the Gospels, dismissed these attestations as guesswork. It was not only the time lag between the Gospels and the patristic testimonies, and not only the apparent discrepancies in the testimonies themselves, that determined this reaction. It was, above all, the temper of the critics, the climate of opinion, that made it almost inevitable. The attack on the credibility of the Gospels as historical documents was simply one facet of a more general assault on the Christian church as a whole, both Protestant and Catholic. The leaders and heirs of the Enlightenment set out with the deliberate intention of destroying the hold of the Christian religion on the educated classes ostensibly because of its association with the political and spiritual thraldom exercised by the governments of the *ancien régime.* One important line of attack was their attempt to prove that there was no direct connection between the Apostles and the Evangelists, who were said to belong to a later period when myth rather than fact reigned.[3] H. S. Reimarus and G. E. Lessing were leading members of the movement that by degrees undermined the confidence of many Christians in the historical character of the Gospels, and consequently their confidence in the churches that continued to affirm their historicity.[4]

On the one hand, there were professors, such as J. J. Griesbach of Jena, who accepted the authenticity of the Gospels but at the same time denied the value of the historical evidence.[5] And on the other hand, the "Tübingen School," and others, denied the value of the historical evidence as well as its authenticity. Thus as soon as there appeared to be no necessity

---

[3]Cf. W. R. Farmer, *The Synoptic Problem* (1964) 19.

[4]The task that H. S. Reimarus set himself was "completely to separate what the Apostles present in their writings [i.e. the Gospels] from what Jesus himself actually said and taught during his lifetime" (from a letter of Reimarus, quoted by W. G. Kümmel, *The New Testament: The History of the Investigations of Its Problems* [1973] 89); cf. also Ralph Martin, *Mark, Evangelist and Theologian* (1973) 32-36.

[5]Cf. *J. J. Griesbach: Synoptic & Text-critical Studies 1776-1976* (Cambridge, 1979) 134.

for dating the Gospels before A.D. 70, the way was open for the advance of the Markan priority hypothesis, although F. C. Baur himself still preferred Greisbach's hypothesis.[6] Under the influence of Heinrich Holtzmann,[7] and with the aid of the synopsis of A. Huck which sought to illustrate his views, the cause of Markan priority advanced rapidly, and had achieved predominance by World War I. By the time that B. H. Streeter came to publish his solution of the synoptic problem in his *The Four Gospels* (1924), the priority of Mark was effectively established in all the universities belonging to the Reformation tradition, and the historical evidence for the priority of Matthew had come to be regarded as too problematical to support the ancient tradition any longer.[8] After World War I the virtual unanimity in academic circles in favor of Markan priority was thought by Bultmann and his school to be a sufficient basis upon which to erect their form-critical theories, still using as their most important tool a revised version of Huck's synopsis, now conveniently divided into the sort of units they were envisaging.[9]

While these changes were taking place in the Protestant faculties of theology in England, Europe, and North America, Roman Catholic scholars for the most part seemed unable to defend the old tradition of Matthean priority, even though, after the Modernist Crisis (1900-1910), they were strictly forbidden to teach the new theories to their students.[10] Only J. H. Chapman and B. C. Butler made serious efforts to vindicate the official assertion of the Biblical Commission that the arguments in favor of the priority of Mark were not sufficient to overturn the ancient tradition.[11] In any case, Pope Pius XII's Encyclical Letter *Divino Afflante Spiritu* (1943) all at once gave Roman Catholic scholars freedom to take advantage of the new perspectives and ideas. They speedily did so, and it is to be noted that

---

[6]Cf. Farmer, *The Synoptic Problem*, 19.

[7]Cf. ibid., 24, 36ff.; cf. also H. J. Holtzmann, *Die synoptischen Evangelien* (1863).

[8]Cf. Farmer, *The Synoptic Problem*, 118ff.

[9]A Huck's *Synopse der drei ersten Evangelien* (1892) was originally composed to illustrate Holtzmann's synoptic theories. Its third edition (1906) was entirely recast but was still framed with the 2DH in mind. The 13th edition (1982), edited by H. Greeven, retains the same outlook. Another popular synopsis, that of K. Aland, *Synopsis Quattuor Evangeliorum* (1963), is based on that of Schmiedel and has a similar perspective.

[10]For the norms that Catholic professors were expected to observe, see "The Replies of the Biblical Commission," trans. E. F. Sutcliffe, in *A Catholic Commentary on Holy Scripture* (1953) §§ 47-53.

[11]Dom John Chapman, *Matthew, Mark, and Luke,* ed. Mgr. J. M. T. Barton (London, 1937); B. C. Butler, *The Originality of St. Matthew* (Cambridge, 1951).

this coming together of Protestant and Catholic scholarship in the third quarter of the twentieth century took place (so far as the New Testament is concerned) on the basis of an acceptance of the priority of Mark and usually of some form or other of the Two Source Theory; only the French biblical school tended to stand aloof from the new conseneus.[12]

The increasing integration of Catholic and Protestant scholarship at the highest academic level brought solid gains in a variety of ways, and particularly from the point of view of ecumenical cooperation and understanding.[13] Nevertheless these advances were made at the cost of jettisoning most of the ancient Christian tradition about the origins of the Gospels, a tradition that had been jointly shared with the Reformed churches down to the end of the nineteenth century.[14] And so the majority of professors in Catholic teaching institutions have now followed the lead of their brethren in the Reformed churches in rejecting the validity of this tradition in the light of the seemingly overwhelming weight of critical evidence for the priority of Mark. If, however, this evidence were now to be seen as no longer compelling, there would be occasion to consider whether the rejection of the tradition may not have been premature. And in fact during the past twenty years the hypothesis of Markan priority has been subjected to such a devastating scrutiny that it is no longer possible to use it as a sure base for exegesis. And if its basis is no longer certain, then it can no longer be used as an argument for the rejection of the historical evidence. It is, then, in the light of these considerations that we shall now attempt a new evaluation of this evidence; but before doing so, it is necessary to complete our survey by chronicling the revival of the alternative solution.

2. The Revival of the Tradition

The first recorded attempt to reverse the trend that led to the rejection of the Tradition came from Dom John Chapman and his disciple and friend, Dom Christopher Butler.[15] Their efforts to gain a fresh hearing for the Tra-

---

[12]See, e.g., X. Léon-Dufour, "Redaktionsgeschichte of Matthew and Literary Criticism," in *Jesus and Man's Hope* (Pittsburgh, 1970) 9-36.

[13]Examples are: the United Bible Societies' *Greek New Testament* ([1]1966, [3]1975); the French TOB (*Traduction oecumenique de la Bible*), and the German *Einheitsübersetzung der Heiligen Schrift: Das Neue Testament* (1979).

[14]For example, in *The Critical Meaning of the Bible* (1981) 38, Professor Raymond Brown writes as follows: "Nor is the appeal to tradition satisfactory, for in questions of authorship the church writers simply copied each other (or expanded what they received with legendary additions). Most of the time the 'tradition' about such an issue, however unanimous, has little more value than the credibility of the first attestation." But for quite a different estimate of the value of the Tradition, see A. N. Sherwin-White, *Roman Society and Roman Law in the New Testament* (Oxford, 1963) 186-93.

[15]See n. 11 above.

dition failed to make any lasting impression, although Chapman had made a powerful plea for the critical and historical evidence to be examined simultaneously, and Butler had succeeded in showing that "Q" was unnecessary. But the seed they had sown finally took root when a young Methodist professor gave it new energy and impetus by linking it up with the earlier researches of J. J. Griesbach and Henry Owen. For in 1964, as a result of reading the works of Chapman and Butler, Professor William R. Farmer, up till then a firm believer in the priority of Mark, risked his academic reputation by publishing his *The Synoptic Problem,* which, for the first time within the liberal Protestant establishment in North America, offered sound critical reasons for believing that the Two Document Hypothesis was really and truly without any solid foundation, and that the correct order of composition was Matthew first, then Luke, and then Mark.[16]

At the time of its publication, and indeed for some years after, Farmer's work was generally ignored where it was not ridiculed;[17] but now, looking back, it can be seen to be the beginning of a new era in Gospel studies. Since its appearance there have been no less than five important international conferences on the relationships between the Gospels, and it has now become clear to a distinguished body of reputable scholars that the existing solution must in all probability be relinquished and other possible solutions envisaged,[18] especially those that take greater account of the tradition. The peculiar strength of the claim of the Two Gospel Hypothesis for a sympathetic hearing lies in the harmony it asserts to exist between the historical and the critical data; and there are some hopeful signs that a bet-

---

[16]Other recent scholarly works arguing for this hypothesis include, H. H. Stoldt, *History and Criticism of the Markan Hypothesis* (Macon GA: Mercer University Press, 1982); *New Synoptic Studies,* ed. William R. Farmer (Macon GA: Mercer University Press, 1983) which contains the main papers of the 1979 Cambridge Griesbach Conference.

[17]See, for example, Professor Beare's caustic review in JBL 84 (1965): 295-97.

[18]These conferences have been: (a) the Pittsburgh Festival of the Gospels, 1970, which published *Jesus and Man's Hope,* 2 vols. (1970-1971); (b) the Münster Griesbach Colloquium, 1976, which published *J. J. Griesbach: Synoptic and Textcritical Studies, 1776-1976* (Cambridge, 1979); (c) the San Antonio Colloquy on the Gospels, 1977, which published *The Relationships among the Gospels* (San Antonio TX: Trinity University Press, 1978); (d) the Cambridge Griesbach Conference, 1979, the papers of which were published in *New Synoptic Studies: The Cambridge Gospel Conference and Beyond* (Macon GA: Mercer University Press, 1983); (e) the Jerusalem Symposium de Interrelatione Evangeliorum, 1984, which was in fulfillment of the unanimous recommendation made at the Cambridge Conference that an international conference should be convened to reopen the whole question of synoptic relationships.

ter appreciation of the maturity of ancient scholarship is now on the way.[19]

The reader is therefore being asked to approach the historical evidence on its own merits, prescinding from any a priori solution of the Synoptic Problem. For the sphere of historical inquiry is a sphere distinct from, and independent of, that of internal literary criticism, and one that has its own recognized principles and methods. Hence the conclusions of the one inquiry are not to be bent or retracted to suit the alleged results of the other; though of course if there is a clash, then there must be further search for agreement. And since all truth is one, the correct conclusion of the one line of inquiry ought to tally with the correct conclusions of the other; disagreement will be a sign that there is still error somewhere. In part one, Harold Riley has proceeded according to the canons of literary criticism; and in this part, I shall proceed according to the canons of historical criticism.

3. Survey of the Emergence of the Written Tradition

A survey of the historical evidence for the authenticity of the Gospels shows that it falls into three distinct phases or epochs:[20]

(a) The first phase is the appearance of the earliest literary evidence for the existence of the Gospels in documents written between the first Penetecost and approximately A.D. 150. In this period we find plenty of what appear to be quotations from the Gospels, though without any specific acknowledgment of their source. This phase will be discussed in chapter 2.

(b) The second phase is that of the conscious recognition and proclamation of the known facts about the four Gospels within the church, and this phase lasts from circa 150-250 and is especially associated with the reaction against the theories of Marcion, who may be taken as representative of those challenging Christian orthodoxy. During this period a number of Christian apologists from different localities within the Empire record what they understand the Tradition had always maintained about the Gospels. Much of their writing has disappeared, but enough

---

[19]Professor E. G. Turner, the great authority on early papyri, has written as follows: "We can now see that the higher criticism of the nineteenth century underrated the value of ancient learning, and therefore at times took a cavalier attitude to the statements of ancient scholars" (*Greek Papyri* [¹1968; this quotation is from the 1980 paperback edition] 99).

[20]The most recent survey of the historical evidence is that of Helmut Merkel, *Die Pluralität der Evangelien*, Traditio Christiana: Texte und Kommentare zur Patristiche Theologie, Band 3 (Bern, 1978). Merkel has printed all the texts in convenient form, but his comments and interpretations need to be received with caution since they are based not only on the premises that govern Markan priority, but also on the "methodical skepticism" that Professor Ben F. Meyer challenges in his *The Aims of Jesus* (London, 1979) 24ff.

has remained for us today to perceive their virtual unanimity. This phase will be discussed in chapter 3.

(c) The third and final phase is dominated by Eusebius of Caesarea, who made a conscious and determined effort to collect and collate in his *Ecclesiastical History* (ca. 305-325) everything of importance written about the Gospels by earlier writers. His presentation was subsequently confirmed in its essentials by Jerome, Augustine, and the later Fathers. This phase will be discussed in chapter 4.

These three phases or periods will be discussed in chronological order. Furthermore, steps will be taken to avoid the error into which so many previous discussions have fallen, namely, to rush impetuously into dealing with the quotations from Papias which are found only in Eusebius's *Ecclesiastical History*. These quotations and the rest of Eusebius's testimony (unless he is quoting from sources of which we already have independent knowledge) are not to be utilized until we reach our third phase. Furthermore, the crucial chapter concerned with Papias (EH III.39) is itself to be first examined according to the historical critical method, for reasons that will become obvious in due course. Hence each piece of written testimony to the authenticity of the Gospels will be discussed in chronological sequence according to the date of the document in which it first appears; and this means that we cannot discuss the testimony of Papias, and also certain passages from Irenaeus and Origen, until we come to Eusebius himself, since his mention of them for his own good reasons is the first certain knowledge we have of their existence. W. G. Kümmel has strongly asserted that the historical evidence for the authenticity of the Gospels is more or less worthless; but while this statement must certainly be rejected, there is no doubt he is right in stating that "it is methodologically improper in connection with the elucidation of the literary relations of the Synoptics to one another, and the origin of Matthew and Mark, to begin with the data of Papias, as is so often done today."[21] What is correct, however, and what will be done, is to take all the evidence in turn in its historical order, beginning with the Letters of Paul; so that by the time Eusebius's *Ecclesiastical History* is reached it will be possible to set his quotations from Papias in their true historical perspective.

---

[21]Cf. W. G. Kümmel, *Introduction to the New Testament* (English edition, 1965) 43.

2

The Matthean Tradition
Before A.D. 150

1. The Quotation of the Matthean Tradition in Paul

This is a vast subject about which nothing conclusive has yet been written, for everything depends on the date of the appearance of our Greek Matthew. Although Henry Owen,[1] an early pioneer of modern critical scholarship, dated all three Synoptic Gospels before A.D. 60, yet, since the general adoption of the hypothesis of Markan Priority and the rise of Form Criticism, the Gospel of Matthew has usually been put back to around A.D. 85; and this date would obviously make it impossible for Paul to have either known or used our Greek Matthew. However, owing to the current decline of confidence in this hypothesis[2] and the reemergence of the possibility of the priority of Matthew and the further possibility of a very early date for it,[3] it becomes reasonable again to take a look at the evidence for Paul's having had direct knowledge, and even the use, of our Greek Matthew. What is certain is that the quality of the references to our Matthew in several of Paul's Letters—for example, Galatians, 1 and 2 Thessalonians, and 1 Corinthians—surpasses the quality of the undoubted Matthean quotations in most of the early Fathers.[4]

Prescinding from attaching any specific dates to any of the Gospels, but being open to the possibility of early datings, the evidence will be outlined

---

[1]Henry Owen, *Observations on the Four Gospels* (London, 1764). Enoch Powell, once Professor of Greek, Sydney University, also believes that the order of dependence is Mt-Lk-Mk; see his essay, ''The Archaeology of Matthew,'' ch. 18 in *Wrestling with the Angel* (Sheldon Press, 1977) 122-23.

[2]See M. E. Boismard, ''The Two-Source Theory at an Impasse,'' NTS 26/1 (1979): 1-17.

[3]See John A. T. Robinson, *Redating the New Testament* (London, 1976) 352-53.

[4]See J. B. Orchard, ''Thessalonians and the Synoptic Gospels,'' *Biblica* 19 (1938): 19-42; also B. Rigaux's critique of Orchard in his *Épîtres aux Thessaloniciens* (Paris, 1956) 96-102.

here for Paul's use of the literary tradition as found in our Greek Matthew. The case of 1 and 2 Thessalonians offers the best and clearest example of Paul's adaptation of the eschatological teaching found chiefly in Matthew, and we recall that the Thessalonian letters were composed during Paul's second missionary journey within a few weeks of each other and that they cannot be dated later then A.D. 51-52.[5] The diagram given below indicates the range and quality of the possible Pauline indebtedness to the synoptic tradition in general.[6] Although the references to Luke and Mark are also given for the sake of completeness, nobody credits either of them with having been written before Thessalonians, so that the problem is simply one of deciding whether the teaching of our Greek Matthew could be a true source of Paul's teaching here.

1, 2 THESSALONIANS		MT	LK	MK
1, 2:14-16	ἀποκτεινάντων . . . τοὺς προφήτας, κτλ.	23:31-39	11:49-50; 13:34-35	----
4:16	σάλπιγγι θεοῦ	24:31	----	----
4:17	ἀπάντησιν	25:6	----	----
5:1	περὶ δὲ τῶν χρόνων, κτλ.	24:36	----	13:32
5:1, 3	περὶ δὲ . . . λέγωσιν . . . αὐτοῖς, κτλ.	24:36, 38	----	----
5:2	κλέπτης ἐν νυκτί, κτλ.	24:42, 43	12:39-40	----
5:3	αἰφνίδιος . . . ἐφίσταται, κτλ.	----	21:34-36	----
5:6, 7	γρηγορῶμεν . . . μεθύουσιν	24:42, 49	12:37, 45	[13:35]
2, 2:1, 7ff.	ὅταν . . . ἐνδοξασθῆναι	24:30; 25:31ff.	21:27	[13:26-32]
2:1	ἐπισυναγωγῆς	24:31	----	13:27
2:2	μηδὲ θροεῖσθαι	24:6	----	13:7
2:3	μή τις ὑμᾶς ἐξαπατήσῃ	24:4	[21:8]	13:5
2:7-10	τῆς ἀνομίας, κτλ.	24:12	----	----
2:8	ἐπιφανείᾳ τῆς παρουσίας	24:27	----	----
2:9-10	τέρασιν ψεύδους, κτλ.	24:24	----	13:22

N.B.: References in brackets indicate a weak or incomplete parallel. It sometimes happens that Mark or Luke is parallel to Matthew without being parallel to Paul, for example, Lk 17:24 = Mt 24:27, but while Mt 24:27 = 2 Thess 2:8 there is no direct parallel between Lk 17:24 and 2 Thess 2:8. In such cases the parallel is not given here since we are only concerned with direct parallels between Thessalonians and each gospel.

---

[5]See Rigaux, ibid.; cf. also P. N. Tarazi, *I Thessalonians* (New York, 1982).

[6]This diagram is taken from my article cited in n. 4 above.

As regards Matthew we must always remember that no matter whether it was put together before 45 or after 85 it remains an amalgam of material put together by an editor of consummate skill. Hence, when one finds concentrated in the eschatological teaching of these two letters the same material, directly or by allusion, as is found similarly concentrated in Matthew 23-25, there is already some ground for thinking that there is some direct borrowing; whereas in Luke there is no ground for thinking in this way, since the references to the same material are scattered widely in chapters 11, 12, 13, and 21. On the contrary, in Matthew 23-25 and in the eschatological sections of both letters, we find the same teaching, the same metaphors and similes and the same key words, some exceedingly rare, like παρουσία, ἀπάντησις, ἐπισυναγωγή, together with an equally striking combination of common words, such as κλέπτης, σάλπιγξ, ἀνομία, τέλος, θροεῖσθαι, γρηγορέω, μεθύω, and so on. For Paul is seen to utilize the same key words and the same illustrations that Matthew uniquely uses with regard to the suddenness of the coming of the Lord: like a thief in the night, like the sudden birth pangs (cf. Mt 24:19), like the sudden arrival (ἀπάντησις) of the bridegroom, like the sudden coming of the flood while life was going on normally (cf. Mt 24:36-38), a coming (παρουσία) in power and glory with his angels and with the sound of a great trumpet.

Other powerful supporting reminiscences of Matthew are found in Galatians 1:12, 16; 1 Corinthians 7:1ff.; 9:14.[7] The inference that Paul both knew and used our Greek Matthew will find further support from the work of E. Massaux in our next section, which will show that the Gospel of Matthew was in fact the basis of the common Christianity of the primitive church from the very beginning. Of course it is certain that Paul made full use of Old Testament eschatological imagery, but some extra details that he himself adds are found together only in Matthew, and argue strongly for his firsthand knowledge of it.

2. The Gospels in Christian Writings Before Justin

In all his monumental work on the use made of the canonical Gospels in all the surviving Christian writings before Irenaeus, E. Massaux methodically and exhaustively sets out the evidence for all to see. Unfortu-

---

[7] See J. H. Chapman, "St Paul and the Revelation to St Peter," *Rev. Ben.* 29 (1912), for a discussion of Gal 1:12, 16; see also D. L. Dungan, *The Sayings of Jesus in the Churches of Paul* (Philadelphia: Fortress Press, 1971) pts. 1 and 2, for a discussion of 1 Cor 7:1ff. and 9:14.

nately, his work is too little known and has not yet been translated.[8] Massaux's conclusion may be summarized as follows:

a. As regards Clement of Rome's First letter (ca. 96) he concludes: (1) "the literary influence of the Gospel of St. Matthew predominates everywhere" (p. 35); (2) "the literary influence of the Second Gospel (Mark) can be considered as nonexistent" (p. 35); (3) "no text of Luke would have appeared to have exercized any clear literary influence on it, though there are a few reminiscences of it"; (4) "there is no real sign of the influence of John"; (5) "but the influence of Paul's writings is certain."

b. As regards the Letters of Ignatius of Antioch (ca. 107), he concludes (1) that "Ignatius certainly knew the Sermon on the Mount (cf. *Ad Smyrn.* 1) and that he was under the general influence throughout of Matthew" (pp. 94-98); (2) "the literary influence of Mark on them is nil" (p. 107); (3) "Luke may have exercized some literary influence" (p. 108); (4) there does not seem to be any direct literary dependence of John, "but it would seem that Ignatius lived and wrote in a milieu impregnated with Johannine ideas, perhaps issuing from John's own preaching, that he [Ignatius] is indebted to them and gives them an original touch, resulting probably from his own personal experience of the Christian life" (p. 112).

c. As regards the *Epistle of Barnabas* (date uncertain, perhaps ca. 150, perhaps 70-100, by an unknown hand), Massaux concludes as follows: (1) "the literary contact is with Matthew rather than with Mark, to whom there does not appear to be any reference" (p. 76); (2) "on the other hand, it is possible to conclude that Matthew was known to Barnabas and exercised a certain influence on the composition of the Epistle" (p. 82).

d. As regards the considerable apocalyptic literature, Massaux concludes as follows: (1) "for the apocalyptic Christian literature, the Gospel of Matthew seems to be the gospel *par excellence;* (2) "it is in the Gospel of Matthew that one finds at this epoch the essence of the Christian message . . . the further one advances into the second century, the more one notices the words of Christ according to Matthew that serve as source of inspiration, and the more one notices that the utilization, for example, of the Parables of Matthew [to construct a development] supposes a very great familiarity with the whole Gospel of Matthew, the rule of the Christian life" (p. 326).

---

[8]E. Massaux, *Influence de l'évangile de saint Matthieu sur la littérature chrétienne avant S. Irénée* (Louvain, 1950). [All the quotations from Massaux in this chapter are my own translations from the French. —J.B.O.]

e. As regards the heretical literature of the period, Massaux points out that "Basilides, Valentinus, and Heracleon also show the influence of Matthew only" (p. 420).

f. As regards Justin Martyr's use of the Gospels, Massaux comments: (1) "the considerable liberty that Justin exercises with regard to our four gospels is an indication that while he knew them perfectly, at the time he wrote there was less concern and preoccupation with the text itself than with the doctrine that it proclaimed" (p. 504); (2) "it has also been established that the apologist uses quotations from the Old Testament according to the form that Matthew gives them, compare *I Apol.* 33.5; 34.1; 35.11; compare also *Dial. Tryph.* 78.1b, where he cites Matthew's version against the LXX"; (3) Massaux also decisively supports the view that Justin knew the Gospel of Mark as "the reminiscences of Peter," compare *Dial Tryph.* 106.3 (pp. 555-56).

g. As regards the *Didache,* Massaux argues that it was composed after A.D. 150, that it certainly used Matthew, and that the *Epistle of Barnabas* was also one of its sources (pp. 605, 620, 641). Others, however, for example, Rordorf-Tuilier, in *Sources Chrétiennes,* argue for a first century date.

Massaux's findings about the use of the Gospels in the first and second centuries are summed up in his general conclusions (pp. 647-54), among which the following may be noted:

(1) The literary influence of Mark on our New Testament writings is nil, while that of Luke, though certain, is very much subsidiary to that of Matthew.

(2) The words of Jesus in Matthew are taken as the norm of the Christian life and it is upon the teachings of Christ drawn out of the Gospel of Matthew that the Common Christianity was established.

(3) Matthew alone showed to the first Christian converts from Judaism what their stance towards the Old Law should be and how to respond, as Jesus did, to the constant enmity of the Jews.

Thus we may again conclude that these findings are compatible with the priority of Mark only with great difficulty; whereas, they are quite naturally compatible with the priority of Matthew.

3

The Anti-Marcionite Reaction
(circa 150-250)

The Second-Century Witnesses to Gospel Authorship

For more than 1,700 years scholars as well as ordinary Christians accepted the tradition that the Gospels were written for the benefit of the Christian church by the persons to whom they are ascribed. But from the middle of the eighteenth century onwards more and more scholars have been asking whether the Gospels were truly composed by Matthew, Mark, Luke, and John in the form in which we now have them. And one of the principal arguments has been the acknowledged lack of mention of the names of any of the four evangelists prior to A.D. 150, though there are a considerable number of recognizable quotations from them in church documents prior to that date. It is claimed that this 100-year gap is too great for us now to be sure that the tradition was handed down correctly. Whether or not this be true, for anyone who wants today to defend the trustworthiness of the existing historical witness, it is essential to offer not only a satisfactory explanation of the long silence but also to prove that the few extant documentary references of the latter half of the second century are in fact reliable historical data.[1]

Our first task will be to examine the witness of Justin Martyr (ca. 100-165), deliberately passing over the witness of Papias, bishop of Hierapolis, who lived circa 60-139, because the latter's most important state-

---

[1]The modern questioning of the apostolic authorship of the Gospels is based on three factors: (1) the inability to find a satisfactory explanation for the lack of direct documentary proof of apostolic authorship before Irenaeus, since most of the apologetical writings that appeared in defence of Christianity about the beginning of the second century have been lost; and what we have left is a tiny random selection (cf. EH III.37); (2) the skepticism of the leaders of the Enlightenment with regard to the value of the Tradition; (3) the avowed aim of the leaders of the Enlightenment (from Reimarus onwards) to establish an unbridgeable gulf between the Apostles and the Gospels in order to discredit the latter. My main guide for the history of this epoch has been Karl Baus, "From the Apostolic Community in Constantine," *History of the Church*, vol. 1., ed. H. Jedin (English edition: London, 1980).

ments come to us only through Eusebius of Caesarea (ca. 260-339), who quotes him not only selectively but probably also tendentiously. Papias's evidence can only be properly evaluated in the light of all that Eusebius has to say about the Gospels in general; and this will require a special chapter (ch. 4) all to itself on account of the peculiar way in which he handled the evidence, some of which indeed is no longer available to us and can only be inferred by careful research. This present chapter therefore will deal only with the evidence that comes to us from documents and writers belonging to the period 150-250, when the Tradition for the first time becomes explicit in its references to the provenance and authorship of the Gospels.

2. Justin (ca. 100-165)

Justin, the son of pagan parents, was born about the year 100 at Flavia Neapolis in Palestine and suffered martyrdom in Rome about 165, which is why he is usually known as Justin *Martyr*. After having studied all contemporary philosophical systems, including the Stoic and Pythagorean, he became a Christian probably about the year 130 at Ephesus, the city where St. John the Apostle had ended his long life only some thirty years before. It is also worth noting that his stay in Ephesus overlapped by some years the last years of the famous Bishop Papias of Hierapolis, a city not far away. About 138 he migrated to Rome and set up as a Christian philosopher and teacher and remained there until his death in 165. Justin must have become a public figure of some importance in the capital because he took it upon himself to address his *First* and *Second Apology* for the Christian community in Rome to the reigning emperor Antoninus Pius and the Roman Senate between 148 and 161. He also refers several times to the official *Acts of Pilate,* now lost, and relates that Christ was born 150 years before under Quirinius (*I Apol.* 35.48, 46). His Dialogue with Trypho is the oldest extant Christian apology against the Jews and was composed between 161 and 165, though his original debate with Trypho seems to have taken place at Ephesus as far back as 135. Because these documents were public defenses of Christianity against persecution by both the Roman State and the Jews, his assertions deserve *prima facie* to be accepted as true in all important particulars, since it is likely that any errors or misstatements would have been instantly and mercilessly exposed by his opponents, who included Marcion, then also living in Rome (cf. *First Apology,* 26.28). Justin was in fact well placed both to know and to pass on the Christian tradition of both East and West. In *I Apol.* 33 he quotes passages from the birth narratives of Matthew and Luke without actually mentioning them by name but simply referring to them as "the teachers who have recorded all that concerns our Saviour Jesus Christ"; and in chapter 66 he again refers to ''the memoirs (ἀπομνημονεύματα) composed by the apostles which are called Gospels.'' Justin is also familiar with the life and teaching of Simon Magus to whom he refers as being ''one of my own nation'' (*Second Ap.* 15).

Justin reveals a thorough mastery of the Septuagint version of the Old Testament in his *Dialogue with Trypho* and a similar mastery of the four Gospels in chapters 98-106 of the same work, quoting several times from all four Gospels in the course of his exegesis of Psalm 21 (22) as a prophecy of the Passion of Christ. In this later section he frequently uses the phrase ''the memoirs of his apostles and of those who followed them'' as the source of his quotations. And in chapter 106.8-11, there can be no doubt that there is an explicit reference to the ''Memoirs of Peter'' in a clear quotation from Mark 3:17. This passage deserves to be quoted in full (*Dial. Tryph.* 106.9-10):

καὶ τὸ εἰπεῖν μετωνομακέναι αὐτὸν Πέτρον ἕνα τῶν ἀποστόλων, καὶ γεγράφθαι ἐν τοῖς ἀπομνημονεύμασιν αὐτοῦ γεγενημένον καὶ τοῦτο μετὰ τοῦ καὶ ἄλλους δύο ἀδελφούς, υἱοὺς Ζεβεδαίου ὄντας, ἐπωνομακέναι ὀνόματι τοῦ Βοανεργές, ὅ ἐστιν υἱοὶ βροντῆς, σημαντικὸν ἦν τοῦ αὐτὸν ἐκεῖνον εἶναι. . . .	And when it is said that he [Jesus] changed the name of one of the apostles to Peter, and when it is written in his memoirs that this happened, as well as that he surnamed other two brothers, who were the sons of Zebedee, with the name of Boanerges, which means Sons of Thunder, this was a signification of. . . .

In this passage the phrase ''in his memoirs'' can only mean ''the memoirs of Peter,'' the apostle himself, from which Justin quotes part of Mark 3:17; for we can be sure that Jesus himself wrote no Memoirs.

It is unfortunate that the Ante-Nicene Fathers' Series translation (Eerdmans reprint, 1977) has rendered the phrase as ''the memoirs of Him,'' implying ''of Jesus''; but this rendering, though grammatically possible, is quite contrary to the sense of the passage and to Justin's own usage.[2] We

---

[2]This mistranslation is due to the influence of I. C. T. Otto's comment on this text in the edition from which our quotation is taken. But E. Massaux confirms the correctness of our present rendering, *Influence,* 555-56. There are some twelve direct references to the four Gospels in chs. 98-107 of the *Dial Tryph.* where Justin is giving an exegesis of Ps. 21 (22) viewed as a prophecy of Christ's passion and death. They are as follows: 100.11; 101.9; 103.16,19; 104.4; 105.4,12,13; 106.7,8-11,16; 107.1. Also in *Dial. Tryph.* 81.4 he specifically attributes the Apocalypse to St. John the Apostle. Cf. also A. J. Bellinzoni, *The Sayings of Jesus in the Writings of Justin Martyr* (Leiden: Brill, 1967); cf. also *Apol.* 66.3. The principal edition of Justin's writings is that of I. C. T. Otto, *S. Iustini Opera,* 2nd ed. (Jena, 1847).

conclude therefore that Justin accepted the tradition that regarded the Gospel of Mark as the Memoirs of Peter.

Justin was also a younger contemporary of Bishop Polycarp of Smyrna (ca. 70-155), who, like Papias, had close connections with St. John the Apostle, as will be recorded in section 4 below in connection with the witness of Irenaeus. There is then every reason to believe that these members of the subapostolic generation shared a firm tradition that the Gospels were "the memoirs of the apostles." For when Justin became a Christian at Ephesus about 130, at a time before Marcion had become a threat to the Church, he found in unquestioned possession the belief that the official records of what Jesus had said and done were properly designated "the memoirs of the apostles." And this helps us to understand why in the earliest days the Gospels were not actively differentiated; for since there was no serious challenge to their authenticity there was no necessity to refer to them explicitly as the work of Matthew, or Mark, or Luke, or John.[3] In any case the evangelists wrote anonymously and the important thing for the primitive church was that all four Gospels were deemed to be authentic memoirs, that is, the recorded memories of the disciples who had lived with and had been formed by Jesus in person.

We may infer from the fact that Justin refers to "his [Peter's] memoirs" that he must have known the names of the other Evangelists as well—such knowledge was part of the tradition that he had inherited—but the lack of any interest in distinguishing the individual authors from one another is merely a sign that the most important thing for churchmen was still the authentic oral tradition about Jesus, either received from men who had known one of the Apostles or who had known men who had known them. The swing-over during the second half of the second century to the individual naming of the Gospels as specifically the work of the Evangelists is to be seen as the public spelling out of the content of the ancient tradition in response to the attack of Marcion; that is to say, the public affirmation that they really were the memoirs of the Apostles themselves and their immediate disciples, namely Matthew, John, Luke, and Mark (this is in fact the order in which the Old Latin versions place the Gospels). In other words, when churchmen had to respond to Marcion, they had to explain exactly what they meant by the phrase "the memoirs of the apostles" and as we shall see they did so clearly and consistently. Finally, Marcion himself by

---

[3]If there had been any such challenge to disturb the tradition between John and Marcion, the repercussions could hardly have failed to reveal themselves either directly or indirectly in the literature of the period, as indeed actually happened when Marcion arose to challenge it. Although none of Marcion's writings survive intact, some of the many tracts against him have survived, and we know the titles of many more (cf. ODCC, "Marcion").

rejecting the fourfold gospel tradition declares himself by this very act a witness of their antiquity (cf. n. 4 below).

3. Marcion (ca. 80-ca. 160)

The chief cause of this new precision was Marcion. Marcion was the son of the bishop of Sinope on the Black Sea and was apparently excommunicated by his father early in his career. It is said that after making (or inheriting) a great fortune as a shipowner he retired from business in order to devote himself to propagating his own brand of Christianity, linked to Gnosticism. For him the Twelve Apostles were completely misinformed about God and Christ and their writings were useless and pernicious. Thus he rejected all four Gospels, simply retaining his own shortened version of Luke, together with ten only of Paul's Epistles. His religion was a peculiar amalgam of Christianity, Gnosticism, and paganism that seemed to suit the mood of many in the forties of the second century.

Unlike other contemporary heretics Marcion was a born organizer as well as a magnetic personality, and the church he set up became a real threat to the universal church. For he created his own hierarchy and rites and centered it on Rome with local churches scattered throughout the Roman Empire. In order to meet his challenge church leaders had to react vigorously, and did so.[4] Every orthodox writer from 150 onwards wrote against him; Justin's treatise against him has in fact perished, but fortunately that of Irenaeus has survived in his work *Against the Heresies*. Thus, it was the irruption of Marcion into Rome about 140 that so rudely disturbed the tranquillity of the church's tradition about the Gospels. The period of the global reference to the Gospels as the "Memoirs of the Apostles" was over, and the church entered upon the age when she set about recalling and specifying the traditions that she had received about them.

---

[4]H. von Campenhausen (*The Formation of the Christian Bible* [English edition: London, 1972]) has well described the shock that the church received as the result of Marcion's attack. But while his book has been rightly acclaimed as a comprehensive and penetrating study, one of his main theses (p. 201)—that our fourfold Gospel canon was first defined by Irenaeus in his *Adv. Haer.* III.1.1—now needs to be radically revealed in the light of the recent discovery by Folker Siegert (see pt. 2, ch. 4, n. 5) that Papias wrote commentaries on both Luke and John. For this means that these two Gospels along with Mt and Mk were being treated as Sacred Scripture as early as the first quarter of the second century by one who knew Disciples of the Lord himself.

4. Irenaeus (ca. 115-ca. 180)

Next in order of time is the witness of Irenaeus, bishop of Lyons, who was born at or near Smyrna before A.D. 120[5] and was martyred some time before the year 200. He was soon universally recognized by the ancient Fathers as the true champion of orthodoxy and as a reliable fount of Christian knowledge and wisdom, since he had personally known Saint Polycarp, the martyr bishop of Smyrna, who in turn had known St. John the Apostle, and he also knew well the Roman traditions. We can be sure of this because Eusebius has preserved a long quotation in the original Greek (EH V.20.4-8) from a letter of Irenaeus written about 177 to Florinus, a Roman presbyter, from which we learn not only that Irenaeus personally frequented Polycarp's house in Smyrna when still a young man, but that he had heard Polycarp telling how he had listened to St. John relating his own memories of what he had heard the Lord say. Irenaeus makes his own affirmation about the Gospels casually in the course of his work against the Gnostics, entitled *Detection and Overthrow of the Pretended but False Knowledge,* which was translated into Latin probably before 200 under the title *Adversus Haereses.* The original Greek text survives only in a large number of disconnected extracts by later writers.[6] However, the Latin translation, which is both faithful and literal, has survived intact; and since it is so much older than Eusebius's quotations, we may use it here and now for our argument. The passage in question occurs in *Adv. Haer.* III.1.1,[7] and runs as follows:

Ita Mattheus in Hebraeis ipsorum lingua scripturam edidit Evangelii, cum Petrus et Paulus Romae evangelizarent et fundarent Ecclesiam.	So Matthew brought out a written Gospel among the Jews in their own tongue, when Peter and Paul were preaching the Gospel at Rome and founding the Church.
Post vero horum excessum Marcus discipulus et interpres Petri et ipse quae a Petro adnuntiata erant per scripta nobis tradidit.	But after their demise, Mark himself the disciple and recorder of Peter, has also handed on to us in writing what had been proclaimed by Peter.

---

[5]Irenaeus speaks of John seeing "the Revelation almost in our own day" (see n. 21 below). Since the vision took place, according to him, in Domitian's reign and Domitian died in 96, Irenaeus must be putting his own life span as beginning well before A.D. 130; he was born probably nearer to 110 than 120. Lawlor & Oulton opt for ca. 115, see vol. 2, p. 188.

[6]See *Eusebius, Ecclesiastical History,* ed. Lawlor and Oulton, vol. 2 (1928) 182-83; also J. Quasten, *Patrology* (Utrecht-Antwerp, [4]1966) 1:291.

[7]See W. W. Harvey, *Sancti Irenaei ep. Lugdunensis libros quinque adversus haereses,* 2 vols. (Cambridge, 1857); cf. also *Adversus Haereses,* ed. Rousseaux, Sources chrétiennes (Paris, 1969) in loc.

Et Lucas autem sectator Pauli quod ab illo praedicabatur Evangelium in libro condidit. Postea et Iohannes discipulus Domini, qui et supra pectus eius recumbebat et ipse edidit Evangelium Ephesi Asiae commorans.	While Luke too, the follower of Paul, put down in a book the Gospel which was being preached by him. Later on too, John, the disciple of the Lord, who had even reclined on his bosom, he too brought out a Gospel while he was dwelling in Ephesus of Asia.

The following comments need to be made:

a. Irenaeus, who was of course himself Greek speaking, has rendered Papias's ἑβραΐδι διαλέκτῳ (Eusebius, EH III.39) as meaning "in the tongue [in the language] of the Jews," mistakenly thinking that Papias was referring to the language in which Matthew was written, whereas Kürzinger[8] has now convincingly shown that Papias really meant "in the Jewish style," that is, that Matthew wrote in the Jewish style and not in the Greek style. This error was to be perpetuated by Origen and all later writers. (For fuller discussion, see ch. 4, 7c.)

b. *Post horum excessum,* "after their demise," certainly means after their martyrdom.

c. *Nobis tradidit.* The Latin *tradidit* fails to render adequately the force of the Greek perfect παραδέδωκεν, that is, "has handed on," which is preserved in EH V.8.2. The true meaning of this much-discussed sentence is that the Gospel that Peter and Paul proclaimed while they were alive continued to be proclaimed after their deaths in the respective Gospels of Mark and Luke.[9]

d. *Interpres Petri,* "the recorder of Peter." This phrase belongs to the oldest stratum of second-century tradition, and is properly understood as Mark "recording" (not "explaining") what Peter had said; it renders the Greek ἑρμηνευτής. (See also ch. 4, 7c.)

e. It is enough to point out here that Irenaeus believed that he was giving the true tradition when he wrote that Matthew was the first Gospel to be written and composed during the lifetime of Peter and Paul; that Mark

---

[8]J. Kürzinger, "Das Papiaszeugnis und die Erstgestalt des Matthäusevangeliums," *Bibl. Zeitschr.,* NF (1960): 19-38. He shows that in that era διάλεκτος was commonly used also for "literary style." However, Kürzinger thinks that Origen was the first to misunderstand Papias; cf. his *Papias von Hierapolis und die Evangelien des N.T.* (Regensburg, 1983) 35-40. See also ch. 4, n.13.

[9]See J. Chapman, "St. Irenaeus and the Dates of the Gospels," *JTS* 6 (1904-1905): 563-69; also G. G. Gamba, "La Testimonianza di St Ireneo in *Adv. Haer.* III.1.1, e la Data di Composizione dei Quattro Vangeli Canonici," *Salesianum* 39 (1977): 545-85.

and Luke contain the traditions authorized by Peter and Paul respectively; that Mark is the *interpres* of Peter and published his Gospel after Peter's death; and that John was the last to appear. This is the sum total of what Irenaeus affirms; it is simple and clear and is entirely consistent with what we have already learned from Justin. Irenaeus mentions these facts just to confirm that the Gospels have truly transmitted to him the apostolic teaching about Christ. Irenaeus, as we shall see (n. 21 below) can get confused over his dating, but there is no reason to think that he errs over his attributions.

5. Clement of Alexandria (ca. 150-215)

Our next witness is Clement of Alexandria, a pupil of Pantaenus, the first great Christian teacher in that city. Alexandria had long possessed a famous pagan university, and, a hundred years before Clement lived, the presence of Philo, the Jewish thinker and exegete (ca. 20 B.C.–A.D. 50), had made it into the chief center of Jewish studies. Philo's thought was to exercise a great influence over Clement, who was destined in his turn to make Alexandria the greatest center of Christian higher learning in the world. Clement's aim was to win over the educated classes of the Empire to Christianity by showing how all the best in ancient pagan culture could be subsumed and elevated through the adoption of Christianity. His influence was immense and was prolonged in his famous pupil Origen, who succeeded him. "Clement is the pioneer of Christian scholarship. . . . We owe it above all to him if scholarly thinking and research are recognized in the Church. He proved that the Faith and philosophy, the Gospel and secular learning, are not enemies, but belong together. . . . His theological work is epoch making and it is no exaggeration to praise him as the founder of speculative theology." These conclusions are the measured words of J. Quasten.[10]

The authority of Clement as a witness to the traditions of the Apostolic Age is recognized a century later by Eusebius when he quotes a passage from Clement's *Stromateis* (*Miscellanies*) where, after indicating the more eminent men of the apostolic succession to which he had reached back, Clement continues in the following terms:

> Now this work is not a writing artfully composed for display, but memoirs which I have stored up against old age, a remedy for forgetfulness, an artless image and outline sketch of those clear and living words which I was privileged to hear, and of those blessed and truly remarkable men. Of these, the Ionian was in Greece, others in Magna Graecia (the one of them came from

---

[10]Cf. J. Quasten, *Patrology* (1953 ed.) 2:6-7, 20.

Coelo-Syria, the other from Egypt); there were others in the East, and in this quarter, the one was from the country of the Assyrians, the other a Hebrew by origin, in Palestine. But when I fell in with the last (who in ability proved to be the first), having run down my quarry as it lay concealed in Egypt—I took my rest. . . . Now these men, preserving the true tradition of the blessed teaching straight from the holy apostles Peter and James, John and Paul, as son inheriting from father (howbeit few sons are like their fathers!), came under God even to our time, to deposit those seeds of their ancestors the apostles.[11]

Clement's credentials are impeccable and Eusebius devotes two chapters of his sixth book to his achievements (EH VI.13-14). However in the present context our plan requires us to make use only of contemporary evidence in its chronological order, and there is in fact still extant a small fragment of an Old Latin translation of Clement's *Adumbrationes in epistolas canonicas*, quite possibly made at the beginning of the third century, a whole century before Eusebius, which throws light on the origins of the Gospel of Mark. Clement is commenting on 1 Peter 5:13 ("She who is at Babylon, who is likewise chosen, sends you greetings and so does my son Mark"). It runs as follows:[12]

Marcus, Petri sectator, praedicante Petro evangelium palam Romae coram quibusdam Caesareanis equitibus et multa Christi testimonia proferente, petitus ab eis, ut possent quae dicebantur memoriae commendare, scripsit ex his quae a Petro dicta sunt evangelium quod secundum Marcum vocitatur; sicut Lucas quoque Actus Apostolorum stilo exsecutus agnoscitur et Pauli ad Hebraeos interpretatus epistolam.	Mark, the follower of Peter, while Peter was publicly preaching the Gospel at Rome in the presence of some of Caesar's knights and uttering many testimonies of Christ, on their asking him to let them have a written record of the things which had been said, wrote the Gospel which is called the Gospel of Mark, from the things said by Peter; just as Luke is recognized as the pen that wrote the Acts of the Apostles and as the translator of the Letter of Paul to the Hebrews.

This account of the origin of the Gospel of Mark is consistent with what we have already learned from Justin and Irenaeus, but goes a good deal further, seeing that it provides the explanation of Irenaeus's phrase "Mark

---

[11]EH V.11; the translation is that of H. J. Lawlor and J. E. L. Oulton, *Eusebius Bishop of Caesarea, The Ecclesiastical History and the Martyrs of Palestine*, vol. 1 (London, 1927) 156.

[12]Cf. Migne, PG 9:730-31; also *Clem. Alex.*, GCS 17:206.

himself, the disciple and recorder of Peter.'' Clement fills in the detail showing how Mark's Gospel was at one and the same time ''the memoirs of Peter'' and also the work of Mark; for Mark is here to be seen as the pen that put the witness of Peter onto paper, just as Luke is recognized as the pen that wrote the Acts of the Apostles, and (according to Clement) as translator of Paul in regard to the Letter to the Hebrews.

Palam Romae coram quibusdam Caesareanis equitibus et multa Christi testimonia proferente. With these words Clement provides us with extra detail that helps to explain the background against which the Gospel of Mark came into existence. For in this text Clement tells us (1) that Peter was preaching the Gospel *palam,* that is speaking it in public and on official occasions; (2) that he was giving ''many testimonies of Christ,'' that is, he was relating his own eyewitness account of Christ's words and deeds; (3) that his audience included a certain number of officers of the knights of Caesar (''in the presence of Caesar's knights'').

Who were these ''knights of Caesar''? Did they belong to the Praetorium? The Epistle of Paul to the Philippians may provide us with a clue. In Philippians 1:13 we read ὥστε τοὺς δεσμούς μου φανεροὺς ἐν Χριστῷ γενέσθαι ἐν ὅλῳ τῷ πραιτορίῳ καὶ τοῖς λοιποῖς πᾶσιν, ''so that it has become known throughout the whole praetorium and to all the rest that my imprisonment is for Christ'' (RSV). And in Philippians 3:22 we read ἀσπάζονται ὑμᾶς πάντες οἱ ἅγιοι, μάλιστα δὲ οἱ ἐκ τῆῳ Καίσαρος οἰκίας, ''All the saints greet you, especially those of Caesar's household'' (RSV).

The Praetorium was the center of the administration of the Roman Empire, and a training organization for its high command. Its career structure was as follows. The Praetorian cohorts were each some 500 strong and were specially selected from the regular army. After five year's service as a *miles* a member could pass into the *equites,* the *militia equestris,* from which after ten years' service, he could become a centurion. (Cf. *Paulus Real-encyclopädie der classischen altertums-wissenschaft,* XXII/2 (1954) col. 1607, ''Praetoriae cohortes.'') Thus the reference of Clement Alexandria is to those serving in the middle ranks of the Praetorium, the *equites.*

The reference in Philippians 4:22 is to nonmilitary personnel in the employ of Caesar, both freedmen and slaves. The Letter to the Philippians is probably the first of the series of letters written by Paul during his imprisonment in Rome,[13] that is, between 60/1–62/3, and it reveals the fact that

---

[13]See, e.g., J. A. Fitzmyer, JBC, in loc.; Ralph P. Martin, *Philippians* (Tyndale, 1983) agrees; and it seems improbable that it was written from a prison in Ephesus. But for another view, see J. Gnilka, *Der Philipperbrief* (Freiburg: Herder, ³1980).

already by this early date Christianity was well established in the very heart of the imperial administration, both military and civil. Thus Clement Alexandria's reference must mean that a number of these influential persons came to listen to Peter.

For a full discussion of Eusebius's important quotation from Clement regarding the order of the Gospels, and known to us only through Eusebius (EH VI.14), see ch. 4, §4 below.

6. Tertullian (ca. 155-220)

Tertullian is a prime witness to the faith of the African church regarding the authenticity of the Gospels despite his later Montanist connection. Being an exact contemporary of Clement of Alexandria, he witnesses to the tradition of all Western Christianity and especially to the tradition of Rome, where he practiced for a time as an advocate. For our present purposes the best account of his writings is to be found in Quasten's *Patrology* (II/4: 246-340). From this source we learn that his *Treatise against Marcion* was composed A.D. 207-212, and that his *De Praescriptione haereticorum* was written about the year 200. Both writings belong to his pre-Montanist period. The following excerpts from his *Adversus Marcionem* show his full support for the main tradition, namely, that Matthew and John are by the apostles with those names, that Mark's Gospel is Peter's, and that Paul was the sponsor of Luke.

Adv. Marcionem IV.2.1-5 (ed. Kroymann, CC 1)

1. . . . Transeo nunc ad evangelii, sane non Iudaici sed Pontici, interim adulterati, demonstrationem, praestructuram, ordinem, quem adgredimur. Constituimus inprimis evangelicum instrumentum apostolos auctores habere, quibus hoc munus evangelii promulgandi ab ipso Domino sit impositum. Si et apostolicos, non tamen solos, sed cum apostolis, quoniam praedicatio discipulorum suspecta fieri posset de gloriae studio, si non adsistat illi auctoritas magistrorum, immo Christi, quae magistros apostolos fecit.

1. . . . I pass on next to show how this [that is, Marcion's] gospel—certainly not Judaic but Pontic—is in places adulterated; and this shall form the basis of my order of approach. I lay it down to begin with that the documents of the gospel have the Apostles for their authors, and that this task of promulgating the gospel was imposed upon them by the Lord himself. If they have also for their authors apostolic men, yet these stand not alone but as companions of apostles, because the preaching of disciples might be made suspect of the desire of vainglory, unless there stood by it the authority of their teachers, or rather the authority of Christ, which made the Apostles teachers.

2. Denique nobis fidem ex apostolis Iohannes et Mattheus insinuant, ex apostolicis Lucas et Marcus instaurant, iisdem regulis exorsi, quantum ad unicum Deum attinet creatorem et Christum eius, natum ex virgine, subplementum legis et prophetarum. Viderit enim, et narrationum dispositio variavit, dummodo de capite fidei conveniat, de quo cum Marcione non convenit.

3. Contra. Marcion evangelio, scilicet suo, nullum abscribit auctorem, quasi non licuerit titulum quoque adfingere, cui nefas non fuit ipsum corpus evertere. Et possem hic iam gradum figere, non agnoscendum contendens opus, quod non erigat frontem, quod nullam constantiam praeferat, nullam fidem repromittat de plenitudine tituli et professione debita auctoris.

4. Sed per omnia congredi malumus, nec dissimulamus quod ex nostro intellegi potest. Nam ex his commentatoribua, quos habemus, Lucam videtur Marcion elegisse, quem caederet. Porro Lucas non apostolus, sed apostolicus, non magister, sed discipulus, utique magistro minor, certe tanto posterior, quanto posterioris apostoli sectator, Pauli sine dubio, ut et si sub ipsius Pauli nomine evangelium Marcion intulisset, non sufficeret ad fidem singularitas instrumenti destituta patrocinio antecessorum.

2. In short, from among the Apostles, John and Matthew implant in us the Faith, while from among apostolic men Luke and Mark reaffirm it, [all of them] beginning with the same rules [of belief,] as far as relates to the one only God, the Creator, and to his Christ, born of a virgin, the fulfilment of the Law and the Prophets. It matters not that the arrangement of their narratives varies, so long as there is agreement on the essentials of the Faith—and on these they show no agreement with Marcion.

3. Marcion, on the other hand, attaches to his gospel no author's name, as though he to whom it was no crime to overturn the whole body, might not assume permission to invent a title for it as well. At this point I might have made a stand, arguing that no recognition is due to a work which cannot lift up its head, which makes no show of courage, which gives no promise of credibility by having a fully descriptive title and the requisite indication of the author's name.

4. But I prefer to join issue at all points, nor am I leaving unmentioned anything that can be taken as being in my favor. For out of those authors whom we possess, Marcion is seen to have chosen Luke as the one to mutilate. Now Luke was not an apostle but an apostolic man, not a master but a disciple, in any case less than his master, and assuredly even more of lesser account as being the follower of a later apostle, Paul, to be sure; so that even if Marcion had introduced his gospel under the name of Paul in person, that one single document would not be adequate for our faith, if destitute of the support of his predecessors.

5. Exigeretur enim id quoque evangelium, quod Paulus invenit, cui fidem dedit, cui mox suum congruere gestiit, siquidem propterea Hierosolymam ascendit ad cognoscendos apostolos et consultandos, ne forte in vacuum cucurrisset, id est ne non secundum illos credidisset et non secundum illos evangelizaret. Denique ut cum auctoribus contulit et convenit de regula fidei, dexteras miscuerunt et exinde officia praedicandi distinxerunt, ut illi in Iudaeos, Paulus in Iudaeos et in nationes. Igitur si ipse inluminator Lucae auctoritatem antecessorum et fidei et praedicationi suae optavit, quanto magis eam evangelio Lucae expostulem, quae evangelio magistri eius fuit necessaria?

5. For we should demand the production of that gospel also which Paul found [in existence], that to which he gave his assent, that with which shortly afterwards he was anxious that his own should agree; for his intention in going up to Jerusalem to know and to consult the Apostles, was lest perchance he had run in vain—that is, lest perchance he had not believed as they did, or was not preaching the gospel in their manner. At length, when he had conferred with the original [Apostles], and there was agreement concerning the rule of the faith, they joined the right hands [of fellowship], and from thenceforth divided their spheres of preaching, so that the others should go to the Jews, but Paul to Jews and Gentiles. If he therefore who gave the light to Luke chose to have his predecessors authority for his faith as well as his preaching, much more must I require for Luke's gospel the authority which was necessary for the gospel of his master.

Ad Marcionem IV.5.3

Habet plane et illud ecclesias, sed suas, tam posteras quam adulteras, quarum si censum requiras, facilius apostaticum quam apostolicum, Marcione scilicet conditore vel aliquo de Marcionis examine. Faciunt faves et vespae, faciunt ecclesias et Marcionitae. Eadem auctoritas ecclesiarum apostolicarum ceteris quoque patrocinabitur evangeliis, quae proinde per illas et secundum illas habemus, Iohannis dico atque Matthei, licet et Marcus quod edidit Petri adfirmetur, cuius interpres Marcus. Nam et Lucae digestum Paulo adscribere solent.

Admittedly that Gospel [of Marcion] too has its churches; but they are its own, of late arrival and spurious: if you search out their ancestry you are more likely to find it apostatic than apostolic, having for founder either Marcion or someone from Marcion's hive. Even wasps make combs, and Marcionites make churches. That same authority of the apostolic churches will stand as witness also for the other gospels, which no less [than Luke's] we possess by their agency and according to their text— I mean John's and Matthew's, though that which Mark produced is stated to be Peter's, whose interpreter Mark was. Luke's narrative also they usually attribute to Paul.

Tertullian then is sure that ''the documents of the Gospels have the Apostles for their authors'' (*constituimus inprimis evangelicum instrumentum apostolos auctore habere*). A man of his stature—an advocate by profession—is not to be lightly accused of failing to have an exact knowledge of the essential facts about the Four Gospels when he takes up the defence of the church's tradition against Marcion, or alternatively, of not knowing that he was unable to get hold of the essential facts! For him there were no grounds at all for setting aside the tradition.

Origen (ca. 185-253)

Origen, the successor of Clement of Alexandria as the principal Christian teacher in that city, embodied the ancient traditions of the church of Alexandria and its great center of learning. Most of his writings have perished, but we give below some pertinent fragments of his homilies on Luke in the original Greek, composed some time during the first half of the third century.[14] These fragments not only show the firmness of Origen's belief in the Four Gospels and in them alone as stemming directly from the Apostles, but also his awareness of and rejection of the numerous apocryphal gospels. Note however that his special emphasis is not so much on the Apostles and Apostolic Men as Evangelists as on the role of the Holy Spirit as the principal author, who enabled the church to distinguish the true from the false and the apocryphal.

Homilia in Lucam I (ed. Rauer, GCS 49)

῞Ωσπερ ἐν τῷ πάλαι λαῷ πολλοὶ προφητείαν ἐπηγγέλοντο, ἀλλὰ τούτων τινὲς μὲν ἦσαν ψευδοπροφῆται, τινὲς δὲ ἀληθῶς προφῆται,	Just as in former times among the chosen people, many exercised prophecy, but some of them were false prophets, but others were true prophets,
καὶ ἦν χάρισμα τῷ λαῷ διάκρισις πνευμάτων, ἀφ' οὗ ἐκρίνετο ὅ τε ἀληθὴς προφήτης καὶ ὁ ψευδώνυμος·	and among the people there was the charisma of discerning spirits, by means of which the true prophet was distinguished from the false,
οὕτω καὶ νῦν ἐν τῇ καινῇ διαθήκῃ τὰ εὐαγγέλια [πολλοὶ] ἠθέλησαν γράψαι, ἀλλ' [οἱ δόκιμοι τραπεζῖται] οὐ πάντα ἐνέκριναν, ἀλλά τινα αὐτῶν ἐξελέξαντο.	so also now in the New Testament "many" have willed to write gospels, but the knowing "money changers" did not accept all, but selected some of them.

---

[14]See GCS 38 (1938), Latin text, ed. E. Klostermann; see also in the same series, 40 (1940), the Greek text of the same; also 41 (1941), fragments and indexes; regarding the number of the apocryphal gospels, see GCS 49, ed. M. Rauer. It is not possible at present to date these fragments as we have no precise chronology for Origen's numerous Homilies.

Τάχα δὲ καὶ τὸ ἐπεχείρησεν λελ-ηθυῖαν ἔχει κατηγορίαν τῶν χωρὶς χαρίσματος ἐλθόντων ἐπὶ τὴν ἀναγραφὴν τῶν εὐαγγελίων. Ματθαῖος γὰρ οὐκ ἐπεχείρησεν ἀλλ' ἔγραψεν ἀπὸ ἁγίου πνεύμα-τος, ὁμοίως καὶ Μᾶρκος καὶ Ἰωάννης, παραπλησίως δὲ καὶ Λουκᾶς.

And probably the phrase "taken in hand" was intended to indicate the category of those who have approached the writing of the gospels without the grace. For Matthew did not "take in hand" but wrote by the Holy Spirit, and so did Mark and John and also equally Luke.

Τὸ μέντοι ἐπιγεγραμμένον κατὰ Αἰγυπτίους εὐαγγέλιον καὶ τὸ ἐπιγεγραμμένον τῶν Δώδεκα εὐαγ-γέλιον οἱ συγγράψαντες ἐπεχ-είρησαν.

The gospel entitled "According to the Egyptians" and the one entitled "The Gospel of the Twelve" are two examples of "those who have taken in hand to write."

Ἤδη δὲ ἐτόλμησε καὶ Βασιλείδης γράψαι κατὰ Βασιλείδην εὐαγ-γέλιον. πολλοὶ μὲν οὖν ἐπεχ-είρησαν. . . .

And Basilides has already dared to write the gospel "According to Basilides." "Many therefore have taken in hand. . . ."

Φέρεται γὰρ καὶ τὸ κατὰ Θωμὰν εὐαγγέλιον καὶ τὸ κατὰ Ματθίαν καὶ ἄλλα πλείονα.

For there is also the gospel "according to Thomas," and that "according to Matthias," and many others.

Ταῦτα ἐστι τῶν ἐπιχειρησ-άντων· τὰ δὲ τέσσερα μόνα προκ-ρίνει ἡ τοῦ Θεοῦ ἐκκλησία.

These are the ones "that have been taken in hand." But the church of God accepts only the four.

As with Tertullian, it is really a slur on Origen's intelligence, on his integrity, and on his scholarship to doubt his word that Matthew and John were written by Matthew and John and that the "apostolic men" Mark and Luke published the Gospels ascribed to them under the authority of Peter and Paul.

8. The Consensus Summaries

We have now examined the witness of the six principal Fathers whose writings have come down to us, who unite in their respective persons the combined traditions of both East and West from apostolic times; and their testimony is congruent, consistent, and complementary. Though they undoubtedly all knew Papias's testimony, they are all in one way or another in touch with other independent sources, such as Polycarp, and other apostolic traditions, such as Peter's. It is now time to turn to the Muratorian Canon and the Anti-Marcionite Prologues to the Gospels. Precisely because they are consensus documents they represent what their anonymous compilers believed to be the general and genuine opinion of the churches in their particular area, for example, Rome, Spain, and elsewhere.

8. a. The Muratorian Canon

The Muratorian Canon is so called because it was discovered by Cardinal Muratori in the Ambrosian Library at Milan and published in 1740. Despite a recent attempt to date it some time in the fourth century,[15] it is still generally held to date from the later second century, because it mentions as contemporaries of the author both Pope Pius I (141-155) and Hermas, the Pope's brother and author of *The Shepherd of Hermas*, as well as the heretics Marcion, Basilides, and Montanus. Its author is unknown, though some have attributed it to Hippolytus. Our Latin text is probably a translation from a Greek original into a barbarous Latin. The text is confirmed, however, by various fragments recently discovered in several places.

Though this Canon contains only an incomplete list of the New Testament writings it gives firm support to the order Matthew and Mark before Luke and John; for the first two lines not only presuppose two earlier Gospels but in the opinion of all scholars seem to refer, indirectly at least, to the Gospel of Mark. The Canon goes on to affirm the unity of doctrine of all four Gospels through the influence of "the one and principal Spirit" (1.19). It also declares Luke to be the disciple of St. Paul and the author of the Acts as well as the Gospel, and it further asserts that the Acts were composed before Peter's martyrdom and Paul's journey to Spain. It is worth noting that the Canon attributes both the Gospel and the Apocalypse to St. John the Apostle. It further claims that Paul's Letters to the churches are seven in number, by a divinely inspired correspondence with the seven Letters of John to the churches in the Apocalypse. It also attributes another Apocalypse to St. Peter "which some of us refuse to have read in Church." However, it denies a place among the inspired books to *The Shepherd of Hermas*, even though its author was the brother of Pope Pius I; and it rejects all the writings of Valentinian, Miltiades, and Marcion.

This list is remarkable for its tone of authority and decisiveness and for the universality of its standpoint; and though it makes no mention of either 1 or 2 Peter or of James or Hebrews, yet with regard to what it actually does mention it is totally definite as to what is and what is not to be accepted as inspired Scripture, that is, as to what is on a level "with the

---

[15]Albert C. Sundberg, Jr., "Canon Muratori: A Fourth Century List," HTR 66/1 (Jan. 1973):1-41. See also G. Brady, "Muratori," DBS, 1399-1408; E. Hennecke, *New Testament Apocrypha* (SCM Press, 1973); also H. von Campenhausen, *Die Enstehung der christlicher Bibel* (Tübingen, 1968) 282-303; also W. Schneemelcher, TRE, vol. 5, art. in loc., who rejects Sundberg's thesis. For the reconstructed Latin Text printed here, see *Florilegium Patristicum*, fasc. 3, ed. G. Rauschen (Bonn, 1905) 27-35.

prophets.'' Hence this ancient Latin document not only witnesses to the firm crystallization of opinion about the origins of the Gospels in an area of the West probably around Rome about 150, but also agrees with all the other ancient witnesses we have previously cited.

The following reconstruction of the text of the Muratorian Fragment is that of G. Rauschen, *Florilegium Patristicum,* fasc. 3 (Bonn, 1905).

1 . . . quibus tamen interfuit et ita posuit.	. . . at which nevertheless he was present and has thus related.
2 Tertium evangelii librum secundum Lucam.	In third place [we have] the book of the Gospel according to Luke.
3 Lucas iste medicus, post adscensum Christi	This Luke, a physician, after the Ascension of Christ,
4 cum eum Paulus quasi iuris studiosum [itineris socium?]	when Paul had taken him, as one studious of Right,
5 secum adsumpsisset, nomine suo	[? to be his follower] at his own request [? in his own name],
6 ex opinione conscripsit, dominum tamen nec ipse	wrote from report, since he himself notwithstanding
7 vidit in carne, et ideo, prout assequi potuit,	had not seen the Lord in the flesh. Yet as far as he could ascertain
8 ita et a nativitate Iohannis incipit dicere.	so indeed he began to relate, beginning at the Birth of John.
9 Quartum evangeliorum Iohannis ex discipulis.	The fourth of the Gospels is John's, one of the Disciples.
10 Cohortantibus condiscipulis et episcopis suis	At the insistence of his fellow-disciples and bishops
11 dixit: 'Conieiunate mihi hodie triduo et quid	he said: Today and for three days fast with me and what
12 cuique fuerit revelatum alterutrum	shall have been revealed to each let us.
13 nobis enarremus. Eadem nocte revelatum	relate to one another. The same night it was revealed
14 Andreae ex apostolis, ut recognoscentibus	to Andrew, one of the Apostles, that whatever
15 cunctis Iohannes suo nomine	should come to the minds of them all John in his own name
16 cuncta describeret. Et ideo, licet varia	should write it all down. And through discrepant
17 singulis evangeliorum libris principia	points in individual Gospels
18 doceantur, nihil tamen differt credentium	may be taught, nothing however disperses the faith of
19 fidei, cum uno ac principali spiritu declarata	believers, since by one and the same supreme Spirit are
20 sint in omnibus omnia de nativitate,	made clear in all things everything concerning the Nativity,
21 de passione, de resurrectione,	concerning the Passion, concerning the Resurrection,
22 de conversatione cum discipulis suis	concerning his intercourse with his disciples

23 ac de gemino eius adventu,

and concerning his twofold Coming,

24 primo in humilitate despecto, quod fuit,

firstly despised in lowliness, which has happened

25 secundo in potestate regali praeclaro,

and secondly in royal power . . . which

26 quod futurum est. Quid ergo

will be glorious. What therefore [is there]

27 mirum, si Iohannes tam constanter

to wonder at if John so constantly

28 singula etiam in epistulis suis proferat

utters statements indeed in his Epistles

29 dicens in semetipsum: "Quae vidimus oculis

saying from his own experience: What we have seen

30 nostris et auribus audivimus et manus

with our eyes and heard with our ears and

31 nostrae palpaverunt, haec scripsimus vobis."

our hands have touched, these things we have written to you?

32 Sic enim non solum visorem se et auditorem

For thus he declares that he is not only an eyewitness and a hearer

33 sed et scriptorem omnium mirabilium domini per ordinem

but also the writer of all the wonders of the Lord in order

34 profitetur. Acta autem omnium apostolorum

However the Acts of the Apostles

35 sub uno libro scripta sunt. Lucas optimo Theophilo

were written in one book. To the excellent Theophilus Luke

36 comprendit, quae sub praesentia eius singula

dedicates [the Acts], some of the events of which

37 gerebantur, sicuti et semota passione Petri

happened in his presence, just as he clearly declares, though

38 evidenter declarat, sed et profectione Pauli ab urbe

with omission of Peter's Passion and Paul's journey

39 ad Spaniam proficiscentis. Epistulae autem

from Rome setting out for Spain. As to the Epistles

40 Pauli quae a quo loco vel qua ex causa directae

of Paul, they themselves make clear to those desiring to

41 sint, volentibus intellegere ipsae declarant;

understand, from what place (they were) directed and for what reason.

42 primum omnium Corinthiis schismae haereses

First of all, to the Corinthians forbidding heretical sects,

43 interdicens, deinceps Galatis circumcisionem,

then to the Galatians (suppressing) circumcision,

44 Romanis autem ordinem scripturarum sed et

to the Romans showing Christ to be . . . (? not) only the order

45 principium earum esse Christum intimans

of the Scriptures but their origin,

46 prolixius scripsit. De quibus singulis necesse

he wrote at greater length. Concerning each of which it is

47 est, a nobis disputari, cum ipse beatus

necessary for us to treat since the Blessed

48 apostolus Paulus sequens prodecessoria sui

Apostle Paul himself, following the arrangment of

49 Iohannis ordinem non nisi nominatim septem

his predecessor John, writes by name to no more than seven

50 ecclesiis scribat ordine tali: ad Corinthios

Churches in this order: to the Corinthians

51 prima, ad Ephesios secunda, ad Phi-
lippenses tertia,

the first, to the Ephesians the second, to the
Philippians the third,

52 ad Colossenses quarta, ad Galatas
quinta,

to the Colossians the fourth, to the Galatians
the fifth,

53 ad Thessalonicenses sexta, ad Roma-
nos

to the Thessalonians the sixth, to the Romans

54 septima. Verum Corinthiis et Thessa-
lonicensibus

the seventh. But though to the Corinthians and
Thessalonians

55 licet pro correptione iteretur, una

a further letter was added by way of a rebuke,

56 tamen per omnem orbem terrae ecclesia

nevertheless the Church dispersed over the
whole world

57 diffusa esse dinoscitur; et Iohannes
enim in

is considered as one. For John too in the

58 apocalypsi licet septem ecclesiis scribat,

Apocalypse, though he writes to seven
Churches,

59 tamen omnibus dicit. Verum ad Phi-
lemonem una

nevertheless he is speaking to all. But to Philemon one

60 et ad Titum una et ad Timotheum duae
pro adfectu

and to Titus one, and to Timothy two out of
loving

61 et dilectione, in honore tamen ecclesiae

affection (which) nevertheless are recognized
in honor

62 catholicae, in ordinatione ecclesiasti-
cae

in the Catholic Church for their ordering of
ecclesiastical

63 disciplinae sanctificatae sunt. Fertur
etiam ad

discipline. There is also said to be one

64 Laodicenses, alia ad Alexandrinos
Pauli nomine

to the Laodiceans, another to the Alexandri-
ans, Paul's name

65 finctae ad haeresem Marcionis et alia
plura,

being forged to (aid) the heresy of Marcion,
and several

66 quae in catholicam ecclesiam recipi non
potest;

others, which cannot be received into the
Catholic Church.

67 fel enim cum melle misceri non congruit.

For it is not fitting to mix gall with honey.

68 Epistula sane Iudae et superscripti

The Epistle of Jude surely, and two

69 Iohannis duae in catholica habentur et
Sapi

with the superscription of John are held in the
Catholic (Church), also

70 entia ab amicis Salomonis in honorem
ipsius

Wisdom written by the friends of Solomon in
his

71 scripta. Apocalypses etiam Iohannis et
Petri

honour. Also the Apocalypses of John and

72 tantum recipimus, quam quidam ex
nostris

of Peter only we receive, which certain persons among us

73 legi in ecclesia nolunt. Pastorem vero

refuse to have read in Church. But The Shepherd

74 nuperrime temporibus nostris in urbe

was written very recently in our times in the
City

75 Roma Hermas conscripsit sedente
cathedra

of Rome by Hermas, when his brother Bishop
Pius was sitting

76 urbis Romae ecclesiae Pio episcopo
fratre

in the Chair of the Church of the City of Rome.

77 eius; et ideo legi eum quidem oportet se	And so it ought also to be read; but indeed
78 publicare vero in ecclesia populo neque inter	it cannot be publicly (read) in Church to the people, neither among
79 prophetas completo numero, neque inter	the Prophets, nor among the Apostles, the number being complete
80 apostolos in finem temporum potest.	to the end of time.
81 Arsinoi autem seu Valentini vel Miltiadis	However we receive nothing whatever of Arisinoo or of Valentine
82 nihil in totum recipimus; quin etiam novum	or of Miltiades;
83 psalmorum librum Marcioni conscripserunt	the Marcionites have written a new book of Psalms
84 una cum Basilide Asiano Cataphrygum	together with Basilides founder of the Catafrigi. . . .
85 constitutore.	

Comment

There are many points of general interest, but we must restrict ourselves to the following.

Line 1. A conjecture: could it be that what he [Mark?] was present at, and that what he related, was the διδασκαλίας of Peter (cf. EH II.15; VI.14)?

Lines 4-5. The transcription, and the translation of these lines, is uncertain and obscure. But they support the tradition that Luke was selected by Paul as his companion and that he wrote ''in Paul's name'' a gospel account based on reports he had obtained, since he had not himself been an eyewitness. The variants concern the epithet that they attach to Luke; ''iuris studiosum,'' ''litteris studiosum,'' and ''itineris socium'' are all possible readings.

Line 28, 68-69. The Canon recognizes two Epistles of John at least, and both 2 John and 3 John are ascribed to ''The Presbyter.'' John was therefore known as ''The Presbyter'' to the compiler of this Canon.

Line 72. This line indicates that some persons, not the author of this Canon, were questioning the authorship of the Apocalypse of John and that of Peter. It is not clear what is meant by the ''Apocalypse of Peter.''

Line 79-80. The author of the Muratorian Canon considers the list of canonical books to have been completed in the time of the Apostles.

Line 81-82. Compare Irenaeus, *Adv. Haer.* IV.6.4.

8. b. The Anti-Marcionite Prologues

These ancient Latin prologues to Mark, Luke, and John, were asserted by Dom de Bruyne in 1928 as being of the second century in origin and anti-Marcionite in character.[16] They are attached to some thirty-eight Latin codices of the Gospel; twenty six of them give a Latin version of a Greek text that originated in Constantinople, twelve of them contain a prologue to Mark, and ten a prologue to John. No prologue to Matthew has been recorded or found.

Although de Bruyne's claim was challenged at the time by Lagrange[17] and others, he received the support of A. Harnack[18] and his attribution was generally accepted until 1969 when J. Regul[19] made a serious attack on his whole theory and gained important support.[20] However, the importance of these prologues is not to be lightly dismissed; for even if their composition was as late as the latter half of the fourth century, they certainly reflect the second-century traditions that we have already noted. And because they are also consensus summaries, they are much more significant for the depth of contemporary opinion than the witness of a single writer, since they represent the distillation of the tradition of a group of churches in more than one area. And since no area within the Roman Empire was isolated from all other areas, such consensuses can be reasonably taken as representing the common view within the Empire as a whole. Modern critics tend to reject all the prologues because of two statements in the Latin prologue to John for which there is no surviving documentary evidence, namely, that Papias was John the Evangelist's amanuensis and that the same John per-

---

[16]Dom D. de Bruyne, "Les plus anciens prologues latins des Évangiles," *Rev. Ben.* 40 (1928): 193-214; E. Gutwenger, "The Anti-Marcionite Prologues," TS 7 (1946): 393-409; W. F. Howard, "The Anti-Marcionite Prologues," *Exp. Times* 47 (1935/6): 534-48; R. G. Heard, "The Old Latin Gospel Prologues," JTS NS 6 (1956): 1-16; J. Chapman, *Notes on the Early History of the Vulgate Gospels* (Oxford 1908); J.-M. Lagrange, *Histoire ancienne du Canon du Nouveau Testament,* pt. 1 (1933); also Robert Grant, "The Oldest Gospel Prologues," *Anglican Theological Review* 23 (1941): 236-43.

[17]J.-M. Lagrange, Review of de Bruyne's article (see n. 16 above), *Rev. Bib.* 38 (1929): 115-21; also J. Quasten, *Patrology,* 2:210-11.

[18]A. Harnack, "Die ältesten Evangelienprologe und die Bildung des NTS," in SPAW, *Phil.-Hist.,* Lk 24 (1928): 322-341.

[19]J. Regul, *Die Antimarcionitischen Evangelienprologe,* Vetus Latina Series (Freiburg, 1969). For the list of these MSS, see De Bruyne (n. 16 above), and Regul, who by his terms of reference is really only interested in the Latin texts of the Prologues. The symbols denoting the various MSS are taken from Regul, 17-29.

[20]See Huck-Greeven, *Synopse* (1981) Introduction, 1,8.

sonally repudiated Marcion. These objections will be dealt with in the sections on the prologue to John (8. f. and g.).

8. c. The Anti-Marcionite Prologue to Luke (Greek Text)

Although Regul is correct in asserting that the Latin text is older than the beginning of the ninth century, his conclusion that the Greek text depends on the Latin by no means follows. For this Greek text has an independent history in the environs of Constantinople, and its reference to "the whole" Gospel of Luke (which is omitted in the Latin versions) is highly significant and argues that it was composed at a time when Marcion's mutilation of the Gospel of Luke was still a live issue, that is, at a time prior to A.D. 200. There is then a considerable degree of probability for thinking that this Greek text is the original and long anterior to the Latin, and that it was directly aimed at Marcion's truncated version of Luke. The Latin version (see below) is a rather slavish rendering of the Greek.

The Greek text given below is that of Regul, following the Greek Minuscule 1828, with the variants of Ms Bodl. Misc. Graec. 141. This Greek manuscript appears to have been brought to Rome about 820 by St. Methodius, patriarch of Constantinople, and presented by him to Pope Paschal I. Since it contains no reference to the transfer of the relics of St. Luke to Constantinople in 356-357 the main paragraph must be earlier than that date. St. Methodius himself regarded it as a precious witness of the early Greek church to Luke and the other evangelists.

Greek Minuscule 1828 with variants of MS Bodl. Misc. Graec. 141

Τοῦτο ἐξ ἰδιοχείρων τοῦ ἁγίου πατριάρχου Μεθοδίου. Ἀνάπαυσις τοῦ ἁγίου ἀποστόλου Λουκᾶ τοῦ εὐαγγελίστου εἰκάδι τοῦ Σεπτεμβρίου μῆνος.
Ἔστιν ὁ ἅγιος Λουκᾶς Ἀντιοχεύς, Σύρος τῷ γένει, ἰατρὸς τὴν τέχνην, μαθητὴς ἀποστόλων γενόμενος καὶ ὕστερον Παύλῳ παρακολουθήσας μέχρις τοῦ μαρτυρίου αὐτοῦ δουλεύσας τῷ Κυρίῳ ἀπερισπάστως, ἀγύναιος, ἄτεκνος, ἐτῶν ὀγδοήκοντα τεσσάρων ἐκοιμήθη ἐν Θήβαις τῇ μητροπόλει τῆς Βοιωτίας πλήρης πνεύματος ἁγίου.*

This is from the holograph of the holy patriarch Methodius. The feast of the passing of the holy apostle Luke the Evangelist, the 20th September.
St. Luke is an Antiochian, a Syrian by birth, by profession a physician, who was first a disciple of the apostles and then a follower of Paul until his martyrdom; having served the Lord without deviation, being unmarried and childless, he went to his rest at the age of eighty-four at Thebes, the metropolis of Boeotia, full of the Holy Spirit.*

οὗτος προυπαρχόντων ἤδη εὐαγγελίων, τοῦ μὲν κατὰ Ματθαῖον ἐν τῇ Ἰουδαίᾳ ἀναγραφέντος, τοῦ δὲ κατὰ Μᾶρκον ἐν τῇ Ἰταλίᾳ, οὗτος προτραπεὶς ὑπὸ πνεύματος ἁγίου ἐν τοῖς περὶ τὴν Ἀχαίαν τὸ πᾶν τοῦτο συνεγράψατο εὐαγγέλιον, δηλῶν διὰ τοῦ προοιμίου τοῦτο αὐτό, ὅτι πρὸ αὐτοῦ ἄλλα ἐστὶ γεγραμμένα καὶ ὅτι ἀναγκαῖον ἦν τοῖς ἐξ ἐθνῶν πιστοῖς τὴν ἀκριβῆ τῆς οἰκονομίας ἐκθέσθαι διήγησιν ὑπὲρ τοῦ μὴ ταῖς Ἰουδαϊκαῖς μυθολογίαις περισπᾶσθαι αὐτοὺς μήτε ταῖς αἱρετικαῖς καὶ κεναῖς φαντασίαις ἀπατωμένους ἀστοχῆναι τῆς ἀληθείας.

ὡς ἀναγκαιοτάτην οὖν οὖσαν εὐθὺς ἐν ἀρχῇ παρειλήφαμεν τὴν τοῦ Ἰωάννου γέννησιν. ὅς ἐστιν ἀρχὴ τοῦ εὐαγγελίου πρόδρομος τοῦ Κυρίου γενόμενος καὶ καινωνὸς ἐν τε τῷ καταρτισμῷ τοῦ εὐαγγελίου καὶ τῇ τοῦ βαπτίσματος διαγωγῇ καὶ τῇ τοῦ πνεύματος κοινωνίᾳ. ταύτης τῆς οἰκονομίας μέμνηται προφήτης ἐν τοῖς δώδεκα.

καὶ δὴ μετέπειτα ἔγραψεν ὁ αὐτὸς Λουκᾶς πράξεις ἀποστόλων. ὕστερον δὲ Ἰωάννης ὁ ἀπόστολος ἐκ τῶν δώδεκα ἔγραψεν τὴν ἀποκάλυψιν ἐν τῇ νήσῳ Πάτμῳ καὶ μετὰ ταῦτα τὸ εὐαγγέλιον.

* For ετων . . . Βοιωτιας, the Bodleian MS reads simply εκοιμηθη εν τη Βοιωτια. This is the only significant variation.

There were already gospels in existence, that according to Matthew, written down in Judaea, and that according to Mark in Italy; but he, guided by the Holy Spirit, composed in the regions around Achaia the whole of this gospel, manifesting by his preface that others had been written before his own and that it was necessary to set forth for believers from among the Gentiles the accurate account of the plan of salvation to prevent them from being wheeled around by Jewish mythical stories and from failing to get to the truth through being deceived by heretical and vain fantasies.

Because therefore it was most necessary, he straightway at the beginning took the birth of John, which is the beginning of the gospel, he who was the forerunner of the Lord and who was his partner in the setting up of the gospel and in the accomplishment of the baptism and in the fellowship of the Holy Spirit. One of the twelve prophets has recorded this plan.

And the same Luke afterwards wrote the Acts of the Apostles. Finally, John the Apostle, one of the Twelve, wrote the Apocalypse on the island of Patmos, and afterwards the Gospel.

* For "at the age . . . Boeotia," the Bodleian MS reads simply "he went to his rest in Boeotia."

Notes and Comments

ἰατρὸς τὴν τέχνην, "by profession a physician" (compare Col 4:14). We find this statement supported by the Muratorian Canon. The other personal details about Luke, that he was a Syrian of Antioch, a celibate, and that he died at Thebes at the age of eighty-four, are not recorded in any other second century document.

προυπαρχόντων ἤδη εὐαγγελίων, "there were already gospels in existence. . . . This statement supports the view that Matthew came first, and that Mark came after Matthew but before Luke, as the Muratorian Canon also suggests. But see part three, chapter 4 for a profounder understanding of this passage.

τὸ πᾶν τοῦτο . . . εὐαγγέλιον, "the whole body of this Gospel." The vital phrase, "this whole," has been omitted by all the Latin recensions, probably because the Latin translators did not perceive its significance. (Indeed, modern commentators have also unaccountably ignored it.) For it is clearly directed against the Marcionites who had deliberately truncated and mutilated the Gospel of Luke, after jettisoning the other three altogether. Among the mutilations was, it seems, the omission of the Lukan birth narrative. The insistence on the existence of the other three Gospels (in a prologue intended for Luke's Gospel only) is to be seen as contradicting Marcion's views about their worthlessness. For good measure, the prologue concludes with the affirmation of the church's acceptance of Luke's Acts of the Apostles, and also of both the Apocalypse and the Gospel as the work of John the Apostle. E. Earle Ellis believes it was "composed about the time of Irenaeus" (*The Gospel of Luke,* [1966] 38). συνεγράψατο, "composed," supports our view that Luke was written to meet the needs of Paul's churches in Achaia; it is also compatible with the view that it was published in that region some time after Paul's stay in Rome.

8. d. The Old Latin Prologue to Luke

This prologue is presented here for the sake of completeness and to illustrate its secondary quality by comparison with the Greek text above. Only recension 1 is printed here since recensions 2 and 3 are almost identical with recension 1.

(MSS: II, 2, S6, M, V1, C)

Est quidem Lucas Antiochensis Syrus, arte medicus, discipulus apostolorum, postea vero Paulum secutus est usque ad confessionem eius, serviens Domino sine crimine.	Luke indeed is a Syrian of Antioch, a physician by profession, a disciple of the apostles, but later followed Paul until his martyrdom, serving the Lord without blame.
Uxorem numquam habuit, filios numquam procreavit, LXXXVIII annorum obiit in Boeotia, plenus Spiritu Sancto.	He never had a wife, he never begot sons, died eighty-eight years old in Boeotia, full of the Holy Spirit.

Igitur cum iam descripta essent evangelia, per Matteum quidem in Iudaea, per Marcum autem in Italia, Sancto instigatus Spiritu in Achaiae partibus hoc descripsit evangelium, significans per principium ante suum alia esse descripta, sed et sibi maximam necessitatem incumbere Graecis fidelibus cum summa diligentia omnem dispositionem enarratione sua exponere,

propterea ne Iudaicis fabulis et stultis sollicitationibus seducti excederent a veritate. Itaque perquam necessariam statim in principio sumpsit a Iohannis nativitate, quae est initium evangelii, praemissus Domini nostri Iesu Christi, et fuit socius ad perfectionem populi item inductionem baptismi atque passionis socius.

Cuius profecto dispositionis exempli meminit Zacharias propheta, unus ex duodecim. Et tamen postremo scripsit idem Lucas Actus Apostolorum; postmodum Iohannes apostolus descripsit primum revelationem in insula Pathmos, deinde evangelium in Asia.

For though Gospels had already been written, by Matthew indeed in Judea, and by Mark in Italy, he, spurred by the Holy Spirit, wrote down this gospel in the regions of Achaia, indicating in the preface that others had been written before his, but that the greatest compulsion lay upon him to expound to the Greek believers with the greatest care the whole economy of salvation in his account,

lest being led astray by Jewish myths and foolish enticements they should depart from the truth. Because therefore it was most necessary, he began at once with the birth of John, which is the beginning of the gospel—he who was the forerunner of our Lord Jesus Christ, and was his partner for the preparation of the people, likewise for the accomplishment of his baptism, and a sharer of his passion.

Zacharias, one of the twelve, actually records an instance of this plan. Moreover this same Luke then also wrote the Acts of the Apostles; subsequently John the Apostle wrote down firstly the Revelation on the island of Patmos, then the Gospel in Asia.

Notes

The following MSS have the Second Recension, B 5-8, P, and the Third Recension, J 2-4, S 1-4, 7, F 4-6, B 1-3. The main differences are: Recensions 2 and 3 have "Bithynia" instead of "Boeotia"; 2 gives Luke's age at his death as "74," while 3 gives it as "84."

Recension 1 speaks of "the whole economy of salvation"; recension 2 interprets this as a "witness to the humanity of God coming in the flesh of Christ," and recension 3 speaks of "the whole plan of Christ coming in the flesh."

Recensions 2 and 3 add to "being led astray" the clause "being solely intent on the fulfilling of the Law."

Where 1 has "Zacharias," 2 and 3 have "Malachias."

These disagreements are all minor, and indicate that Recension 1 is the earliest. For further comments on this text, see the notes on the Greek text above.

8. e. The Old Latin Prologue to Mark: Recensions 1 and 2

There are two recensions of the prologue to Mark. Recension 1 (the shorter text) shows Mark as the recorder of Peter's memoirs and as publishing them after Peter's death; recension 2 (the longer text) explains in greater detail how Mark came to be both the recorder and the publisher of Peter's memoirs. The intention of both recensions seems to be to prove that Mark had Peter's confidence and faithfully recorded his memoirs during Peter's lifetime.

Recension 1
(MSS: B4, M VI, C)

. . . Marcus adseruit, qui colobodactylus est nominatus, ideo quod ad ceteram corporis proceritatem digitos minores habuisset. Iste interpres fuit Petri. Post excessionem ipsius Petri, descripsit idem hoc in Italiae partibut evangelium.	. . . Mark asserted, who was called Stubfinger because he had shorter fingers in relation to the other dimension of the body. He had been the recorder of Peter. After the demise of Peter himself, the same [Mark] published this Gospel in the regions of Italy.

Recension 2
(MSS: J2, S2-4, 7)

. . . Marcus qui et colobodactylus est nominatus, ideo quod a cetera corporis proceritate digitos minores habuisset.	. . . Mark who was also called Stubfinger, because he had shorter fingers with regard to the other dimension of his body.
Hic discipulus et interpres fuit Petri, quem secutus, sicut ipsum audierat referentem. Rogatus Romae a fratribus hoc breve evangelium in Italiae partibus scripsit; quod cum Petrus audisset probavit ecclesiaeque legendum auctoritate firmavit.	He had been the disciple and recorder of Peter, whom he followed, just as he had heard him relating. Having been asked by the brethren in Rome he wrote this short Gospel in the regions of Italy; when Peter heard about it, he approved and authorized it to be read to the church with [his own] authority.
Verum post discessum Petri assumpto hoc evangelio quod ipse confecerat perrexit Aegyptum et primus Alexandriae episcopus ordinatus, Christum adnuntians constituit illic ecclesiam. Tantae doctrinae et vitae continentiae fuit ut omnes sectatores Christi ad suum cogeret imitari exemplum.	But after the demise of Peter, taking this Gospel that he had composed, he journeyed to Egypt and being ordained the first bishop of Alexandria he founded a Church there, preaching Christ. He was a man of such great learning and austerity of life that he induced all the followers of Christ to imitate his example.

Notes and Comments

Recension 1 is found in three MSS of German provenance, and in a fourth in the Vatican Library. Recension 2 is found in one Vatican MS and in four others of Spanish origin.

Recension 1 seems to require the following comments: *Marcus adseruit,* "Mark asserted." It is as curious as it is unfortunate that none of the MSS have retained the earlier part of the first sentence of what appears to be the real beginning of the prologue. It would seem that all these MSS were copied from the same defective copy of a still earlier date. It is difficult to make any plausible guess as to what it was that Mark had asserted. Is it simply a coincidence that the Muratorian Canon has also lost its opening sentence in a similar way? (Cf. above, 8.a.)

Colobodactylus, "stub-fingered." This is a Greek nickname, but supports the theory of a Roman origin for this recension; for the only other second century writer to mention this physical defect is Hippolytus (170-236) who taught in Rome (cf. his *Syntagma* VII.30.1).

Interpres Petri, "the recorder of Peter." The term *interpres* was ordinarily used to denote the function of Mercury, the messenger of the Gods; it is the exact equivalent of the Greek ἑρμηνευτής, which Papias used about Mark (EH III.39.15). It means one who transmits or exactly records what he has been told to say, a "go-between" or an "agent." The root meaning is that of one who accurately presents the teaching or message of another; and from this we get the more common meanings of "interpreter" or "translator" (cf. Liddell & Scott; Lampe, *A Patristic Greek Lexicon*).

Post excessionem ipsius Petri, "After the demise of Peter himself." This bears out Irenaeus's statement (Adv. Haer. III.1.1) that Mark did not publish his Gospel until after the death of Peter.

Descripsit . . . in Italiae partibus, "wrote down . . . in the regions of Italy," that is, wrote down his Gospel. This statement does not, however, compel us to assume that the Gospel of Mark was actually compiled after the death of Peter, or that it did not first of all circulate privately, but only that Mark himself did not publish it until after Peter's death. It does not contradict the statement of Papias's presbyter that Mark himself heard what Peter had said. Indeed our present text assumes that Mark recorded what Peter has said while he was alive but did not publish it until after Peter's death.

As regards recension 2, the following additional comments are required: The compiler of this recension certainly had recension 1 before him and deliberately set out to clear up possible ambiguities in it. He has nothing to add to the first sentence, but in the second he makes it clear that Mark was the disciple as well as the recorder of Peter, thus witnessing to a living contact between them.

Quem secutus sicut ipsum audierat referentem, "whom he followed, just as he had heard him relating." This makes it doubly clear that he not only followed Peter but heard what he related, and recorded it.

Rogatus . . . scripsit, "Having been asked . . . he wrote." For good measure the compiler of this recension 2 explains the origin of Mark. It seems that neither Peter nor Mark had any intention of composing another gospel, but Peter's reminiscences were so interesting that some of the Roman brethren prevailed on Mark to write out for them what Peter had said. And the compiler is also able to add the assurance that Peter both saw and approved of what had been done. This statement seems to depend on what Clement of Alexandria related (see ch. 4), the only addition here being that the compiler, writing a hundred or so years later, can with hindsight add that Peter's recognition of it gave it authority to be read in church. This is a gloss of the compiler, but one that is justified *post factum*.

Post discessum Petri, "after the demise of Peter." This phrase indicates that, for the church of the compiler of recension 2, Mark's taking the gospel to Egypt meant that it was no longer a private document but one intended for other Churches. His final argument is that the sanctity of Mark was to be regarded as a further proof of the holy nature of Mark's Gospel. The dependence of recension 2 on recension 1 is clear, but it is also equally clear that the compiler of recension 1 is in full command of the tradition about the origin of Mark that Clement of Alexandria had. And there is no discrepancy between them, but merely the clarifications that a later situation allowed to be brought out and which the compiler of recension 1 did not include. We shall see in the next chapter that Eusebius himself regarded the traditions recorded in recension 2 as worthy of credit and that he incorporated them in his overall picture (ch. 4, 4).

8. f. The Old Latin Prologue to John: Recensions 1 and 2

This prologue requires to be examined here because of the possible connection with the prologue to Mark, and because of the important reference to Papias (see also ch. 4 below). The text is taken from Regul.

Recension 1
(MSS: M, VI, 2, C)

Evangelium Iohannis manifestatum est ecclesiis ab Iohanne adhuc in corpore constituto, sicut Papias nomine Hierapolitanus, discipulus Iohannis carus, in exotericis, id est in extremis, quinque libris retulit; descripsit vero evangelium dictante Iohanne recte.	The Gospel of John was published to the churches by John while still living in the flesh, as the [Bishop] of Hierapolis, Papias by name, dear disciple of John, has related in the "exoteric," that is, in the last five books; for he wrote down the Gospel correctly at John's dictation.
Verum Marcion hereticus cum ab eo esset improbatus eo quod contraria sentiebat, abiectus est ab Iohanne.	But the heretic Marcion, when he had been disavowed by him because he held contrary opinions, was expelled by John.
Is vero scripta vel epistolas ad eum pertulerat a fratribus, qui in Ponto fuerant.	For he had brought him writings and letters from the brethren who were in Pontus.

Recension 2
MSS: S2, 3, 7, 8)

Iohannes apostolus, quem Dominus Iesus amavit plurimum, novissimus scripsit hoc evangelium postulantibus Asiae episcopis adversus Cerinthum aliosque hereticos et maxime tunc Ebionitarum dogma consurgens,

qui asserunt stultitiae suae pravitate, sic enim Ebionitae appellantur, Christum antequam de Maria nasceretur non fuisse nec natum ante saecula de Deo patre.

Unde etiam conpulsus est divinam eius a patre nativitatem dicere.

Sed et aliam causam conscripti huis evangelii ferunt, quia, cum legisset Matthaei, Marci et Lucae de evangelio volumina, probaverit quidem textum historiae et vera eos dixisse firmaverit, sed unius tantum anni in quo et passus est post carcerem Iohannis historiam texuisse.

Praetermisso itaque anno, cuius acta a tribus exposita fuerant, superioris temporis, antequam Iohannes clauderetur in carcere, gesta narravit, sicut manifestuam esse poterit his, qui quattuor evangeliorum volumina legerint diligenter.

Hoc igitur evangelium post apocalypsin scriptum manifestum et datum est ecclesiis in Asia a Iohanne adhuc in corpore constituto, sicut Papias nomine Hierapolitanus episcopus, discipulus Iohannis et carus, in exotericis suis, id est in extremis, quinque libris retulit; quit hoc evangelium Iohanne sibi dictante conscripsit.

Verum Marcion hereticus, cum ab eo fuisset reprobatus eo quod contraria sentiret, proiectus est a a Iohanne.

John the Apostle, whom the Lord Jesus loved exceedingly, last of all wrote this Gospel at the request of the bishops of Asia against Cerinthus and other heretics and especially the teaching of the Ebionites then arising,

who assert in the perversity of their folly (for that is why they are called Ebionites) that before Christ was born of Mary he neither existed nor was he born of God the Father before time began.

For this reason he was obliged to declare his divine birth from the Father.

But they also say that there was another reason for this Gospel being written, because after reading the volumes of Matthew, Mark, and Luke on the gospel, he of course approved the text of their accounts and confirmed the truth of what they had said, but [perceived] that they had provided the account of one year only in which he suffered after the imprisonment of John.

Omitting therefore the year whose happenings were recorded by the three, he related the events that occurred at an earlier period before John was shut up in prison, as will be able to be clear to those who have carefully read the books of the four Gospels.

This Gospel therefore, written after the Apocalypse, was also given to the churches in Asia by John while still living in the flesh, as the bishop of Hierapolis, Papias by name, a dear disciple of John, has related in his "exoteric," that is, in [his] last, five books, who wrote out this Gospel, John dictating it to him.

But the herectic Marcion, when he had been reproved by him for holding contrary opinions, was expelled by John.

| Hic vero scripta vel epistulas ad eum pertulerat a fratribus missus, qui in Ponto erant fideles in Christo Iesu Domino nostro. | For he had brought him writings and letters, having been sent by the brethren who were in Pontus, ones who were faithful in Christ Jesus our Lord. |

Notes and Comments

Recension 1 is found in two MSS of German provenance and in two others in the Vatican Library. Recension 2 is found in four MSS of Spanish provenance (see Regul). Recension 2 is in agreement with, but is also a considerable expansion of, recension 1, namely, by explaining that John wrote at the request of the bishop of Asia to refute Cerinthus and the Ebionites, by adding that John knew the Synoptics and wrote to supplement them, and that he wrote the Apocalypse before the Gospel. Irenaeus, writing circa 180, also expressly declares that John wrote to refute Cerinthus (*Adv. Haer* III.1.1), and Jerome also agrees (*De Vir. Illus.* IX).

Iohanne adhuc in corpore constituto, "while John was still living." The unusual and precise form of this Latin phrase suggests that contemporaries of the compiler of recension 1 were refuting the assertion (so often made today) that his Gospel was in fact only published after his death on the responsibility of some of his disciples.[21] It may also be that this statement was inserted to refute not only Cerinthus but the Alogi, who claimed that Cerinthus was the author of both the Gospel and the Apocalypse.[22] Particularly notable is the agreement of both recensions that the authority for John publishing "while still in the body" is Papias, bishop of Hierapolis, the

---

[21]This is neither the occasion nor the place to get involved in the critical arguments regarding the date and authorship of St. John's Gospel; we are concerned solely with the intrinsic value of the historical evidence taken by itself. But in *Adv. Haer.* V.30.3 Irenaeus made a statement that goes contrary to all the other early witnesses that place the Apocalypse before the Gospel of John, and in the reign of Nero, i.e., not later than 68/69; whereas Irenaeus in the above passage states that "the apocalyptic vision was seen not very long time since, but almost in our own day." The evidence for the early date is so strong that it seems best to consider that Irenaeus suffered from a momentary lapse of concentration, and that he really meant to say that John, "the one who saw the apocalyptic vision" died soon after completing his Gospel and not so many years before Irenaeus himself was born.

[22]On the Alogi, see ODCC, art. "Alogi." Epiphanius seems to be the authority regarding the Alogi's attribution of both the Gospel and the Apocalypse of John to the Docete Cerinthus (Epiphanius, *Haer.* LI.3; PG. XLI, col. 892). But the Roman priest Caius or Gaius (flor. ca. 200), whom Eusebius thought to be an orthodox believer (EH II.25.6), is also stated by Hippolytus (Comm. in Apoc.) to have attributed the Gospel of John and the Apocalypse to Cerinthus, a heretic and Millenarianist, cf. Bardy, "Cérinthe," *Rev. Bib.* (1921): 344-73; cf. also DTC, "Cérinthe" cols. 2151-55, by G. Bareille; cf. also A. Bludau, "Die ersten Gegner der Johannesschriften," *Bib. Studien* 22, Heft 1 and 2 (1925) 1-230. See also Stuart G. Hall, "Aloger," TRE 2, 1/2 (Berlin/New York, 1981-).

"dear disciple of John," and that it is to be found in his five books, that is, in his *The Exegesis of the Sayings of the Lord,* a work Eusebius dates before A.D. 110 (see ch. 4 below in loc).

In exotericis suis, id est, in extremis, quinque libris retulit, "In his exoteric, that is in the last, five books." This work of Papias is mentioned by Eusbius (EH III.39.1). No scholar has so far offered a satisfactory explanation of either "exoteric" or of "extreme." "Extremis" seems to be an attempt to elucidate "exotericis," which is the transliteration of a Greek word meaning "the one or that which is outside." But this cryptic phrase must have conveyed something important and exact to those who knew Papias's five books in their original Greek.

Dictante Iohanne recte / Iohanne sibi dictante, "John dictating rightly / John dictating to him." Both recensions unambiguously state that Papias wrote while John dicated.[23] A final suggestion: John 21 can be said to be "that which is outside" the main story of the Gospel, in fact an addition, that is, it is "exoteric," and it is also *in extremis,* that is, at the very end of the Gospel, and no doubt also very near the end of John's life. Is the compiler trying to tell us in some kind of shorthand way that Papias was called in by John in some emergency to write down at John's dictation just the last chapter of the Gospel? This would not be an unreasonable conjecture; but it remains a guess.

Verum Marcion hereticus, "but the heretic Marcion. . . . " Not only do both recensions tell the same story about Marcion's encounter with John, but they both support it with the reason that the brethren in Pontus sent him to John in the hope that he might be the one person to convince him of the error of his ways.

8. g. The Credibility of the Prologue to John

Modern critical scholarship has for the most part, however, peremptorily rejected as pure fantasy the notion that John might have dictated any part of his Gospel to Papias or that he could have met and rejected Marcion; and mainly on these grounds it has regarded these prologues as historically unreliable and these two stories as "legendary accretions." These judgments are for too sweeping.

---

[23]B. W. Bacon thinks that *recte* should be understood as part of the following statement about Marcion, because it can, grammatically speaking, with some difficulty, be taken with "expelled," i.e., that John *rightly* expelled him. But this is rather forced, and the word is naturally and with good sense to be understood as confirming that Papias made no attempt to modify what John dictated but did it correctly. See. B. W. Bacon, "The Anti-Marcionite Prologue to John," JBL 49 (1930): 43-54.

Firstly, as regards the possibility of Marcion having met John, this is quite feasible since Marcion was almost the exact contemporary of Polycarp, who had himself listened to John at his house (EH IV.14). Now Polycarp died a martyr at the age of 86 in 155/6, so that he was born circa 70. Marcion seems to have died circa 160, so that if he had been about the same age as Polycarp, he could have been born in the 70s also, which would have allowed time for him to have been in his early 20s in the last years of John, circa 98/100, and so a meeting between them is possible and cannot be ruled out as absurd.

Secondly, as regards Papias both knowing and being a friend of John in the latter's old age, there are good grounds for acknowledging it. Papias's dates are usually given as circa 60-134/8 and since he was remarkable enough to be selected to become Bishop of Hierapolis at the beginning of the second century it is very likely that John knew about him and that he himself would have been drawn to get to know the last surviving apostle. If Irenaeus was not deceived in his belief that Papias was truly the ἀκουστης of John, as we hope to show in the next chapter, then there is nothing extraordinary in his having acted as his amanuensis. Indeed some such connection is needed to explain the great fame and prestige of Papias that was only dimmed after Eusebius succeeded two centuries later in denigrating him.

However, the main historical argument against the credibility of these statements is reckoned to be the complete silence of both Irenaeus and Eusebius on both of them.[24] To answer this it will be necessary to utilize the conclusion arrived at in chapter 4 below regarding Eusebius himself and his "the presbyter John." The argument from silence can only have force if it can be shown that our authors ought to have mentioned these matters when they had the opportunity of doing so and then failed to take advantage of it.

As regards the silence of Irenaeus regarding Papias being the amanuensis of John the Evangelist, we must be careful not to transfer our own modern concern as to how the Gospels were composed back upon the Fathers. Their prime and almost exclusive interest was centered upon the authority of the author, that is, whether he was an actual eyewitness or not, and upon the particular nature of his relationship with Jesus, and, where the author was not an Apostle, upon the nature of his relationship with a particular Apostle, as in the case of Mark with Peter. Christians wanted to be sure that the Evangelists were actually disciples of Jesus and that they had seen

---

[24]See R. G. Heard (JTS [1956]: 16) who asserts that "the Prologue of John dates from 5th to 6th century, and its material is of no historical value."

and heard with their own eyes and ears the words and deeds of Jesus. And if they were not eyewitnesses, as in the case of Luke and Mark, they wanted to be sure that their writings had been approved by an Apostle.[25] The actual mechanics of transmission, by comparison, did not really matter; for the use of shorthand writers and amanuenses was commonplace and their presence could normally be assumed whenever important speeches were to be made. However, the most effective way of refuting the assertion that Cerinthus had composed the Gospel of John was the compiler's ability to quote Papias's own statement in his five books that he himself had acted as amanuensis to the Beloved Disciple. But Irenaeus, who must have known this fact (as he had read the five books), had no need to recall it since Marcion never denied John's authorship so far as we know.

And now for the silence of Eusebius. The first part of the answer is that the part played by Papias was a purely mechanical one (and if my surmise is correct the dictation may only have concerned the last chapter); he was simply the ''pen'' of John and no more. But in the case of Eusebius there was a real reason for his keeping silence in any event both because of his animosity towards Papias on the one hand and, on the other, of his theory that Papias did not know John, but only ''the presbyter John.'' For if Eusebius once allowed Papias to know John the Apostle, then he had no way of avoiding the conclusion that Irenaeus was right in attributing the Apocalypse to the Apostle, and, by doing so, he would be destroying his pet theory that the Apocalypse was not an inspired book and therefore not in the canon of Scripture. For further proof that in this instance Eusebius (normally an honest scholar) was disingeneous in his treatment of Papias, the reader is referred to the appropriate section of the following chapter. In this case the argument from silence has no value whatever.

8. h. An Evaluation of the A.-M. Gospel Prologues

It must be recognized that J. Regul seems to have proved that Dom de Bruyne was mistaken in positing a second-century Catholic anti-Marcionite edition of the Gospels with these prologues; there was none in fact. De Bruyne may also well be mistaken in attributing the ten Pauline prologues accepted into the Vulgate as in origin Marcionite documents.[26] Moreover

---

[25]This is the measured judgment of E. Massaux, in his final summing up at the conclusion of his study, *Influence de l'évangile de saint Matthieu*, 550ff.

[26]Dom D. de Bruyne had already earlier put forward the theory that the Latin Prologues to the Pauline Epistles were of Marcionite origin, a theory that was basically rejected by J.-M. Lagrange; cf. de Bruyne, ''Prologues bibliques d'origine marcionite,'' *Rev. Ben.* (1907): 1-16, which was answered by Lagrange in ''Les Prologues prétendus marcionites,'' *Rev. Bib.* 35 (1925): 161-73.

there seems now to be general agreement that (1) the Latin texts of the prologues to Mark and to John were originally composed in Greek as well as the prologue to Luke (though Regul seems to be alone in thinking that the text of the Greek prologue is not original but derived from a Latin translation of the original); (2) the Latin texts of the prologues to Mark and John were translated from the Greek during the third century in Africa; (3) Regul is correct in holding that it cannot be shown that the three prologues all stem from the same hand; so that each must be evaluated separately and on its own merits;[27] (4) Regul is also correct in holding that the Monarchian prologues are a later expansion of these three prologues and are Priscillianist in origin and date from the latter part of the fourth century,[28] though this makes it certain that our Prologues were already regarded as ancient and authoritative at that time. Hence the original Greek texts must go back at least to the beginning of the third century; (5) there is no clear evidence that either Marcion or any of his immediate followers wrote prologues either for the ten epistles of Paul which he acknowledged, or for his mutilated version of Luke. But though so far as we know he did not deny the apostolic authorships, his open contempt for the apostles as misguided men who had failed to understand the message of Jesus makes it all the more probable that individual orthodox bishops and patrons of editions of the Gospels would very early have hit on the device of having some short notice of authenticity prefaced to new copies of the Gospels. Thus the mere fact of stressing apostolic authorship would make them anti-Marcionite in character; for they fully support the common teaching on Gospel authorship that we find in Justin, Irenaeus, Clement of Alexandria, Tertullian, and Origen, and they differ only by adding some further details that are consonant with the foregoing. The unanimity and harmony of all the evidence so far available (including the support of the Gnostics), and the lack of all contrary evidence of value in what was a sensitive area of Christian belief, are strong indications that these prologues are in the authentic tradition. Our inquiry also suggests that the lack of documentary, that is, written, confirmation of apostolic authorship before Irenaeus is not in itself a good argument for questioning the reliability of the tradition.

---

[27]Cf. Regul, *Die Antimarcion. Ev.*, 266.

[28]Chapman had already come to this same conclusion in his *Notes on the Early History of the Vulgate Gospels* (Oxford, 1908) 217-88.

4

Eusebius and the Gospel Tradition

1. The Scholar and his *Ecclesiastical History*

The testimony of Eusebius Pamphili (ca. 260-340), bishop of Caesarea in Palestine and the author of the *Ecclesiastical History,* is central to the whole discussion of the sequential order, origin, and relationships between the Gospels, in the sense that he sums up in a magisterial manner the evidence available in his day, including much that has since perished. But it has been necessary in the earlier chapters to detail the evidence of those who went before him from the beginning in order now to be in a position to judge the value of his work by comparing his witness with theirs.

There is universal agreement that Eusebius was the greatest scholar of his age, the period when the church first gained her political and cultural freedom to expand according to her inner dynamism; and that he had at his disposal the best library facilities and the most complete documentation of early Christian literature ever assembled. For at Caesarea, where he spent most of his life, he had become the literary heir of his teacher and friend, the martyr Pamphilus, who had inherited the library of Origen and developed it into a comprehensive collection of the earliest literature of the Christian church; while through the continuing influence of Origen (d. 253), who had spent the last twenty years of his life in Caesarea, and through his inheritance of the writings and correspondence of St. Dionysius of Alexandria (d. 264), he was in command of the unrivalled scholarly traditions of the ancient church of Alexandria. And the city of Alexandria itself, where the Septuagint translation of the Old Testament had been made and which had been graced by the scholarship of Philo, was the place where Christian scholarship first began, and which (according to Eusebius EH II.16.24 and to the Old Latin Prologue to the Gospel of Mark) had had St. Mark himself as its first bishop.

Eusebius was a man of many parts: an assiduous courtier of the Emperor, who played a part in the Council of Nicaea (325); a theologian, whose outlook was somewhat tainted with Arianism; but at the same time a great biblical critic to whom his martyr friend Pamphilus had imparted his own devotion to the Bible and above all to the New Testament, in the formation of the canon of which he was keen to play his part. He put all succeeding generations of Christians in his debt by his work in producing critical texts and new editions of the Scriptures based on Origen's Hexapla (see Quasten, *Patrology,* 2:146). He was an ambitious man, and it was his own realization that he was in this unique and powerful position and so able to sum up all that had gone before him since the church began that motivated him, at the dawn of the new era of freedom for the church under Constantine, to carry out between 303 and 325 his grand design for a history of the church from its origins to his own time, the first work of its kind. It was also part of his plan to show the Empire of Constantine as the earthly counterpart and protector of God's Holy Church. However, apart from the successions of the Roman pontiffs and the martyrs of Gaul, he pays no attention whatever to the church in Western Europe; his interest is in its development in the East.

The Ecclesiastical History consists of ten books, of which the first seven recount the history of the church from the beginning down to A.D. 303, while the last three deal with some events of Eusebius's own lifetime down to the events leading up to the Council of Nicaea. In Book I he deals with the time of Jesus; in Book II with the apostles down to the destruction of Jerusalem, A.D. 30/33-67; in Book III with the remaining apostles and with the "apostolic men" who committed the Tradition to writing, A.D. 67-108; Book IV deals with the period A.D. 109-177; Book V with the period A.D. 177-200; Book VI with the period A.D. 200-260; and Book VII with the period A.D. 260-303; and Books VIII-X review the situation of the church in the period A.D. 303-325, and especially extol the glorious freedom given it by Constantine.

Each of these books fills up a normal commercial roll, which goes to show incidentally that as late as A.D. 325 the roll and not the codex was still a common vehicle of book publication for everything except the Bible.[1]

---

[1]Cf. E. G. Turner, *Greek Papyri: An Introduction* (Oxford: Clarendon, 1980) 11; B. M. Metzger, *The Text of the New Testament* (Oxford: Clarendon, ²1973) 5-8. Two critical editions of the *Ecclesiastical History* have been used: H. J. Lawlor and J. E. L. Oulton, *Eusebius, Bishop of Caesarea, Ecclesiastical History and Martyrs of Palestine,* vol. 1: translation; vol. 2: introduction, notes, and index (London: S.P.C.K., 1927-1928; reprinted 1954); B. G. Bardy, *Eusèbe de Césarée, Histoire Ecclésiastique,* Sources chrétiennes, 4 vols. (19bis, 41, 55, 73) (Paris, 1952-1960). Reference also will be made to the scholarly Penguin edition trans. and ed. by G. A. Williamson (1965, and reprinted 1967); see also Quasten, *Patrology* 3 (1963): 311-13 for an account of Eusebius's Chronicle; see also Robert M. Grant, *Eusebius as Church Historian* (Oxford: Clarendon, 1980) esp. 22-

The way in which the *Ecclesiastical History* is set out in modern printed editions tends to mask the fact that Eusebius is following a strictly chronological order throughout. Earlier in his career, about 303, he had published his *Chronici Canones,* which he was to use in an amended form in the present work. He also made use of the chronological table that Clement of Alexandria had set in the first volume of his *Stromata* (EH VI.6) and also Africanus's *Dictionary of Dates* (EH VI.31). He declares himself especially interested in providing the following sets of information: (a) the succession of bishops from the time of the Holy Apostles down to his own day; but on account of the wealth of material available, and in order to simplify his task and to reduce it to manageable proportions, he actually selected only the four apostolic sees nearest to him, namely, Rome, Alexandria, Jerusalem, and Antioch, with the dates of the corresponding Roman emperors (EH I.1.1). (b) the accounts of those pastors and evangelists, who being in the first succession from the Apostles, have preserved in writing the apostolic teachings (EH III.37.4). Out of a vast number of these latter he selected three, namely Clement of Alexandria, Ignatius of Antioch, and Papias Bishop of Hierapolis, as the most important. (c) Information about the "accepted" books, the "disputed" books, and the "rejected" books of the New Testament.

The question of Eusebius's personal views on the origins and relationships among the Gospels and the other Books of the New Testament is very important for the purposes of this study. His references to them are dispersed throughout the first seven books. For he set down and collated what he believed to be the absolutely sure traditions of the ancient authorities in their chronological sequence. And so in order to find out his views on each book—which ones he regarded as to be "accepted," which he held to be still "disputed," and which to be "rejected"—it is necessary for us to correlate a considerable number of passages throughout the work, namely, II.15-16; III.3; III.24-25; III.39; 15-16; V.8.1-5; VI.14.5-7; VI.25.10; VII.25. It will be best to take these texts in the following order: that on the four Gospels, III.24-25; on Irenaeus, V.8.1-5; on Clement Alexandria, II.15-16.1; VI.14.5-7; on Origen, VI.25.3-6; on Papias, III.39.1-17. The investigation will conclude with two special studies of questions that crop up during its course.

28; also A. A. Mosshammer, *The Chronology of Eusebius and Greek Chronographic Tradition* (Lewisburg PA: Bucknell University Press, 1979) reviewed by Averil Cameron, Heythrop Journal 22/4 (October 1981): 448-49; E. des Places, *Eusèbe de Césarée commentateur* (Paris, 1982). See also J. Kürzinger's excellent monograph cited above; also Timothy D. Barnes, *Constantine and Eusebius* (Cambridge MA: Harvard University Press, 1981).

As regards Eusebius's chronological scheme, we need only note that it is by far the most reliable that we have, since he made it his business to work out the chronology of early church history in a series of scholarly studies of a comprehensive character. His chronology is therefore to be accepted except where it can be proved to be either wrong or doubtful, which is seldom.[2]

2. Eusebius on the Four Gospels, EH III.24-25

Following out his chronological method, Eusebius at III.3 provides the reader with information about the Letters of Paul and Peter immediately after recording their martyrdoms; and so, having brought his chronological survey down to the death of St. John the Apostle about the year 100, he pauses at III.24-25 in order to recapitulate and to confirm what he has to tell us about the Gospels, that is, the written teaching about Jesus. As he has been relating stories about John the Apostle he first mentions the Fourth Gospel as John's (III.24.1), but goes on to remind the reader that the Apostles regarded the matter of actually writing down their preaching of the Word as a secondary affair, and that they ultimately did it only as a confirmation of their oral preaching. He then records that only two Apostles, Matthew and John, "left records (ὑπομνήματα) of the Lord's deeds." (Ὑπομνήματα are authentic records made to assist memory, and/or authentic records based on personal memory [compare Liddell and Scott, in loc.].) He then goes on to explain the purpose of Matthew. And then, passing over Mark and Luke, he informs us that eventually copies of all three came into the hands of John, who wrote to confirm their accuracy and also to record the earlier part of the ministry of Jesus which the Synoptics had omitted. He then goes on to say that as he has already explained the origin of Mark (II.15), he is able to pass straight on to the origin of the Gospel of Luke, who was able to "furnish in his own Gospel an authentic account of the events of which he had learned the undoubted truth, thanks to his association and intercourse with Paul and his conversations with the other Apostles" (III.24.15). He concludes his exposition by mentioning other writings attributed to John, and the doubts some had about 2 John and 3 John and the Apocalypse, doubts he himself shared.

3. Eusebius on Irenaeus, EH V.8.1-5

It is necessary to review here again (but from another standpoint) the witness of Irenaeus because Eusebius alone has preserved for us in this passage the original Greek text of *Adv. Haer.* III.1.1, the full impact of

---

[2]For further discussion of his chronology see Barnes, *Constantine and Eusebius,* 120; also J. B. Orchard, "Some Guidelines for the Interpretation of Eusebius's Hist. Eccl. 3.34-39," in *The New Testament Age: Essays in Honor of Bo Reicke* (Macon GA: Mercer University Press, 1984) 2:393-404.

which the Latin translation failed to convey. The context of the statement of Irenaeus that we are now about to quote is this. He has already composed two books against the Gnostics, in the first of which he sets down their perverse doctrines in order to refute them in the second book. In this third book he now proceeds to set forth the true Christian doctrine of the gospel which has come down to him by direct personal succession from the Twelve Apostles, who at the first Pentecost had been filled with the Holy Spirit and received the mandate to go forth and preach the gospel. He continues to confirm his competence to hand on the tradition by mentioning the origin and authenticity of the Four Gospels which contain the true apostolic teaching, from which he is going to draw out the whole Christian economy of salvation in Christ. And so in his second chapter he makes it clear that this authentic teaching tradition of the Twelve has come to him by being handed down by word of mouth by means of "the successions of presbyters in the Churches," first of all in the Church of Rome, quoting by name the full list of the successors of St. Peter down to Eleutherius, the contemporary bishop of Rome. For further proof of the authenticity of his teaching he mentions Bishop Polycarp of Smyrna, whom he knew personally and who had personally learned from the Apostle John. He also mentions the concurrent witness of the church of Ephesus, dwelt in by John himself, who lived to see the reign of Trajan (compare EH IV.14).

We should therefore perceive Irenaeus's references to the Evangelists to be simply a brief summary of what was common knowledge to all Christians, because he feels entitled to omit many other proofs that he could have alleged if it had been necessary to do so (*Adv. Haer.*, III.4.1). (Our text is that of G. Bardy, *Sources Chrétiennes*, in loc.)

EH V.8.1-5

§1. Ἐπεὶ δὲ ἀρχόμενοι τῆς πραγματείας ὑπόσχεσιν πεποιήμεθα παραθήσεσθαι κατὰ καιρὸν εἰπόντες τὰς τῶν ἀρχαίων ἐκκλησιαστικῶν πρεσβυτέρων τε καὶ συγγραφέων φωνὰς ἐν αἷς τὰς περὶ τῶν ἐνδιαθήκων γραφῶν εἰς αὐτοὺς κατελθούσας παραδόσεις γραφῇ παραδεδώκασιν, τούτων δὲ καὶ ὁ Εἰρηναῖος ἦν, φέρε, καὶ τὰς αὐτοῦ παραθώμεθα λέξεις,

§1. Since at the beginning of this undertaking we made a promise to relate at the right time [cf. III.3.3] the utterances of the "archaic" church's elders and writers, in which they have handed on in written form the traditions that had come down to them about the testamentary writings, and of whom Irenaeus also was one, so now we shall quote his remarks.

§2. καὶ πρώτας γε τὰς περὶ τῶν ἱερῶν εὐαγγελίων οὕτως ἐχούσας·
ὁ μὲν δὴ Ματθαῖος ἐν τοῖς Ἑβραίοις τῇ ἰδίᾳ αὐτῶν διαλέκτῳ καὶ γραφὴν ἐξήνεγκεν εὐαγγελίου, τοῦ Πέτρου καὶ τοῦ Παύλου ἐν Ῥώμῃ εὐαγγελιζομένων καὶ θεμελιούντων τὴν ἐκκλησίαν.

§2. And firstly these about the holy gospels.
Now Matthew brought out a written gospel among the Jews in their own dialect, while Peter and Paul were evangelizing in Rome and founding the church.

§3. μετὰ δὲ τὴν τούτων ἔξοδον Μάρκος, ὁ μαθητὴς καὶ ἑρμηνευτὴς Πέτρου, καὶ αὐτὸς τὰ ὑπὸ Πέτρου κηρυσσόμενα ἐγγράφως ἡμῖν παραδέδωκεν.

§3. And after their demise Mark, the disciple and recorder of Peter, he too has handed on to us in writing what Peter had preached.

καὶ Λουκᾶς δέ, ὁ ἀκόλουθος Παύλου, τὸ ὑπ' ἐκείνου κηρυσσόμενον εὐαγγέλιον ἐν βίβλῳ κατέθετο.

And Luke too, Paul's follower, set down in a book the gospel preached by him.

§4. ἔπειτα Ἰωάννης, ὁ μαθητὴς τοῦ Κυρίου, ὁ καὶ ἐπὶ τὸ στῆθος αὐτοῦ ἀναπεσών, καὶ αὐτὸς ἐξέδωκεν τὸ εὐαγγέλιον, ἐν Ἐφέσῳ τῆς Ἀσίας διατρίβων.

Then John, the disciple of the Lord, he who also reclined on his bosom, he too published the gospel, while he was living in Asia at Ephesus.

§5. ταῦτα μὲν οὖν ἐν τρίτῳ τῆς εἰρημένης ὑποθέσεως προδηλωθέντι εἴρηται, . . .

§5. These things are the ones he has related in the third book of the aforesaid work, . . .

The following comments on this text are in order at this point:

Kata kairon, "at the right time." This promise was made by Eusebius at EH III.3.3; by "the right time" he really means at the appropriate chronological moment in his History.

Τὰς τῶν ἀρχαίων ἐκκλησιαστικῶν πρεσβυτέρων, "[the utterances] of the 'archaic' church elders." Ἀρχαίων is used in a technical sense of those who have a real link with the origins of the Faith; Eusebius regards Irenaeus as qualifying for this epithet as a result of his connection with Polycarp, who in his turn knew St. John.

Ἐν τοῖς Ἑβραίοις τῇ ἰδία αὐτῶν διαλέκτῳ, "among the Jews in their own dialect." The common view of the critics is that this phrase shows that Irenaeus knew Papias's five books. However, as we shall see presently, Irenaeus has changed Papias's "in a Jewish dialect" (EH III.39.16) into "among the Jews in their own dialect," thus missing Papias's point, which referred to Matthew's style, and not to the language in which he wrote (see excursus 3).

Τοῦ Πέτρου καὶ τοῦ Παύλου ἐν Ῥώμῃ εὐαγγελιζομένων καὶ θεμελιούντων τὴν ἐκκλησίαν, "while Peter and Paul were evangelizing and founding the Church at Rome." Thus, for Irenaeus Matthew is the first written Gospel, Peter and Paul are the joint founders of the church of Rome (*Adv. Haer.* III.3), and their Gospels (Mark and Luke) are subsequent to Matthew's.

Μετὰ δὲ τὴν τούτων ἔξοδον, "and after their demise." In modern times nearly all critics, under the influence of the opinion that all the Gospels were written after the death of Peter and Paul, have interpreted this phrase as proving that Irenaeus thought that Mark and Luke wrote after the death of Peter and Paul. But it was pointed out by Chapman some seventy years ago and recently again by Gamba,[3] that this is a serious misunderstanding of Irenaeus, a misunderstanding fostered by the Latin rendering of παραδέδωκεν as *tradidit,* thus failing to do justice to the force of the Greek perfect tense, which implies that the Gospels of Mark and Luke have handed on the traditions taught by Peter and Paul when they were still alive.

In other words, Irenaeus is not making any reference to the date of the composition of Mark and Luke; he is simply concerned with pointing out that just as the traditions of Matthew and John continue to live on in their respective Gospels, so do those of Peter and Paul in the Gospels of Mark and Luke. That is to say, as long as Peter and Paul lived they preached their own Gospels personally by word of mouth, but after their demise their preaching also continued in the Gospels in which their followers had already recorded their teaching. Eusebius himself may be claimed in support of this view, for in section 1 he says he is going to show how the elders of the church have *in their turn* handed on the traditions, following the examples of the Apostles.

Καὶ Λουκᾶς . . . κατα . . . κατέθετο, "Luke . . . set down." The Greek aorist tense suggests a less intimate connection between Paul and the Gospel of Luke than that between Peter and the Gospel of Mark.

Ἔπειτα Ἰωάννης . . . καὶ αὐτὸς ἐξέδωκεν τὸ εὐαγγέλιον, "then John . . . he too published the Gospel." The witness of Irenaeus is categorical that the Apostle John published his own Gospel while he was living in Ephesus and confirms the statements we found in the Old Latin Prologue to John.

In conclusion, this text of Irenaeus, recorded by Eusebius in its original Greek, should no longer be claimed in support of the conjecture that both Mark and Luke were composed after the death of Peter and Paul, for it offers no evidence for this claim. This means that there is no contradiction or discrepancy between the testimony of Irenaeus and the large amount of witness in favour of Mark and Luke having both been written and published during the lifetime of Peter and Paul. Consequently the evidence of Irenaeus is in harmony with the rest.

4. Eusebius on Clement of Alexandria, EH II.15-16.1; VI.14.5-7

In chapter 3, section 5 above, the background and authority of Clement were fully explained. The special information for which Eusebius turns to Clement is to be found in EH VI.14 where he quotes a passage from the

---

[3]J. Chapman, "St. Irenaeus and the Dates of the Gospel," JTS 6 (1904-1905): 563-69; G. G. Gamba, "La Testimonianza di S. Ireneo in Adv. Haer. III, e la Data di Composizione dei Quattro Vangeli Canonici," Salesianum 39 (1977): 545-85.

Outlines ('Υποτυπωσεις) describing Peter's part in the composition of Mark's Gospel, although he has already used this text in a dramatic account of the formation of the same Gospel in EH II.15, a text which also refers to EH III.39.[4] These three texts are set side by side below together with the Latin Anti-Marcionite Prologue to Mark and the passage from Clement's *Adumbrationes in Ep. Can. in 1 Peter 5:13* in order to demonstrate the harmony existing between all five items. It will be more effective to first take VI.14 because it will lead us back to II.15.

The meaning of VI.14 appears to be quite clear, namely, that Matthew and Luke came into existence before Mark; but, as support for the 2GH has grown there have been renewed attempts to understand it differently (see Orchard's Response to Merkel, in the Jerusalem Gospel Symposium [1984] papers).[5] Some notes seem called for.

Παράδοσιν τῶν ἀνέκαθεν πρεσβυτέρων, "the tradition of the early time," that is, those of the subapostolic age.

Περὶ τῆς τάξεως τῶν εὐαγγελίων, "regarding the order of the Gospels." Τάξις, has different shades of meaning according to the context. Since it is connected with the verb προγράφω which comes later in the second half of the sentence, the prefix προ- confirms that *taxis* must here refer to chronological order.

Τὰ περιέχοντα τὰς γενεαλογίας, "those having the genealogies," that is, Matthew and Luke only.

Προγεγράφθαι, "to have been written beforehand," that is, in point of time.

Τὸ δὲ κατὰ Μάρκον ταύτην, ἐσχηκέναι τὴν οἰκονομίαν, "but that according to Mark to have had this formation." The δε ("but") is normally adversative, and Eusebius himself takes it as such; for, after extract-

---

[4]That there was a need in the second century to stress that Mark's Gospel was composed with Peter's cooperation during his lifetime but not published officially until after his death is strongly suggested by the amplification of this point in the longer text of the Old Latin prologue to Mark when compared with the shorter.

[5]If this text is authentic and its normal interpretation is allowed to stand, then it of course destroys the last vestige of external support for the priority of Mark as well as providing strong external support for the 2GH. It is therefore not at all surprising that at the Jerusalem Gospel Symposium (1984) no less than seven alternative interpretations of it were tabled as having been at one time or another proposed in order to make it compatible with Markan priority. All of them however founder on the fact that Eusebius himself substantially accepts it as authentic, for in EH II.15 he quotes it in support of his statement that Mark in Rome recorded exactly what he had heard Peter relate; and though in quoting it he does not actually mention the detail that we are here most interested in, namely, that Mark was composed after Matthew and Luke, this is because his purpose was simply to tell his readers that the Gospel of Mark was the verbatim record of Peter's discourses.

Papias's Presbyter on Mark (EH III.39.15)

15. Καὶ τοῦθ' ὁ πρεσβύτερος ἔλεγεν· Μάρκος μὲν ἑρμηνευτὴς Πέτρου γενόμενος, ὅσα ἐμνημόνευσεν ἀκριβῶς ἔγραψεν οὐ μέντοι τάξει τὰ ὑπὸ τοῦ Κυρίου ἢ λεχθέντα ἢ πραχθέντα. οὔτε γὰρ ἤκουσεν τοῦ Κυρίου οὔτε παρηκολούθησεν αὐτῷ, ὕστερον δὲ, ὡς ἔφην, Πέτρῳ· ὃς πρὸς τὰς χρείας ἐποιεῖτο τὰς διδασκαλίας, ἀλλ' οὐχ ὥσπερ σύνταξιν τῶν κυριακῶν ποιούμενος λογίων, ὥστε οὐδὲν ἥμαρτεν Μάρκος οὕτως ἔνια γράψας ὡς ἀπεμνημόνευσεν. ἑνὸς γὰρ ἐποιήσατο πρόνοιαν, τοῦ μηδὲν ὧν ἤκουσεν παραλιπεῖν ἢ ψεύσασθαί τι ἐν αὐτοῖς.

16. ταῦτα μὲν οὖν ἱστόρηται τῷ Παπίᾳ περὶ Μάρκου.

From Clem. Alex.'s Outlines as quoted by Eusebius (EH VI.14.5-7)

5. αὖθις δ' ἐν τοῖς αὐτοῖς ὁ Κλήμης βιβλίοις περὶ τῆς τάξεως τῶν εὐαγγελίων παράδοσιν τῶν ἀνέκαθεν πρεσβυτέρων τέθειται, τοῦτον ἔχουσαν τὸν τρόπον προγεγράφθαι ἔλεγεν τῶν εὐαγγελίων τὰ περιέχοντα τὰς γενεαλογίας,

6. τὸ δὲ κατὰ Μάρκον ταύτην ἐσχηκέναι τὴν οἰκονομίαν· τοῦ Πέτρου δημοσίᾳ ἐν Ῥώμῃ κηρύξαντος τὸν λόγον καὶ πνεύματι τὸ εὐαγγέλιον ἐξειπόντος, τοὺς παρόντας, πολλοὺς ὄντας, παρακαλέσαι τὸν Μάρκον, ὡς ἂν ἀκολουθήσαντα αὐτῷ πόρρωθεν καὶ μεμνημένον τῶν λεχθέντων, ἀναγράψαι τὰ εἰρημένα, ποιήσαντα δὲ τὸ εὐαγγέλιον μεταδοῦναι τοῖς δεομένοις αὐτοῦ.

7. ὅπερ ἐπιγνόντα τὸν Πέτρον προτρεπτικῶς μήτε κωλῦσαι μήτε προτρέψασθαι.

Eusebius (EH II.15.1-16.1)

1. οὕτω δὴ οὖν ἐπιδημήσαντος αὐτοῖς τοῦ θείου λόγου, ἡ μὲν τοῦ Σίμωνος ἀπέσβη καὶ παραχρῆμα σὺν καὶ τῷ ἀνδρὶ κατελέλυτο δύναμις.

Τοσοῦτον δ' ἐπέλαμψεν ταῖς τῶν ἀκροατῶν τοῦ Πέτρου διανοίαις εὐσεβείας φέγγος, ὡς μὴ τῇ εἰς ἅπαξ ἱκανῶς ἔχειν ἀρκεῖσθαι ἀκοῇ μηδὲ τῇ ἀγράφῳ τοῦ θείου κηρύγματος διδασκαλίᾳ. παρακλήσεσιν δὲ παντοίαις Μάρκον, οὗ τὸ εὐαγγέλιον φέρεται ἀκόλουθον ὄντα Πέτρου, λιπαρῆσαι, ὡς ἂν καὶ διὰ γραφῆς ὑπόμνημα τῆς διὰ λόγου παραδοθείσης αὐτοῖς καταλείποιεν διδασκαλίας, μὴ πρότερόν τε ἀνεῖναι ἢ κατεργάσασθαι τὸν ἄνδρα, καὶ ταύτῃ αἰτίους γενέσθαι τῆς τοῦ λεγομένου κατὰ Μάρκον εὐαγγελίου γραφῆς.

2. γνόντα δὲ τὸ πραχθέν φασι τὸν ἀπόστολον ἀποκαλύψαντος αὐτῷ τοῦ πνεύματος ἡσθῆναι τῇ τῶν ἀνδρῶν προθυμίᾳ κυρῶσαί τε τὴν γραφὴν εἰς ἔντευξιν ταῖς ἐκκλησίαις.

Κλήμης ἐν ἕκτῳ τῶν Ὑποτυπώσεων παρατέθειται τὴν ἱστορίαν, συνεπιμαρτυρεῖ δὲ αὐτῷ καὶ ὁ Ἱεραπολίτης ἐπίσκοπος ὀνόματι Παπίας, τοῦ δὲ Μάρκου μνημονεύειν τὸν Πέτρον ἐν τῇ προτέρᾳ ἐπιστολῇ, ἣν καὶ συντάξαι φασὶν ἐπ' αὐτῆς Ῥώμης, σημαίνειν τε τοῦτ' αὐτόν, τὴν πόλιν τροπικώτερον Βαβυλῶνα προσειπόντα διὰ τούτων· ἀσπάζεται ὑμᾶς ἐν Βαβυλῶνι συνεκλεκτὴ καὶ Μάρκος ὁ υἱός μου.

16.1. τοῦτον δὲ Μάρκον πρῶτον φασιν ἐπὶ τῆς Αἰγύπτου στειλάμενον, τὸ εὐαγγέλιον, ὃ δὴ καὶ συνεγράψατο, κηρῦξαι, ἐκκλησίας τε πρῶτον ἐπ' αὐτῆς Ἀλεξανδρείας συστήσασθαι.

Clem. Alex., Adumbr. in Ep. can. in 1 Pet 5:13

Marcus Petri sectator praedicante Petro evangelium palam Romae coram quibusdam Caesareanis equitibus et multa Christi testimonia proferente, petitus ab eis, ut possent quae dicebantur memoriae commendare, scripsit ex his quae a Petro dicta sunt evangelium quod secundum Marcum vocitatur; sicut Lucas quoque Actus Apostolorum stilo exsecutus agnoscitur et Pauli ad Hebraeos interpretatus epistolam.

[The Greek text of the above has been lost. There is a note in Migne, Patr. Graeca, IX. 729-30 suggesting that the above Latin text was translated by Cassiodorus from a part of Clement's *Outlines* that is no longer extant.]

Anti-Marcionite Prologue to Mark Shorter Text

. . . Marcus adseruit, qui colobodactylus est nominatus, ideo quod ad ceteram corporis proceritatem digitos minores habuisset. Iste interpres fuit Petri. Post excessionem ipsius Petri descripsit idem hoc in partibus Italiae evangelium.

Longer Text

. . . Marcus adseruit, qui colobodactylus est nominatus, ideo quod ad ceteram corporis proceritatem digitos minores habuisset. Hic discipulus et interpres fuit Petri, quem secutus sicut ipsum audierat referentem. Rogatus Romae a fratribus hoc breve evangelium in Italiae partibus scripsit. Quod cum Petrus audisset probavit ecclesiaeque legendum sua auctoritate firmavit. Verum post discessum Petri adsumpto hoc evangelio quod ipse confecerat perrexit Aegyptum, et primus Alexandriae episcopus ordinatus, Christum adnuntians constituit illic ecclesiam, tantae doctrinae et vitae continentiae fuit ut omnes sectatores Christi ad suum cogeret imitari exemplum.

Greek Anti-Marcionite Prologue to Luke

Οὗτος [Λουκᾶς]. . . . προϋπαρχόντων ἤδη εὐαγγελίων, τοῦ μὲν κατὰ Ματθαῖον ἐν τῇ Ἰουδαίᾳ ἀναγραφέντος, τοῦ δὲ κατὰ Μάρκον ἐν τῇ Ἰταλίᾳ. . . .

Anti-Marcionite Prologue to Mark Shorter Text

. . . Mark asserted, who was called "Stubfinger" because he had short fingers in relation to the size of his body. He had been the recorder of Peter. After the demise of the above Peter he himself published this gospel in the land of Italy.

Longer Text

. . . Mark who was also called "Stubfinger" because he had short fingers in relation to the size of his body.

He had been the disciple and recorder of Peter, whom he followed, just as he had heard him relating. Having been asked by the brethren in Rome he wrote this short gospel in the region of Italy. When Peter heard about it, he approved and authorized it to be read to the church with [his own] authority.

But after the demise of Peter, taking this gospel that he had composed, he journeyed to Egypt and being ordained the first bishop of Alexandria he founded a church there, preaching Christ.

He was a man of such great learning and austerity of life that he induced all the followers of Christ to follow his example.

Greek Anti-Marcionite Prologue to Luke

This [Luke]. . . . There were already gospels in existence, that according to Matthew, written down in Judea, and that according to Mark in Italy. . . .

Clem. Alex., Adumbr. in Ep. can. in 1 Pet 5:13

Mark, the follower of Peter, while Peter was publicly preaching the gospel at Rome before some of Caesar's knights and producing many testimonies about Christ, on their asking him to let them have the opportunity of committing to memory the things that had been said, wrote the gospel which is called the Gospel of Mark from the things said by Peter—just as Luke is recognized as the pen that wrote the Acts of the Apostles and as the translator of the Letter of Paul to the Hebrews.

Eusebius (EH II.15.1-16.1)

1. So then, when the divine word made its home among them [the Romans], the power of Simon [Magus] was extinguished and straightway destroyed with the man himself. So greatly then did the brightness of true religion light up the minds of Peter's hearers that they were not satisfied to have a once-for-all hearing nor with the unwritten teaching of the divine proclamation, but with appeals of every kind begged Mark, the follower of Peter, whose gospel we have, to leave them too a memorial in writing of the teaching given them by word of mouth. Nor did they cease until they had persuaded the man, and in this way became the cause of the written gospel according to Mark.

2. And it is said that the apostle, when the fact became known to him through the revelation of the Spirit, was pleased with the eagerness of the men and approved the writing for use in the churches. Clement relates the anecdote in the sixth book of the *Outlines*, and Papias, bishop of Hierapolis, also bears witness to it and to Peter mentioning Mark in his earlier letter. Indeed they say that he composed it at Rome itself, and that he indicates this when referring figuratively to the city as Babylon in these words: "The elect [church] that is in Babylon greets you and so does my son Mark" [1 Pet 5:13].

16.1. They also say that this Mark set out for Egypt and was the first to proclaim the gospel which he had written, and was the first to set up churches in Alexandria itself.

From Clem. Alex.'s Outlines as quoted by Eusebius (EH VI.14.5-7)

5. And again in the same books [the Outlines], Clement states a tradition of the very earliest presbyters about the order of the gospels; and it has this form.

He used to say that the first written of the gospels were those having the genealogies,

6. and that the Gospel of Mark had this formation. While Peter was publicly preaching the Word in Rome and proclaiming the gospel by the the Spirit, the audience, which was numerous, begged Mark, as one who had followed him for a long time and remembered what had been said, to write down the things he had said. And he did so, handing over the Gospel to those who had asked for it.

7. And when Peter got to know about it, he exerted no pressure either to forbid it or to promote it.

Papias's Presbyter on Mark (EH III.39.15)

15. And this the Presbyter used to say: Mark, being the recorder of Peter, wrote accurately but not in [literary] order whatever he [Peter] remembered of the things either said or done by the Lord. For he had neither heard the Lord nor followed him, but later, as I said, Peter, who used to make his teachings according to the chreias, but not making [them] as a literary composition of the Lord's sayings; so that Mark did not err at all when he wrote certain things just as he [Peter] had recalled [them]. For he had but one intention, not to leave out anything he had heard, nor to falsify anything in them.

16. This is what was related by Papias about Mark.

ing this quotation from its context in Clement, he transfers the essence of it to II.15, in order to illustrate the special formation of Mark from the point of view of Peter.

Ὅπερ ἐπιγνόντα τὸν Πέτρον προτρεπτικῶς μήτε κωλῦσαι μήτε προτρέψασθαι, "and when Peter got to know about it he exerted no pressure either to forbid it or to promote it." Προτρεπτικῶς is an adverb meaning "by way of exhortation." That is to say, Peter made no personal effort either to withhold it or to encourage its circulation. This indifference on his part to a wider circulation of his teachings about Christ suggests that there must have been other gospel accounts available, or he could hardly have failed to promote such an important witness as his. But if there were already in existence one or more standard accounts, then his lack of eagerness to promote his own account is easily understandable.

Turning now to EH II.15, it is agreed that it is indebted both to VI.14 and to III.39, and it is also true that Eusebius somewhat dramatizes the situation. It was the power of Peter's eloquence in defeating Simon Magus and the power of his teaching of the divine proclamation that leads Eusebius on to describing what he had learned from Clement to be the written record of Peter's preaching. But he does not deviate in any essential from the story as told by Clement, even when he says that it was the insistence of the audience that was the cause of Mark being written down. In the next section (2) Eusebius borrows the exact words of the Anti-Marcionite prologue to Mark, though with two minor embellishments, namely, that Peter learned of Mark's action "through the revelation of the Spirit" and that he "was pleased with the eagerness of the men." Both are fully in line with the situation as Clement presented it; while the positive statement that Peter "authorized" it for use in the churches can be truthfully inferred from hindsight, and from Clement's final remark that Peter "exerted no pressure either to forbid it or to promote it," that is, he was quite content to trust Mark not to have misrepresented what he had said, and so to allow him to give it out to all who asked for it.

Therefore when Eusebius comes to deal with the origins of the Gospels in his *locus classicus* (EH III.24-25), he says that he has already explained about the composition of Mark and simply refers the reader back to II.15 where his own conclusions about its origins are to be found.

We may synthesize the statements by Eusebius about the origins of Mark in the following way.

1. Eusebius records here the composition of the Gospel of Mark from the point of view of Peter himself, stressing the authenticity of his witness to the tradition about Jesus; whereas Clement of Alexandria is quoted by him at VI.14 from the point of view of a question about the actual chronological order of the Gospels.

2. An interesting point that emerges from this comparison is that Eusebius himself took over the longer text of the Old Latin Prologue to Mark pretty well verbally, while his use of the verb φασι ("they say") in section 2 seems to imply an anonymous authority such as this Prologue.

3. What Eusebius has to say about the Gospels in III.39 will be discussed in the succeeding sections, but we can already see that it looks like being in full conformity with II.15, though it will throw important new light on the partnership of Peter and Mark. Thus we have learned from Clement of Alexandria some important facts regarding the complex situation that led to the publication of Mark, namely, the following:

   a. The Gospel of Mark is the authentic record of some public discourses of Peter given (it is said) in Rome before an enthusiastic audience.

   b. Mark was persuaded by the persistence of some members of this audience to make available to them a transcript of what Peter had said.

   c. Peter had had no previous intention of writing a book of his proclamation of the gospel, nor had Mark.

   d. Peter, however, did not oppose its private circulation when he learned what Mark had done.

   e. All this took place while Peter was alive and active.

   f. Peter's tacit acquiescence was soon regarded by the churches as tantamount to approval of the work.

   g. Eusebius specifically notes here that Papias in his five books asserted that the "Mark" of 1 Peter 5:13 is our Evangelist.

5. Eusebius on Origen, EH VI.25.3b-6

We come next to the witness of Origen in a text that survives in the quotation that Eusebius has inserted into his history at this place from Origen's Commentary on Matthew, composed at Caesarea after 244.

3. . . . ἐν δὲ τῷ πρώτῳ τῶν εἰς τὸ κατὰ Ματθαῖον, τὸν ἐκκλησιαστικὸν φυλάττων κανόνα, μόνα τέσσαρα εἰδέναι εὐαγγέλια μαρτύρεται, ὧδέ πως γράφων:

4. ὡς ἐν παραδόσει μαθὼν περὶ τῶν τεσσάρων εὐαγγελίων, ἃ καὶ μόνα ἀναντίρρητά ἐστιν ἐν τῷ ὑπὸ τὸν οὐρανὸν ἐκκλησίᾳ τοῦ θεοῦ, ὅτι πρῶτον μὲν γέγραπται τὸ κατὰ τόν ποτε τελώνην, ὕστερον δὲ ἀπόστολον Ἰησοῦ Χριστοῦ Ματθαῖον, ἐκδεδωκότα αὐτὸ τοῖς ἀπὸ Ἰουδαϊσμοῦ πιστεύσασιν, γράμμασιν Ἑβραϊκοῖς συντεταγμένον.

5. δεύτερον δὲ τὸ κατὰ Μάρκον, ὡς Πέτρος ὑφηγήσατο αὐτῷ, ποιήσαντα, ὃν καὶ υἱὸν ἐν τῇ καθολικῇ ἐπιστολῇ διὰ τούτων, ὡμολόγησεν φάσκων· ἀσπάζεται ὑμᾶς ἡ ἐν Βαβυλῶνι συνεκλεκτὴ καὶ Μάρκος ὁ υἱός μου.

6. καὶ τρίτον τὸ κατὰ Λουκᾶν, τὸ ὑπὸ Παύλου ἐπαινούμενον εὐαγγέλιον τοῖς ἀπὸ τῶν ἐθνῶν πεποιηκότα·
ἐπὶ πᾶσιν τὸ κατὰ Ἰωάννου·

3. . . . and in the first [book of his commentaries] on the [Gospel] according to Matthew, when defending the ecclesiastical canon, he testifies that he knows only four gospels, writing as follows:

4. As [I have] learned in the tradition about the four gospels, which are alone uncontested in the church of God under heaven, namely, the first written was that according to the one-time tax collector but later apostle of Jesus Christ, Matthew, who published it for the believers from Judaism, composed in Hebrew characters;

5. And second, that according to Mark, composed as Peter guided, whom he also proclaimed to be his son in the catholic epistle, speaking thus: "She that is in Babylon jointly chosen [with you] greets you, and my son Mark too" [1 Pet 5:13].

6. And third, that according to Luke, the gospel praised by Paul, composed for those from the Gentiles.

Finally, that according to John.

It will be noted that Origen refers to the Gospels in the same order as Irenaeus and that he knows that the Gospel of Mark "was composed as Peter guided." For his belief that Matthew was also composed "in Hebrew characters," see excursus 3. It is of course for him the work of the apostle Matthew.

6. Eusebius on Papias

The material of the thirty-ninth chapter of EH III, which records all that Eusebius wished to tell about the testimony of Papias, bishop of Hierapolis (ca. 60-138), is firmly situated in the pontificate of Pope Evaristus (101-109) (compare III.34 and IV.1). In III.36 we were informed that in Asia at that time, Polycarp, a companion of the apostles, was preeminent, and that other famous contemporaries were Papias, who "to this day is universally remembered," and Ignatius, bishop of Antioch. In the next chapter (37) he gives his readers the following reason for specially mentioning at this point Clement of Rome, Ignatius, and Papias: "As it is impossible to enumerate by name all who in the first succession from the apostles became pastors or evangelists throughout the world, we have set down the record of those alone who are actually known by name to have written, and whose transmission of the apostolic teaching has come to us through memoirs" (III.37.4). That is to say, Eusebius regards Papias as one of the three most important transmitters of "the succession from the Apostles," and hence allows him a whole chapter to himself, partly for his intrinsic importance, but still more (as we shall learn) for the incidental assistance that Papias will be able to provide for the furtherance of his own opinion about the authorship of the Apocalypse.

This chapter 39, "About the writings of Papias," has been a *crux interpretum* for the past 200 years, and even today there is little or no agreement about its value and interpretation. For so many scholars have made elaborate efforts to find support in it for so many different synoptic theories that there is today a great skepticism about its value as evidence, and this has resulted in a general aversion to considering it at all. Nevertheless a rational and scientific approach in the light of recent research, after clearing away the confusions and misunderstandings of many generations, will enable us to grasp the peculiar logic of Eusebius and to demonstrate that the evidence of this chapter actually endorses what he has related elsewhere.

As we turn to III.39 let us remind ourselves that in studying it we are expected by Eusebius to bear in mind all that he has previously said or referred with regard to the Gospels and the rest of the New Testament. In III.31.6, he writes:

> In these pages [chapter 24-30] I have set down all the facts that have come to my knowledge regarding the apostles and the apostolic period; the sacred writings they have left us; the books which though disputed are nevertheless constantly used by many in most churches; those that are unmistakeably spurious and foreign to apostolic orthodoxy.
>
> (Trans. G. A. Williamson, Penguin ed., 1967).

So we must bear in mind that Eusebius himself not only believed that the three Synoptic Gospels were written before the death of Peter (ca. 65/67), but also knew that Papias had the same belief and was in full agreement with him on this point. Unlike Eusebius, we today lack all sight of Papias's five books so that we cannot directly check up on this point. But we may be sure that if Eusebius had any reason to doubt Papias's knowledge of the same Four Gospels, he would not have failed to note it and to exploit it on account of his strong bias against him (compare EH III.39.13). Interesting confirmation that Papias knew and used all four Gospels has appeared in a recent article by Folker Siegert who discovered that medieval Armenian scholars[6] have recorded comments by Papias on both John 19:39 and on Luke 10:8. This means that Papias's seeming silence regarding both Luke and John must no longer be taken as arguing that he did not know about them; on the contrary, this whole chapter may now be interpreted in the light of the fact that Papias knew all four evangelists well, but that Eusebius for his own good reasons only quoted passages referring to Mark and Matthew.

It will also be as well at this point to draw the reader's attention to another unique characteristic of this chapter, namely, that it is the only chapter in the whole *Ecclesiastical History* in which Eusebius questions the theological orthodoxy, accuracy, and good judgment of two of the most respected fathers of the early church, Papias and Irenaeus, while also blaming the former for "the meanness of his intelligence" and for his misrepresentation of apostolic teaching that led (so he asserts) such a theologian as Irenaeus into millenarian errors (cf. III.39.12-13).

Very little is known about Papias himself, and some things that were formerly accepted about him are today denied by the majority of scholars. The agreed facts seem to be these: Papias lived circa 60-134/8, and for perhaps as long as forty years he was bishop of Hierapolis in the valley of the river Lycus not far from its confluence with the river Meander. Colossae and Laodicea were neighbouring cities, and Hierapolis was only some hundred miles along a good road from Ephesus where St. John lived and died about the year 99. Papias was the author of a work of five books entitled *The Expositions of the Lord's Sayings,* which has entirely disappeared, only a few scrappy quotations surviving, including those recorded by Eusebius. His reputation and his fame in the second century, and later, rested on the belief of the ancient fathers that he was actually a disciple of St. John the Apostle and wrote down the Gospel at John's dictation, at least according to the Old Latin prologue to that Gospel, which, as we have seen above, quotes his five books of Expositions as its authority for this statement. We shall deal below with the question whether Papias really knew John the Apostle personally, or whether he was only directly acquainted with another "John," the so-called "Presbyter John." What is certain is

---

[6]Folker Siegert in a recent article ("Unbeachtete Papiaszitate bei Armenischen Schriftstellern," NTS 27:605-14) has shown (1) that Vardan, a thirteenth-century Armenian scholar, quotes Papias's exegesis of Jn 19:39 on ἀλόης, which in the New Testament is found only in John; (2) that Papias would appear to have referred to Lk 10:8 in a quotation of his found in an Armenian fragment on the Apocalypse of John; (3) that Vardan also asserts that "Papias, a pupil of John, wrote the story of a woman taken in adultery." Cf. Jn 7:53-8:11; EH III.39.17; J. Kürzinger, *Papias von Hierapolis,* 94-138.

that his lifespan overlapped that of St. John by 30 to 40 years and that he lived within easy communication by road.[7]

7. Introduction to EH III.39 (about the Writings of Papias)

This chapter (EH III.39) has three divisions:

(1) Sections 1-8a are concerned with Eusebius's attempt to use Papias's preface to his five books of *Expositions of the Lord's Sayings* to support his own theory that the Apocalypse is not by John the Apostle but by another person of the same name.

(2) Sections 8b-13 quote in a condescending manner various matters matters that Papias has seemingly related on his own authority, and also bitterly attack him for his lack of critical judgement.

(3) Sections 14-17 relate two genuine traditions from Papias that Eusebius is forced to accept as additional authentic items of witness to the composition of the Gospels among the dross that he claims to have found elsewhere in Papias's books.

Each of these divisions will require separate treatment, but first we must state the presuppositions with which this chapter must be approached if we are to elucidate its full meaning:

Firstly, both Irenaeus and Eusebius have carefully read and digested Papias's Five Books, now entirely lost to us, whereas we have to read Papias's mind through what Eusebius has written about him.

Secondly, Eusebius knew full well that Irenaeus, Justin (cf. *Dial. Tryph.* 81), and all orthodox writers from the beginning down to Origen inclusive, were unanimous (save Dionysius of Alexandria) in believing the tradition that the Apostle John wrote the Apocalypse as well as the Gospel.

Thirdly, Eusebius knew that Irenaeus believed Papias to be a reliable witness to the original apostolic tradition. Hence, if Papias had ever expressed in his Books any doubt at all about the authorship of the Apocalypse, Irenaeus would not have spoken so categorically about John's authorship of it, while Eusebius would have pounced on any such doubt to support his own and Dionysius's opposing conjecture.

Fourthly, if Eusebius had found in Papias either any contradiction or any lack of support for his own presentation of the Gospel evidence as given

---

[7]See M. Jourjon, "Papias," DBS 6 (1960): 1104-1109; John F. Bligh, "The Prologue of Papias," TS 13 (1952): 234-40; also "Papias," in ODCC; also D. M. Yarbrough, "The Date of Papias for Reassessment," *Journal of the Evangelical Theological Society* 26/2 (1983): 181-92, supports Eusebius's dating of Papias's five books as being prior to A.D. 110. See also ch. 3, n. 8.

in his own III.24-25, we can be quite sure that he would have been quite pitiless in exposing the gaps. But he makes no such charge against him.

Fifthly, not only does Eusebius expect his readers to bear in mind all the information about the gospels that he has already accumulated in Book 2 and Book 3, but he writes as if he takes it for granted that he and Papias are in agreement over the list of the Gospels and of the other sacred books including 1 John and 1 Peter (III.39.17). Moreover, although in the citations there is no actual mention by Papias of Luke by name, there is in fact a strong reminiscence of Luke's Prologue in section 15.

Sixthly, Eusebius also knew that 2 John and 3 John were very ancient letters attributed to John the Apostle, and that, though John's name is never mentioned in either of them, it was common knowledge at the time that their actual superscription, "The Presbyter," stood for the Apostle John (cf. III.25.3).

Seventhly, Eusebius was not an original thinker, but he had very definite views on the major questions of his age and was a strong supporter of the theological opinions of Archbishop St. Dionysius of Alexandria (died ca. 264), to whose memory he was extremely devoted. Thus in the *Ecclesiastical History* we have three particular examples of his tenacity in following the opinions of Dionysius: his acceptance of the Pauline authorship of Hebrews (VI.41.6) against the opinion of Origen (cf. Excursus 3); his tenacious attachment to Dionysius's rejection of the Johannine authorship of the Apocalypse (VII.25); his fanatical hatred of millenarianism (VII.24). The second and third of these opinions have controlled his interpretation of Papias in this chapter.

The text, which is quite secure and follows that of G. Bardy (see n. 1 above), is given below with a fresh translation, followed by a commentary.

a. "The Presbyter, John" (EH III.39.1-8a)

Περὶ τῶν Παπία συγγραμμάτων	About the Compositions of Papias
[1] τοῦ δὲ Παπία συγγράμματα πέντε τὸν ἀριθμὸν φέρεται, ἃ καὶ ἐπιγέγραπται Λογίων κυριακῶν ἐξηγήσεως. τούτων καὶ Εἰρηναῖος, ὡς μόνων αὐτῷ γραφέντων μνημονεύει, ὧδέ πως λέγων· ταῦτα δὲ καὶ Παπίας ὁ Ἰωάννου μὲν ἀκουστής, Πολυκάρπου δὲ ἑταῖρος γεγονώς, ἀρχαῖος ἀνήρ, ἐγγράφως ἐπιμαρτυρεῖ ἐν τῇ τετάρτῃ τῶν ἑαυτοῦ βιβλίων. ἔστιν γὰρ αὐτῷ πέντε βιβλία συντεταγμένα.	[1] The compositions of Papias are reproted to be five in number, and they are entitled "An Exposition of the Lord's Sayings." And Irenaeus records these as his only writings, speaking here as follows: And to these things too witness is borne in writing by Papias, the hearer of John, who was also the companion of Polycarp, an "original" man, in the fourth of his volumes, for he had composed five.

[2] καὶ ὁ μὲν Εἰρηναῖος ταῦτα. αὐτός γε μὴν ὁ Παπίας κατὰ τὸ προοίμιον τῶν αὐτοῦ λόγων ἀκροατὴν μὲν καὶ αὐτόπτην οὐδαμῶς ἑαυτὸν γενέσθαι τῶν ἱερῶν ἀποστόλων ἐμφαίνει, παρειληφέναι δὲ τὰ τῆς πίστεως παρὰ τῶν ἐκείνοις γνωρίμων διδάσκει δι' ὧν φησιν λέξεων·

[3] οὐκ ὀκνήσω δέ σοι καὶ ὅσα ποτὲ παρὰ τῶν πρεσβυτέρων καλῶς ἔμαθον καὶ καλῶς ἐμνημόνευσα, συγκατατάξαι ταῖς ἑρμηνείαις, διαβεβαιούμενος ὑπὲρ αὐτῶν ἀλήθειαν. οὐ γὰρ τοῖς τὰ πολλὰ λέγουσιν ἔχαιρον ὥσπερ οἱ πολλοί, ἀλλὰ τοῖς τἀληθῆ διδάσκουσιν, οὐδὲ τοῖς τὰς ἀλλοτρίας ἐντολὰς μνημονεύουσιν, ἀλλὰ τοῖς τὰς παρὰ τοῦ Κυρίου τῇ πίστει δεδομένας καὶ ἀπ' αὐτῆς παραγινομένας τῆς ἀληθείας·

[4] εἰ δέ που καὶ παρηκολουθηκώς τις τοῖς πρεσβυτέροις ἔλθοι, τοὺς τῶν πρεσβυτέρων ἀνέκρινον λόγους, τί Ἀνδρέας ἢ τί Πέτρος εἶπεν ἢ τί Φίλιππος ἢ τί Θωμᾶς ἢ Ἰάκωβος ἢ τί Ἰωάννης ἢ Ματθαῖος ἢ τισ ἕτερος τῶν Κυρίου μαθητῶν ἅ τε Ἀριστίων καὶ ὁ πρεσβύτερος Ἰωάννης, τοῦ Κυρίου μαθηταί, λέγουσιν. οὐ γὰρ τὰ ἐκ τῶν βιβλίων τοσοῦτόν με ὠφελεῖν ὑπελάμβανον ὅσον τὰ παρὰ ζώσης φωνῆς καὶ μενούσης.

[5] ἔνθα καὶ ἐπιστῆσαι ἄξιον δὶς καθαριθμοῦντι αὐτῷ τὸ Ἰωάννου ὄνομα, ὧν τὸν μὲν πρότερον Πέτρῳ καὶ Ἰακώβῳ καὶ Ματθαίῳ καὶ τοῖς λοιποῖς ἀποστόλοις συγκαταλέγει, σαφῶς δηλῶν τὸν εὐαγγελιστήν, τὸν δ' ἕτερον Ἰωάννην, διαστείλας τὸν λόγον, ἑτέροις παρὰ τὸν τῶν ἀποστόλων ἀριθμὸν κατατάσσει, προτάξας αὐτοῦ τὸν Ἀριστίωνα, σαφῶς τε αὐτὸν πρεσβύτερον ὀνομάζει·

[2] So says Irenaeus. Yet Papias himself, according to the preface of his book, in no wise makes it apparent that he was really a hearer and eyewitness of the holy apostles, but teaches that he had received the facts of the faith from their acquaintances, for he speaks as follows:

[3] And for thee I shall not hesitate also to classify with the sacred records whatever at any time I had both duly learned from the presbyters and duly remembered, being absolutely confident of their truth. For I was not one to take pleasure, like so many people, in those who talk at great length but in those whose teaching is true; nor in those who remember the directives of others, but in those who remember the ones given by the Lord to the Faith and that come from the truth itself.

[4] If then indeed someone who had followed the presbyters happened to come along, I used to inquire the words of the presbyters—what Andrew or Peter had said, or what Philip, or what Thomas or James or what John or Matthew, or any other of the disciples of the Lord—and what Aristion and the presbyter John, disciples of the Lord, were still saying. For I reckoned that whatever is got out of the books is not as useful to me as the [utterances] of a living and abiding voice.

[5] It is here worth noting that he twice counts the name of John, ranking the former of them with Peter and James and Matthew and the rest of the apostles, clearly referring to the evangelist; but as regards the other "John," by separating the expression he lists him with others outside the number of the apostles, putting Aristion before him and clearly calling him a presbyter.

[6] ὡς καὶ διὰ τούτων ἀποδείκνυ-σθαι τὴν ἱστορίαν ἀληθῆ τῶν δύο κατὰ τὴν ᾿Ασίαν ὁμωνυμίᾳ κεχρῆσθαι εἰρηκότων, δύο τε ἐν ᾿Εφέσῳ γενέσθαι μνήματα καὶ ἑκ-άτερον ᾿Ιωάννου ἔτι νῦν λέγε-σθαι· οἷς καὶ ἀναγκαῖον προσέχειν τὸν νοῦν, εἰκὸς γὰρ τὸν δεύτερον, εἰ μή τις ἐθέλοι τὸν πρῶτον, τὴν ἐπ' ὀνόματος φερομένην ᾿Ιωάννου ἀποκάλυψιν ἑορακέναι.
[7] καὶ ὁ νῦν δὲ ἡμῖν δηλούμενος Παπίας τοὺς μὲν τῶν ἀποστόλων λόγους παρὰ τῶν αὐτοῖς παρηκο-λουθηκότων ὁμολογεῖ παρε-ιληφέναι, ᾿Αριστίωνος δὲ καὶ τοῦ πρεσβυτέρου ᾿Ιωάννου αὐτήκοον ἑαυτον φησι γενέσθαι· ὀνομαστί γοῦν πολλάκις αὐτῶν μνημονεύ-σας ἐν τοῖς αὐτοῦ συγγράμμασιν τίθησιν αὐτῶν παραδόσεις.
[8] καὶ ταῦτα δ'ἡμῖν οὐκ εἰς τὸ ἄχρηστον εἰρήσθω.

[6] And so by these words is demon-strated the truth of the assertion that there were two men in Asia said to be possessed of the same name and that there were two tombs in Ephesus, and each even now is said to be John's.

Now it is necessary to draw attention to these matters, for it is likely that the lat-ter—unless anyone prefers the for-mer—beheld the revelation that carries the name of John.
[7] And the Papias whom we are now discussing declares that he has received the words of the apostles from those who had followed them, but he also says that he actually heard Aristion and the presbyter John with his own ears. For he records them often by name and re-lates their traditions in his writings.
[8] And the recounting of these things is not without value for us.

Notes to "The Presbyter, John" (EH III.39.1-8a)

[1] τούτων . . . ὡς μόνων, "these . . . as only (writings)." Eusebius is saying that from among Papias's writings, Irenaeus quotes only from Papias's Five Books. The actual reference here is to Adv. Haer. V.33.4. By means of this quotation Eusebius prepares the way for his hypothesis that there were simultaneously two Johns in Asia, one who wrote the Gospel, and the other—the Presbyter—who wrote the Apocalypse (cf. Quasten, II:37ff.).

ταῦτα, "these things." The reference is to a long excerpt by Irenaeus, Adv. Haer. V.33.3, from Papias's fourth volume. This excerpt deals with one aspect of the Millen-nium, and it is clear that here Irenaeus is relying on the authority of Papias, who in turn presents it as coming to him on the authority of "the elders who saw John, the disciple of the Lord," who claimed that they had heard from him how the Lord used to speak about it (see below §7b).

ἀρχαῖος ἀνήρ, "an original man," that is, one with sure knowledge based on per-sonal contact with original members of the church. For Irenaeus, Polycarp was a presbyter with knowledge of the origins (cf. EH V.8.1).

ἐν τῇ τετάρτῃ, "in the fourth (book)." Eusebius is specific about the passage in question, and gives the exact reference.

[2] κατὰ τὸ προοίμιον τῶν αὐτοῦ λόγων, "according to the preface of his book." This use of "logos" to denote the actual book of the Exposition of the Lord's Sayings is noteworthy. Similarly the "logia" of Matthew denotes our Gospel of Matthew (compare EH III.39.16).

τὰ τῆς πίστεως, "the facts of the Faith." This seems to be the earliest recorded example in the Fathers of the use of πίστις to denote the Christian Religion.

[3] ταῖς ἑρμηνείαις, "the Sacred Records." Modern translators usually render this word as "interpretations," a rendering that is meaningless. It would rather seem to be a technical term for "the Sacred Writings," a view which is supported by the use of the cognate noun and the corresponding verb in two other surviving fragments from Papias: namely, in the one case the noun means "the words of Jesus," while in the other case the verb indicates "the translation of St. Matthew's Gospel" (cf. BAG, ἑρμηνεία, ἑρμηνεύω).

παρὰ τῶν πρεσβυτέρων, "from the Presbyters." Both here and in [4] this term means the Apostles, as Eusebius himself recognizes when in [7] he writes "Apostles" instead of "Presbyters" when he quotes directly from this part of Papias's preface [4]. Of course in other contexts and in later ecclesiastical writers, the term usually means either "the followers of the Apostles" or "their followers' followers" or simply "the elders of the church." But Dom John Chapman, whose *John the Presbyter* (Oxford, 1911, §§2-4) still remains the most devastating dismissal of "the Presbyter John" legend created by Eusebius, seems to be at fault on this point. For his interpretation of τοὺς τῶν πρεσβυτέρων ἀνέκρινον λόγους, τί ᾿Ανδρέας ἢ τί Πέτρος εἶπεν κτλ. [4] seems unduly forced. Chapman preferred to understand the meaning as: "I used to enquire the words of the Presbyters, what *they said* Peter and Andrew said" (italics added), instead of the straightforward "I used to enquire the words of the Presbyters, what Peter and Andrew said." Chapman also denies that Papias meant "the Apostles" when he referred to the Presbyters here in [3], and he sought support from Irenaeus's own usage. But he seems to have overlooked that the usage of the term "presbyter" may well have changed during the interval between Papias and Irenaeus. But in other respects Chapman's arguments still remain valid today.

[4] εἰ δέ που καὶ, "If then indeed. . . . " The protasis that governs the sentence "I used to enquire the words of the Presbyters . . . or any other of the Disciples of the Lord," strictly speaking also governs "what Aristion and the Presbyter John are saying." But it is clear that Eusebius did not take it in this way. For in fact Papias has changed the construction during the course of the sentence. Thus Eusebius understands Papias to mean simply this: "And I also used to enquire what Aristion and the Presbyter John were still saying." And this is how we too must take it. "Disciples of the Lord" means all those whom Jesus himself personally taught, that is, not only the Twelve, but others like Aristion. Note also that Matthew and John, the Evangelists, are linked together here.

λέγουσιν, "were still saying." The present tense (rendered by "were saying" in indirect speech) implies that Papias personally heard with his own ears both Aristion and "the Presbyter John."

ζώσης φωνῆς καὶ μενούσης, "of a living and abiding voice." Papias means the direct contact with Christ through the voices of those who had been personally Disciples of the Lord, that is, Aristion and "the Presbyter John." There was all the difference between this and secondhand contact with the Twelve.

[5] The argument of this section will be explained below in the Commentary.

[6] τὴν ἱστορίαν ἀληθῆ, "the truth of the assertion." A clear exaggeration on the part of Eusebius; his own interpretation is no more than a possible one, owing to an ambiguity in the syntax of Papias. The story of the "two men" and "the two tombs" first appears in the writings of Dionysius of Alexandria (see EH VII.25.12-16), some two generations earlier, and so far as we know it is peculiar to him alone.

ἀναγκαῖον, "necessary." Eusebius feels compelled to justify his procedure in [5] and [6] for claiming some tangible support for his theory in this context.

τὸν πρῶτον, "the former." Eusebius means that one of these tombs was that of the Apostle, and the other that of "The Presbyter"; and that the reader can take his choice. It does not seem to have struck the commentators that if there had really been two tombs there, the odds are that their respective custodians would have been noisy rivals each claiming to possess the true body of the Apostle John!

[7] παρὰ τῶν αὐτοῖς παρηκολουθηκότων, "from those who had followed them." As noted above, Eusebius is here repeating Papias's phrase in [4] and simply substituting "Apostles" for "Presbyters." ὀνομαστί, "by name." Eusebius is of course quite prepared to accept (indeed he cannot deny) Papias's claim to have heard both Aristion and "the Presbyter John" with his own ears, provided that "Presbyter John" does not mean John the Apostle. The real question is whether Papias himself anywhere else in his Five Books used again the phrase "the Presbyter John," or whether he always spoke either of "John" or of "The Presbyter." Although Eusebius is careful to use the phrase "the Presbyter John," we shall find some reason for thinking that he describes each occurrence of "the John-that-Papias-heard" as "the Presbyter John," simply because his theory demanded it.

[8] εἰς τὸ ἄχρηστον, "be not without usefulness." The purpose of the hypothesis of the "two Johns" is to offer an argument for the Apocalypse not being the work of John the Apostle, and so for being apocryphal (cf. EH III.25.4). His argument on this topic concluded, he turns to destroying the theological reputation of Papias.

Commentary

Coming now to deal explicitly with the problems facing us in this first part (§§1-8a) of the chapter, our preliminary task will be to clear up as best we can some seeming ambiguities that reveal themselves in Papias's preface, ambiguities that have been made a great fuss of by many scholars. The disputed points are three:

i. Who are the "presbyters" in [3]? Are they the seven Apostles referred to in [4], or are they merely the disciples of these seven?

ii. Did Papias hear Aristion and the Presbyter John with his own ears or not? For [4] is ambiguous owing to the loose construction of the sentence, which allows one to assume either that Papias did actually hear them with his own ears, or that they were alive when he was collecting information though he did not hear them personally.

iii. Is the Presbyter John, [4], identical with John the Apostle mentioned earlier in the same sentence along with six other Apostles, or is he a different person?

As to i, Eusebius equates the "Presbyters" in [3] with the "Apostles" in [4], because in [7] he writes: "Papias . . . asserts that he has received the words of the Apostles from those who had followed them, but also says he actually heard Aristion and the Presbyter John with his own ears." This is a quotation from [4] where Eusebius simply has "Presbyters" in place of "Apostles." Thus our first question is answered: the "Presbyters" in [3] are the "Apostles" of [4].

As to ii, the latter part of the above sentence confirms that in his preface Eusebius rightly understands Papias to be claiming that he himself heard Aristion and the Presbyter John with his own ears (cf. the note on [4]). But this brings us no nearer to a solution of the third question, the identity of the Presbyter John.

As to iii, all we know for certain at the moment is that both the "Presbyter John" and Aristion were true "Disciples of the Lord" and that Papias heard them both with his own ears. But the first part of this chapter was composed by Eusebius with the object of convincing the reader that the reference is not to John the Apostle but to another contemporary with the same name. His motive is, as we have seen above, his desire to promote the view of Dionysius of Alexandria (see EH VII.25) that the Apocalypse for critical reasons simply cannot be from the pen of the author of the Fourth Gospel and so show it to be "apocryphal." His dislike of the Apocalypse seems to stem from what it says about a Millennium in Apocalypse 20:1-6. What then is the value of Eusebius's conjecture about the identity of "the Presbyter John"? The quotation from Irenaeus (*Adv. Haer.* V.33.4), that stands at the beginning of our chapter 39, is crucial for Eusebius; for here and here only in his extant writings does Irenaeus, who recognized John the Apostle as the author both of the Apocalypse and of the Fourth Gospel, definitely speak of Papias as "the hearer of John." If Eusebius was to stand any chance of convincing the world of his time that John could not be the author of the Apocalypse he had to find sound evidence to show that Irenaeus had here unwittingly misinterpreted Papias and confused the Apostle John with another John, a contemporary of the Apostle.

Now in this quotation "these things" refers to an extract that Irenaeus has made from the writings of Papias about the Millennium and of which he (Papias) shows his approval when he adds, "Now these things are credible to believers" (*Adv. Haer.* V.33.4). The extract in question certainly seems to possess a mythical character and is quite unlike any of the Gospel sayings of Jesus. Eusebius therefore seems to have had good reason for suspecting not only that Papias's judgment was here at fault but that Irenaeus too had been misled by the prestige of Papias into accepting his teaching on the Millennium. And so, by asserting that he has also found in the preface to Papias's Five Books a clear reference to a "second John," he considers that he has some positive support for suggesting that Irenaeus was not only led astray by Papias's gullibility over the Millennium but was also led astray in the very same passage by Papias's statement that he was "the hearer of John." If we grant these premises to Eusebius, he is then able to dispose of the witness of two of the most authoritative Fathers of the Subapostolic Age and able to show some support for the suggestion of

St. Dionysius that the Apocalypse was written by another John, to whom Eusebius gives the title of "The Presbyter"; and with St. John no longer the author, the Apocalypse becomes suspect of being apocryphal! This chain of reasoning he further supports by a hearsay report of there being two tombs of John at Ephesus and therefore two different occupants of them! All this argumentation lies behind the seemingly innocent presentation in the first part of this chapter.

Now there are two factors that have predisposed modern scholars to accept Eusebius's thesis without bothering too much about the strength of his arguments: firstly, the prestige of two such great scholars as Dionysius and Eusebius, both Greek speakers and both discussing a work written in Greek not long before their own time, both seemingly unbiased, and persons who therefore must really know best;[8] secondly, the common modern belief that internal critical grounds preclude assigning the Apocalypse to John the Apostle. But of course from the point of view of our present enquiry it does not matter whether John is its author or not; for the only question to be decided here is whether Eusebius has or has not found good arguments for the separate existence of such a person as "the Presbyter John."

Eusebius's first argument is from the fact that the name John appears twice in the same long and involved sentence in two distinct but related contexts. This of course proves nothing at all unless it is supported by other independent evidence.

His second argument is that Papias lists the "second John" with another unknown "Disciple of the Lord," namely, Aristion. But this is a *petitio principii*, while the phrase "Disciple of the Lord" occurring earlier in the same sentence is already a title ascribed to those of the Twelve mentioned there.

His third argument is that there was a report that there were at one time two tombs at Ephesus dedicated to John. These are the only arguments he has to propose, apart from the internal critical argument against Johannine authorship of the Apocalypse, which is here quite irrelevant.

---

[8]B. G. Bardy (*Eusèbe de Césarée*, 1:155n2) capitulates to Eusebius's suggestion for quite insufficient reasons, when he writes: "Eusèbe interprète à sa facon le texte du Papias et ne prétend pas s'appuyer pour cela, sur une tradition. Mais il est intelligent, instruit de l'antiquité chrétienne plus que tout autre, et il sait bien le grec. Aussi peut-on lui faire confiance lorsqu'il affirme la distinction des deux Jean." On the other hand, G. A. Williamson, editor of the Penguin edition of *The History of the Church* (1965), dismisses Eusebius's reasoning as "unsatisfactory" (see 151n1). Lawlor and Oulton (*Eusebius, Bishop of Caesarea*, 114) sum up the matter as follows: "The reasoning of Eusebius seems unconvincing; and the argument of others who have reached the same conclusion on other lines is of doubtful validity."

Since the first argument is no argument at all in itself, we turn to the second, the double mention of the name of "John." Eusebius finds it very significant that Papias lists "John" in the second instance outside the number of the Apostles, putting Aristion, who was not one of the Twelve, before him and clearly calling this "John" a Presbyter. But there is no force in this argument, since he has already referred to the other Apostles as presbyters in [4]. Furthermore, he has just called the other Apostles the "Disciples of the Lord" and now also calls both Aristion and the Presbyter John "Disciples of the Lord." This "second John" is therefore doubly identified as both "Presbyter" and "Disciple of the Lord," that is to say, he is identified by two terms that equally apply to St. John the Apostle. Nor is there anything against the identification of this "second John" with the Evangelist simply on the grounds that Aristion is mentioned before him, for the second place is the more emphatic and better suited if he is indeed the Apostle John. Eusebius in [7] says that Papias often mentions in his work Aristion and the Presbyter John by name. What we would like to know is how Papias normally referred to St. John the Apostle in the rest of his Five Books: does he refer to him simply as "John" as in his first mention of his name in [4], or does he refer to him as "The Presbyter," or does he ever use again the phrase "the Presbyter John"? It will be argued here and now that Papias normally used to refer to the Apostle John as "John" or as "the Presbyter"; for in §§14-15 Eusebius tells us that he is going to give us some traditions of "The Presbyter John," and then proceeds to quote Papias what "The Presbyter used to say. . . . " Now this seems to indicate that when Eusebius found in Papias's writings the phrase "The Presbyter," he wanted to understand it in his own special sense as the "second John," "the Presbyter John." It rather begins to look as if Papias may have used the phrase "The Presbyter John" only this once (in his preface) in order to clear up any chance of ambiguity that might result from his mentioning the Apostle John twice in the one sentence in a rather clumsy fashion.

As to the third argument—the hearsay, first mentioned by Dionysius (EH VII.25) and resumed by Eusebius here, that there were two tombs of John at Ephesus—all commentators agree that even if there was any historical or archaeological evidence for two tombs (which there is not) their existence would be no proper argument for their being two Johns (cf. Oulton and Lawlor, 2:114 in loc.).

So much then for the positive arguments of Eusebius; they have in fact no probative value whatever. Given his unrivalled knowledge of, and access to, early Christian literature, the paucity of these arguments can only mean that he can find nothing else in Papias or elsewhere to support his thesis. And so far as his extant writings are concerned he never alluded again to this strange thesis of his. It would seem to have been an impulsive *jeu d'esprit,* motivated by his theological zeal, which he was later glad to forget. Unfortunately, what he wrote remained on record and had an immense influence in course of time.

But how then are the peculiarities of Papias's preface to be explained? First of all, this extract is, it seems, a good example of his involved and none too easy style, a fault that Eusebius himself suffers from, Papias is trying to tell the reader that his work contains two categories of witness; most of it is secondhand, but some of it is in fact firsthand, and as good as "Gospel" (cf. §3). That is to say, the first category contains the results of his inquiries from those who had known the Apostles when they were alive; the second category contains the results of his inquiries from two disciples of the Lord whom he had heard with his own ears, namely, Aristion and the Presbyter John. Indeed, Papias was not born in time to have known any Apostle personally save John. Our question therefore is: Was John the Apostle in both categories? That is to say, did Papias not only hear the words of John about the Lord after John's death from those who had known John in his lifetime, but did he not also himself personally hear about the Lord from the lips of John the Apostle himself as well as from Aristion? There is nothing whatever in [4] to prevent us from understanding "The Presbyter John" as the same person as the "John" mentioned with the other Apostles earlier in the same sentence, except the clumsiness of the juxtaposition and the problem (if it is really a problem?) of the qualification "the Presbyter" being prefixed to "John."

From the practical point of view, Papias was quite old enough to have known the Apostle well personally (as the Old Latin prologue to John asserts), for as a contemporary of the daughters of Philip he must have been over thirty years of age when John died about the year 100. Furthermore he wrote his Five Books only a few years after John's death, that is, between 101-109, according to Eusebius's chronology; and Hierapolis itself is within easy communication with Ephesus. The ancient fame of Papias in the second century and his authority and prestige are surely the result of the common belief of the time that he knew John the Apostle very well, and was in a position to pass on his traditions to the second-century Christians.

Therefore, though Eusebius, on account of his views on the Apocalypse and his dislike of Papias's views about the Millennium, insisted that Papias meant to refer to a "second John," we are in no way obliged to go along with him. On the contrary, nobody before Dionysius (d. 264) ever dreamed of John the Apostle having a "double," a *doppelganger;* nor is there any record in the 200 years between Papias and Eusebius of any writer attributing such a theory to Papias, though the latter's Five Books were a common possession. Nor does Eusebius introduce this "second John" into any of the later editions of his famous chronicle. This guess then seems to have been the result of a momentary impulse, the wish to find a "double" being father to the thought.

Why then, we may ask, did Papias use this phrase "The Presbyter John" at all? So far as we can tell, Papias used it once only, and that in his preface here. Eusebius however picks it up and repeats it twice in this chapter, giving it his own connotation, while also seeming to infer that it is Papias's usage too. Yet this phrase did not suggest to any of the ancient Fathers, or early Christian writers before 325, the meaning that Eusebius now attaches to it. Nevertheless to Eusebius belongs the doubtful credit of supporting the ambiguity and of deciding to exploit it in the interests of his (and Dionysius's) theory about Johannine authorship of the Apocalypse! And for us moderns the irritating thing is that there would probably be no problem at all if Papias's Five Books had survived and not been totally lost!

But could there not be another and perfectly simple explanation for our conundrum? Could it not be that in the course of dictating his preface Papias became aware of the possibility of an ambiguity arising, and that he took the only step possible to avoid it without having to recast the whole sentence? For, having mentioned John once among the seven Apostles, "the disciples of the Lord," he realizes that he is going to mention him a second time in the same sentence, because John comes into both categories that he has set up. So he decides to use for the second occurrence the famous and affectionate title by which John was at that time known, "The Presbyter," since to write "John" again *tout court* would at the least be inelegant and would also cause momentary surprise to the reader at the repetition. But no sooner has he uttered "The Presbyter" than he realized that this familiar title, appearing in the same sentence, might itself seem to imply a distinction not intended; and so he avoids, to his own satisfaction at least, any ambiguity by at once adding "(John)"; and to make trebly sure that there should be no misunderstanding in the reader's mind he further adds "disciples of the Lord."[9] These clarifications were quite sufficient

---

[9]It can of course be argued that if Papias had just wanted to correct the notion that he was unintentionally appearing to make a distinction between "John" (obviously the Apostle) and "the Presbyter" by dictating ὁ πρεσβυτερος alone, he would have done best to add to ὁ πρεσβυτερος the phrase ὁ αὐτος Ἰωαννης; but surely the context is clear enough for him simply to add Ἰωαννης as an aside, since all knew that John knew himself to be referred to during his own lifetime as ὁ πρεσβυτερος (see 2 and 3 John). It was not necessary to make such a ponderous and solemn affirmation as ὁ αὐτος Ἰωαννης, for it was superfluous in the climate of that time.

for all the readers of Papias's preface for 200 years to leave them in no doubt that only John the Apostle, "The Presbyter," "the Disciple of the Lord," was intended—until it became Eusebius's distinction to be the first scholar to misinterpret the mind of Papias. With our own hindsight we can now see that when Papias clumsily sought to avoid this ambiguity he un-intentionality left room for Eusebius to exploit the very ambigiuty he had tried to remove. And Eusebius uses it to prove the very opposite to the in-tention of Papias, and all because he had acquired a vested interest in cre-ating another John against the unanimous testimony of all the ancient Fathers and the ancient prologues. Eusebius is here surely behaving dis-ingenuously and irresponsibly by totally ignoring in this context certain facts he himself has recorded elsewhere; he acts disingenuously in ignoring what he knew very well, that the whole world knew that the ascription "the Presbyter" in two contemporary letters, 2 John and 3 John, was known to refer to John the Apostle (EH III.25.3). His irresponsibility is shown by his recklessly appearing to suggest that "The Presbyter" could have writ-ten the Gospel of John if he did not write the Apocalypse ("unless anyone prefers the former," EH III.39.6)—so desperate was he to win support for Dionysius's suggestion.

And once we consider the larger context in which the question of the presbyter John must be considered, the final shreds of Eusebius's argu-ments disappear. For if ever there had been two such men as John—both Disciples of the Lord, both well known in Ephesus, both of advanced age, both there at the same time, both men of outstanding authority—it is im-possible but that some one somewhere would have dropped something more than the one very ambiguous and doubtful hint with which Eusebius has to make do; indeed, it is really impossible that we should not have received some further inkling of his existence from the early Church writers.[10]

Our conclusion therefore is that there are no solid reasons for arguing that Papias had ever thought of a second elder called John in contrast to the Apostle John. The arguments that Eusebius advanced were, and remain,

---

[10]J. H. Chapman (*John the Presbyter* [Oxford, 1911] 41ff.) had already pointed out that it was quite impossible for Irenaeus to have been mistaken as to the witness of Papias that there was only one John, the Apostle and disciple of the Lord, and also universally known as "the Presbyter" (2 and 3 Jn). The fact of John's authorship is so basic that any diver-gence would have been noted and recorded somewhere before 300 had it come from Pa-pias. It is sometimes argued that Papias is the "bottleneck" through which the Johannine traditions have reached us, so that if he were mistaken then the error of Irenaeus is feasible and understandable. But though Papias is undoubtedly a major source, there were other sources at least partially independent of him, though in full agreement, such as the Old Latin prologues and the Muratorian Canon; only Eusebius and Dionysius, his source, think differently, but they have no historical grounds to support their theory of a second John.

special pleading, flimsy and invalid, and he would never have advanced them but for his personal interest and patent involvement in promoting the theory of Dionysius about the authorship of the Apocalypse. Papias then, despite the efforts of Eusebius, is to be reckoned as one with the rest of the ancient Fathers in believing that there was only one disciple of the Lord called John, the very same person who called himself "The Presbyter" in the two brief letters of his that have survived from the epoch in which Papias himself lived and wrote. "The Presbyter John" of Eusebius and Papias's "The Presbyter" are one and the same person, and this person is St. John the Apostle, the disciple of the Lord, the Evangelist, otherwise known as "The Presbyter."

Why then did some Fathers, such as Jerome, later give support to the notion of "The Presbyter John"? Firstly, because of the reputation of Eusebius as a scholar; secondly, because critical scholarship of the fourth century, like that of the twentieth, saw in Eusebius's guess a possible solution of the problem of the authorship of the Apocalypse. Indeed, the subsequent history of the whole question of the Presbyter John provides a fine commentary on the aphorism of Étienne Gilson, who in another context wrote that "the discoveries of historical criticism are so often simply commentaries on misconceptions" (*Héloise and Abelard* [ET: London, 1953] 155).

And what a misconception! We are now in a position to assert (in agreement with Chapman in his *John the Presbyter*) that "The Presbyter John" is a pure invention on the part of Eusebius, and that if the text of Papias's preface be read again with proper punctuation, that is, by bracketing "John" thus: "The Presbyter (John)," the whole problem vanishes, and the Grand Old Man, John the Disciple of the Lord, is left in sole possession of the field.

b. "The Stupidity of Papias" (EH III.39.8b-13)

[8b] ἄξιον δὲ ταῖς ἀποδοθείσαις τοῦ Παπία φωναῖς προσάψαι λέξεις ἑτέρας αὐτοῦ, δι' ὧν παράδοξά τινα ἱστορεῖ καὶ ἄλλα ὡς ἂν ἐκ παραδόσεως εἰς αὐτὸν ἐλθόντα.

[9] τὸ μὲν οὖν κατὰ τὴν Ἱεράπολιν Φίλιππον τὸν ἀπόστολον ἅμα ταῖς θυγατράσιν διατρῖψαι διὰ τῶν πρόσθεν δεδήλωται· ὡς δὲ κατὰ τοὺς αὐτοὺς ὁ Παπίας γενόμενος, διήγησιν παρειληφέναι θαυμασίαν ὑπὸ τῶν τοῦ Φιλίππου θυγατέρων μνημονεύει,
τὰ νῦν σημειωτέον·

[8b] It is now proper to attach to the utterances of Papias already given some other sayings of his, by means of which he relates some things hard to believe and others that seemingly come to him from the Tradition.
[9] It has already been mentioned above that the apostle Philip together with his daughters had lived at Hierapolis; and how Papias, who was a contemporary, records a wonderful narrative that he had received from the daughters of Philip.

These things are now to be noted.

νεκροῦ γὰρ ἀνάστασιν κατ' αὐτὸν γεγονυῖαν ἱστορεῖ καὶ αὖ πάλιν ἕτερον παράδοξον περὶ 'Ιοῦστον τὸν ἐπικληθέντα Βαρσαβᾶν γεγονός, ὡς δηλητήριον φάρμακον ἐμπιόντος καὶ μηδὲν ἀηδὲς διὰ τὴν τοῦ Κυρίου χάριν ὑπομείναντος.

[10] τοῦτον δὲ τὸν 'Ιοῦστον μετὰ τὴν τοῦ Σωτῆρος ἀνάληψιν τοὺς ἱεροὺς ἀποστόλους μετὰ Ματθία στῆσαί τε καὶ ἐπεύξασθαι ἀντὶ τοῦ προδότου 'Ιούδα ἐπὶ τὸν κλῆρον τῆς ἀναπληρώσεως τοῦ αὐτῶν ἀριθμοῦ ἡ τῶν Πράξεων ὧδέ πως ἱστορεῖ γραφή· καὶ ἔστησαν δύο, 'Ιωσὴφ τὸν καλούμενον Βαρσαβᾶν, ὃς ἐπεκλήθη 'Ιοῦστος, καὶ Ματθίαν· καὶ προσευξάμενοι εἶπαν· . . .

[11] καὶ ἄλλα δὲ ὁ αὐτὸς ὡς ἐκ παραδόσεως ἀγράφου εἰς αὐτὸν ἥκοντα παρατέθειται ξένας τέ τινας παραβολὰς τοῦ Σωτῆρος καὶ διδασκαλίας αὐτοῦ καί τινα ἄλλα μυθικώτερα·

[12] ἐν οἷς καὶ χιλιάδα τινά φησιν ἐτῶν ἔσεσθαι μετὰ τὴν ἐκ νεκρῶν ἀνάστασιν, σωματικῶς τῆς Χριστοῦ Βασιλείας ἐπὶ ταυτησὶ τῆς γῆς ὑποστησομένης· ἃ καὶ ἡγοῦμαι τὰς ἀποστολικὰς παρεκδεξάμενον διηγήσεις ὑπολαβεῖν, τὰ ἐν ὑποδείγμασι πρὸς αὐτῶν μυστικῶς εἰρημένα μὴ συνεορακότα.

[13] σφόδρα γάρ τοι σμικρὸς ὢν τὸν νοῦν, ὡς ἂν ἐκ τῶν αὐτοῦ λόγων τεκμηράμενον εἰπεῖν, φαίνεται, πλὴν καὶ τοῖς μετ' αὐτὸν πλείστοις ὅσοις τῶν ἐκκλησιαστικῶν τῆς ὁμοίας αὐτῷ δόξης παραίτιος γέγονεν τὴν ἀρχαιότητα τἀνδρὸς προβεβλημένοις, ὥσπερ οὖν Εἰρηναίῳ καὶ εἴ τις ἄλλος τὰ ὅμοια φρονῶν ἀναπέφηνεν.

For he relates a resurrection of a dead man that happened in his own day, and again a further extraordinary event about Justus the one surnamed Barsabbas, how after drinking a poisoned cup he survived without any ill effect by the grace of the Lord.

[10] This Justus is the one whom, after the Ascension of the Savior, the holy apostles put with Matthias and prayed over for the casting of lots for the filling up of their number after the traitor Judas, as the Book of the Acts relates: "And they put two, Joseph called Barsabas and surnamed Justus, and Matthias, and they prayed, saying. . . . "

[11] And the said [Papias] has added things that came to him from the unwritten tradition, that is, some strange parables of the Savior and teachings of His, and some other things of a somewhat mythical character.

[12] Among which he also says that there will be a thousand years or so after the resurrrection of the dead when the kingdom of Christ will be corporally set up on this earth. I think indeed that he took up these matters misconstruing the apostolic teachings, not having grasped that they had been said by them in figures in a mystical sense.

[13] For he appears to have been a man of exceedingly small intelligence insofar as can be shown from his books. Moreover he has been partly the cause of quite a large number of churchmen after him holding the same opinions as his, for they relied on the ancient connection of the man, as has happened to Irenaeus and any others thinking likewise.

Notes to "The Stupidity of Papias" (EH III.39.8b-13)

[9] Φίλιππον τὸν ἀπόστολον, "the Apostle Philip." Not only does Eusebius here use the term "apostle" in a loose sense (which custom permitted) but he makes the mistake of confusing Philip the Apostle with Philip the Evangelist. The reference is to EH III.31.3-5, cf. also Acts 21:8.

δὲ κατὰ τοὺς αὐτοὺς ὁ Παπίας γενόμενος, "Papias who was a contemporary." Eusebius here reckons Papias as a contemporary of the daughters of Philip the Evangelist, that is, he regards Papias as someone who must have been in his thirties before the end of the first century. Consequently he was certainly old enough to have been very well acquainted with St. John the Apostle at Ephesus during the latter's last years.

[11] τινα ἄλλα μυθικώτερα, "of a somewhat mythical character." This mild condemnation is meant to excuse Irenaeus, and seems especially to refer to the quotation that Irenaeus drew from Papias about the Millennium (EH V.33.3, see above).

[12] μυστικῶς. "in a mystical sense." The doctrine of the Millennium was never officially condemned by the church, but the quotation that Irenaeus drew from Papias (EH V.33.3) seems farfetched and altogether uncharacteristic of the sayings of Jesus in the Gospels, so that Eusebius's disapproval has a good deal of justification.

[13] σφόδρα γάρ τοι σμικρὸς ὢν τὸν νοῦν, "a man of exceedingly small intelligence." This cutting comment has been far too often taken at its face value by modern scholars, who fail to realize the degree of *odium theologicum* that animated it.

τὰ ὅμοια φρονῶν, "holding the same opinions." Eusebius seems to be correct in claiming that both Justin and Irenaeus relied on Papias's connection with John for their teaching on the Millennium. And Eusebius follows Dionysius of Alexandria in his vehement desire to uproot this doctrine (cf. EH VII.24). For a defence of Irenaeus against the imputations of Eusebius, see M. Jourjon, "Papias," DBS 6.

Commentary

Eusebius's purpose in this part is to present material for which Papias vouches on his own authority or else on his mistaken understanding of the Tradition, thus demonstrating that his judgment is not always to be trusted. Eusebius excerpts a couple of miracles that Papias had learned about from the daughters of Philip the Evangelist. He then notes that Papias has related "some things that had come to him from the Unwritten Tradition, including some otherwise unknown parables of the Saviour and discourses of His and some other things of a more mythical character." Among these things he mentions Papias's teaching about the Millennium, that the Kingdom of Christ would be established on the earth for a thousand years after The Resurrection of the Dead and before the final consummation and the descent of the Heavenly Jerusalem. Eusebius roundly claims that Papias has misunderstood the apostolic teachings, failing to interpret them in a mystical sense. He then refers to him contemptuously as a "man of exceedingly small intelligence" for his lack of good sense and of theological insight, and blames him for misleading Irenaeus and many others in the matter of the Millennium.

The matter for which Eusebius condemns Papias for misleading Irenaeus is to be found in *Adv. Haer.* book 5, chapters 33-36. Irenaeus appears to have held that after the Resurrection of the Just, the Kingdom of
Christ would be established on earth for a thousand years, and then the final judgment would come and the general Resurrection. The passage that
led Eusebius to hold that Papias had culpably misunderstood the apostolic
tradition is the following text which Irenaeus claims that he has had from
Papias's Fourth Book and which he accepts because he understands that
Papias has had it directly from the elders who followed John (*Adv. Haer.*
V.33.3.4).

§3. The predicted blessing, therefore belongs unquestionably to the times
of the Kingdom [cf. Apoc. 20:1-6], when the righteous shall bear rule upon
their rising from the dead; when also the creation, having been renovated and
set free, shall fructify with an abundance of all kinds of food, from the dew
of heaven and from the fertility of the earth, just as the elders who saw John,
the disciple of the Lord, related that they had heard from him how the Lord
used to teach in regard to these times [the Millennium], and say: The days
will come, in which vines shall grow, each having ten thousand branches,
and in each branch ten thousand twigs, and in each true twig ten thousand
clusters, and on every one of the clusters ten thousand grapes, and every grape
when pressed will give five and twenty measures of wine. And when anyone
of the saints shall lay hold of a cluster, another shall cry out, "I am a better
cluster; take me; bless the Lord through me." In like manner [the Lord de-
clared] that a grain of wheat would produce ten thousand ears, and that every
ear should have ten thousand grains, and every grain would yield ten pounds
of clear, pure, fine flour; and that all other fruit-bearing trees, and seeds and
grass, would produce in similar proportions; and that all animals feeding [only]
on the produce of the earth, should [in those days] become peaceful and har-
monious among each other, and be in perfect subjection to man.

§4. And these things are borne witness to in writing by Papias, the hearer
of John, and a companion of Polycarp, in his fourth book; for there were five
books compiled by him. And he says in addition, "Now these things are
credible to believers." And he says that, "when the traitor Judas did not give
credit to them, and put the question, 'How then can things about to bring forth
so abundantly be wrought by the Lord?', the Lord declared, 'They who shall
come to these [times] shall see.' "

We must agree with Eusebius that this parable cannot be a genuine saying
of Jesus in its present form, and that it is in fact rather absurd. Yet it would
seem that Irenaeus accepted this unlikely story solely because of his belief
that Papias had such a very close connection with John (cf. §[13]). Though
Irenaeus is not approving anything strictly heretical, Eusebius refuses to
make any allowances for Papias because of his own total opposition to the
doctrine of the Millennium.

c. Testimony of Papias and the Presbyter to Mark and Matthew
(EH III.39.14-17)

[14] καὶ ἄλλας δὲ τῇ ἰδίᾳ γραφῇ παρ-
αδίδωσιν Ἀριστίωνος τοῦ πρόσθεν
δεδηλωμένον τῶν τοῦ Κυρίου λόγων
διηγήσεις καὶ τοῦ πρεσβυτέρου
Ἰωάννου παραδόσεις· ἐφ᾽ ἃς τοὺς
φιλομαθεῖς ἀναπέμψαντες.
ἀναγκαίως νῦν προσθήσομεν ταῖς
προεκτεθείσαις αὐτοῦ φωναῖς παράδοσιν ἣν περὶ Μάρκου τοῦ τὸ εὐαγγέλιον γεγραφότος ἐκτέθειται διὰ
τούτων·
[15] καὶ τοῦθ᾽ ὁ πρεσβύτερος ἔλε-
γεν· Μάρκος μὲν ἑρμηνευτὴς Πέτρου γενόμενος, ὅσα ἐμνημόνευσεν
ἀκριβῶς ἔγραψεν οὐ μέντοι τάξει
τὰ ὑπὸ Κυρίου ἢ λεχθέντα ἢ πραχθέντα.
οὔτε γὰρ ἤκουσεν τοῦ Κυρίου οὔτε
παρηκολούθησεν αὐτῷ
ὕστερον δὲ ὡς ἔφην Πέτρῳ· ὃς πρὸς
τὰς χρείας ἐποιεῖτο τὰς διδασκαλίας ἀλλ᾽ οὐχ ὥσπερ σύνταξιν τῶν
κυριακῶν λογίων, ὥστε οὐδὲν ἥμαρτεν Μάρκος οὕτως ἔνια γράψας ὡς
ἀπεμνημόνευσεν.

ἑνὸς γὰρ ἐποιήσατο πρόνοιαν τοῦ
μηδὲν ὧν ἤκουσεν παραλιπεῖν ἢ ψεύσασθαί τι ἐν αὐτοῖς. ταῦτα μὲν οὖν
ἱστόρηται τῷ Παπίᾳ περὶ τοῦ Μάρκου.
[16] περὶ δὲ τοῦ Ματθαίου ταῦτ᾽ εἴ-
ρηται·
Ματθαῖος μὲν οὖν Ἑβραΐδι
διαλέκτῳ τὰ λόγια συνετάξατο,
ἡρμήνευσεν δ᾽ αὐτὰ ὡς ἦν δυνατὸς
ἕκαστος.
[17] κέχρηται δ᾽ ὁ αὐτὸς μαρτυρίαις ἀπὸ τῆς Ἰωάννου προτέρας
ἐπιστολῆς καὶ ἀπὸ τῆς Πέτρου
ὁμοίως, ἐκτέθειται δὲ καὶ ἄλλην ἱστορίαν περὶ γυναικὸς ἐπὶ πολλαῖς
ἁμαρτίαις διαβληθείσης ἐπὶ τοῦ
Κυρίου, ἣν τὸ καθ᾽ Ἑβραίους εὐαγγέλιον περιέχει.

[14] And also in his own book he
hands on other accounts of the
above-mentioned Aristion of the
words of the Lord and traditions of
the presbyter John, to which we refer those eager for instruction.
At this point we shall, of necessity
add to his utterances made above a
tradition which he has expounded
about Mark who wrote the gospel,
as follows:
[15] And this the presbyter used to
say: Mark, being the recorder of Peter, wrote accurately but not in order
whatever he [Peter] remembered of
the things either said or done by the
Lord.
For he had neither heard the Lord nor
followed him,
but later Peter, as I said, who used to
make [his] discourses according to
the chreias, but not making as it were
a literary composition of the Lord's
sayings, so that Mark did not err at
all when he wrote certain things just
as he [Peter] recalled them.
For he had but one intention, not to
leave out anything he had heard nor
to falsify anything in them. This is
what was related by Papias about the
[Gospel] of Mark.
[16] But about [that] of Matthew this
was said:
For Matthew composed the logia in
a Hebraic style; but each recorded
them as he was in a position to.

[17] And he has made use of testimonies from the First Letter of John
and likewise from the First Letter of
Peter; and he has also set down another story about a woman accused
of many sins before the Lord, which
the gospel According to the Hebrews contains.

καὶ ταῦτα δ᾽ ἡμῖν ἀναγκαίως πρὸς τοῖς ἐκτεθεῖσιν ἐπιτετηρήσθω.

And so these things are of necessity to have been noted down by us in addition to what has been set out.

Notes to "Testimony of Papias and the Presbyter"

[14] Ἀριστίωνος . . . διηγήσεις καὶ τοῦ πρεσβυτέρου Ἰωάννου παραδόσεις, "accounts of Aristion . . . and the traditions of the Presbyter John." Note how Eusebius distinguishes between the "accounts" of Aristion and the "traditions" of the Presbyter John: the latter's statements seem to have for him the authority of the main Tradition.

ἀναγκαίως, "of necessity." Despite all his derogatory remarks about Papias, Eusebius finds himself constrained (ἀναγκαίως) by his scholarly integrity as a historian to record two traditions from Papias which he regards as authentic. Also Eusebius actually equates the person whom he calls "the Presbyter John" with "the Presbyter" of Papias. It would seem that Papias thinks the plain title "the Presbyter" is sufficient identification. The repetition of ἀναγκαίως in [17] shows that everything in between is to be regarded as coming from the Tradition by virtue of "inclusion."

ταῖς προεκτεθείσαις αὐτοῦ φωναῖς, "to his utterances made above," that is, in §§8b-13. (G. Bardy, in loc., correctly sees here a reference to EH II.15.2.)

τὸ εὐαγγέλιον, "the Gospel." Note that Eusebius, who has read Papias's Five Books, declares that Papias is speaking about the Gospel of Mark, our Mark, the Mark that Eusebius knows. This seems to be the earliest clear use of the term "euaggelion" to denote one of the four canonical Gospels.

[15] ὁ πρεσβύτερος, "the Presbyter." This expression, as we have shown above, must refer to our Apostle John; it is a term of affection, one that the Apostle applied to himself in 2 John and 3 John, and is a usage of which Eusebius is aware (cf. EH III.25.3). It is really somewhat disingenuous for the majority of critics to profess, as they do, complete ignorance regarding the identity of this Presbyter; the Apostle John is in any case the most likely candidate, and the most obvious.

ἔλεγεν, "used to say." The imperfect tense implies that the Presbyter would reiterate this comment whenever the occasion arose. And this in turn implies that there was something either in the nature or in the origin of the Gospel of Mark that was an ongoing problem.

Μάρκος μὲν ἑρμηνευτὴς Πέτρου γενόμενος, "Mark being the recorder of Peter." ἑρμηνευτής is used here in its root meaning of one who simply transmits or records what he has been told; it does not mean one who "explains." γενόμενος means quite simply "who was," or "when he was," though Lawlor and Oulton (2:113) prefer to render "who had been," thus possibly implying that Peter had died before the Second Gospel was written. (Also see Riley's treatment of this passage above, pt. 2, ch. 7, §6.) For *interpres* meaning *amanuensis,* see Jerome *Ep.* 120.11.

ὅσα ἐμνημόνευσεν, "whatever he [Peter] remembered." Though the third singular, "he," grammatically speaking, can refer to Mark, as many translators make it do, yet to link them is to go against the sense of the passage, because Mark had no deeds or sayings of the Lord to remember, not having followed him. For our text says that it is Peter who recalls what the Lord said and did, and it is Mark's function to write it all down carefully. In any case, Eusebius understood the sentence in this way (EH II.15), and this should be decisive.

ἀκριβῶς ἔγραψεν οὐ μέντοι τάξει, "wrote accurately but not in order." τάξις can be equally used for indicating either literary or chronological order; the context alone can decide. Here the context demands the notion of literary order, the order required in a true literary composition (though it does not exclude the other sense). This clause has a strong reminiscence of Luke 1:3 (ἀκριβῶς καθεξῆς σοι γράψαι) and it is worth noting that in EH III.24.14-15 Eusebius says of Luke that "at the beginning of his Gospel he has provided the reason why he has fashioned the σύνταξις (προύθηκεν δι᾽ ἣν πεποίηται τὴν σύνταξιν). σύνταξις is the identical word that Eusebius uses in the next sentence to indicate what the Gospel of Mark is not!

πρὸς τὰς χρείας, "according to the Chreias." J. Kürzinger is correct in understanding χρεία as the contemporary grammatical term for a special kind of anecdote with a striking conclusion.[11] The Gospel of Mark consists of a series of χρεία and ἀπομνημονεύματα (a longer form of χρεία as a rule). (Cf. also pt. 2, ch. 3, §4.a.)

ἀλλ᾽ οὐχ ὥσπερ σύνταξιν, "not as it were a syntaxis." The Presbyter is saying that Mark is not a syntaxis or literary composition according to the rules of the grammarians, whereas Luke is. This phrase is epexegetical of "not in order (ταξις)."

ὥστε οὐδὲν ἥμαρτεν Μάρκος, "so that Mark did not err at all." The Presbyter seems to be implying that Mark had been criticized not only with regard to his lack of literary style, probably by unfavourable comparison with some other available material, but also for errors (cf. Mk 1:2—Isaiah instead of "Malachi").

οὕτως ἔνια γράψας ὡς ἀπεμνημόνευσεν "thus writing some things just as he [Peter] had recalled [them]." In the whole of this passage it is Mark who is doing the "recording" and Peter who in his utterances is doing the "remembering"; it is disingenuous to argue, as many critics do, that Mark is remembering what Peter had remembered!

ἢ ψεύσασθαί τι ἐν αὐτοῖς "or to falsify anything in them." The Presbyter hints at certain difficulties in the text, but asserts that Mark made no attempt to "improve" either by addition or alteration.

περὶ δὲ τοῦ Μάρκου, "and about the [Gospel] of Mark." Eusebius is speaking here, and he recognizes that Papias has the same Gospel of Mark as he himself.

[16] περὶ δὲ τοῦ Ματθαίου, "and about (that) of Matthew." Eusebius, who had Papias's Five Books at his disposal, is clear that Papias is also speaking about Eusebius's own Gospel of Matthew, that is, about our own Greek Gospel of Matthew.

Ἑβραΐδι διαλέκτῳ, "in a Hebraic [Jewish] style." J. Kürzinger has demonstrated that this phrase in its present context must be rendered as "in a Jewish style [of composition]" ("Das Papiaszeugnis und die Erstgestalt des Matthäus Evangeliums," Bib Zeitschr. NF [1960]: 19-38).

τὰ λόγια συνετάξατο, "composed the Logia." It is not quite clear whether Eusebius is here quoting Papias himself or Papias's Presbyter. In either case the assertion is authoritative; the meaning of "composed" is that Matthew collected and put in order the sayings,

---

[11]See Kürzinger, *Papias von Hierapolis und die Evangelien des N.T.* (Regensburg, 1983) ch. 3, n. 8. In Liddell and Scott's lexicon, the fifth category of meaning of χρεία is given as "(Rhet.) pregnant sentence, maxim, frequently illustrated by an anecdote"; it also gives references to various authors including Theon, the famous rhetor contemporary with Papias. Kürzinger gives a number of examples to show that χρεία was in common use at that period to describe the literary form of the kind of story units we find in Mark. Cf. also R. O. P. Taylor, *The Groundwork of the Gospel*, 78.

which of course are the sayings of the Lord. (The sentence cannot be understood to mean that Matthew "invented" the Sayings.) Eusebius, it seems, is quoting what Papias has to say about Eusebius's (and our) Gospel of Matthew. It follows therefore that λόγια is simply a way of describing the Gospel of Matthew by means of its contents, for it is *par excellence* a compilation of the sayings of Jesus.[12]

ἡρμήνευσεν δ'αὐτὰ ὡς ἦν δυνατὸς ἕκαστος, "but each recorded them as he was in a position to." We know for certain that Papias knew and used all four gospels (see n. 6 above). The key word in this sentence is ἕκαστος, ("each of two") which is usually taken to refer to any or all of those who delved into and utilized the λόγια, whoever they were. But ἕκαστος is too specific to be interpreted in this way, if another more plausible interpretation can be found.

Now although Papias's Presbyter does not specifically refer to Luke, now that we know that he did know and did use Luke, we can see that the Presbyter (and Papias) are contrasting Mark's lack of τάξις with both Luke's σύνταξις (that is, his normal Greek style) and Matthew's Ἑβραΐδι διαλέκτῳ (Jewish literary style). And speaking here about Matthew, Eusebius is telling us that Papias sees the other two, that is, each (ἕκαστος), as extracting material from Matthew, each according to his need. And this interpretation is not only legitimate but agrees with what Clement of Alexandria wrote about Mark being the third gospel in point of time.

[17] μαρτυρίαις ἀπὸ . . . Ἰωάννου . . . Πέτρου, "testimonies from . . . John . . . Peter." Eusebius reaffirms Papias's knowledge of 1 Peter (cf. EH II.15) with its reference to our evangelist Mark at 5:13.

ἀλλην ἱστορίαν περὶ γυναικός, "another story about a woman." Most commentators take this as a reference to John 7:53–8:11, a pericope which had several resting places before it finally came to rest in John.

ἀναγκαίως, "of necessity." This use of ἀναγκαίως coupled with its appearance in [14] marks an *inclusio* that contains two important traditions recorded by Papias.

ἐπιτετηρήσθω, "are to have been noted down." The use of the third person imperative is a trick of style often employed by Eusebius when he comes to the end of a particular discussion (cf. I.6.11). (See Robert M. Grant *Eusebius as Church Historian* [Oxford: Clarendon Press, 1980] 24.) Eusebius is here instructing the reader to relate what has been told him in these sections with what he has recorded elsewhere, for example, EH III.24.25.

Commentary

What has been attempted here is to view Papias in a consistent manner through the eyes of Eusebius with all his learning and with all his prejudices, in accord with the principles of historical criticism. In the past

---

[12]See W. G. Kümmel, *Introduction to the New Testament* (London: SCM Press, 1965) 43-44, who concurs that here *logia* means our Gospel of Matthew, and quotes J. Munck, "Presbyters and Disciples of the Lord in Papias," HTR (1959): 223-43. It would seem from Justin's use of the term "gospel" (εὐαγγελιον) that it was in fairly general use by A.D. 150; but before that date our gospels seem to have been referred to by a number of different terms, e.g., ἑρμηνειαι, ἀπομνημονευματα. In each case the book of the gospel is indicated by a term descriptive of its contents. So is it here with *logia*, which Eusebius here regards as the equivalent of the Gospel of Matthew. Cf. J. Donovan, *The Logia in Ancient and Recent Literature* (Cambridge: Heffer, 1924); cf. also EH III.24.5 where Matthew and John are described as ὑπομνηματα.

scholars and critics have invariably sought to wrestle with the obscurities of Eusebius's extracts from the lost Five Books of Papias without invoking the aid of Eusebius himself who, having not only read them but also having sifted all that had been passed on to him by the earliest Fathers and Apologists, knew exactly what he still needed to take from Papias to complete the synthesis he was making. The key to the full understanding of this chapter is to examine what Eusebius has already set forth here and elsewhere (in his discursive and chronological manner) in the light of his special theological interests and prejudices, which he did not hesitate to bring into his historical record. He was passionately interested in the final formation of the canon of Scripture and saw no reason why he should not bring his own views, and his arguments for them, into his *Ecclesiastical History*. From St. Dionysius of Alexandria he inherited a strong aversion to Millenarianism and so to the Apocalypse of John which seemed to provide a foundation for this doctrine. He also inherited, through Origen and Dionysius, the Alexandrian School's interest in literary criticism and he understood very well the literary and critical problems caused by the tradition that John the Apostle wrote both the Apocalypse and the Gospel. These convictions, coupled with his surely justified view that Papias showed great lack of judgment over the extract about the Millennium (that misled even Irenaeus), tended to dominate his selection of material from Papias. Thus two-thirds of chapter 39 are devoted to what he thought, at the time, to be a new argument for the Apocalypse not being by John the Apostle, and also to dismissing the greater part of Papias's work as gossip of uncertain value. Nevertheless he could not in fairness conclude the chapter without quoting two pieces of information from Papias which as a historian he knew to be sound tradition and which he needed in order to complete his own synthesis about the origin and authenticity of the Gospels. In the light of his awareness that Papias already enjoyed the use of our four gospels, each of the extracts he selected from Papias throws light on problems that were then in process of discussion and solution.

The first extract concerns the problem of the origin and composition of Mark. The two recensions of the Old Latin prologue to Mark make it clear that the precise relationship of the Gospel of Mark to Peter was a matter that needed clarification. Eusebius's quotation from Papias makes it clear that Mark really and truly recorded what he had heard from the lips of Peter himself, but it also gives us a glimpse of some controversy about both the style and the accuracy of Mark's Gospel. That is to say, its style was, it seems, being compared unfavorably with the literary style of both Luke and Matthew; moreover there were also, it seems, certain discrepancies between Mark and the other Gospels over matters of fact, or what appeared to be such (cf. 1:2; 6:8). Eusebius then proceeds to quote Papias's record of the actual words of "The Presbyter," whom we have now identified as St. John the Apostle, in order to delete any idea that Mark's Gospel was not an entirely factual and literal record of what Peter had said; so that if there were any such discrepancies they were not to be resolved by saying that Mark had erred. The rather odd phrase that "Peter . . . made his teachings according to the *chreiai*" supports the view that Peter was not writing a book but in this instance at any rate giving his teachings or reminiscences in the form of a series of anecdotes or *chreiai*.

Neither Papias nor the Presbyter tells us why Peter chose this particular form for his teaching; at least if they did, Eusebius did not think it necessary to tell us. The Presbyter is at any rate clear that what Peter said and Mark wrote down did not conform to the contemporary idea of the literary style that an author would adopt. Finally, this new information about Peter and Mark's Gospel is intended to be taken together with what we learn about Mark in EH II.15 and VI.14.

We come now to the second piece of information that is meant to dovetail into what Eusebius has already written elsewhere. In EH III.15, and here (III.39.14-17), he has authenticated the Gospel of Mark, and in VI.14 he has told us that the Gospel of Mark is subsequent to both Matthew and Luke, the Gospels with the genealogies. With his interest in critical and literary questions relating to the New Testament writings,[13] Eusebius is now able to complete his instruction by producing Papias's explanation of the relationship between Matthew and the other two Synoptic Gospels. As we have already shown, Eusebius assumes that Papias is referring to the Gospel of Matthew we all know, and not to a proto-Matthew or a collection of Sayings, such as "Q" is reputed to be. For Papias, and for Eusebius, "Matthew" is of course the Apostle referred to in his preface, and Papias's description of the Gospel of Matthew as the *logia,* that is the Sayings of the Lord, is peculiarly apt. Papias, and Eusebius too, make it clear that Matthew is unlike Mark in that it has a very definite literary style, a Jewish style, just as Luke conforms on the whole to the normal conventional Greek style of "bios" literature.

We have now arrived at the position where we can see that Papias and Eusebius recognized that whereas Luke was composed in the contemporary style of a Greek book and Matthew composed in the style acceptable to the Jews, Mark conformed to neither style but was composed in rather unique circumstances by Mark and Peter working together as explained above. This being so, it was natural for Eusebius to ask himself the question: What then is the relationships between these three documents? And

---

[13]See "Excursus 1: Eusebius's Bias for Hebrews and against the Apocalypse."

he finds in Papias an answer that fits in perfectly with what Clement of Alexandria had said; and the answer is that each, that is, Luke and Mark, recorded, that is, utilized, the logia of Matthew "as he was in a position to" (or as Kürzinger wrote, "wie er dazu in der Lage war"). Luke and Mark therefore took of the Sayings of Matthew into their respective Gospels just what they needed for their own particular situation and requirements.[14]

The final section [17] confirms Papias's knowledge of 1 John and of 1 Peter (compare EH II.15.2). The story "about the woman accused of many sins before the Lord" is generally agreed to be that found now in John 7:53–8:11. We have no sure information about the "Gospel of the Hebrews" in which it is said also to be recorded; but this would indicate that it cannot be identical with our Gospel of Matthew.

8. Summary of the Findings
on Eusebius's Treatment of Papias's Statements

The above exhaustive examination of Eusebius's teaching on Gospel origins enables us to make the following judgments:

a. Eusebius has collected together in his own chronological manner all the trustworthy information about the Gospels that was available to him, and, as we shall see in the next chapter, nothing of consequence was added thereafter. He himself did not make a strict synthesis of it, though he held all the elements of the synthesis in his own mind, as is clear from the cross references he makes from time to time. For him, Matthew is the first writ-

---

[14]It is worth noting that Robert H. Gundry in his *Matthew: A Commentary on His Literary and Theological Art* (Grand Rapids MI: Eerdmans, 1982) has independently arrived at most of these conclusions; cf. his appendix: "Some Higher-Critical Conclusions," 599-613. For he concludes as follows (620): (1) that Papias's five books were composed before A.D. 110 (and not ca. 135), and thus only some ten years after the death of John the Apostle; (2) that "the Presbyter John" and St. John the Apostle are one and the same, despite the efforts of Eusebius to make them into separate persons; (3) that Eusebius's attempt to distinguish two persons was motivated by his dislike of the Apocalypse for its reference to the millennium and by his overriding desire to dissociate it from St. John the Apostle; (4) that ἑβραΐδι διαλέκτῳ means "in a Hebrew [literary] style," and not "in the Hebrew language or dialect," so that both Irenaeus and Origen were wrong in thinking that it meant that Matthew was originally published in Aramaic; (5) that the Apostle Matthew is the true author of the Gospel that bears his name.

These surprising conclusions are—in the opinion of the present writer—all correct, but number 5 also produces acute embarrassment for Gundry since he accepts the priority of Mark. For he then has, among other problems, the difficult task of explaining why the Apostle Matthew should feel obliged to be dependent on the work of Mark, who was not an apostle and who never heard or saw Jesus. He is thus unable to perceive the true meaning of Papias's statement that "each recorded them according to his needs" (EH III.39.16).

ten Gospel, composed in Judea by the Apostle Matthew for the Jews ''in their own tongue.'' Mark is next dealt with in the second place (EH III.24) and is regarded as the memoirs of Peter faithfully recorded at Rome by his disciple Mark (EH II.15). Nonetheless, Eusebius accepts the statement of Clement of Alexandria that Mark came after Matthew and Luke, so far as chronological order is concerned. The Gospel of Luke of course was written by Paul's disciple Luke for the benefit of his Greek churches. The relationship between the three Synoptic Gospels is completed by Eusebius with the quotation from Papias that both the others made use of the logia of Matthew. Thus we have two statements: (1) Matthew and Luke are prior to Mark, and (2) Luke and Mark both made use of the ''logia'' of Matthew.

b. Eusebius's judgements on Papias and Irenaeus in regard to St. John the Apostle and ''the Presbyter John'' cannot be accepted without making due allowance for his bias against Millenarianism on the one hand, and for his unique deference to the judgment of Dionysius on the other. There can be no doubt that *odium theologicum* is at the root of his contempt of Papias.

c. The critical grounds advanced by Dionysius against Johannine authorshp of the Apocalypse, which appear overwhelming to so many modern scholars, are of course in fundamental opposition with the practically unanimous voice of tradition that John was indeed its author. To decide whether the critics or the tradition is right is not our concern here. What is certain is that Eusebius's own arguments for affirming the existence of two Johns are of no value whatever, and the critics must find another answer to their problem, since his arguments do not stand up to critical examination.

Excursus 1
Eusebius's Bias for Hebrews and against the Apocalypse

Perhaps the most noteworthy aspect of Eusebius's treatment of Hebrews and the Apocalypse in his *Ecclesiastical History* is his dependence on the views of St. Dionysius of Alexandria, a dependence that is not unexpected in view of the praise he accords him in Book VI. Three points need to be made.

1. Eusebius and Hebrews

Eusebius declares that there is only one universally recognized Letter of Clement of Rome ''which he sent in the name of the Roman Church to the Church of Corinth'' (EH III.38.1), and that the so-called Second Letter attributed to him was not recognized by the Early Fathers, nor were various other more recent forgeries. And he goes on to say that 1 Clement

echoes many thoughts from the Epistle to the Hebrews, and indeed makes many verbal quotations from it, proving beyond doubt that the document [Hebrews] was not of recent origin, and making it seem quite natural to include it with the rest of the list of the Apostle's writings. Paul had communicated with the Hebrews by writing to them in their native tongue; and some say that the evangelist Luke, others that this same Clement, translated the original text. The second suggestion is the more convincing, in view of the similarity of phraseology shown throughout by the Epistle of Clement and the Epistle to the Hebrews, and of the absence of any great different between the two works in the underlying thought. (EH III.38.2-3)

Dionysius, in a letter recorded by Eusebius (EH VI.41.6), quotes Heb 10:34 as being Paul's, and writes that in their endurance the martyrs of Alexandria were "like those to whom Paul paid tribute: 'They took with cheerfulness the plundering of their belongings.' " And Clement of Alexandria supports his assertion of Pauline authorship by affirming that our Hebrews is Luke's Greek version made from the original Hebrew of Paul, the omission of whose signature to the Letter is explained in a quotation from "the blessed presbyter" (EH VI.14.4). Furthermore, Eusebius himself approves the suggestion of Origen that Clement may have translated it since 1 Clement contains many verbal quotations from Hebrews, besides great similarity of thought and phraseology (compare 1 Clem 17 = Heb 11:37; 1 Clem 21 = Heb 4:12; 1 Clem 27 = Heb 10:23; 1 Clem 36 = Heb 2:17,18, and so forth). Nevertheless, despite his recognition of the lack of the support of the church of Rome for the Pauline authorship (III.3.5), despite the declaration of Origen that "God alone knows who wrote it," Eusebius prefers to adhere to the affirmative opinion of Dionysius, supported by the general tradition of the Eastern churches, that Paul is the author. The full list of references to Hebrews in EH is as follows: II.17; III.3, 38; VI.13, 14, 20, 25, 41.

2. Eusebius and the Style of Dionysius

There is an interesting example of Eusebius's deference to Dionysius even as regards literary style in EH IX.3-4, where he plagiarizes the phraseology of the latter's letter which he has already quoted in VII.10.4. (See G. A. Williamson, 360n2.)

3. Eusebius and the Apocalypse

But the most interesting example of all is Eusebius's treatment of the Apocalypse. The list of references is as follows: III.18; III.24.15; III.25.2-4; III.28; III.39.6; IV.18; IV.24; V.8; V.18.24; VI.25; VII.24; VII.25. In

III.18 Eusebius speaks of "what is called" the Apocalypse of John. In III.24.15, he states that the views of "most peole to this day are evenly divided" about the authorship, which his further quotations hardly support. For in III.25 he seems to admit that the Apocalypse of John is one of the "recognized" books, but in III.25.4 he actually puts it among the "spurious" books, though with the qualification "if this be thought to be the right place for it." In III.28 he refers the reader to the lengthy statements from Dionysius of Alexandria in VII.25 about the authorship of the Apocalypse. In III.29 he notes that the Nicolaitans are mentioned in it. In III.39.6 he mentions for the first time his own view that "the Presbyter John" might be the author of the Apocalypse. In IV.18 he explicitly acknowledges that Justin Martyr stated that the Apocalypse was the work of John the Apostle. In IV.24 there is a passing reference to the Apocalypse. In V.8 Eusebius says that Irenaeus makes a definite statement about John being the author of the Apocalypse. In V.18.24 he tells us that the heretic Apollonius makes use of texts taken from the Apocalypse of John. In VI.25 he quotes the statement of Origen, without any comment, that John the Evangelist wrote the Apocalypse. In VII.24 he refers to Nepos, an Egyptian bishop who used the Apocalypse to support a doctrine of Millenarianism which was refuted in a pamphlet of Dionysius from which Eusebius quotes at some length. And finally in VII.25 he sets out in full the arguments advanced by Dionysius for the Apocalypse not being written by John the Evangelist, and it is here that is first found the suggestion of a second man with the name John, who may also have been buried in a tomb in Ephesus distinct from the tomb of John the Apostle.

Eusebius was in an quandary over the Apocalypse. He knew very well that all the earliest writers and Fathers of the Church down to his own time (he ignores the doubtful witness of Cerinthus and the Roman priest Gaius) accepted Johannine authorship, except his own favorite author, St. Dionysius of Alexandria, who when faced with the difficult problem of the conflicting styles of Gospel and Apocalypse made a tentative suggestion about there being a "second John." Nobody took up his suggestion about there being a "second John." Nobody took up his suggestion for another fifty years until Eusebius himself decided to refloat the idea afresh upon what is now seen to be meretricious evidence. It is true that Jerome in his account of Papias and John, in his *De Vir.* III.9 and 18, speaks guardedly in favor of Eusebius's suggestion; but it should be noted that he also clearly refers to Papias as "the pupil of John," meaning the Apostle, and he also restricts the authorship of "The Presbyter" to 2 and 3 John (Acts of the Council of Rome, 382). Nowhere indeed does Jerome support Eusebius in his denial that Papias knew John personally—an assertion that is cardinal for the acceptance of Eusebius's theory; on the contrary, he accepts that he was the disciple of St. John and never questions John's authorship of the Apocalypse.

In conclusion, it seems clear that most modern critics have let themselves be deceived by Eusebius's opportunist advocacy of a personal whim, based on a misconception fostered by Papias's clumsy style. The real reason for giving undue weight to Eusebius's biased view has been the conviction, on grounds of internal criticism, that the Apocalypse simply cannot be by the author of the Fourth Gospel, and that Eusebius is on the right side anyway. But if his arguments for the existence of "the Presbyter John" cannot stand—and they cannot—then no one is any longer entitled to claim any support from Papias or Eusebius. Moreover the common modern view that Papias is an untrustworthy "pinhead" is a gross caricature based on the same false premises. It is indeed quite astounding the degree of infallibility that has been attributed to an *obiter dictum* that is contrary to all the evidence once it is probed.

Excursus 2
The Origin of the Notion
of an "Aramaic" Gospel of Matthew

The notion stems from the phrase of Papias quoted by Eusebius in EH III.39.16, Ἑβραΐδι διαλέκτῳ. The modern discussion of its meaning was initiated by J. Kürzinger (see ch. 3, n. 8), and continued in his *Papias von Hierapolis*. Kürzinger explains that in the first century διάλεκτος commonly meant both "language" and "style," so that our phrase could mean either "in a Jewish Language" or "in a Jewish style," depending on the context. In the present instance Kürzinger pointed out, and we agree with him, that it is clear from the context that the Presbyter had been explaining some problems of the style and/or content of Mark, since it possessed neither the Jewish style of Matthew nor the normal literary style of a Greek biography such as Luke, but was the result of some quite special collaboration between Peter and Mark.

When Irenaeus came to write some seventy or so years later, about 180, the controversy over the style of Mark would seem to have been forgotten, but Irenaeus, who must have read the Five Books of Papias, had not forgotten the pregnant phrase and in fact paraphrased it as follows: "Matthew published a written Gospel among the Jews *in their own dialect.*" (For the Greek text, see ch. 4, §3.)

In rephrasing the words of Papias as "among the Jews in their own dialect" he opened the way to a future misunderstanding, even if, as is possible, he himself properly understood what Papias meant. For though "in their own dialect" can equally well mean "in their own style," yet when divorced from its context in connection with Mark, it would be natural to understand it to mean "in their own language" instead of "in the Jewish style." And Irenaeus's great work was soon translated into Latin and diffused throughout the Roman Empire. Thus it was natural too for Origen, some sixty or so years later in his Commentary on Matthew, to make still more explicit the phrase "in their own language" by writing "in Jewish characters." And this gradual transition was all the easier because everyone knew not only that Matthew was written for a people who spoke Aramaic among themselves, but that Jesus himself also spoke it.

Kürzinger however prefers to argue that Irenaeus himself did not misunderstand Papias's "in their own dialect," but that it was Origen who was misled by the ambiguous phrase into assuming that Irenaeus meant "in their own *language*" (cf. *Papias von Hierapolis,* 35-40).

Last of all, Eusebius, writing another seventy or so years later, about 320, in the same city of Caesarea in Palestine, where Origen had ended his days, finally put his seal on this misconception when he wrote (EH III.24): Ματθαῖος τε γὰρ πρότερον ᾽Εβραίοις κηρύξας, ὡς ἤμελλεν καὶ ἐφ᾽ ἑτέρους ἰέναι, πατρίῳ γλώττῃ γραφῇ παραδοὺς τὸ κατ᾽ αὐτὸν εὐαγγέλιον ("Now Matthew in the first place having preached to the Jews, when he decided to go to others also, committed his own Gospel to writing in his native tongue").

Thus the sequence in the development of the misunderstanding is complete, and the legend of the Aramaic Gospel of Matthew was confirmed. (For the texts, see above, ch. 3, §7.)

5

Fourth-Century Tradition After Eusebius

It will not be necessary to set out in full the witness of the fourth-century Fathers since that has been completely done in a recent work by H. Merkel;[1] it will be enough to indicate where they add peripheral details to, or differ from, the hard core of the Gospel tradition which they all accept, and which has been recorded in chapters 2, 3, and 4 above.

1. Ephraem Syrus (ca. 306-373)

Ephraem Syrus, a deacon of Edessa, wrote exclusively in Syriac, but his writings were later translated into Greek and Latin. He wrote a commentary on the Diatessaron of Tatian, who was a pupil of Justin Martyr at Rome. The Diatessaron (ca. 150-180) is a notable witness to the authority already enjoyed by the four Gospels. In his commentary[2] Ephraem explained that the Gospels are not "concordant," because the Evangelists wrote at different times and in response to different situations. Ephraem thought that Matthew was written originally in Hebrew and later turned into Greek; Mark was composed at Rome in Latin (seemingly his own unsupported guess) and that it was derived from Simon Peter; that Luke wrote in Greek and that John was the last to write a Gospel and lived into the reign of Trajan.

2. Epiphanius (ca. 315-403)

Epiphanius, bishop of Salamis, a stern upholder of the faith of Nicaea, firmly adhered to the tradition that the Apostle John wrote both the Gospel and the Apocalypse, while attacking some heretics (whom he called Al-

---

[1]*Die Pluralität der Evangelien;* cf. above, ch. 1, n. 20. Merkel also instances Julius Africanus, *Epist. ad. Aristides* (p. 534); Dionysius Alex., *Epist. ad Basilides;* Apollinaris Laodicensis, *Comm. in Matt.* (ante 390) ed. Reuss, fragments 46, 100, 106, 130, 132, 135; Theodore of Mopsuestia, *Comm. in Ioann. Ap.* (ca. 400) which contains a long account of how John came to write his Gospel at the request of the brethren of Ephesus—in fact, an elaboration of the anti-Marcionite prologue; John Chrysostom, *Hom, in Matt.* I (ca. 390); Ambrose, *Comm. on Luke, Prol.,* 1-4, 7-8. But none of these add anything important to the matter presented in this chapter, and therefore do not require to be printed here.

[2]Cf. *Comm. in Diatess. Tatiani* (sec. ms. Ch. Beatty 709, ed. Leloir [1963] 250ff.); also *Vers. arm. add.* (ed. Leloir, CSCO 137/145, app. 1).

ogi) who asserted that Cerinthus and not John was the author of both. Like Ephraem, Epiphanius saw no real conflict between the seemingly discordant passages in the Gospels. For him the Apostle Matthew wrote first in Hebrew characters (following Origen). He is also clear that Mark's Gospel was composed in Peter's lifetime, that Mark was a followers of St. Peter and was entrusted by him with the task of setting out his Gospel; but he also thought that Mark was one of the seventy-two disciples (*Panarion haer.* 51.6.10-12, ed. Holl, GCS 31).

3. Ambrosiaster (fl. ca. 370-400)

Ambrosiaster is the name originally given by Erasmus of Rotterdam to a set of Latin commentaries on the Old Latin text of thirteen letters of Paul that were attributed throughout the Middle Ages to St. Ambrose. It seems, however, to have been established by modern scholars that this attribution is wrong, but there is still no agreement about their true author, save that he must be a late fourth-century commentator of great importance and reliability. To Ambrosiaster, however, must now almost certainly be ascribed *Liber Quaestionum Veteris et Novi Testamenti* (ed. A. Souter, CSEL [908]), once attributed to St. Augustine (cf. ODCC in loc.). In this manuscript there is the following interesting passage on the order of the Gospels.

Ad IV. Quoniam constat quattuor libros rite conscriptow gestorum et dictorum Domini, sciendum quis eorum ordo sit. Evangelium ordinatione colligitur magis quam tempore.	In respect of IV. Given that there are only four duly composed gospels of the words and deeds of the Lord, we now inquire what is their order. The gospel is arranged according to the order [of their contents] rather than in chronological order.
Matthaeus ergo primus ponendus est, quia ab ipsa promissione sumpsit initium, id est, ab Abraham, cui facta promission est incarnationis domini Iesu Christi. Post hunc Lucas, quia incarnationem hanc quomodo facta est narrat. Tertius Marcus, qui evangelium quod praedictum est a Christo, testatur in lege promissum.	Therefore, Matthew is put in the first place because he begins from the promise, that is, from Abraham to whom was made the promise of the incarnation of our Lord Jesus Christ. Next comes Luke, because he relates how this incarnation took place. Third comes Mark, who witnesses that the gospel preached by Christ has been promised in the Law.

Quartus autem Ioannes, quia hunc, promissum est Abrahae incarnandus et a Luca quem ad modum incarnatus est dictum est et a Marco evangelium eius iuxta Esiae prophetiam praedicatum ostensum est, aperta voce ostendit Deum dicens: In principio erat verbum et verbum erat apud Deum et Deus erat verbum.

Fourthly John, who, in the sentence "In the beginning was the Word and the Word was with God and the Word was God," shows in clear language that he indeed was God whose incarnation was promised to Abraham and whose manner of becoming incarnate was related by Luke, while Isaiah's prophecy of the gospel was proclaimed by Mark.

4. Jerome (ca. 342-420)

Jerome was able to synthesize the traditions regarding the origins of the Gospels.[3] His teachings may be summarized as follows:

a. The Apostle *Matthew*, the former tax collector wrote the first gospel "in Hebrew characters" (following Origen), but Jerome did not know who later translated it into Greek. He claims to have seen and actually to have transcribed the Hebrew text of Matthew in the library at Caesarea assembled by Pamphilus and used by Eusebius, and adds that this Hebrew text was in use in his time by the Nazarenes in Beroea, a city of Syria. Modern scholars, however, mostly think this must have been a version made earlier from the Greek original.

b. As to *Luke*, Jerome accepts the tradition of the Muratorian Canon that he was the author of the Third Gospel, and that he was a physician; and also the tradition of the Greek anti-Marcionite prologue that he was a Syrian from Antioch and the companion of Paul on much of his journeying, so that the Acts was composed by him largely from firsthand information.

c. As to *Mark*, among Jerome's authorities are Clement of Alexandria's Sixth Book of *Hypotypōses* and also what Papias of Hierapolis wrote in his Five Books. He accepts the tradition that Mark is the person referred to in 1 Peter 5:13, and that he died in Alexandria, a dating in which he follows Eusebius (EH II.24.1—and which presents some difficulties with regard to chronology). To sum up, for Jerome, Mark is "Marcum, cuius evangelium Petro narrante et illo scribente" ("Mark is he whose Gospel consists of Peter's narration and Mark's writing" —*Ep.* 120.11).

d. As regards *John*, Jerome accepts the tradition found in the longer text of the Old Latin prologue that his gospel was composed at the request of the bishops of Asia against the errors of Cerinthus and other heretics such as the Ebionites. He seems to follow Irenaeus in dating the Apocalypse in

---

[3]Cf. *De vir. ill.* I.1, III, VI, VIII, IX, ed. E. C. Richardson, TU. For Jerome's prologue to the four Gospels, see Wordsworth and White, *Novum Testamentum DNJC*, 1.

the reign of Domitian (81-96) rather than in that of Nero (54-68), thus making the fourteenth year of Domitian, A.D. 94, as the date of John's banishment to Patmos; but he agrees with the other testimonies in putting John's death some time after the accession of Trajan (98-117) in the sixty-eighth year after the Crucifixion. But as we saw above (ch. 3, n. 21), Irenaeus was probably making an inadvertent error that Jerome copied, since internal evidence as well as all other external witnesses connect the Apocalypse with Nero.

When Jerome comes to refer to "the Presbyter John," we are able easily to identify the source of his information, that is, Eusebius, EH III.39. It is also worth noting that in the decree of Pope Damasus, *De Explanatione Fidei*, made at the Council of Rome in 382, there is a list of the canonical Scriptures, undoubtedly composed with the aid of Jerome who was present at the council, where we find the final list in which Paul is credited with fourteen Letters; but as regards the Letters of John we read: "One of John the Apostle, two of another John the Presbyter." However, much later in the pontificate of Hormisdas (514-523), in a recension of the Decree of Gelasius, which repeats the above-mentioned Decree of Damasus, we find a return to "the three Letters of the Apostle John,"[4] thus rejecting Jerome's opinion on this point, where we believe he was misled by Eusebius. The attentive reader of the texts of Jerome that follow below will note his reliance on the basic texts we have examined in previous chapters; for he was satisfied that his sources were sound.

De viris inlustribus III (ed. Richardson, TU XIV.1)

Matthew, also called Levi, apostle and previously a publican, first composed the gospel of Christ in Hebrew letters and words for the sake of those of the circumcision who believed. Who it was who later translated it into Greek is not quite certain. However, the Hebrew itself is preserved even now in the library at Caesarea which Pamphilus the martyr so carefully assembled. I also was given the opportunity of transcribing this volume by the Nazarenes who use it in Beroea, a city of Syria. It should be noted that in it, whenever the evangelist has occasion to make use of the witness of the Old Testament—whether it be in his own person or in that of our Lord and Saviour—he does not follow the authority of the Septuagint translators, but that of the Hebrew. Whence are those two forms: "Out of Egypt I have called my son" (2:15) and "For he shall be called a Nazarene" (2:23).

De vir. ill. VII (ed. Richardson, TU XIV.1)

Luke, a physician from Antioch, indicated by his writings that he knew Greek, and that he was a follower of the apostle Paul and the companion of all his journeying: he wrote a gospel about which the same Paul says, "We

---

[4]Cf. Denzinger-Schönmetzer, *Enchiridion Symbolorum, Definitionum et Declarationum de rebus fidei et morum* (Friburg: Herder, 1963) §180m.

have sent with him a brother whose praise is in the gospel thoughout all the
churches'' (2 Cor 8:18), and to the Colossians ''Luke the beloved physician
greets you'' (4:14), and to Timothy ''Luke only is with me'' (2 Tim 4:11).
He also published another outstanding work which is known by the title *Acts
of the Apostles:* its subject matter runs to the second year of Paul's stay at
Rome, that is, the fourth year of Nero. From this we understand that the book
was composed in the same city. However, the *Journeys of Paul and Thecla*
and the whole of the story about the baptized lion we reckon among the apocryphal writings: for how is it that the inseparable companion of the apostle
in his other dealings knew nothing of this one event? Besides Tertullian, who
lived close to that period, relates that a certain presbyter in Asia, an adherent
of the apostle Paul, was convicted by John of being the author of the book:
he admitted that he had done it for love of Paul and gave up his post. Some
people think that whenever Paul says in his epistles ''according to my gospel'' (Rom 16:25) he is referring to Luke's book, and that Luke was taught
the gospel not only by the apostle Paul, who had never been with the Lord in
the flesh, but also by the other apostles. This he himself declares at the beginning of his book where he says, ''Just as they have instructed us who from
the beginning were eyewitnesses and ministers of the word'' (Lk 1:2). Thus
he wrote his gospel in accordance with what he had heard; but he composed
the *Acts of the Apostles* in accordance with what he himself had seen. He is
buried at Constantinople to which city his bones, together with the relics of
Andrew the apostle, were translated in the twentieth year of Constantius.

De vir. ill. VIII (ed. Richardson, TU XIV.1)

Mark, the disciple and interpreter of Peter, wrote a short gospel at the request
of the brethren in Rome in accordance with what he had heard Peter relate. When
Peter heard of it, he approved and by his own authority gave it out to be read by
the churches, as Clement writes in the sixth book of his *Hypotypōses,* and also
Papias, bishop of Hierapolis. Peter himself calls this Mark to mind in that first
epistle where he indicates Rome figuratively by the name of Babylon: ''She who
is elected together with you in Babylon sends greetings, and so does my son
Mark'' (1 Pet 5:13). Accordingly, taking with him the gospel which he had himself composed, he went to Egypt and, first preaching Christ at Alexandria, he
established a church so distinguished for her teaching and sobriety of life that
she constrained all followers of Christ to conform to her example. Philo, that
most sagacious of Jews, seeing that the first church in Alexandria had still a Jewish flavor, wrote a book on their mode of life as though in praise of his own
nation, and just as Luke tells how the believers in Jerusalem had all things in
common, so he made a record of what he saw being done at Alexandria under
the learned Mark. Mark died in the eighth year of Nero and was buried at Alexandria. Annianus succeeded him.

De vir. ill. IX (ed. Richardson, TU XIV.1)

John, the apostle whom Jesus greatly loved, son of Zebedee and brother
of the apostle James whom Herod beheaded after the Lord's passion, wrote
his gospel last of all at the request of the bishops of Asia, against Cerinthus

and other heretics and particularly against the doctrine of the Ebionites which was then springing up with its assertion that Christ did not exist before Mary. For this reason he was obliged to maintain his divine nativity. But there is said to be yet another reason for this work, for when he had read the books of Matthew, Mark and Luke he approved the text of their narration and confirmed the truth of what they said, but they had treated of that one year only in which he had suffered after John's imprisonment. So leaving aside the year whose events had been recounted by the other three, he dealt with what had happened in the earlier time before John was shut up in prison, as may clearly be seen by those who read the books of the four evangelists with care. This fact further removes the discord which seems to obtain between John and the others.

He also wrote a single epistle which begins as follows: "That which was from the beginning, which we have heard and seen with our eyes, which we have looked upon and which our hands have touched, concerning the word of life" (1 Jn 1:1); this is accepted by all men of the church and of learning. The other two of which the first is "The elder to the elect lady and her children" (2 Jn 1) and the next "The elder to the beloved Gaius whom I love in the truth" (3 Jn 1) are said to be John the Presbyter's, whose tomb is shown at Ephesus even today. However, some think that both the memorials are John the evangelist's: we shall discuss this theory when, in due time, we come to Papias, his hearer.

In the fourteenth year, on Domitian initiating the second persecution after Nero, John was banished to the island of Patmos where he wrote his *Apocalypse* which Justin Martyr and Irenaeus have expounded. But when Domitian had been put to death and his decrees abrogated by the senate because of their excessive severity, he returned to Ephesus during the reign of Nerva. There he continued until the emperor Trajan's time, establishing and ordering all the churches of Asia. He died in the sixty-eighth year after the Lord's passion worn out by old age, and he is buried close by that same city.

On Paul, Peter and Mark (*Epistula* 120.11, ed. Hilberg, CSEL 55)

We have often remarked that the apostle Paul was a most learned man and that he was educated at the feet of Gamaliel. The latter addressed the people in the Acts of the Apostles, saying: "And now what have you to do with men such as these? For if [this undertaking] is of God, it will endure; but if it is of men, it shall be destroyed" (Acts 5:38-39). However, although [Paul] had a knowledge of Holy Scripture and of discourse, and although he possessed the gift of a variety of languages so that he might boast in the Lord, saying "I give thanks to God that I speak in tongues more than all of them" (1 Cor 14:18), he was not able adequately to express the grandeur of the divine message in the terms of Greek speech. And he had Titus as a recorder, just as blessed Peter had Mark, whose gospel consists of Peter's narration and the latter's writing. Again the two letters which are said to be Peter's differ from one another in style, character and syntax; from this we deduce that he used different recorders as various circumstances might determine.

Prologus quattuor evangeliorum (praefatio in comm. in Mattheum)
(Wordsworth-White 1:11-14)

There have been many who wrote gospels as Luke the evangelist testifies saying, "Inasmuch as many have endeavoured to set in order the narrative of the things that have been accomplished among us, just as they were delivered to us by those who from the beginning were eyewitnesses and ministers of the word" (1:1-2). Those of the documents that are even now extant, being published by a variety of authors, were the origins of a variety of heresies: examples are the Gospel of the Egyptians, of Thomas, of Matthias, of Bartholomew, even of the Twelve Apostles, of Basilides and of Apelles, and of all the others whom it would take too long to list, since for present purposes it need only be remarked that certain people, lacking the Spirit and grace of God, have endeavoured more "to set in order the narrative" than to expound historical truth.

To such as these one may fittingly apply the prophecy (Ez 13:3, 6) "Woe to those who prophesy from their own heart, who follow their own desire. . . . Who say, 'Thus says the Lord,' and the Lord has not sent them." Of these even the Saviour speaks in the gospel of John (10:8), saying, "All who came before me were thieves and robbers." "Who came," not "who were sent." For he himself said, "They came, yet I was not sending them." Those who come display rash presumption; those who are sent, true obedience. Now the church which has been set upon the rock by the Lord's voice, whom the king has led to his bedchamber and towards whom he secretly stretched out his hand through the opening, is like a little fallow deer, a young stag; like paradise it is the source of four rivers, and it has four corners and four rings by means of which it is carried by moveable poles as was the ark of the covenant—the receptacle for the law of the Lord.

First of all was *Matthew,* the publican, surnamed Levi, who published the gospel in Judea in the Hebrew tongue particularly for the sake of those of the Jews who had believed in Jesus, that they might preserve the gospel without the shadow of the Law stealing back.

Second was *Mark,* Peter's recorder and the first bishop of the church in Alexandria. In fact he himself had not seen the Lord and Saviour, so he recounted the things he had heard his master preach in accordance with faith rather than the order of events.

Third was *Luke* the physician, a native of Antioch in Syria, whose gospel is his glory. Moreover he was himself a disciple of the apostle Paul in Achaia and Boeotia where he wrote his book, repeating some things with greater emphasis and, as he himself admits in his preface, describing things he had heard rather than seen.

Last was *John,* the apostle and evangelist, whom Jesus loved the most. He, reclining upon the Lord's breast, drank in the most pure streams of doctrine and alone was worthy to hear from the cross "Behold thy mother" (Jn 19:27). He was in Asia at the time when the seeds of heresy were sprouting, especially that of Cerinthus the Ebionite and of those others who deny that

Christ came in the flesh. John himself brands them in his epistle as anti-christs, and the apostle Paul often attacked them. At that time John was compelled by almost all the bishops of Asia and by delegations from many churches to write more fully of the Savior's divinity and to "burst forth" so to say, with the question of the Word of God with a boldness that would be not offensive but opportune. Church tradition tells us that when he was compelled by the brethren to write, he answered that he would do so provided that when a fast had been proclaimed all together would offer praise to God: when this was done he was filled with enlightenment and burst forth into that preface which comes to us from heaven: "In the beginning was the Word, and the Word was with God, and God was this Word: this was in the beginning with God" (Jn 1:1-2).

That these four gospels were long ago foretold, the book of Ezekiel proves, for here the first vision runs as follows: "And in the midst there was the likeness of four animals" (1:5), "and in their countenances were the face of a man and the face of a lion and the face of an ox and the face of an eagle" (1:10). The first face of a man signifies Matthew who began to write as if concerning a man: "The book of the generation of Jesus Christ, the son of David the son of Abraham" (1:1). The second signifies Mark, in whose gospel the voice of a lion roaring in the wilderness is heard: "The voice of one crying in the wilderness, 'Prepare the way of the Lord, make straight his paths' " (1:3). The third face, being that of an ox, prefigured Luke the evangelist's beginning with Zacharias the priest. The fourth signifies John the evangelist who, having taken the wings of an eagle and hastening above, treats of the Word of God. The other things that follow are there to the same purpose. "Their legs were straight and their feet feathered" (Ez 1:7); "and whenever the Spirit went they also went and came not back" (1:12); "and their backs were filled with eyes" (1:18); "and sparks and lamps moving swiftly to and fro in the midst" (1:13); "and a wheel within a wheel" (1:16), and each one had four faces. For this reason John's Apocalypse, after dealing with the four-and-twenty elders who holding lutes and censers worship the Lamb of God, brings in thunder and lightning and seven spirits running to and fro and the sea of glass and "four animals full of eyes" (Apoc 4:6) saying, "The first animal was like a lion and the second like an ox and the third like a man and the fourth like a flying eagle" (4:7). And a little later it says, "They were full of eyes and they rested not day or night, proclaiming, 'Holy, holy, holy is the Lord God almighty who was and who is and who is to come' " (4:8). From all these things it is perfectly clear that only four gospels should be accepted and that all the dirges of the apocryphal books should be sung by dead heretics rather than by the men of the church who yet live.

Commentarius in Epistolam S. Pauli ad Galatas (PL 26.462)

Blessed John the evangelist, while dwelling at Ephesus, would even in extreme old age be borne with difficulty in the hands of his disciples into the church. He had not the strength for many words, yet he was in the habit of saying nothing in each of his prayers but this: "Little children, love one another.'' At last the disciples and brethren who were present, being irritated by always hearing the same things, said: ''Master, why do you keep on saying this?'' John's answer was wholly characteristic: ''Because it is the Lord's command, and if it were that alone, it would be enough.'' Hence this present command of the apostle: ''Let us do good to all, but especially to members of the household of the faith.''

5. The Monarchian Prologues (ca. 380)

(For a critical survey see J. H. Chapman, *Notes on the Early History of the Vulgate Gospels* [Oxford, 1908] 217-88; H. Lietzmann, *Kleine Texte* series, no. 1 [1902; ⁴1933]; also ''Monarchian Prologues,'' ODCC.)

The four Monarchian Prologues, are now generally recognized to be late fourth-century documents, and appear to be dependent on the Old Latin prologues, though they are different in style, and in content also, to a large extent. They give the impression of being the work of an individual, and Dom John Chapman's view that they were the work of the Spanish heretic bishop Priscillian (d. 386) seems now to be generally accepted. Their purpose was to promote the Monarchian heresy; for example, Christ is everywhere referred to as ''God,'' since the Monarchians held that the Son was not a different person from the Father. Nevertheless the theological parts of these Prologues are written in such an involved and labored style that it is almost impossible fully to understand what they are trying to convey! Chapman also notes that the prologue to John comes next after that of Matthew, and Mark in fourth place, and explains this as follows: ''[This order reveals that] the writer of the prologue used an Old Latin codex, having the Latin order of the gospels universal before Jerome, viz., Matthew, John, Luke, Mark—for as the prologue says, Though he [John] is said to have written after all the others, yet in the disposition of the ordered canon, he is placed after Matthew'' (Chapman, 228-29). The following is a brief summary of their contents so far as they concern us here:

Matthew. The evangelist is indeed Matthew himself, the ''publican'' of our Gospels, and one of the Twelve. He was the first to write and he wrote in Judea. Nothing is said here about the original language of Matthew.

John. John too is one of the Twelve, who are here called ''the disciples of God.'' He was a virgin and always remained one; he wrote his Gospel in Asia after he had written the Apocalypse on the island of Patmos. He died in Ephesus.

Luke. Luke was a Syrian of Antioch by race, by profession a physician, first of all a disciple of the Apostles and then of Paul whom he followed until Paul's martyrdom. He wrote his Gospel in the regions of Achaia after Matthew had written in Judea and Mark in Italy. He also wrote the Acts of the Apostles. Note also the many close resemblances of this prologue to the anti-Marcionite prologue to Luke in Greek (II.3.8c).

Mark. Mark was the spiritual son and disciple of Peter, and is also said to have been a Levite. After his conversion he wrote his Gospel in Italy. He is also said to have cut off his thumb after he had received the faith in order that he might be accounted unfit for the priesthood. Despite this mutilation he later became the bishop of Alexandria, according to an old tradition.

The main facts therefore are in accord with those furnished by the earliest of our authorities. The extra details are peripheral and in no wise affect the complete agreement with the main tradition; for they are simply personal details about the evangelists themselves. The one important discrepancy, namely, that Luke wrote in Achaia after Mark had written in Italy can be easily resolved if "written" is understood in the sense of "publication" of Luke. That is, perhaps Luke could have been written before Mark but published after it, in Achaia (see pt. 3, below, chs. 3 and 4 passim). The details not mentioned in previous accounts are the following: that John was a virgin; that Mark had been a Levite; and an explanation of Mark having cut off his thumb to debar himself from the priesthood, which seems to be a clarification of Hippolytus's *colobodactylus*. Most remarkable of all is a sentence that seems to imply (if the true reading is "viderat" rather than "vicerat")[5] that Mark knew the contents of both Matthew and Luke, that is, that the compiler of this prologue believed Mark had the other two Gospels in front of him as he wrote: Denique perfecti evangelii opus intrans, et a baptismo Domini praedicare Deum inchoans, non laboravit nativitatem carnis quam in prioribus viderat dicere ("For setting out on the perfect work of the Gospel, and starting to preach God from the Lord's baptism, he did not bother with the nativity story which he had seen related in the former [Gospels]").

6. The Vulgate Prologues (5th century)

The Vulgate prologues are in all essentials identical with the Monarchian Prologues. The critical text is to be found in the edition of the Vulgate prepared by J. Wordsworth and H. J. White (1889-1954) 1:15-17, 171-

---

[5]Chapman (*Notes . . . in loc.*) had rendered this sentence as "which he had already conquered in what preceded." But his text was defective in reading *vicerat* instead of *viderat,* and he also failed to note the significance of *in prioribus.* The compiler of this prologue perceived that Mark was able to omit the birth narratives because he had already seen them in the "prior" Gospels. For this suggestion, I am indebted to a private communication from Professor G. G. Gamba, Salesian University Rome. See also ch. 3, n. 38; ch. 4, n. 2.

73. No one has as yet given an entirely satisfactory explanation of how and why they came to be incorporated with the Vulgate. Their appearance in this context may indicate, among other things, that no new information about the Gospels was forthcoming.

7. Augustine of Hippo (354-430)

Augustine is important for us for his part in the formation of the canon and for his views on the interrelationships of the Synoptic Gospels.

a. On the Canon of Scripture

Augustine was ordained priest by Valerian, bishop of Hippo Regio, in 391; in 393 he was consecrated Valerian's coadjutor; and from 396 until his death he presided as sole bishop of the see. His views can be ascertained from his known influence in 397. Denzinger[6] has the following entry regarding this latter council.

> Canon 47 of this Council gives the list of canonical books, which with minimal changes only, are said to be those of canon 36 of the Council of Hippo Regio held on 8 October 393. The list is repeated almost identically in canon 29 of the Council of Carthage of 419, which ends with the following statement: "Let this [list] be imparted to our brother and fellowpriest the holy Boniface, bishop of the city of Rome, and to other bishops of these regions for the confirmation of this canon. This canon reads:
> It is our good pleasure that . . . nothing be read in the Church under the title of the Divine Scriptures except the canonical Scriptures. The canonical Scriptures are these: Genesis, Exodus, Leviticus, Numbers, Deuteronomy, Joshua, Judges. Ruth, four Books of Kings, two Books of Chronicles, Job, the Psalter of David, five Books of Solomon, twelve Books of the Prophets, Isaiah, Jeremiah, Daniel, Ezechiel, Tobias, Judith, Esther, two Books of Esdras, two Books of Machabees. Of the New Testament: Four Books of the Gospels, one Book of the Acts of the Apostles, thirteen Epistles of the Apostle Paul, one (Epistle) of the same to the Hebrews, two of Peter, three of John, one of James, one of Jude, the Apocalypse of John.
> Some codices add: "that the Church across-the-sea should be consulted about the confirmation of this canon."

b. *De Consensu Evangelistarum*

It will be appropriate to conclude this part 2 with the summary of the views on Gospel interrelationshps reached, as a result of intensive study, by Augustine, that paragon of theologians, in the first and last books of his

---

[6]Denzinger-Schönmetzer, *Enchiridion*, §186.

De Consensu Evangelistarum.[7] It is easy to see that Augustine writes in a manner untouched by the post-Reformation view of the Scriptures as the sole rule of salvation, but that he views them as part and parcel of the whole tradition inherited from the Apostles. For him, there are only four canonical Gospels, and he sees no problem in concluding that no evangelist wrote in ignorance of his predecessor, this again being part of the tradition, although each felt free to retain or to add or to subtract material from his predecessor or predecessors in accordance with his own literary plan. Nor did he see any problem in asserting in Book I that the order of dignity was Matthew, John, Mark, Luke; that the received order of writing was Matthew, Mark, Luke, John; or finally in Book IV that the order of theological development was Matthew, Luke, Mark, John. This last point has particular relevance for our present study; for it indicates that at the end of his intensive investigation of the discrepancies between the evangelists he had considerably modified his view of Mark; for he finally sees that Mark is not really the *pedisequus,* the footman, or the abbreviator, of Matthew, but has rather adopted characteristics drawn from both Matthew and Luke. In other words, he sees that in the order of theological ideas Mark has drawn on and combined ideas from both Matthew and Luke respectively.[8] It was no great disadvantage that by having to work with the Vulgate he was precluded from discussing their literary relationshps in the light of the original text, although this would have made matters still clearer to him; for the Vulgate faithfully reflects the main ideas of the Greek. For him then, Matthew seems to emphasize Christ's Kingship, to which he appends the symbol of the Lion, while Luke emphasizes his Priesthood, to which he appends the symbol of the Bull. Augustine concludes that Kingship and Priesthood together signify the fullness of his humanity, notes that both attributes are found together in Mark, and signifies his perception of their union in Mark's portrait of Christ by the symbol of the Man. Thus Christ is the perfect Man in virtue of being both Priest and King. We may therefore argue with credibility that in Augustine's thought Mark has fused the ideas of Matthew and Luke into his portrait of Christ. The relevant texts from Book I and Book IV of *De Cons. Ev.* are printed below in Englsh translation, and the Latin text is in the attached Appendix.

---

[7]*Sancti Aurelii Augustini, de Consensu Evangelistarum,* Libri Quattuor, ed. Weihrich, CSEL (1904).

[8]Dr. David Peabody was the first to draw my attention to the final opinion of Augustine on Gospel relationships; cf. his "Augustine and 'The Augustinian Hypotheses,' " in *New Synoptic Studies: The Cambridge Gospel Conference and Beyond,"* ed. W. R. Farmer (Macon GA: Mercer University Press, 1983).

I.1. Among all the divine authorities found in Holy Writ the Gospel excels in merit. For what the Law and the Prophets foretold would come to pass, is seen to be effected and completed in the Gospels. The first Apostles were its preachers who saw our Lord and Saviour Jesus Christ himself present in the flesh; and on account of the task of evangelizing imposed on them, they took care to proclaim to the human race not only those words and deeds of his which they remembered either from hearing them from his mouth or from seeing him perform them before their eyes, but also those matters wrought by God and worthy of record concerning his birth and infancy and childhood which they were able to discover and to learn either from him or from his parents or from other persons. And two of these Apostles, namely Matthew and John, each produced a book containing what they considered should be written about him.

I.2. And lest in the matter of grasping and preaching the Gospel, it should be thought to matter whether those should proclaim it who had followed the same Lord appearing here in the flesh while serving their discipleship, or whether those should proclaim it who believed what they had faithfully learned from them, it was arranged by Divine Providence through the Holy Spirit that the authority not just for proclaiming but also for writing a true Gospel should also be granted to some of those who followed the first Apostles, namely to Mark and Luke. But other men who attemped or dared to write things about the deeds of the Lord or of the Apostles did not appear in their own times as persons respecting whom the Church could trust or grant to their writings the canonical authority of the Holy Books, not only because they were not persons whose stories were fit to be trusted but also because they set down in their writings some things which the catholic and apostolic faith and sound doctrine condemns.

I.3. Therefore these four Evangelists, well known to the whole world, four in number, perhaps because of the four parts of the world, are said to have written in this order: first Matthew, then Mark, thirdly Luke, lastly John. Thus they have one order as regards knowing and preaching, and another order as regards actual composition. As regards knowing and preaching, first came the two who heard and saw the Lord speaking while present in the flesh, and who were sent by his personal utterance to evangelize.

But in the writing of the Gospel, which we are to believe to have been divinely ordained, two of the number of those whom the Lord chose before his Passion hold the first and the last place, namely first Matthew, and John last. So that the other two, who were not of that number, but had followed Christ speaking in them, should be supported by them on each side, like sons to be embraced and in fact set up in the middle place.

I.4. Of the four, Matthew alone is said to have been written in the Hebrew language, the others in Greek, and although each of them seems to have retained his own particular literary sequence of writing, nevertheless each of them is found not to have desired to write in ignorance of his predecessor,

nor to have omitted what the other is found to have written except by deliberate purpose; but each has added without any superfluity the cooperation of
his own work, according to the manner in which he was inspired. For Matthew is seen to have dealt with the incarnation of the Lord according to the
kingly line of descent and a great many deeds and sayings according to the
present life of men. Mark seems to have followed him as his footman and
abbreviator; for with John alone he, Mark, says nothing, he himself alone
says very few things, with Luke alone a few more, but with Matthew he says
many things—and just as many things almost in the very same words—either
with Matthew alone or with both the others. But Luke appears more occupied
with the priestly connection and person of the Lord. For he goes back to David not following the line of the kings but a different route through those who
were not kings to Nathan, son of David, who was not himself a king. Not so
Matthew, who descends through King Solomon, and pursues in order the other
kings, preserving in them the mystic number of which we shall speak later.

I.3.6. Since Matthew was concerned with the person of the King and Luke
with the Priest, they both strongly commended the humanity of Christ. Christ
as Man was made King and Priest, to whom God gave the throne of his father
David, so that his kingdom would have no end and so that Christ the mediator
of God and men would be pleading for us. But Luke, unlike Matthew, did
not have Mark as an abbreviator to him; and this probably has a symbolical
meaning, because kings do not go about without the service of attendants.
And so the one who had undertaken to narrate the kingly person of Christ had
a sort of companion attached to him, who in a certain way followed in his
footsteps; whereas on the other hand, as the priest used to enter alone into the
Holy of Holies, Luke, whose concern was with the Priesthood of Christ, did
not have a companion and follower who would in some way abbreviate his
narrative.

I.4.7. So while these three Evangelists especially dwelt on those matters
which Christ performed in the world through his humn flesh, John on the other
hand, was above all concerned with the divinity of the Lord and his equality
with the Father, and was at pains in his Gospel to commend it as far as he
believed it to suffice among men. . . .

IV.10.11. We are now left with John and there is none with whom he may
be compared. For whatever each evangelist said that was not also recorded
by the others, can hardly be said to be the cause of any contradiction between
them! And therefore it is quite clear that Matthew, Mark, and Luke have dealt
especially with the humanity of our Lord Jesus Christ in respect of his being
both King and Priest; and therefore Mark (who in the mysterious symbolism
of the four living creatures seems to symbolize the figure of the Man) either
appears rather as one who goes with Matthew because together with him he
relates a greater number of things respecting the kingly figure (which as we
have noted in Book I is usually acompanied by an attendant) or more probably he goes in step with both. For although he agrees with Matthew in many

things, yet in some things he agrees more with Luke, so that by this very fact he may be shown to share the symbolism of the Lion and the Bull (for Christ is a Man), which symbolism Mark possesses as he shares both aspects [the kingly and the priestly figure]. But the divinity of Christ . . . is presented by John with special commendation . . . under the symbol of the Eagle.

Conclusions: Fourth-Century Traditions After Eusebius

The later fourth century Fathers neither add nor subtract anything substantial to what they had received from their predecessors. They all accept without question the tradition that the Apostle Matthew wrote the First Gospel in Judea, that Luke was the disciple of Paul and that John wrote the Fourth Gospel. As regards the Gospel of Mark, Jerome summed up the universal tradition when he wrote: [Paulus] habebat ergo Titum interpretem sicut beatus Petrus Marcum, cuius evangelium Petro narrante et illo scribente compositum est ("[Paul] had Titus as a recorder just as blessed Peter had Mark, whose Gospel consists of Peter's narration and the latter's writings." —Letter 120.11, ed. Hilberg, CSEL 55). Furthermore they all seem quite content with the Gospel order Matthew-Mark-Luke-John, and none of them sought to contrast or to oppose this order with Clement of Alexandria's statement that the two Gospels with genealogies were written prior to Mark, although they knew about it. Nevertheless there were occasional allusions to a certain priority of Luke over Mark, for example, Ambrosiaster; while Augustine, in his later work, certainly saw the Gospel of Mark as conflating and harmonizing the thought of Matthew and Luke. Sometimes the Fathers confirm peripheral personal details that had appeared sporadically in earlier writers, for example, that Mark was *Kolobodaktylos* (Hippolytus), or that Luke was a physician (Muratorian Canon). Sometimes they may draw the wrong inference from the received data, for example, that Matthew was written "in Hebrew characters" (Origen), or that Mark was originally composed in Latin (Ephraem Syrus). But their deviations from the main tradition are practically insignificant.

Appendix
Latin Texts of Jerome and Augustine
Jerome
De viris illustribus III (ed. Richardson, TU XIV.1)

Matthaeus qui et Levi, ex publicano apostolus, primus in Iudaea, propter eos qui ex circumcisione crediderunt, Evangelium Christi Hebraeis litteris verbisque conposuit; quod quis postea in Graecum transtulerit, non satis certum est. Porro ipsum Hebraicum habetur usque hodie in Caesariensi bibliotheca, quam Pamphilus martyr studiosissime confecit. Mihi quoque a Nazaraeis qui in Beroea, urbe Syriae, hoc volumine utuntur, describendi facultas fuit. In quo animadvertendum, quod ubicumque evangelista, sive ex persona sua sive ex Domini Salvatoris veteris scripturae testimoniis abutitur, non sequatur Septuaginta translatorum auctoritatem, sed Hebraicam. E quibus illa duo sint: Ex Aegypto vocavi Filium meum, et: Quoniam Nazaraeus vocabitur.

De viris illustribus VII (ed. Richardson, TU XIV.1)

Lucas, medicus Antiochensus, ut eius scripta indicant, Graeci sermonis non ignarus fuit, sector apostoli Pauli et omnis eius peregrinationis comes, scripsit Evangelium, de quo idem Paulus: Misimus, inquit, cum illo fratrem cuius laus est in evangelio per omnes ecclesias; et ad Colossenses: Salutat vos lucas medicus carissimus; et ad Timotheum:Lucas est mecum solus. Aliud quoque edidit volumen egregium quod titulo Apostolicorum *praxēon* praenotatur, cuius historia usque ad biennium Romae commorantis Pauli pervenit, id est usque ad quartum Neronis annum. Ex quo intelligimus in eadem urbe librum esse conpositum. Igitur *periodous* Pauli et Theclae et totam baptizati leonis fabulam inter apocryphas scripturas conputemus. Quale enim est, ut individuus comes apostoli inter ceteras eius res hoc solum ignoraverit? Sed et Tertullianus, vicinus illorum temporum, refert presbyterum quendam in Asia, *spoudastēn* apostoli Pauli, convictum apud Iohannem quod auctor esset libri, et confessum se hoc Pauli amore fecisse, loco excidisse. Quidam suspicantur, quotiescumque Paulus in epistulis suis dicat 'iuxta evangelium meum', de Lucae significare volumine et Lucam non solum ab apostolo Paulo didicisse evangelium, qui cum Domino in carne non fuerat, sed et a ceteris apostolis. Quod ipse quoque in principio voluminis sui declarat dicens: Sicut tradiderunt nobis qui a principio ipsi viderunt et ministri fuerunt sermonis. Igitur Evangelium, sicut audierat scripsit: Acta vero apostolorum, sicut viderat ipse, conposuit. Sepultus est Constantinopolim, ad quam urbem, vicesimo Constantiii anno, ossa eius, cum reliquiis Andreae apostoli, translata sunt.

De viris illustribus VIII (ed. Richardson, TU XIV.1)

Marcus, discipulus et interpres Petri iuxta quod Petrum referentem audierat, rogatus Romae a fratribus breve scripsit evangelium. Quod cum Petrus audisset, probavit et ecclesiis legendum sua auctoritate edidit, sicut scribit

Clemens in sexto 'Ypotypōseōn libro et Papias Hierapolitanus episcopus. Meminit huius Marci et Petrus in prima epistola, sub nomine Babylonis figuraliter Romam significans: Salutat vos quae est in Babylone coélecta et Marcus filius meus. Adsumpto itaque evangelio quod ipse confecerat, perrexit Aegyptum et primus Alexandriae Christum adnuncians constituit ecclesiam tanta doctrina et vitat continentia, ut omnes sectatores Christi ad exemplus sui cogeret. Denique Philon, dissertissimus Iudaeorum, videns Alexandriae primam ecclesiam adhuc Iudaizantem quasi in laudem gentis suae librum super eorum conversatione scripsit, et quomodo lucas narrat Hierosolymae credentes omnia habuisse communia, sic ille quod Alexandriae, sub Marco fieri doctore cernebat memoriae tradidit. Mortuus est autem octavo Neronis anno et sepultus Alexandriae, succedente sibi Anniano.

De viris illustribus IX (ed. Richardson, TU XIV.1)

Iohannes apostolus quem Iesus amavit plurimum, filius Zebedaei et frater Iacobi apostoli quem Herodes post passionem Domini decollavit, novissimus omnium scripsit Evangelium, rogatus ab Asiae episcopis, adversus Cerinthum aliosque hæreticos et maxime tunc Ebionitarum dogma consurgens, qui adserunt Christum ante Mariam non fuisse. Unde etiam conpulsus est divinam eius nativitatem edicere. Sed et aliam causam huius scripturae ferunt, quod, cum legisset Matthaei, Marci et Lucae volumina, probaverit quidem textum historiae et vera eos dixisse firmaverit, sed unius tantum anni quo et passus est post carcerem Iohannis, historiam texuisse. Praetermisso itaque anno cuius acta a tribus exposita fuerant, superioris temporis, antequam Iohannes clauderetur in carcerem, gesta narravit, sicut manifestum esse poterit his qui diligenter quattuor Evangeliorum volumina legerint. Quae res et *diaphonian*, quae videtur Iohannis esse cum ceteris, tollit. Scripsit autem et unam Epistolam cuius exordium est: Quod fuit ab initio, quod audivimus et vidimus oculis nostris, quod perspeximus et manus nostrae temptaverunt de verbo vitae, quae ab universis ecclesiasticis et eruditis viris probatur. Reliquae autem duae quarum principium est: Senior electae dominae et natis eius, et sequentis: Senior Gaio carissimo, quem ego diligo in veritate, iohannis presbyteri adseruntur, cuius et hodie alterum sepulcrum apud Ephesum ostenditur; et nonnulli putant duas memorias eiusdem Iohannis evangelistate esse; super qua re, cum per ordinem ad Papiam auditorem eius ventum fuerit, disseremus. Quarto decimo igitur anno. secundam post Neronem persecutionem movente Domitiano, in Patmo insulam relegatus, scripsit Apocalypsin, quam interpretantur Iustunus martyr et Irenaeus. Interfecto autem Domitiano et actis eius ob nimiam crudelitatem a senatu rescissis, sub Nerva redit Ephesum ibique usuque ad Traianun principem perseverans totas Asiae fundavit rexitque ecclesias et confectus senio et sexagesimo octavo post passionem Domini anno mortuus, iuxta eandem urbem sepultus est.

On Paul, Peter, and Mark (*Epistula* 120.11, ed. Hilberg, CSEL 55)

Aliquotiens diximus apostolum Paulum virum fuisse doctissimum et eruditum ad pedes Gamalihel, qui in apostolorum Actibus contionatur et dicit: Et nunc quid habetis cum hominibus istis? Si enim a Deo est, stabit, si ex hominibus, destruetur. cumque haberet sanctarum scientiam scripturarum et sermonis diversarumque linguarum gratiam possideret—unde ipse gloriatur in Domino et dicit: Gratias ago Deo, quod omnium eorum magis linguis loquor, divinorum sensum maiestatem digno non poterat Graeci eloquii explicare sermone. habebit ergo Titum interpretem sicut beatus Petrus Marcum, cuius evangelium Petro narrante et illo scribente conpositum est. denique et duae epistolae, quae feruntur Petri, stilo inter se et caractere discrepant structuraque verborum; ex quo intellegimus pro necessitate rerum diversis eum usum interpretibus.

Prologus quattuor evangeliorum (praefatio in comm. in Mattheum)
(Wordsworth-White 1:11-14)

Plures fuisse qui evangelia scripserunt, et Lucas evangelista testatur dicens: Quoniam quidem multi conati sunt ordinare narrationem rerum quae in nobis conpletae sunt sicut tradiderunt nobis qui ab initio ipsi viderunt sermonem et ministraverunt ei; et perseverantia usque ad praesens tempus monumenta declarant, quae a diversis auctoribus edita diversarum heresium fuere principia: ut est illud iuxta Aegyptios et Thoman et Bartholomeum, duodecim quoque apostolorum, et Basilidis et Apellis, ac reliquorum quos enumerare longissimum est, cum hoc tantum in praesentiarum necesse sit dicere, extitisse quosdam qui sine spiritu et gratia Dei conati sunt magis ordinare narrationem quam historiae texere veritatem. Quibus iure potest illud propheticum coaptari: Vae qui prophetant de corde suo, qui ambulant post spiritum suum, (et:) qui dicunt Dicit Dominus, et Dominus non misit eos. De quibus et Salvator in evangelio Iohannis loquitur: Omnes qui ante me venerunt fures fuerunt et latrones. Qui venerunt, non qui missi sunt. Ipse enim ait, Veniebant, et ego non mittebam eos. In venientibus praesumtio temeritatis, in missis obsequium veritatis est. Ecclesia autem supra petram Domini voce fundata est, quam introduxit rex in cubiculum suum et ad quam per foramen descensionis occulte misit manum suam, similis dammulae hinnuloque cervorum, quattuor flumina paradisi instar eructans, quattuor et angulos et anulos habet, per quos quasi arca testamenti et custos legis Domini lignis mobilibus vehitur.

Primus omnium Mattheus est publicanus cognomento Levi, qui evangelium in Iudaea hebreo sermone edidit, ob eorum vel maxime causam qui in Iesum crediderant ex Iudaeis et nequaquam legis umbra succedente evangelii veritatem servabant.

Secundus Marcus interpres apostoli Petri et Alexandrinae ecclesiae primus episcopus, qui Dominum quidem salvatorem ipse non vidit, sed ea quae magistrum audierat praedicantem iuxta fidem magis gestorum narravit quam ordinem.

Tertius Lucas medicus, natione Syrus Antiochensis, cuius laus in evangelio, qui et ipse discipulus apostoli Pauli in Achaiae Boeotiaeque partibus volumen condidit, quaedam altius repetens et, ut ipse in prohemio confitetur, audita magis quam visa describens.

Ultimus Iohannes apostolus et evangelista, quem Iesus amavit plurimum, qui super pectus Domini recumbens purissima doctrinarum fluenta potavit, et qui solus de cruce meruit audire: Ecce mater tua. Is cum esset in Asia et iam tunc hereticorum semina pullularent, Cerinthi Hebionis et ceterorum qui negant Christum in carne venisse, quos et ipse in epistola sua antichristos vocat et apostolus Paulus frequenter percutit, coactus est ab omnibus paene tunc Asiae episcopis et multarum ecclesiarum legationibus, de divinitate Salvatoris altius scribere et ad ipsum ut ita dicam Dei Verbum non tam audaci quam felici temeritate prorumpere, ut ecclesiastica narrat historia, cum a fratribus cogeretur ut scriberet, ita facturum respondisse si indicto ieunio in commune omnes Deum deprecarentur; quo expleto revelatione saturatus in illud prohemium caelo veniens eructavit: In principio erat verbum, et verbum erat Deum, et Deus erat hoc verbum: hoc erat in principio apud Deum.

Haec igitur quattuor evangelia multum ante praedicta Ezechielis quoque volumen probat, in quo prima visio ita contexitur: Et in medio sicut similitudo quattuor animalium (et: Et Vultus eorum facies hominis et facies leonis et facies vituli et facies aquilae. Prima hominis facies Mattheum significat, qui quasi de homine exorsus est scribere: Liber generationis Iesu christi filii David filii Abraham.

Secunda Marcum, in quo vox leonis in eremo rugientis auditur: Vox clamantis in deserto, Parate viam Domini, rectas facite semitas eius.

Tertia vituli, quae evangelistam lucam a Zacharia sacerdote sumsisse initium praefiguravit.

Quarta Iohannem evangelistam, qui adsumtis pennis aquilae et ad altiora festinans de Verbo Dei disputat.

Cetera quae sequuntur in eundem sensum proficiant: Crura eorum recta et pinnati pedes (et:) et quocumque spiritus ibat ibant et non revertebantur, et: dorsa eorum plena oculis (et:) et scintillae ac lampades in medio discurrentes (et:) et rota in rota, et in singulis quattuor facies. Unde et Apocalypsis Iohannis post expositionem viginta quattuor seniorum, qui tenentes citharas et fialas adorant agnum Dei, introducit fulgura et tonitrua et septem spiritus discurrentes et mare vitreum, et: quattuor animalia plena oculis, dicens: Animal primum simile leoni, et secundum simile vitulo, et tertium simile hominis, et quartum simile acquilae volanti. Et post paululum: Plena, inquit, erant oculis, et requiem non habebant die ac nocte, dicentia Sanctus sanctus sanctus Dominus Deus omnipotens, qui erat et qui est et qui venturus est. Quibus cunctis perspicue ostenditur quattuor tantum debere evangelia suscipi, et omnes apocriforum nenias mortuis magis hereticis quam ecclesiasticis vivis canendas.

Commentarius in Epistolam S. Pauli ad Galatas (PL 26.462)

Beatus Iohannes evangelista cum Ephesi moraretur usque ad ultimam senectutem et vix inter discipulorum manus ad ecclesiam deferretur nec posset in plura vocem verba contexere, nihil aliud per singulas solebat proferre collectas, nisi hoc; Filioli, diligite alterurum. Tandem discipuli et fratres qui aderant, taedio affecti, quod eadem semper audirent, dixerunt; Magister, quare

semper hoc loqueris? Qui respondit dignam Iohanne sententiam: Quia prae-
ceptum Domini est, et si solum fiat, sufficit. Hoc propter praesens Apostoli
mandatum: Operemur bonum ad omnes, maxime autem ad domesticos fidei.

Augustine
De Consensu Evangelistarum

Bk. I.1. Inter omnes divinas auctoritates, quae sanctis litteris continentur,
evangelium merito excellit. quod enim lex et prophetae futurum praenun-
tiaverunt, hoc redditum adque conpletum in evangelio demonstratur. cuius
primi praedicatores apostoli fuerunt, qui dominum ipsum et salvatorem nos-
trum Iesum Christum etiam presentem in carne viderunt, cuius non solum ea,
quae ex ore eius audita vel ab illo sub oculis suis operata dicta et facta mem-
inerant, verum etiam quae, priusquam illi per discipulatum adhaeserant, in
eius nativitate vel infantia vel pueritia divinitus gesta et digna memoria sive
ab ipso sive a parentibus eius sive quibuslibet aliis certissimis indiciis et fi-
delissimis testimoniis requirere et cognoscere potuerunt, inposito sibi evan-
gelizandi munere generi humano adnuntiare curarunt. quorum quidam, hoc
est Mattheus et Iohannes, etiam scripta de illo, quae scribenda visa sunt, libris singulis ediderunt.

2. Ac ne putaretur, quod adtinet ad percipiendum et praedicandum evangelium, interesse aliquid, utrum illi adnuntient, qui eundem dominum hic in
carne apparentem discipulatu famulante secuti sunt, an hi, qui ex illis fide-
liter conperta crediderunt, divina providentia procuratum est per spiritum
sanctum, ut quibusdam etiam ex illis, qui primos apostolos squenbantur, non
solum adnuntiandi, verum etiam scribendi evangelium tribueretur auctoritas.
hi sunt Marcus et Lucas. ceteri autem homines, qui de domini vel de apostolorum actibus aliqua scribere conati sunt vel ausi sunt, non tales suis temporibus extiterunt, ut eis fidem haberet ecclesia adque in auctoritatem
canonicam sanctorum librorum eorum scripta reciperet, nec solum quia illi
non tales erant, quibus narrantibus credi oporteret, sed etiam quia scriptis suis
quaedam fallaciter indiderunt, quae catholica adque apostolica regula fidei
et sana doctrina condemnat.

3. Isti igitur quattuor evangelistae universo terrarum orbe notissimi, et ob
hoc fortasse quattuor, quoniam quattuor sunt partes orbis terrae, per cuius
universitatem Christi ecclesiam dilatari ipso sui numeri sancramento quodammodo declararunt, hoc ordine scripsisse perhibentur: primus Mattheus,
deinde Marcus, tertio Lucas, ultimo Ioannes, unde alius eis fuit ordo cog-
noscendi adque praedicandi, alius scribendi. ad cognoscendum quippe adque
praedicandum primi utique fuerunt qui secuti dominum in carne presentem
dicentem audierunt facientemque viderunt adque ex eius ore ad evangelizan-
dum missi sunt, sed in conscribendo evangelio, quod divinitus ordinatum esse
credendum est, ex numero eorum, quos ante passionem dominus elegit, primum adque ultimul locum duo tenuerunt, primum Mattheum, ultimum Iohannes, ut reliqui duo, qui ex illo numero non erant, sed tamen Christum in

illis loquentem secuti erant, tamquam filii amplectendi ac per hoc in loco medio constituti utroque ab eis latere munirentur.

4. Horum sane quattuor solus Mattheus hebraeo scripsisse perhibetur eloquio, ceteri Graeco, et quamvis singuli suum quendam narrandi ordinem tenuisse videantur, non tamen unusquisque eorum velut alterius praecedentis ignarus voluisse scribere repperitur vel ignorata praetermisisse, quae scripsisse alius invenitur, sed sicut unicuique inspiratum est non superfluam cooperationem sui laboris adiunxit. nam Mattheus suscepisse intellegitur incarnationem domini secundum stirpem regiam et pleraque secundum hominum presentem vitam facta et dicta eius. Marcus eum subsecutus tamquam pedisequus et breviator eius videtur. Cum solo quippe Iohanne nihil dixit, solus ipse perpauca, cum solo Luca pauciora, cum Mattheo vero plurima et multa paene totidem adque ipsis verbis sive cum solo sive cum ceteris consonante. Lucas autem circa sacerdotalem domini stirpem adque personam magis occupatus apparet. nam et ad ipsum David non regium stemma secutus ascendit, sed per eos, qui reges non fuerunt, exit ad Nathan filium David, qui nec ipse rex fuit, non sicut Mattheus, qui per Salomonem regem descendens ceteros etiam reges ex ordine persecutus est servans in eis de quo postea loquemur, mysticum numerum.

3.6. Cum ergo Mattheus circa regis, Lucas circa sacedotis personam gereret intentionem, utique humanitatem Christi maxime commendarunt, secundum hominem quippe Christus et rex et sacerdos effectus est, cui dedit deus sedem David patris sui, ut regni eius non esset finis et esset ad interpellandum pro nobis mediator dei et hominum homo Christus Iesus, non autem habuit tamquam breviatorem coniunctum Lucas sicut Marcum Mattheus, et hoc forte non sine aliquo sacramento, quia regum est non esse sine comitem obsequio, unde ille, qui regiam personam Christi narrandam susceperat, habuit sibi tamquam comitem adiunctum, qui sua vestigia quodammodo sequeretur, sacerdos autem quoniam in sancta sanctorum solus intrabat, propterea Lucas, cuius circa sacerdotium Christi erat intentio, non habuit tamquam socium subsequentem, qui suam narrationem quodammodo breviaret.

4.7. Tres tamen isti evangelistae in his rebus maxime deversati sunt, quas Christus per humanam carnem temporaliter gessit; porro autem Iohannes ipsam maxime divinitatem domini, qua patri est aequalis, intendit eamque praecipue suo evangelio, quantum inter homines sufficere credidit, commendare curavit. . . .

Bk IV.10. Iohannes est reliquus, qui iam non restat cui conferatur. quidquid enim singuli dixerunt, quae ab aliis non dicta sunt, difficile est, ut habeant aliquam repugnantiae quaestionem. ac per hoc liquido constat tres istos, Mattheum scilicet, Marcum et Lucam, maxime circa humanitatem domini nostri Iesu Christi esse versatos, secundum quam et rex et sacerdos est. et ideo Marcus, qui in illo mysterio quattuor animalium hominis videtur demonstrare personam, vel Matthei magis comes videtur, quia cum illo plura dicit propter regiam personam, quae incomitata esse non solet, quod in primo libro commemoravi, vel, quod probabilius intellegitur, cum ambobus incedit. nam quamvis Mattheo in pluribus, tamen in aliis nonnullis Lucae magis congruit, ut hoc ipso demonstretur ad leonem et ad vitulum, hoc est et ad regalem, quam Mattheus, et ad sacerdotalem, quam Lucas insinuat personam, id quod Christus homo est, pertinere, quam figuram Marcus gerit pertinens ad utrumque. divinitas vero Christi . . . a Iohanne maxime commendanda suscepta est, . . . sicut aquila. . . .

6

The Value of the External Testimonies
to the Gospels

The relative scarcity of the external evidence for the existence of the Gospels between A.D. 50 and 150 ought not to be interpreted as a sign that the tradition was not continuous from the beginning. For as long as St. John the Apostle remained alive in Ephesus, as the tradition says, he above all would have been recognized as the source of authentic information about the Twelve, and about the traditions connected with Jesus; and we ought not to expect his junior contemporaries to have posed as authorities about the Gospels during his lifetime. And indeed Eusebius, who had access to all the available sources, only knew of three subapostolic men who actually transmitted the apostolic teaching in writing, namely, Clement of Rome, Ignatius of Antioch, and Papias of Hierapolis (EH III.37.4). Nevertheless he was aware that immediately after the death of John there was a great spate of works from apologists of all kinds in defence of the Faith (EH IV.3), nearly all of which have since been lost through attrition or wilful destruction. He also knew that from the beginning Christianity had communicated itself by word of mouth rather than by the written word, and he specifically declared that his tradition was that each Gospel was specially composed at a particular time to meet some particular need of the church or some crisis in her history (EH III.24.7). For the written word was always considered to be secondary to the living voice of the tradition, as Papias had enunciated in his preface (EH III.39).

It is also noteworthy that all four evangelists hid their authorship under the cloak of anonymity, so that Justin preferred to refer to the Gospels collectively as "the reminiscences of the Apostles," while at the same time revealing that he was aware of the distinctive character of the contents of each of them.

The question now arises: if the Gospels were in fact the work and responsibility of the original Twelve, one would be entitled to expect to find some allusions to them in the other N.T. writings, and especially in the letters of Paul. There are, in fact, some striking allusions to the Greek text of the Gospel of Matthew in Galatians, in 1 and 2 Thessalonians, and in

Romans, which have been rejected by most modern critics on the ground that Matthew's Gospel was not then even thought of, and that the most that can be conceded would be that they reflect an early stage of the "Matthean tradition." However, if on the other grounds it could be shown that a very early date for Matthew were feasible, then there would be but little doubt that Paul had in mind our actual Greek text of such passages, as Matthew 23–25. And of course the early Fathers quoted from Matthew almost exclusively, as we have also seen above in part 2, chapter 2.

The first known attack on the value of the Synoptic Gospels as records of Jesus' thought, words, and ministry was that of Marcion (ca. 140), and it led to the strong reaction in support of them that was championed by Justin and Irenaeus. The universal diffusion of the *Adversus Haereses* in the West in the third century by means of its translation into Latin was the acknowledgment by the whole Christian church that Irenaeus was an authentic conveyor of the tradition that all four Gospels were apostolic documents, two of them composed by Apostles, and the other two sponsored by Peter and Paul. Contrary to the opinion commonly expressed today, we hope to have shown that the church writers, scholars, and theologians of the second phase (150-300) were in complete agreement on all essentials with those who came before and after them; that is to say, they were all convinced that the Gospels were given to the church personally and publicly by the apostolic persons to whom they were attributed. Eusebius of Caesarea (263-338) then appeared with his ten-volume *Ecclesiastical History* containing almost all the data of the tradition, his own emphasis, like that of all the early Fathers, being on their authenticity, that is, on their apostolic authorship and/or authority. Thus for him too, the Gospels were the work of the eyewitnesses Matthew and John, and of Mark and Luke, disciples of Peter and Paul. However, careful study of Eusebius's treatment of Papias has revealed not only his strong bias against him—an *odium theologicum*—but also a certain selectivity in his quotations from the latter's lost treatise *The Exegesis of the Lord's Sayings,* in all probability the first-ever commentary on the Gospels. Eusebius has undoubtedly selected his quotations from Papias's work for his own ends in a disingenuous manner in order to prove that the Apostle John did not write the Apocalypse. This selectivity has, as a side effect, enabled modern critics to understand Eusebius's interpretation of Papias as favoring Markan priority, whereas it really does no such thing but rather tends to support the Two-Gospel Hypothesis. Papias is not to be distrusted when he speaks of traditions he has received; it is rather Eusebius who has to be carefully watched on account of his bias. Later in the fourth century Jerome will confirm and synthesize the data collected by Eusebius in the light of his own researches; he will reject Eusebius's view about the Apocalypse but accept a modified view of a "second John."

We have suggested in the first chapter of this part that the root cause of the modern distrust of the positive value of the external evidence is an ideological one, namely, disbelief that the Christian church could have transmitted, without fatal distortion, traditions received directly from the Apostles themselves. We will prescind from argument on this question at this point, but it is important to point out that the practical arguments adduced by most writers are faulty. Among these arguments are the following:

(1) that the testimony of the tradition is either contradictory or vitiated by important discrepancies;
(2) that the external evidence is worthless since the earliest testimonies are untrustworthy and the early writers simply copied one another;
(3) that the external evidence must be wrong since internal evidence has "proved" the priority of the Gospel of Mark;
(4) that first-and second-century writers had different ideas from ours about the meaning of "authorship."

To these arguments we reply as follows.

As to (1), our analysis of all the relevant passages has shown that they are neither contradictory nor discrepant, and that on the contrary there is a strong inner unity between all the contributory texts. The discrepancies that exist are peripheral only, and there is a reasonable explanation for each of them.

As to (2), of course the early writers quoted and copied what they believed to be true on good authority; no other course was possible. But the earliest attestations and witnesses—Justin, Irenaeus, Clement of Alexandria, and Papias too (as related by Eusebius)—all had a wide range of contacts with those who had known the Apostles; the Gnostic heretics also affirmed the apostolic authorship. If any of the sources of any of these witnesses had disagreed about the authorship, it would certainly have come to light at the time of the anti-Marcionite reaction, but there is no record of any disagreement.

As to (3), it has been shown in part 1 that the priority of Mark is too insecure to build anything at all on it nowadays.

As to (4), the alleged parallels with historians such as Thucydides are not really parallels at all. The Gospels are not claimed to be "histories"; they are always the personal reminiscences of able men who sacrificed their lives for the truth. It is the tradition that they wrote solely at the request of the particular Christian church to which they belonged to give it the facts about the Founder. The facts they recorded in their writings were all well known to many other members of their church; the possibility of successful forgery was nil, as the exposure of the apocryphal gospels attests. Again, the suggestion is still sometimes made to account for the attributions of the Gospels to Matthew and John, namely, that their names were added to the anonymous work of other Christian scribes in order to gain them acceptance in the early Church. However, from the beginning two of the Gospels were acknowldged to be the work of secondary personages, that is to say, the Gospels of Mark and Luke were acceptable only because they were known to have been sponsored by Peter and Paul. If Matthew and John had originated in the same way, the church would have had no problem in admitting it. The fact that Matthew and John are named as authors therefore argues that they were.

Further to the question of the ability of an ancient institution to verify its own origins, we may at this point invoke the legal historian A. N. Sherwin-White against the contemporary historical skepticism.[1] He wrote: "The basis of the confidence of secular professors of ancient history in the ability to acquire sure knowledge is the external confirmation and the working of the synoptic principle; . . . the criticism of sources tends to reveal the existence of a basic unitary tradition beneath the manifold divergencies in detail in rival narratives." In our present field our claim is that there is in fact a basic unitary tradition that has always existed in the Christian church as a living historical institution, one that holds on tenaciously to what has been passed down, and one that is always suspicious of innovation. And we may also quote Sherwin-White in reply to those who would argue that the century or so that elapsed between the time of the Apostles, the reputed authors and sponsors of the Gospels, and the inauguration of the written tradition in the time of Justin and Irenaeus and the other anti-Marcionite apologists, was long enough to allow the mythical tendency to prevail over the hard core of the oral tradition. For he has written: "The Thucydidean version of the death of Hipparchus is a salutary warning that even a century after a major event it is possible in a relatively small or enclosed community for a determined inquirer to establish a remarkably detailed account of a major event, by inquiry within the inner circle of the descendants of those concerned with the event itself." And in our present research the reader will recall that this is exactly what Clement of Alexandria did.

Thus the historical evidence gives firm support for the following statements:

---

[1]A. N. Sherwin-White, *Roman Society and Roman Law in the New Testament* (Oxford, 1963) esp. lecture 8, "The Historicity of the Gospels and Graeco-Roman Historiography," 186-93.

1. That our Matthew was the first Gospel to be written and that it was written in Judea by the apostle himself; the tradition that it was originally composed in Aramaic seems to stem from a misunderstanding of Papias by Irenaeus, which was adopted by Origen and later taken over by Eusebius of Caesarea.
2. According to a tradition that reflects a late-first-century belief, Mark is the recorder of Peter's reminiscences personally communicated to him, and written down (as another very early tradition states) in Rome or in Italy during Peter's lifetime, though not published by him personally until after Peter's death. Some copies, however, were earlier passed to friends privately on request.
3. Luke, the disciple of Paul, also wrote a Gospel, which was published in Achaia.
4. John the Apostle was the author of the Gospel and the Apocalypse. There is no vestige of truth in the suggestion that there were two men with the name of John in Asia, one the Apostle and the other "the Presbyter."
5. As regards the relationship between Luke and Mark, a very early usage in the church puts Mark before Luke, for example, the Muratorian Canon. There is in fact no single agreed order of the Gospels in the second century, but by the time of Origen, the order is normally given as Matthew, Mark, Luke, and John. But, on the other hand, Clement of Alexandria, who is the only early writer specifically to discuss the chronological order, clearly stated that Matthew and Luke were composed before Mark. Eusebius, too, can also be understood without difficulty as having indicated that Luke and Mark each took from Matthew what they needed for their respective purposes.

In conclusion, we are surely fully entitled on critical grounds to propound the thesis that there are extremely strong arguments for the rehabilitation of the substance of the ancient traditions about the authorship and origin of the Gospels.

Part Three
HOW
THE SYNOPTIC GOSPELS
CAME INTO EXISTENCE

(A tentative reconstruction
of the history of their composition
by means of a synthesis of the evidence
drawn from parts one and two)

Bernard Orchard

Foundations
for a Synthesis

1. The Problem and a Tentative Solution

The problem that now faces us is that of comparing the conclusions of part one with those of part two, noting where they agree and where they differ or fail to match up, in order to formulate a theory of synoptic origins that will take account of everything.

In part one Riley has shown that the internal evidence, critically evaluated, indicates that the first of the three Synoptic Gospels to be written was our Greek Matthew; that Luke was written second, being partly dependent on, partly independent of Matthew; and that Mark was third, using both Matthew and Luke. This conclusion is based solely on the literary evidence available to all critics in the current texts of the respective Gospels. This literary evidence bears only on the question of the sequence in which the Gospels were composed; it does not tell us when or where or how or by whom the Gospels were written.

In part two Orchard has shown that the external evidence, critically evaluated, indicates that the Greek Matthew was first, and that John was the fourth and last. Thus far the fundamental critical conclusions of part one and part two converge and fully support each other; that is to say, the major conclusion that Matthew was the first and foundational Gospel is supported by both the internal and the external evidence. This conclusion is of vital importance because it demonstrates that the hypothesis of the priority of Mark is contradicted by the hard critical evidence and so is no longer tenable. While it does not of itself solve the Synoptic Problem, it does involve a revolution in synoptic studies; and it clears out of the way the most important obstacle to finding the complete solution.

For if independent internal critical examination vindicates the conclusion of the external evidence that Matthew is after all the first Gospel in order of time and also in an important sense the source of the other two, there is a *prima facie* likelihood that the tradition furnished by the external evidence may also be correct in other respects. That is to say, we now have solid grounds for erecting a new hypothesis to explain how the Gospels are related and how they came into separate existence. We are now justified in scanning the history of the primitive church anew to see how all three Gospels could be responses to real-life situations quite other than those normally envisaged. If Matthew is the first, then we must now look for new explanations for the precise relationship between Matthew and Luke and for new reasons why Luke may be second in order.

Again, if Matthew is first, there will be three possible ways of dating the Synoptics: either all three could be pre-70, or they could all three be post-70, or they might straddle the watershed of 70. And if it is possible for all three to be pre-70, then a new angle appears; for whereas Markan priority requires Matthew to be the work of some late-first-century Christian scribe, the early date admits the possibility and the reasonableness of ascribing Matthew directly to the tax collector turned Apostle.

We have therefore the solid fact that the tradition and the internal evidence agree on the priority of Matthew, though the internal evidence gives no direct support to the second conclusion of the external evidence, namely that the Gospels are the personal reminiscences of some of the Apostles. Thus our task in this part is to explore and probe further the external evidence and to attempt to read between the lines, so to speak, of the New Testament literature, with a view to formulating a comprehensive hypothesis of the coming to be of our Gospels, one that will make sense of the remaining discrepancies. Such a hypothesis for instance, must make full allowance for the fact that there are two traditions about the relative order of Mark and Luke; either could be correct, or both may be correct from different standpoints. For the critical mind cannot rest until some credible reason is furnished for the discrepancy between the tradition that Mark was second and Clement of Alexandria's contention that Mark was third in order of writing. Again, Markan priorists, on their own premises of course, have a serious difficulty in understanding how the author of Mark, who (according to Riley) had before him the texts of our Matthew and our Luke and composed his text mostly out of these two earlier Gospels, could at the same time have been the ''interpreter'' of Peter, and the agent for publishing a gospel based on Peter's preaching.

The doctrine of the priority of Mark over Matthew and Luke has been the sheet anchor for refusing to countenance any approach to the Synoptic Gospels that would see them as the actual product of the pre-70 struggle between the Circumcision and the Uncircumcision and/or the result of the personal initiatives of the apostolic leaders, namely, Peter and Paul. Nevertheless since the external evidence for the priority of Matthew has now been corroborated by a convincing presentation of the internal evidence, there is now no intrinsic reason why the same external evidence should not also prove reliable in assigning all three Synoptic Gospels to the pre-70 period.

Part three therefore sets out to break new ground in more than one way. In the first place, for the first time the external evidence for the Gospels is presented in the light of the Two-Gospel Hypothesis, and the history of the primitive church is interpreted as it appears in the light of the same hypothesis. Nor has anyone ever before attempted to apply compositional criticism to the Gospels in the light of the Two-Gospel Hypothesis. This new standpoint throws an entirely new light not only on the Gospels but also on the history of the first thirty years of the church's existence.

Some scholars of course are bound to register shock when they see where the strict application of the principles applied in part one and part two lead to in part three. However, it must be recognized that every scrap of tradition has been sifted and marshaled and that every single item finds its own proper place in our synthesis. That is to say, our synthesis is scientifically based and forms a consistent whole. And the further probing of the external evidence continues to show it to be consistent with itself and also with the internal critical evidence.

The key to the whole problem is the nature of the Gospel of Mark. We have already seen in part two that there was never any controversy or doubt among the earliest witnesses about the provenance of either Matthew or Luke. But from the earliest time of which we have record (that of Papias) the sources all indicate that there was a real problem regarding the character and provenance of the Gospel of Mark. This problem reveals itself to us first in the defensive remarks of Papias's Presbyter defending Mark's accuracy and veracity; secondly, in the fact that Mark is never spoken of as the ''author'' of his Gospel, but always as the ''interpreter'' (ἑρμηνευτής) of Peter, a term which means ''agent'' or ''messenger'' or ''recorder''; thirdly, as we have already noted, it reveals itself in the double tradition about the order of Mark, that is, the tradition of Clement of Alexandria which puts Mark after Matthew and Luke, and the tradition of the Muratorian Canon which placed Mark between Matthew and Luke; fourthly and lastly, it reveals itself in the problem of Mark 16:9-20, which is present in longer or shorter form in about half of the best manuscripts and which is missing in the remainder. With these phenomena, we may also include the fact that the whole of Mark, less about 26 verses, is found either in Matthew or Luke or in both together, although Mark has a large number of vivid phrases not found in the other two. The conclusion is obvious, that the solution to the Synoptic Problem depends on the proper understanding of the connection between Mark and Matthew and Luke taken together.

It was said earlier that now that the priority has been restored to Matthew there are three options available for the dating of the Synoptics, the early, the intermediate, and the late dating. The late dating would place Matthew in the middle 70s or 80s and Mark and Luke in the 80s or 90s; this late dating would best suit those who still rely on the elaborate "scenario" or *Sitz im Leben* that has been built up around Markan priority over the past century, including the possibility of various recensions of one or more of the Gospels with time allowed for their respective circulation and for their copying. This late date is also the one favored by Professor Farmer in his recent book (1982), *Jesus and the Gospel.* The intermediate dating, however, which would imply that Matthew at least was before 70, has never found favor and presents various difficulties which need not detain us here. The third option, the one which we shall be presenting in this part, leaves the date of Mark where the majority of scholars would place it, ± 65, with Luke and Matthew correspondingly earlier, that is, Matthew before 45 and Luke not later than 61. This third option will now be presented as a viable alternative solution of the problem which we have just outlined. In the course of the following chapters we shall be asking the following questions:

(1) Did the right conditions exist for the composition of the Gospel of Matthew between A.D. 30-44? And does it fit into the situation revealed in Acts 1-12?

(2) Given the existence of the Gospel of Matthew as the expression of the faith of the primitive church of Jerusalem, was there by the time Paul had completed his third missionary journey a need for a new gospel manifesto, one this time slanted towards the needs of Paul's Gentile churches (compare Ac 13:28)? In other words, granted the existence of the Jerusalem tradition of the Circumcision Party and the corresponding existence of the strong Greek tradition of Paul's churches, was there a need by the time of his imprisonment at Caesarea for a mediating document such as the Gospel of Mark, in order to bring together the two traditions?

(3) Could anything less than the witness, the authority, and the mediating role of Peter be adequate to unify the two traditions thus juxtaposed?

Much of the evidence already presented in part two of this book will be new to many readers, since never before has the evidence from the early church tradition been laid out in a methodologically correct form in a single volume. Hence it will not be uncritical for the reader who has always thought that such evidence was unworthy of serious consideration, to reappraise his position and to entertain the possibility that it is of more historical value than he had heretofore realized. In any case it is hard to see how the proper interpretation of the evidence presented in parts one and two can lead to any other conclusions. Certainly the results of these two parts are independent of the conclusions of part three. The fact is that the restoration of the priority of Matthew immediately opens up, willy-nilly, the possibility of a very early date for the Gospel of Matthew; and this part illustrates one of the possible solutions.

We assume the basic historicity of the Acts of the Apostles and of the Pauline corpus, including the letters of the Roman captivity,[1] for they are the nearest contemporary accounts of the affairs of the church created by the Apostles, who in their turn, according to the tradition, created the Gospels.

2. Some Facts about the Gospel of Matthew[2]

(1) In the first place, Matthew is evidently concerned with matters in which the first Christians and their potential converts were deeply and passionately interested, for example, the genealogy of the Messiah, the relation of Jesus and his teaching to the Torah and to its rabbinic interpretation. It is a document addressed to readers who want to know how Christ actually fulfilled the Old Testament prophecies about the Messiah. Lamar Cope is right in holding that the author of Matthew consciously used the O.T. in constructing his Gospel (see n. 2).

(2) It assumes that its readers understood and practiced the Temple ritual worship and its prescriptions, and also understood the interpretation of the rabbis and the Pharisees (cf. Mt 5:12-20; 19:1-9).

(3) It assumes that its readers were familiar with the views and customs of the groups named as the scribes, the Pharisees, the Herodians, and the Sadducees. It never explains who they are.

---

[1] Cf. F. F. Bruce, *The Acts of the Apostles* (London, ²1952, 7th ptg.); M. Hengel, *Acts and the History of Earliest Christianity* (Philadelphia: Fortress, 1980); also the latter's *Studies in the Gospel of Mark* (London: SCM Press, 1985). As regards the epistles of the captivity, our assumption is that they were written from Rome by Paul himself, although a small but significant number of scholars are now holding that they are pseudepigraphical.

[2] The following commentaries on the Gospel of Matthew have been helpful: G. D. Kilpatrick, *The Origins of the Gospel according to St. Matthew* (Oxford, 1946); M.-J. Lagrange, *L'Évangile selon saint Matthieu* (Paris, 1928); Lohmeyer/Schmauch, *Das Evangelium des Matthäus* (Göttingen, 1967); O. Lamar Cope, *Matthew: A Scribe trained for the Kingdom of Heaven,* CBQ monograph series 5 (Washington DC, 1976); R. H. Gundry, *Matthew: A Commentary on His Literary and Theological Art* (Grand Rapids: Eerdmans, 1982) has some important appendixes; also W. F. Albright and C. S. Mann, *Matthew,* Anchor Bible series (New York, 1971).

(4) It assumes that its readers know why these groups were so hostile to Jesus, and that they were aware of the conflict between the Law of Moses as interpreted by the Pharisees and the teaching of Jesus (cf. Mt 12:22-45).

(5) It assumes that some of its readers at least had a problem of conscience about paying the temple tax (cf. Mt 17:24-27).

(6) It indicates a situation in which its readers were used to being harassed by the high priests, scribes and Pharisees (Mt 10:17-22; 23:1-12; cf. Ac 1-9).

(7) It lacks any evidence that the church had already started officially to evangelize the Gentiles, an event that forms the watershed of the first part of the Acts (cf. 11:18), though of course there are naturally some forecasts of what was to come, for example, Matthew 8:11-13; 28:16-20. The horizon of the evangelist is still basically limited to the homeland of Jesus (cf. Mt 10:5-7).

(8) John A. T. Robinson has argued very cogently that if Matthew had been composed after 70 it would not have been possible to have omitted some reference to the destruction of the Temple and the Holy City as the fulfilment of Jesus' prophecy.[3] For this prophecy was an integral part of Jesus' eschatological teaching, which was a matter of great concern to communities like the Thessalonians[4] (cf. also the accusation against Stephen, Ac. 6:14).

(9) The so-called allusion to the destruction of the Holy City in Matthew's Parable of the Marriage Feast (Mt 22:7), which Jesus' hearers would have rightly taken as a warning to them about the future of the Holy City, cannot be justly pressed to conclude that the destruction had already taken place when Matthew was composed. The warning is given in the context of a parable relating what was then the recognized penalty for a rebellious city. The warning is there indeed, but the presence of the parable in the text of Matthew can in no way be pressed to mean that the destruction had already happened (cf. Bo Reicke, n. 3 above).

(10) There are two texts that, taken straightforwardly, indicate that the social milieu of Jesus' time was still intact when Matthew was written, that is, the phrase "even unto this day" (Mt 27:8; 28:15).

---

[3]John A. T. Robinson, *Redating the New Testament* (1976) 13-30, 342, 360. Cf. also C. H. Dodd, "The Fall of Jerusalem and the 'Abomination of Desolation'," JRS 37 (1947): 47-54; B. Reicke, "Synoptic Prophecies on the Destruction of Jerusalem," in *Studies in New Testament and Early Christian Literature: Essays in Honour of Allen P. Wikgren,* ed. D. W. Aune, Nov. Test. Supp. 33 (Leiden, 1972) 121-34.

[4]Cf. Mt 24:2; 1 Thess 4:13ff.; 2 Thess 2:1-2.

(11) An important theme of the Gospel, namely, that Jesus is the successor of Moses as the Giver of the New Law, was a theme that appealed to the religious patriotism of the Jews, but had no appeal to the Gentiles. Like Moses, Jesus is revealed in Matthew as the one who ascends the mountain to announce the revision and fulfilment of the Law of Moses; and the Evangelist arranged that Jesus should give a great discourse on it[5] just as Moses did in Deuteronomuy (cf. 4:41–29:69).

(12) Among the Twelve, Matthew, the former tax collector, would probably have been the one best qualified by education and worldly experience (at least after the defection of Judas) to collect and edit the sayings of Jesus into a coherent whole in the Greek language.[6]

(13) R. H. Gundry has shown that the author or final redactor of Matthew was familiar with the three languages then in simultaneous use only in Palestine, namely, Aramaic, Greek, and Hebrew, because the allusive O.T. quotations reveal familiarity with all three languages.[7] That is to say, the "final redactor" of Matthew must have been a Greek-speaking Palestinian who, in quoting from the Hebrew O.T. or the Septuagint, from time to time modifies his quotations with Aramaic touches, precisely because he is addressing a pre-70 audience.

The above observations fit in very well with what we have learned about Matthew in part two. For as to authorship, though part one offers no direct evidence, it certainly poses no obstacle to the tradition that the author was the Apostle Matthew, the former tax collector. As to the addressees, internal reasons agree with the external evidence that they were Palestinian Jewish Christians. Our part one, chapter 3, also supports in general a Palestinian provenance.

As to the language in which Matthew was written, modern critics are almost unanimous that it was in Koine Greek. On the other hand the tradition from Irenaeus onwards was that it was originally composed in Aramaic. This view seems to be the result of a misunderstanding of Papias by Irenaeus, as has been explained in part two, excursus 2.

---

[5]Cf. J. B. Orchard, MLM, table 1, pp. 41-42.

[6]M. Hengel, *Acts,* 115: "At the very beginning of our era Greek education was firmly established even in Jerusalem"; R. H. Gundry, "The Language Milieu of First Century Palestine," JBL 83 (1964): 404-405; cf. also R. Riesner, *Jesus als Lehrer* (Tübingen, 1981) 123-99. This is the most recent and comprehensive account of Jewish education.

[7]Cf. R. H. Gundry, *The Use of the Old Testament in St. Matthew's Gospel* (Leiden: E. J. Brill, 1967; Suppl. to Novum Testamentum XVIII) 177-78. Cf. also Gundry, *Matthew,* 599-622, "Some Higher-critical Conclusions," for the date and authorship of Matthew.

As to the date of the Gospel, internal evidence is not opposed, and much of it is favorable, to a date before 70, and even before Paul's first missionary journey (47-49), that is, even to a date prior to the departure of Peter from Jerusalem about A.D. 44 (cf. Ac 12). As to Matthew's relationship with the other Gospels, the tradition does not concern itself with the strictly literary relationships existing between them, unless Papias's cryptic phrase "but each recorded the logia of Matthew as he was in a position to" (Eusebius EH III.39.16), can be understood as a reference to the dependence of Luke and Mark on Matthew; it is certainly open to such an understanding. On the other hand, the internal critical evidence of our part one comes down firmly on the side of Matthew being the first and original Gospel.

3. Some Facts about the Gospel of Luke

In part one, chapters 3 and 5, Riley has given cogent reasons for holding that Luke is dependent on Matthew and not on Mark or "Q", and he is supported by many modern critics, among whom one of the most important is M. D. Goulder.[8]

The strongest argument offered by those who think that Luke is later than Mark is said to be the assertion that the so-called reference in Luke 21:20 to the destruction of Jerusalem is a prophecy *post eventum*.[9] But this is to read into the text much more than it can truly bear, and it can be true only *if* Mark really did precede Matthew. Thus the historical and the critical evidence regarding Luke agree on the following:

(1) Authorship. Almost all modern authorities agree that the tradition is correct in ascribing Luke-Acts to our Luke, the companion of Paul. Nor is there anything in either work to contradict the view that he was a native of Antioch and a physician.[10]

(2) There is everything to be said in favor of, and almost nothing against, his having written for a predominantly Gentile audience, such as was to be found in the churches that Paul had founded during his three mis-

---

[8]M. D. Goulder, "On putting Q to the Test," NTS 20 (1978): 219-34; and his *Midrash and Lection in Matthew* (London: S.P.C.K., 1974); but cf. C. M. Tuckett, "On the Relationship between Matthew and Luke," NTS 30:130-42. Cf. C. J. Hemer "Luke the Historian," BJRL 60 (1977-1978): 28-51.

[9]See Joseph A. Fitzmyer, *The Gospel according to Luke*, 2 vols. (Garden City NY: Doubleday, 1982, 1985) introduction and passim. For further study of the literary relationship of Luke to Matthew, see B. C. Butler, *The Originality of St. Matthew* (Oxford, 1951); J. B. Orchard, MLM.

[10]Cf. Fitzmyer, *Luke*, intro. and ch. 2.

sionary journeys.[11]

(3) Internal evidence would allow Luke to have been published anywhere in the Greek-speaking world, so that there is no bar to the tradition that it was first written and/or published in Achaia.[12]

(4) If Luke was composed before Acts, as all scholars agree, and if, as Riley has shown, Mark is dependent on Luke, then Luke could have been completed as early as 61, the date which best suits our thesis.[13]

4. Some Facts about the Gospel of Mark[14]

The reader of this work will have noted that never at any time in the history of the early church was any criticism advanced against the authorship of the Gospels of Matthew and Luke. But from the time of the earliest mention of Mark, that of Papias, there was acknowledged to be some complication about its authorship. The following points may be noted.

(1) The historical and critical evidence both agree, as we have seen above in parts one and two, in placing Mark after Matthew, but the only definite statement that Mark was third in order of time after Matthew and Luke comes to us on the authority of Clement of Alexandria (Eusebius, EH VI.14).

(2) As regards authorship, there is no direct internal evidence for the gospel having been composed by Mark himself, but modern critics usually accept without qualification that Mark was the author. The external evidence, however, affirms only that Mark was the ''agent'' (ἑρμηνευτής) of Peter as regards composition, and that publication after Peter's death was Mark's responsibility alone. It is significant that in the ancient documents Mark is never spoken of as ''the author.'' However Riley has no alternative but to speak of Mark as the author, without attempting to distinguish between the respective roles of author, editor, and publisher, as we shall do below. It is of course clear that Mark 1:1–16:8 covers the period of Peter's personal eyewitness, so that there is nothing in the internal evidence to contradict the view

---

[11]Cf. ibid., intro. and ch. 2 §3.

[12]Cf. Anti-Marcionite prologue to Luke in Greek, pt. 2, ch. 3, 6b.

[13]Cf. Bruce *Acts,* 10-14; but Fitzmyer, having opted for Markan priority over Luke, has to date Luke ca. A.D. 85, so that Acts would then be later still.

[14]The work of Ralph Martin, *Mark, Evangelist and Theologian* (Grand Rapids: Zondervan, 1972) is one of the best commentaries interpreting Mark on the basis of Markan priority over Matthew and Luke. On the importance of Peter in connection with the formation of the Gospel of Mark, see M. Hengel, ''Probleme des Markusevangeliums,'' in *Das Evangelium und die Evangelien* (Tübingen, 1983) 221-66.

of Jerome that "the Gospel of Mark consists of Peter's narration and [Mark's] writing."[15] Indeed Papias's presbyter is specially quoted as saying that Mark was particularly careful not to tamper in any way with what Peter had said (Eusebius EH III.39.15).

(3) The addressees. Most commentators agree that Mark was addressed to a predominantly Greek-speaking audience that knew little or nothing about Jewish customs; this is by far the best way to account for the explanations made by Mark from time to time (for example, 7:1-4, 19).

(4) Provenance. The tradition that Mark was composed in Italy and at Rome was the only tradition known to the ancients. There are also some indications in the text itself that suit a Roman provenance (for example the *quadrans* of 12:42, and the reference to the Roman law that permitted a woman to divorce her husband (10:12).

(5) The language in which Mark was written was certainly Greek, but is not that of a practiced writer (see pt. one, ch. 7, §3). The vividness of the detail in certain places suggests that the composer was an eyewitness of what he described, and that he used Greek very forcefully but like a second language.

(6) According to Clement, the text was circulated privately in Peter's lifetime by Mark. A date before 64, when Nero's persecution began, perhaps A.D. 62, is a likely date (compare Eusebius, EH II.25). It was only after Peter's martyrdom, 65/67, that Mark himself published the Gospel. Eusebius's chronology is however confused because he noted (EH II.16.24) that Annianus succeeded Mark at Alexandria in the eighth year of Nero (that is, 63).

---

[15]Cf. Jerome *Ep*. 120.11; see pt. two, ch. 5, appendix.

2

The Composition
of the Gospel of Matthew

1. The Jerusalem Church of Acts 1–12

Although the majority of the Twelve Apostles would not have had a Greek education (so far as we know),[1] Greek influence in Palestine was strong and they would have had a sound grounding in all essentials in the local synagogue, and one based on the study of the Old Testament.[2] The leading three, Peter, James, and John, were levelheaded, practical fishermen with good, native intelligence. Moreover they were to prove themselves to be persons possessed of wisdom, energy, directness, integrity, and the ability to manage men, as the Acts shows (compare Ac 6:1ff.). There is reason to think that although they began by being relatively unsophisticated they learned with remarkable speed the basic lessons that evangelizing a harsh and incredulous world could teach them.

That they were able from the beginning to interest and win over to the faith many of the priests (Ac 6:7) and the cosmopolitan crowds visiting Jerusalem for the Feast of Pentecost (Ac 2:1ff.), is proof enough that Jesus had chosen as his apostles determined men who could convince not only their own peers but also the intelligent, the wealthy, and the powerful of this world. Peter and James and John (the latter, by the way, seems to have moved easily in high-priestly circles, Jn 18:16) were also humble enough to realize that they needed the help of heaven-sent persons like Paul, whose education and talent were exactly what was needed to make the right impact on the pagan, Greek-speaking world (Gal 2:1-10). However, after

---

[1]Cf. E. G. Turner, *Greek Papyri* (Oxford, [2]1980) ch. 6 passim.

[2]Matthew, John, and Judas Iscariot may well have had a Greek education: see ch. 1, n. 6. For an account of the synagogue, and its educational value, see *New Westminster Dictionary of the Bible*, "Synagogue"; also ODCC, in loc. See also B. Reicke, *The New Testament Era* (London: A. & C. Black, 1974) 119-24; R. Riesner, *Jesus als Lehrer* (Tübingen, 1981) 123-99, for an authoritative discussion; and Gerard Mussies, "Greek as the Vehicle of Early Christianity," NTS 29/3 (July 1983): 356-69.

Pentecost their first task was to make sure that they preached the Gospel unitedly and effectively to their own fellow countrymen in the very place where the movement began, namely in Jerusalem itself, starting from the place where 120 or so had first received the Holy Spirit. Guided by the same Spirit they revealed remarkable powers of organization and improvisation in the face of fierce opposition from the powerful and all-pervasive influence of the Jewish high priesthood which had set itself to eradicate this "detestable sect."[3]

Paul, writing to the Thessalonians (1 Thess 2:14-16) some twenty-two years after the Resurrection, feelingly records the sufferings of the primitive church of Jerusalem, which had the task of defending itself not only against the physical violence of its enemies but also against the sophisms of the rabbis and the Pharisees who had tried in vain to entrap Jesus in his speech.[4]

The sourcebook of their apologetic was the Septuagint, and especially those passages that spoke of the future Messiah. As K. Stendahl has noted, what the Jerusalem Church needed was a handbook, at once apologetic, didactic, and administrative, that would sum up in simple form the gospel of the kingdom.[5] What was needed to give cohension and courage to the little flock and to confute the calumnies of its enemies was another "writing" to prove to the Jewish nation that Jesus was indeed the fulfilment of ancient prophecy. It is true of course that the gospel message was meant to be communicated primarily by word of mouth, from heart to heart, for Jesus himself did not write anything; but a written document of the "new Torah," containing the sayings and way of life of the Master, would be the fitting answer to all their critics and in addition a useful handbook or *vade mecum*, for all the new itinerant preachers.

The Acts of the Apostles indicates that the Twelve stayed in Jerusalem for some years after the first Pentecost and did not disperse even when persecution drove many to escape from the Holy City (Ac 8:1). Acts also records the setting up of an orderly way of life, namely, that the first converts "devoted themselves to the apostles' teaching and fellowship, to the breaking of bread and the prayers" (Ac 2:42). Little reflection is needed

---

[3]There is no solid reason for doubting the correctness of Luke's account in Ac 1-12, which in our opinion he put together not more than thirty years after the events therein recorded. See M. Hengel, *Acts and the History of Earliest Christianity* (Philadelphia: Fortress 1980); F. F. Bruce, *The Acts of the Apostles* ([2]1952); J. Dupont, *The Sources of Acts* (1964) 167ff. E. Haenchen, *The Acts of the Apostles* (Oxford, 1971) gives another view.

[4]Cf. also Peter's speeches in Ac 2:14-39; 3:11-26.

[5]K. Stendahl, "Commentary on Matthew," *Peake's Commentary,* ([6]1962) §673c.

to realize that the pastoral, liturgical theological, and social activity involved in setting up in such a thorough manner the Christian commune in that hostile environment was a complex task that required the highest skills and must have taxed all the wisdom, mutual charity, prudence, and energy of the Twelve over a lengthy period. Among other things, it involved the setting up of house-churches, since the Temple was no place for them to celebrate the Christian liturgy (cf. Ac 2:46, and 12:12—the church in the house of Mark); the care of the widows of both the Hellenists and the Hebrews; and the construction of an ecclesial organization that would leave the Twelve free "to devote themselves to prayer and the ministry of the Word" (Ac 6:4). Most important of all, however, was the need to draw up a common statement of their faith, the gospel message.

2. The Church's Need Met by the Gospel of Matthew

Thus it is highly probable that the Jerusalem church made it one of its highest priorities to formulate the teaching of the Master not only in oral form but also in writing. For a literate people like the Jews, the notion of recording the life and teaching of Jesus in a book would be no novelty. It is therefore sensible to infer that the Apostles would have been urged to put down and into circulation their memories of Jesus while these were still fresh and fully relevant to their immediate situation. Not to have done so would have been to lose a great opportunity. Indeed, it would in any case have been an eminently sensible action for these brilliant organizers to commission a book like the Gospel of Matthew to strengthen their unity and their apologetic. And once decided upon, who more capable than Matthew? Eusebius has recorded the tradition that each evangelist in turn "took to writing of necessity" (EH III.24.5); and in Acts 1–12 we have just such a situation that called for the sort of document that Matthew undoubtedly is. For it met all the requirements of the predicament in which the nascent Church found itself at that time. The Gospel of Matthew furnishes the precise answers to the pressing questions that then confronted the Jerusalem community.[6] It is important to note that it is always the Twelve, in asso-

---

[6]The early date of Matthew, that is, prior to A.D. 44, hereby presupposed, finds firm support from the way in which the Gospel slots into the situation depicted in Ac 1–12. Markan priorists, already committed to a post-80 date for Matthew, are forced (a) to say that Ac 1–12 does not give a true picture (Haenchen, *Acts,* passim), and (b) to create a "scenario" to justify a post-80 dating, either by creating an anachronistic Christian Jewish community or enclave situated between Damascus and Antioch about 75-90, or by linking Matthew's hostility to the Pharisees with the obscure workings of the so-called Synod of Jamnia (ca. 91) in order to account for Jewish hostility towards the Christians. All these are in reality conjectures that rely for their credibility on the soundness of Markan priority.

ciation with Peter, who strictly control the teaching of the Jerusalem Church, that is, the tradition coming directly from Jesus himself (cf. Ac 2:42); it is never the faithful rank and file. The Apostles both shaped and controlled the tradition, to which Paul himself considered himself subject (Gal 2:1-2; 1 Cor 11:2; 2 Thess 2:15; 3:6). Because of their unique relationship to Jesus during his earthly ministry they alone possessed the full inner story of what Jesus said and did (cf. Ac 1:21); and no one attempted to question their authority and right to speak and to teach. They were also surely brimful of memories of the Master individually and collectively, and their problem was simply that of knowing which were the best ones to select for the benefit of the Jerusalem church.

On the first Pentecost itself (Ac 2:1ff.), the enthusiastic response of the multinational audience must have made them realize that the world was calling for their "good news" and that their apostolate would be worldwide; their speaking in tongues was a portent of this. The medium of their apostolate would of course have to be the Koine Greek, the language of the whole Roman world and beyond; it was also fortunately the second langage of all educated people in Palestine.

However, some years were to pass before the church was ready to pass from its homeland to set up and monitor churches abroad (cf. Ac 8:4, 14, 25; 9:31-32; 11:1-18; 22-23). During this period, and for some time later, the Jerusalem Church remained the mother church, monitoring all the while any new developments (cf. Barnabas's mission to Antioch). Our belief is that the Gospel of Matthew saw the light in these earliest years and thus rightly came to be regarded as "the Gospel of the Church," the principal source for the logia of Jesus, and the doctrinal norm for the first stage of apostolic evangelization. It is also the only Gospel that provides the necessary continuity between the Old Covenant and the New, between the time of preparation and the time of fulfilment, between the Law of Moses and the Law of Christ. Let us now see how Matthew was constructed.

3. The Construction of the Gospel of Matthew

Basing ourselves on the researches chronicled above it is reasonable to conclude that the Gospel of Matthew is no more and no less than the written record of the tradition which the Apostles had personally received from Jesus himself during the years that they had accompanied him in his ministry. Of course their primary task after Pentecost was to hand on intact this oral tradition, the teaching that they had received from him by word of mouth; and to do this they had to make a synthesis of his sayings and behavior that would at least comprise all that was immediately important for the situation of the primitive church in the Holy City and in Judea.[7] They had to make up their minds not only what to put in but also what to leave out, and no doubt most would have to be left out for lack of space. But they were not without external guidance regarding the process that had to be followed in order to make the tradition available. They had only to follow the example both of the rabbis and also of the Greek world in order to pass on the tradition exactly. R. O. P. Taylor has described the process thus: "Tradition, in the first century at least, stood for a system of ensuring the retention of information . . . ; though it also meant a written record, it was still more a fixing in men's memories. . . . For the Jew of that time the only legitimate way of conveying the facts was the imparting of the exact words of the record, in this case Jesus himself. Nothing less was required of him, and nothing less was expected of the pupils."[8]

An urgent task of the Twelve therefore would have been to reduce their memories of Jesus to a form suitable for an oral catechesis. The orderly way in which the church is seen to develop after the first Pentecost indicates that it set about this task in the same orderly manner. Taylor has pointed out that Greek education and the work of Greek grammarians were also well known in first-century Palestine. That is to say, educated contempoary Jews knew and used the five principal literary forms of good writing, namely, the γνώμη (the maxim or pregnant saying), the παραβολή (an effort to put an idea before the mind's eye), the διήγησις (straightforward narrative), the χρεία (a pithy anecdote), and the ἀπομνημόνευμα (a recollection, the natural artless form in which an incident would be remembered).[9] For the purpose of evangelization the words and deeds of Jesus had to be set down within these categories, and this was no mean task. But the Gospel of Matthew is proof that this task was faithfully carried out. There was obviously an enormous number of such memories

---

[7]B. Gerhardsson, *Memory and Manuscript* (Uppsala, 1961) explains the methods used by the contemporary rabbis to teach their disciples. Jesus would have taught his disciples similarly by word and example.

[8]R. O. P. Taylor, *The Groundwork of the Gospels* (Oxford, 1946), quoted in MLM, 31-34.

[9]See MLM, 32. The carefully contrived form of the pericopes is illustrated in J. B. Orchard, "The 'Common Step' Phenomenon," in *New Synoptic Studies: The Cambridge Gospel Conference and Beyond* (Macon GA: Mercer University Press, 1983). The categories of pericopes popularized by Bultmann and others, e.g., miracle stories, pronouncement stories, controversy stories, are mainly subjective and are largely based on outmoded theological views or attitudes, such as that the first Christians were specially interested in miracles; see E. Massaux, *Influence de l'Évangile de Saint Matthieu sur la littérature chrétienne avant S. Irénée* (Louvain, 1950) 647-55.

to choose from (cf. Jn 21:25). But barring one or two agrapha the only units that have survived out of the vast repertoire possessed by the Twelve Apostles are the ones found in our Matthew and the other Gospels. Naturally they are all in an easily memorable form, and, especially in the Synoptic Gospels, there is a common pattern both for the stories and for the sayings, although within this pattern there is some degree of minor variation. For our present purpose the most interesting fact is that the evangelist Matthew not only employs all these five literary forms, but that in most cases his χρεῖαι and ἀπομνημονεύματα are the shortest, Luke's are correspondingly longer, and Mark's longest of all. In other words, there is a presumption that Matthew has the shortest and most original form of each story unit, that Luke amplifies it somewhat, and that Mark amplifies it still more; but the basic pattern remains the same in each.[10]

As soon as these oral forms of the primitive catechesis had been fixed by "the pillars" of the Jerusalem Church, the way would have been open to putting them down in writing. The Gospel of Matthew seems to be the first literary fixation of the Palestinian oral catechesis and forms a concise, coherent, and comprehensive collection of material for a rounded picture of the Founder's teaching. And because its length was determined by the normal length of a commerical roll of papyrus or parchment, the Gospel of Matthew had to be restricted to some 2,600 stichoi, or lines to the manuscript column. In the light of these considerations, let us now take a closer look at the content of Matthew's Gospel in order to note the essential elements of the tradition as articulated by the primitive church.

4. The Essential Content of the Gospel of Matthew

Matthew begins abruptly with the assertion that Jesus is the Christ, and proves by his genealogy that he is the Son of David by legal adoption on the part of Joseph, whose fiancée Mary had unexpectedly conceived by the power of the Holy Spirit (Mt 1).

As contemporary Jews were unfamiliar with the idea of a "suffering Messiah," it was also necessary to record his Resurrection which alone could vindicate his entire mission after its seeming total failure (cf. Mt 12:38-42; 16:22-23; 28:11-20). Again, Matthew stresses the importance of the witness of John the Baptist, his prophesied forerunner, whom the whole nation had revered as a prophet of God (Mt 3:1-17; 11:2-19; 21:23-27). Again, his claim to have the authority both to fulfill and to complete the Law of Moses, and even to abrogate some of its rules, made it essential to show him superior to Moses and greater than Jonah and Solomon (5:17-

---

[10]See n. 9 above.

48; 12:38-42). Hence too the construction of five great discourses (chapters 5-7, 10, 13, 18, 23-25), which show him remolding the Law given to Moses (cf. Ex 20–24; Dt 1:5–4:40; 5:1–26:19; 29:1–30:20). These discourses are interspersed by a carefully chosen selection of story units illustrating various aspects of the person and powers of the Christ. And there is no mitigation of the stark fact that the priestly leaders of the Jewish people in Jerusalem itself were responsible for the death of the Christ, the revered founder of the church of the Apostles (cf. Ez 33:5; Mt 27:25). The Gospel also makes it clear that he is condemned to death for his claim to be the Son of God and his further claim that his enemies would one day see him coming on the clouds of Heaven, in fulfilment of the prophecy of Daniel (Mt 26:64).

Thus we see that the Gospel of Matthew can be viewed as the Gospel of the church of Jerusalem as we see it flourishing in Acts 1-12; and could therefore be the true prototype of the gospel genre.[11] Thus we see how the first document of the church about Jesus Christ could have evolved within the Jerusalem church itself in response to its existential needs. As to its date, we shall see in our next chapter (ch. 3, n. 4) that is likely to have appeared not only before 1 and 2 Thessalonians and Galatians but probably before Paul's second visit to Jerusalem "after fourteen years" (Gal 2:1; Ac 11:27-30, 12:25), that is to say, before 46/47; so that its formation could have taken place in the first decade of the church's life; moreover, it was in all probability known to Paul before he began his first missionary journey (46/47) and was thus the main literary source of his knowledge of the earthly life of Jesus.[12]

---

[11]The usual claim that Mark is the first exemplar of the gospel genre stands or falls on the degree of probability of Markan priority.

[12]If Matthew was composed before A.D. 44, then it must certainly have been known to Paul. Support for this view is to be found in an article by J. Chapman (see pt. 2, ch. 2, n. 7). For Paul's use of Matthew in 1 and 2 Thess see J. B. Orchard, "Thessalonians and the Synoptic Gospels," *Biblica* (1938): 19-42 (see pt. 2, ch. 2, n. 4). For the use of Matthew in 1 Corinthians, see D. L. Dungan, *The Sayings of Jesus in the Churches of Paul* (Philadelphia: Fortress, 1971) 139ff.

3

The Composition of Luke-Acts

1. The Circumcision Question and the Roles of Peter and Paul

It is remarkable that we have hardly any certain knowledge of the missionary activities of the Twelve Apostles, except what we learn from Acts about Peter, James, and John. How do we account for this ignorance?

The short answer is to state that it is because we depend largely on Luke, their contemporary and the first Church historian, and because Luke, who had had the opportunity of finding out what they were doing, or had done, when he was researching in Palestine, kept silent about them. The little he tells us when he records Pentecost and its consequences for the Twelve is that their main function was to be witnesses to the Resurrection of Jesus and that the qualification for this was "to have accompanied Jesus all the time he went in and out among them from the baptism of John until the day of his ascension" (cf. Ac 1:12ff.). Thereafter Luke makes no mention by name of any of them except those three. And why did he still keep silent? It can only be because he had no intention of writing a general history of the church and of the adventures of the Twelve as they set out for different parts of the world.[1] Indeed, at the time he had completed Luke-Acts (ca. 60/62),[2] he clearly saw the main evolution of the church in terms of the respective ministries of Peter and Paul, Peter representing mainly the tradition of the circumcision (περιτομή), and Paul representing the arrival of the uncircumcision (ἀκροβυστία), that is to say, the mass entrance of the Greco-Roman world into the new Israel of God (cf. Eph 2:11-22). And so Luke restricts himself to those aspects of their ministries of which he either had personal knowledge or had been able to research during the years

---

[1]For a vindication of Luke as a historiographer, see W. C. Van Unnik, "Luke's Second Book and the Rules of Hellenistic Historiography," in *Les Actes des Apôtres: Tradition rédaction, théologie*, ed. J. Kremer (Leuven University Press, 1979) 37-60.

[2]The basis of my chronology is the normal view that the Acts was completed before Paul's release, i.e., about A.D. 62; cf. Bruce, *Acts*, 10ff.

of Paul's detention in Caesarea.[3] Furthermore, he makes clear to his readers that he saw the post-Resurrection development of the church as taking place in two phases. The first phase was the firm establishment of the church among those who had inherited the Old Testament, namely, among Jewish converts, proselytes, and "God-fearers" (Ac 1-12). The second phrase was its extension to the Gentiles (Ac 13-28), and it began with the first missionary journey of Paul and Barnabas, starting from Antioch, the most important city of the East, where the church already had a secure foothold. But we also learn from Paul's own admission that the opening of the second phase had been preceded by a vital agreement between Paul and the "Three Pillars" of the Jerualem church, Peter, James, and John (cf. Gal 2:1-10; Ac 11:27-30; 12:25).[4]

---

[3]The "we" passages, Ac 21:7; 27:1; 28:16, would seem to indicate that the author of Acts was not far from Paul all during his period of imprisonment at Caesarea, and down to his arrival in Rome (cf. Bruce, *Acts,* in loc). Of his contacts with any other members of the Twelve we have no documentary record, unless James of Jerusalem was one; cf. also Van Unnik's article above, n.1, with comment on the "we" passages.

[4]In the view followed here, the Letter to the Galatians was not written about the time of Romans, ca. 57, but was sent off by Paul while on his way up to the Council of 49, as soon as he heard that his Judaizing opponents of Ac 15:1ff. had gone "behind his back" and won over his Galatian converts to their views. Thus Paul's second visit to Jerusalem after fourteen years is identical with his second visit in Acts (11:27-30; 12:25). Hence this meeting with the "three pillars" must be considered as having taken place before his first missionary journey, probably in 46 (see Bruce, *Acts,* 241). This meeting now takes on an altogether new significance; for in addition to the other reasons for his journey, the Holy Spirit was prompting Paul to secure in advance the official support of the Apostles against the day when he would need it, namely, at the Council of 49. Thus the "false brethren" mentioned in Gal 2:4 had nothing to do with his second visit, but are either the persons (or the allies of those) whom he had been arguing with in Ac. 15:1-3. The key to this interpretation lies in realizing that the ellipsis of Gal 2:4 is to be understood as Paul's elliptical lament that the whole controversy raging when he wrote (including the defection of his Galatians) was due to the machinations of the false brethren so recently introduced among them. I must here assume the reader's familiarity with th work of Professor F. F. Bruce, especially in his *Commentary on Galatians* (1982) and in his series of articles, "Galatians Problems," which appeared in the *Bulletin of the John Rylands Library* (1969-1973). See also J. B. Orchard, "The Problem of Acts and Galatians," CBQ (1945): 377-97; "Thessalonians and the Synoptic Gospels," *Biblica* 18 (1938): 19-42; "The Ellipsis between Gal 2:4 and Gal 2:4," *Biblica* 54 (1973):469-81; "Once again the Ellipsis between Gal 2:3 and 2:4," *Biblica* 57 (1976):254-55; and "Ellipsis and Parenthesis in Gal 2:1-10 and 2 Thess 2:1-12," in *Paul de Tarse—Apôtre de notre temps* (Rome: Basilica di San Paolo f-l-m, 1979). The whole modern problem regarding the three visits has arisen from a misconception of the meaning of Gal 2:4. On the other hand, the chief argument for the late date of Galatians—its thematic parallel with Romans—has been countered by B. N. Kaye in "To the Romans and Others," *Nov. Test.* 18/1 (January 1976). On Paul's purpose in writing to the Romans, see C. E. B. Cranfield, *Romans* (1979) 2:814-23, "Essay I: Paul's Purpose or Purposes in writing Romans."

The purpose of the agreement was to make provision regarding the circumcision question that was to rack the church for the next twenty years. At their meeting Peter and the other pillars had recognized the special responsibility that had been given to Paul by the Holy Spirit for the opening up of the church to the Gentiles. It was indeed a momentous meeting because it cleared the way for Paul's missionary enterprise to begin with Jerusalem's official support. The need for this support was to become evident a couple of years later when the success of Paul's mission in Galatia aroused the jealous hostility of the circumcision party in the Holy City, the point in dispute being recognized as requiring a special council of the Apostles with Paul (Ac 15:1-36).

2. The Purpose of Luke's Gospel

By the time Paul was brought down to Caesarea as the prisoner of Felix (ca. 57), he would (according to our hypothesis) have had the use of Matthew's Gospel for at least ten years. These had been years of extraordinary successful evangelization during which he had planted churches in a number of strategic places, such as Ephesus, Philippi, and Corinth; and during this time he would have been able to assess both the advantages and the disadvantages of the first gospel as an instrument of evangelization in the Greek-speaking world. We have already seen that it had been originally written for the church of Jerusalem before Paul's mission to the Gentiles had begun, and that it had been specifically aimed at convincing the Jewish nation that Jesus was indeed their Messiah. It made no attempt to envisage the mentality or the specific needs of the other inhabitants of the Roman Empire, who of course included all his Gentile converts who were by then far more numerous in his churches than the original nucleus of Jews and "God-fearers." The Gospel of Matthew was perfect for its original purpose, but it did not attempt to answer the new questions about the gospel that the men of Greek culture were asking. But now, in this situation, Paul would have come to realize that what he needed was a rewriting of the message of Matthew in order to set the ministry of Jesus in a light that would appeal to his Greek converts, learned and unlearned alike. This of course would be a major undertaking. The very idea of such a rewriting of the original gospel was one that would certainly upset the circumcision party. It would also require not only the most careful preparation, but much research to expand and adapt existing stories and also to recover some of the many stories that Matthew had had to pass over in the life of Jesus. It would also require a tranquil period for study and reflection when Luke, as a member of Paul's entourage, would not be constantly on the move from place to place. Such a favorable opportunity occurred when Paul found himself a prisoner at Caesarea, yet with access to his friends and his assistants, Luke among them.[5] When first the idea of a new gospel document entered Paul's mind we do not know, but a guess will be hazarded that he was already thinking of it when he remarked that after visiting Jerusalem next time he would also have to visit Rome (Ac 19:21; see next section). At all events, when Paul was under arrest at Caesarea, his friend and assistant Luke, probably also his personal physician, had the time and the freedom to go fact-finding in Galilee and Samaria, and in Jerusalem and Judea, and the opportunity to look up and question the survivors of those who had personally known Jesus nearly thirty years before. For the Gospel of Luke not only adds further details to Matthew's existing stories but adds a number of new ones from each of the above areas. While Luke was collecting his material Paul would have been reflecting on his past experiences and envisaging the sort of Gospel he wanted Luke to write.[6]

An examination of the Gospel itself suggests that his first principle was to make as few changes in Matthew's order as would be compatible with his chronological scheme, to follow as far as possible the pattern of Matthew, and to avoid offending the conservative-minded. His second principle was to compose a volume as far as possible (given the Jewish character of the material) in the contemporary Greek biographical style. His third principle was to include as far as possible everything of importance found in Matthew that was of direct interest to his Greek churches. His fourth principle was to retain only so much of the references to the Law as was necessary for an educated Greek to appreciate the Jewish background of

---

[5]Cf. F. F. Bruce, *Acts,* 14. The "we" passages imply Luke's presence at Caesarea.

[6]In his important and well-researched volume, *The Purpose of Luke-Acts* (Edinburgh, 1982), R. Maddox takes up the question of Luke's purpose in writing (pp. 1, 19-23), and devotes a final chapter to some conclusions about it. The matter clearly intrigues him and, having discarded a number of past suggestions, he concludes that Luke wrote to reassure the Christian community and to show how Jesus' message had been fulfilled. But this view neither adds anything new nor does it satisfy fully as a reason. Maddox makes a vital point (p. 1) when he writes "that we find it more natural today to say, with C. K. Barrett that 'the Church in Luke's day had reached a point at which a variety of considerations . . . called for the sort of book that Luke wrote' (*Luke the Historian,* 53)." But, unfortunately, since Maddox has felt obliged to adopt the current Markan priority hypothesis, which forces him to place Luke's Gospel between 70 and 90, he can never ascertain the real reason for Luke having written such as we have formulated it. All the theories Maddox mentions on pp. 19-23 suffer greatly from the same defect. Wrong dating spoils the results of so much otherwise excellent scholarship. Bernard Lonergan has well said: "Questions of date and authenticity, which might be thought secondary in biblical theology, really have a decisive importance" (*Method in Theology* [1972] 171). J. L. Houlden's important article "The Purpose of Luke" (JSOT 21 [1984]: 53-65) appeared too late for full consideration here; it provides a qualification of Maddox's thesis to the effect that Luke was neither anti-Jewish nor pro-Jewish, and that his theology moved, as we too believe, on a higher plane.

Jesus. His fifth principle was to emphasize that Jesus was also the Savior of the Gentiles as well as of the Jews, and the one who could show the way to overcoming all the social evils of the time, which of course meant bringing in many new stories and discarding others of interest chiefly to Jews. To achieve all this in the space of one commercial roll required great editorial skill and the omission of duplicate stories wherever possible, for example, the Feeding of the Four Thousand. The result of putting all these principles into action was the Gospel of Luke as we know it; and it may well have been ready by the time that Paul embarked at Caesarea for Rome under the guard of the centurion Julius with his companions Aristarchus and Luke (cf. Ac 27:2; Col 4:10; Philem 24). Though Paul goes to Rome as a prisoner, he realized that this was the way in which the Holy Spirit wished him to witness to Christ in the capital of the Roman Empire (Ac 23:11). This will also be a convenient place to pause in order to consider more closely Paul's own reasons for wanting to visit Rome.

3. Some Reasons for Paul's Desire to Visit Rome

It is pertinent at this stage to ask two questions:
(1) Why did Paul want to go to Rome at all in the first place, seeing that it had already been evangelized by somebody else (Rom 15:20), and seeing that he also professed himself fully satisfied about their faith and practice (Rom 15:4)?
(2) Why did he write the Romans such a long and elaborate treatise if he was so satisfied with them?

The two questions would seem to be intimately connected and they will be answered together. The information at our disposal (namely, Rom 15:14-21, Ac 19:21, 23:11) has to be viewed in the overall perspective that we have been slowly building up with regard to the two gospels of Matthew and Luke and the relationship to the great question of the epoch, that of cementing the union of Jew and Gentile in Christ and of fully understanding all its theological implications. The real reasons will finally appear when we have succeeded in coordinating the facts at our disposal with the Apostle's overarching plan.

In the first place, it is strange and intriguing for Luke, who is so economical with his words, to insert, seemingly gratuitously, into his narrative of the Third Journey the sentence about seeing Rome after revisiting Jerusalem. The whole sentence is as follows: "Now after these events [in Ephesus] Paul resolved in the Spirit (ἔθετο . . . ἐν τῇ πνεύματι) to pass through Macedonia and Achaia and go to Jerusalem, saying 'After I have been there, I must also see Rome' " (Ac 19:21). Luke never wastes his words, and he must have had some special reason for inserting this statement in this particular context. F. F. Bruce agrees that the reference to the Holy Spirit is "more likely," and goes on to comment that "in the light of these passages [Ac 19:21; Rom 1:11f. and 15:23ff.] this verse reveals what [W. M.] Ramsay calls 'the clear conception of a far-reaching plan' to proceed via the Imperial City to evangelize 'the chief seat of Roman civilization in the West' (i.e. Spain). This decision thus marks a crisis in Paul's career" (*Acts*, 361). The instinct of these two commentators is surely correct, but there is even more to it than they have stated. For on his way through Macedonia, Paul fetched Luke to go with him, as is revealed by the "we" passage beginning at Acts 20:5-6. The fact that Luke also records the message of the Lord's appearance to Paul in the night (Ac 23:11) confirms the importance attached to the Roman visit by the Holy Spirit as well as by Luke. Luke records five other visions of Paul sent either to direct or to encourage him at moments of crisis, (cf. Ac 9:4; 16:9; 18:9; 22:17; 27:23). Clearly his Roman visit is to be momentous for the spread of the Gospel. Thus Luke sees the Spirit of Jesus encouraging Paul to make a visit which (as we shall see) in the event turned out to be the occasion for a final recognition of his special apostolate by his colleague Peter, thus reinforcing the pact of Galatians 2:7-10, a recognition that would in due time take on the form of Mark's Gospel.

In the second place, in Romans 15:28 Paul gives further details of his itinerary, saying that he would go on to Spain by way of Rome. Rome would of course be a natural stopping place on his way to the West, and especially because he had so many friends there (Rom 16:1 ff.).

In the third place, he still thought that the Judaizers within the church presented a grave danger to peace and unity (Rom 15:31), and by addressing to the Romans such a long and intense treatise on faith in Christ and on the Jewish question, in the expectation that they would have quite a long time to assimilate it before he arrived, he surely indicated that he wanted to prepare them very thoroughly for his coming and to make sure that they fully understod the importance of his work and of the discussions that he wished to initiate about the place of the Gentiles in the church. Romans was therefore intended to give them the background reading for what he would have to say to them when he arrived. In fact, as it worked out, they had plenty of time—between five and six years—in which to digest it all and to get ready to receive him.

In the fourth place, the centrality and importance of the capital city of the Empire made it the most advantageous place from which to launch a doctrinal treatise that put the whole question in a nutshell and that would have repercussions for every church in the world.

In the fifth place, we must interrogate very carefully the crucial passage (Rom 15:14-21) to discover exactly what it was that Paul hoped to add to the spiritual life of the Romans. It will be best be quote first the whole passage.

> [15:14]I myself am satisfied about you, my brethren, that you yourselves are full of goodness, filled with all knowledge, and able to instruct one another. [15]But on some points I have written to you very boldly by way of reminder, because of the grace given me by God, [16]to be a minister (λειτουργόν) of Christ Jesus to the Gentiles in the priestly service (ἱερουργοῦντα) of the gospel of God, so that the offering (προσφορά) of the Gentiles may be acceptable, sanctified by the Holy Spirit. [17]In Christ Jesus, then, I have reason to be proud of my work for God. [18]For I will not venture to speak of anything except what Christ has wrought through me to win obedience from the Gentiles, by word and deed, [19]by the power of signs and wonders, by the power of the Holy Spirit, so that from Jerusalem and as far round as Illyricum I have fully preached the gospel of Christ, [20]thus making it my ambition to preach the gospel, not where Christ has already been named, lest I build on another man's foundation, [21]but as it is written: They shall see who have never been told of him, and they shall understand, who have never heard of him.

It seems clear that Paul had something to show them and also some request to make of them, and gave two reasons why they should listen to him and do what he wanted them to do. The first was that he would come to them as the ambassador and plenipotentiary of the Gentiles, because he had been made their sacred minister with the function of offering up their "sacrifice" (προσφορά); his credentials were impeccable because God himself has made him their "priest" to make offering on their behalf.

Secondly, the enormous success of his work proved that God had set his seal on it fully. This work was the very work he set out to do after the meeting with Peter, James, and John, the three pillars, as he has described in Galatians 2:1-10. This work had now been brought to complete success, and it is clear from his Epistle to the Romans (1:8-15; 11:13-14) that he wanted the Romans to recognize the fact, that is, to give complete and public recognition to the new status of equality[7] that the Gentiles had achieved in the church as a result of his missionary work, to declare acceptable the offering of the Gentiles. Given this situation, a symbolic gesture from Peter his "opposite number" would suffice; that is to say, an outward sign to give parity of status in the church to the Gentile Christians, and this could be done by formal recognition of the written Gospel that Luke had composed on Paul's behalf to meet the spiritual needs of his Churches.

---

[7]Père J. M. R. Tillard, approaching the question from a different standpoint, has also divined the mind of Paul in his recent work, *The Bishop of Rome* (S.P.C.K., 1983), when he writes: "Paul wanted his vocation [the mission to the Gentiles] to be in some way received by the mother Church [of Rome]" (116).

Just as the Gospel of Matthew was the manifesto for the church of Jerusalem and for all that it stood for, so now Paul wanted the church of the Romans to accept and recommend the Gospel of Luke as the Christian manifesto designed especially for the Gentile converts, so that it could be proudly displayed side by side with the Gospel of Matthew. The Gospel of Matthew had been the charter for Jewish converts to Christ and the justification for their belief that they were indeed the true Israel and the true sons of Abraham, despite the defection of their former leaders, the old high priesthood. And now the Gospel of Luke was to become the corresponding charter for the right of the Gentile converts to have equal honor in the new Kingdom, for by faith in Christ they too had become true sons of Abraham (cf. Zacchaeus, Lk 19:1-10).[8]

Paul must have seen that owing to the strength and tenacity of the conservative forces still at work in Jewish-Christian society (Ac 21:20; Rom 15:31) there would be no chance for a controversial figure like himself securing a general acceptance of this new Gospel of Luke (which encapsulated his own presentation of Jesus) without the full backing of the same "pillars" who many years before had given him full support for, and recognition of, his unique apostolate. If he was to attain his objective and get Luke's work into circulation without an uproar even among his own churches (where there were anyway many converted Jews), he would have to make sure in advance that its publication would not antagonize those for whom the Gospel of Matthew had been composed long before. Not only common courtesy but essential diplomacy required that he should consult the other church leaders available and get their agreement, in order to forestall Luke's new volume becoming a "bone of contention" and a cause of renewed internal strife between the two distinct cultural traditions now within the church. The problem was above all one that converts from Judaism had to come to terms with, seeing that they were by now in the minority as a result of Paul's apostolate. His statesmanlike aim would have to be to make sure that the "Gentile shoot" was properly grafted onto the original parent stem of Israel in a manner that would last for all time. While it would be exceedingly helpful to obtain full recognition from the church of the Christians of Rome whom he so much admired, it would be most

---

[8]It is interesting to note that the Second Letter of Peter speaks of the Gentiles precisely in these terms, for it is addressed "to those who have obtained a faith of equal standing (ἰσότιμον) with ours in the righteousness of our God and Saviour Jesus Christ" (2 Pet 1:1). It is also noteworthy that whereas 1 Peter seems to be addressed primarily to the Jewish-Christian tradition, 2 Peter is addressed to the Gentile-Christian tradition that Paul had created. Despite the generally held late date of 2 Peter, there is little doubt it reflects a tradition contemporary with Peter himself.

satisfactory of all if he could secure from those same pillars the acknowledgment that he had fulfilled his part of the bargain he had struck with them. James had not been too helpful recently; but Peter and John were still alive.

Finally, looking back, it seems probable that Paul already had Luke in mind as the author of his Gospel manifesto when he fetched him to accompany him to Jerusalem (Ac 20:6). It is also probable that Luke had written his Gospel before he took ship with Paul for Rome; so that Paul would have had no difficulty in apprising James of Jerusalem before leaving Palestine of his intention to consult if possible the other two original "pillars" with regard to the publication of Luke's Gospel.

4. Could Peter and Paul Have Collaborated and/or Met After 49?

Although we have a great deal of information in Acts about Paul's movements between his first missionary journey in 47-49 and his Roman captivity in about 61-63, we know nothing for certain about Peter's movements. There is the tradition that he went to Antioch (Gal 2:11-15), and he was of course in Jerusalem for the Council of 49. We also know that he was well known to the Corinthians (1 Cor 1:12), and the fact that 1 Peter is addressed to the Christians of Pontus, Galatia, Cappadocia, Asia, and Bithynia suggests that he may have visited these distant regions of the Empire. And of course we know that 1 Peter was written from Rome. Furthermore it is entirely reasonable to assume that the two men whom Luke regarded as the founders of Christianity in the West should have been in constant touch all along, as their respective apostolates developed. What sort of collaboration, if any, could there have been between Peter and Paul in the years between the Council of Jerusalem and Paul's Roman captivity (ca. 60-62)? F. F. Bruce has shown that Galatians was the earliest Pauline epistle and was composed on the eve of the Council of Jerusalem (cf. n. 4 above). This in turn suggests that Paul's famous rebuke of Peter (Gal 2:11-14) took place several years before the Council, so that Peter's collaboration with Paul on the circumcision question proved that their disagreement had been only temporary and that they were again in full harmony.

In any event, the mere absence of any documentary proof of fruitful contact between them during this period is no argument for it not having taken place either occasionally or at regular intervals. The only history of the period that we possess—the Acts of the Apostles—is not a history of the growth of the Christian church, for it does not mention the activities of two-thirds of the original band of Twelve whom Jesus sent out (Mt 28:16-20). Indeed, it does little more than sum up the respective parts played by Peter and Paul in establishing the Jewish and Gentile wings of the Church in its first thirty years. But it is important to notice that Paul's churches were encouraged by him to support the beleaguered church of Jerusalem, in the foundation of which Peter had played a principle part (cf. Ac 11:26-30; 12:24-25; Gal. 2:10). Furthermore, the Acts and the Pauline letters afford proof of intercommunication between the churches of Paul and the churches of Jerusalem and Rome, for example the arrival of Priscilla and Aquila, refugees from Rome, who are welcomed in Paul's Church (Ac 18:1-2).

Again, the fact that Paul was constrained by a divine revelation to consult the "three pillars" at Jerusalem about his teaching on the circumcision question (Gal 2), together with their favorable reception of him at that time, would have predisposed him to consult them again if a further matter were to arise involving other aspects of this very question, which continued to simmer right down to the end of his life (cf. Phil 3:2-3). This time the Holy Spirit was urgently directing him to go instead to Rome for some equally weighty reason that was probably already known to him in principle (cf. Ac 23:11), though we can now only discover it by indirect means in virtue of our hindsight.

Finally, there is no doubt that there remains in the mind of the reader of Acts, as he comes to the end of the final chapter (28), a feeling that something yet remains to be settled, a kind of question mark about the union of the Jewish- and Gentile-Christian traditions, that is to say, of the Jerusalem church of Acts 1:12, 15 and 21 with the Pauline churches of Acts 13-28.

On our assumption that Luke-Acts had been more or less completed some time during Paul's detention in Rome at Caesar's pleasure, we already have some important reasons for bringing the two apostles once more into contact. There is, however, one further consideration that we may adduce at this point. It is this. Paul was no longer his own master, free to come and go as the needs of his apostolate dictated. It was known to all that he was in the custody of the Roman legal system and Rome was inexorably his destination and residence until his case was settled.

The lack of communication between Malta and the mainland during the winter he spent there may have led the church to think that he had been drowned. But when the news that he and the whole ship's company had been saved reached the outside world, the surviving "pillars," Peter and John (and James if still alive by then), would have realized that someone would have to go to visit him at the place of his confinement. His dangerous predicament would have been a signal for Peter, who seems to have been a wandering apostle, like Paul himself, to go to the capital to meet him and to plan for all eventualities, for Paul's execution at that time would have endangered the future of all his churches.

5. Peter in Rome

It is of course true that we have no explicit statement in the New Testament that Peter was ever in Rome before he wrote 1 Peter in that city (ca. 62; cf. 1 Pet 5:12-13). Peter could have been anywhere in the Roman Empire at the time Paul determined to go there (Ac 19:21). But G. Edmundson (*The Church in Rome in the First Century* [London, 1913] 30-47) argues strongly for Peter being the founder of the Roman Church, and that he was there in residence at least from 62-65. That the City of Rome itself is meant by the reference to "Babylon" (1 Pet 5:13) is quite certain, for the Sibylline Oracles (Book V) refer to Rome simply as "Babylon." Furthermore, the conveying of Paul to Rome as a prisoner could have been the clinching argument for Peter to go there to support him at his trial. We can also be sure that Paul would have had no difficulty in contacting Peter at any time by messenger or by letter; and it could even have been that he asked Peter to meet him there to discuss his momentous business. G. Edmundson (*The Church in Rome in the First Century,* 121) has also pointed out that the author of 1 Peter was well aware of Paul's letters to the Romans and Ephesians, as is shown by his many allusions to the text of both. Furthermore, the author of 2 Peter (even assuming it belongs to the period 90-100) was aware of an old tradition that Peter had studied Paul's letters and had found them difficult (cf. 2 Peter 3:15-16). 2 Peter is primarily directed to Gentile Christians, in fact to the same category of persons as the recipients of Paul's letters dealing with the Parousia (cf. 1 and 2 Thess and 1 Cor), and it reflects the interest shown by Peter in Paul's teaching. Consequently, there are many reasons for believing that their correspondence was reciprocal on the many issues facing the apostolic church, and that their common interest in the progress of the churches would urge them to keep in touch, and to meet when convenient and urgent to do so.

6. Roman Friends and Collaborators of Peter and Paul

Our knowledge of the persons residing at Rome and already known to Paul derives from the lists of persons he mentions in Romans 16:1ff., and from the names he mentions in the letters to the Ephesians, Philippians, Colossians, and Philemon, all written during his Roman captivity (60-62/63).

Whether these letters are pseudonymous or not does not concern us here, since the details of the names can be taken as authentic in any event.[9] In

---

[9]In recent years an increasing number of scholars and commentators on the epistles of the captivity, the Pastoral Epistles, and 2 Peter have declared them to be pseudepigraphical, and therefore of a later date than Paul by persons unknown but friendly to him, one of

addition to these thirty or so persons, men and women, to whom he sent affectionate greetings to Rome five years or more earlier,[10] Paul refers in Colossians and Philemon to Luke and to Mark with whom he is clearly in exceedingly close touch; in Philemon 24 they are linked together directly, and are both with Paul in Colossians 4:10, 14. The tradition has always identified this Luke with our evangelist; and thus we find two disciples called Mark and Luke, in Paul's intimate circle in Rome during his captivity there. Moreover Papias is on record (Eusebius, EH III.15) as asserting that the Mark referred to by Peter in 1 Peter 5:12-13 as "his son" is indeed the evangelist; he must surely be the same as the Mark of Colossians 4:10 and 14. Again the messenger who delivered Peter's first letter was no other than Sylvanus, who is correctly identified by modern exegetes as Silas, Paul's companion on his second missionary journey (Ac 15:31, 40; 2 Cor 1-19; 1 Pet 5:12). All these were members of a peripatetic team of younger men who worked, it seems, for both apostles (cf. also Ac 20:4-5). The fact that these younger men worked at one time for Peter and at another time for Paul, and vice versa, reveals a strong bond of cooperation between all of them, and a fortiori argues for a similar bond between Peter and Paul. Again, whatever the true status of the second letter of Peter, the letter's reference to Paul as "our beloved brother" (3:15) must surely faithfully reflect their lifelong personal collaboration.[11]

---

the chief reasons being the belief that they contain the theology of anything up to forty years later. This is, however, still a highly controversial issue; and even if it were to be solidly proved it would not invalidate our assertion that the catalogue of persons named in these letters accurately reflects the list of Paul's friends and fellow workers at the time of his Roman captivity. For if such details had not been accurate, there would have been many elderly churchmen alive and active even forty years later (such as Clement of Rome) who would have remembered and noticed discrepancies, and so voided the purpose of those who wished to pass them off as Paul's own work. Again, the attempt to prove that these "captivity" epistles were written from Caesarea has never won general acceptance; they are far too "Roman" in tone (cf. Reicke, ch. 2, n.2).

[10]Regarding the problem posed by the text of Rom 16:1ff., see Cranfield, *Romans,* 1:5-11, for a measured judgement of their authenticity.

[11]The view that Peter and Paul were rival "poles" of Christianity, and sometimes at loggerheads, goes back at least to F. C. Baur and the Tübingen School, and is based chiefly on Gal 2:11-14. The most recent, and best, treatment of this difficult passage is that of F. F. Bruce (*Galatians* [1982] 128-34). There is no need to minimize Paul's rebuke to Peter for a temporary failure to stand by his principles because of pressure from Judaizing elements. But this incident does not in any way negate the general statement of their full collaboration. Moreover, on the assumption (which I share with Professor Bruce) that Galatians was written and sent off before the Council of Jerusalem, it is clear that his rebuke of Peter took place before his second visit to Jerusalem, A.D. 46-47 (Ac 11:27; 12:24-25), and that by the time the Council met in A.D. 49 they were again in full harmony.

7. The Collaboration of Peter and Paul

How close did Peter and Paul come to each other during Paul's Roman captivity? We may answer this question as follows. First of all, if the entourage of Peter and Paul lived and worked for the church in the same city and knew each other, it is very hard to believe that the principals themselves were not in regular communication.

Secondly, Paul's Roman captivity seems to have lasted at least from 60-62/63,[12] and the first letter of Peter seems to have been sent from Rome before the persecution of Nero began in 64. There is therefore a considerable *prima-facie* likelihood that their periods of residence overlapped in the city at some time or other between these dates.

Thirdly, given the relative ease of communication within the Empire, the news of Paul's imprisonment and of his subsequent movements towards Rome would have been brought to Peter's notice wherever he happened to be; indeed, because of the delay of the shipwreck on Malta, Peter would have heard of Paul's appeal to Caesar at least a year before the latter's arrival in Rome. Moreover, Paul's own churches would have passed the news around at once and we know that at least the Philippians on two occasions sent financial help to him at Rome.

Finally, given the immense importance of Paul to the church as a whole, his fate was a matter of personal concern to all other church leaders and especially to the three "pillars," James (Gal 1:19; 2:9; Ac 15:13; 21:18), the leader of the church in Jerusalem, John, who was later to settle at Ephesus, and especially to Peter. It can be taken as certain that if Peter was there he would have visited Paul not only out of human friendship and compassion for Paul's suffering for the faith, but also in response to the Lord's injunction to "visit the imprisoned" (Mt 25:36), and would have sought to comfort and cheer in every possible way the most distinguished confessor of Christ yet to visit the capital.[13] Indeed, because of the role that Luke gives to them both in Acts, it may justly be inferred that in whatever distant part of the Empire Peter might have been when he heard that Paul was being

---

[12]However B. Reicke thinks that Paul was set free in Caesarea sometime in A.D. 62; cf. *The New Testament Era* (London, 1974) 220ff.

[13]Reicke suggests 63-65 as the years of Peter's residence in Rome (ibid., 223-24), but we must remember that all dates in this respect are conjectural. What is certain is that Peter must have labored in Rome for a sufficient number of years before his martyrdom to qualify as a founder of its church, while the conjunction of Paul with Peter as founder suggests that they had collaborated together in the evangelization of the city of Rome. See also, G. Edmundson (*The Church in Rome in the First Century*, 47), who reckons that Peter was in Rome 62-65, as well as at earlier dates, about 44 and 57.

taken to Rome to stand his trial there, he would have amended his travel schedule to be at his friend's side at the critical moment. Nor is it in the least surprising that no reference to their encounter at this juncture appears in New Testament annals. For instance, it is only because Paul felt it to be necessary to demonstrate his own independence of Peter and and the other Jerusalem apostles that he bothered to relate his own relevant personal movements and the nature of his contacts with them in Galatians 2. In this present case, we shall be arguing that the record of their renewed contact is to be seen "writ large" in the very existence of the Gospel of Mark.

8. The Original Format of the Gospels of Matthew and Luke

It would seem that the gospel book that Luke brought with him to Rome must have been in the normal format of that era, namely, the roll. B. M. Metzger tells us that "the Gospel of Luke and the Book of the Acts—the two longest books in the New Testament—would each have filled an ordinary papyrus roll of 31 or 32 feet in length; and that this is one of the reasons why Luke-Acts was issued in two volumes instead of one."[14]

Since Luke is just the full length of an ordinary commerical papyrus roll, and since the codex was not for a long time to be in commercial use, we may safely assume that Luke's original copy was on such a roll. Matthew, slightly shorter than Luke, must also originally have been in a roll format. But had it already been copied into a codex for use in the church's liturgy? In fact, not a single example of a Gospel in the form of a roll has survived from antiquity, and the earliest Gospel texts that have survived from the end of the second century are invariably in codex form; so it is just conceivable, though most unlikely, that the Gospel of Matthew, which had been in circulation for fifteen years or so, had already been transcribed into a codex for liturgical use.

The point of this inquiry is that anyone reading from the roll of Luke's Gospel needed to hold it in both hands in order to read it, unrolling it with the right hand and rolling it up again with the left hand. Thus the reader could not have used the roll of Matthew (that is, had it open in his hand) while actually reading from the roll of Luke. When he was reading from Luke, the roll of Matthew would have been lying beside him and open at the last place at which he had been reading from it. Again, when the reader was reading from Matthew's roll, Luke's roll would have been lying beside and open at the last place from which he had been reading. This point will be seen to be important when we come to consider why Mark passes from Matthew to Luke and back during the course of his narrative; for it

---

[14]Cf. B. M. Metzger, *The Text of the New Testament* (Oxford, ²1968) 5-6.

will greatly help us to understand Griesbach's claim that Mark "had Matthew and Luke before him when he wrote." We therefore assume this copy of Matthew still to be in roll format, and Luke too, of course.[15]

9. The Problem Posed by Luke's Gospel for the Non-Pauline Churches

The appearance of the Gospel of Luke—a counter-Gospel to that of Matthew, and a work specifically aimed at meeting the needs of the churches of Paul—raised a problem that concerned the Christian church everywhere. For while each apostle appears to have been recognized as supreme in his own mission territory, books have no boundaries; indeed they transcend all individual mission fields. Hence the arrival of this Gospel was a matter of concern to all the churches, Pauline and non-Pauline, wherever Greek was spoken; for it impinged on the teaching area of every apostle; and, in the present case, especially on the sphere of Peter, whose apostolic area certainly adjoined that of Paul in many places in Europe (cf. 1 Cor 1:11-12). Since all the Apostles were of equal authority as witnesses of Jesus' ministry and Resurrection they would all have a right to judge its worth for the spread of the faith. In other words, what sort of agreement ought the leaders of the Church, and especially Peter and Paul, to come to over this matter, and what sort of "censorship" should they impose by virtue of their unique knowledge of the teaching of Jesus? It is easy to see that if the new Gospel (compiled by one who had not been an eyewitness) were to relate facts or to teach doctrines different from those of the First Gospel, the truth of the message and the unity of the Church would be in danger.

Now we have already seen that there was a precedent for consultation, namely, the one mentioned by Paul in Galatians 2, when Paul, directed by the Spirit, met with Peter, James, and John (the three "pillars," as Paul calls them) to lay before them his teaching with respect to the practice of circumcision in relation to the law of Christ. This meeting ended with full agreement on doctrine and on defining their respective areas of evangelization, namely, that Paul should have responsibility for the Noncircumcision and the other three for the Circumcision. This was a sensible and practicable proposal; it worked for Paul, and we may presume that it worked out well for the other apostles. But when Paul arrived in Rome, with Luke and his Gospel in his company, it would seem that the Holy Spirit had ar-

---

[15]This discussion about the feasibility of handling two rolls at the same time has been used as an argument against the 2GH, for it has been said to require some sleight of hand. In the next chapter I hope to show not only that this is not required but also that the alternate use of the rolls of Matthew and Luke helps to explain the phenomenona of the order found in Mark.

ranged a conjunction of events and persons that would not merely consolidate the gains already made but that would once and for all fuse together the two separate areas and would finally eliminate the distinction between the Circumcision and the Noncircumcision that still dogged the thinking of many Jewish Christians. Paul has come to Rome as a prisoner, although he would have come in any case if he had been free, because of the Spirit's prompting. With him is Luke who will have finished his Luke-Acts during the two years of Paul's custody there. Peter and Mark have also come to Rome, one possible reason at least being in order to offer fraternal assistance to Paul in his forthcoming trial before Caesar (1 Pet 5:12-13). What Paul wants from Peter is "clearance" for the use of Luke's Gospel among the many groups of his converts living within Peter's area of evangelization, that is, within the Petrine churches. If he can secure this from Peter, he will then feel at ease in his own mind when he published Luke's Gospel in his own area of evangelization in Achaia and elsewhere. He knows moreover that if the Romans react favorably to Luke's Gospel it will get support everywhere owing to the presence of many of Paul's converts in what (in Paul's own estimation) was the most prestigious church in the world (cf. Rom 1:8).

But such clearance could not be given lightly because this new Gospel was not merely a piece of research in a style that conformed to the literary standards of the time, but also because it was potentially capable of disrupting the still delicate equilibrium between the active adherents of the circumcision party and the advocates of the freedom of the Gentiles. As an important leader, Peter would have to bear in mind on the one hand the susceptibilities of the church of Jerusalem and the circumcision party. And on the other hand, since Luke differed considerably in style, layout, and content from the original Gospel of Matthew, it would be necessary for him to evaluate its contents in considerable detail. There were various ways in which this might be done, either in writing or by word of mouth or by a combination of both. But in fact in those days there was no adequate substitute for a personal public declaration by a respected figure who was also a competent witness; this was generally regarded at the time as the recognized way of putting out the truth.[16] A mere written statement of the same truth would not have had the same impact and would in any case have done no more than confirm, for other and later times and generations, the truths of the original proclamation. The evidence we are gathering will lead us

---

[16]Cf. H. I. Marrou, "History of Education," *Encyclopaedia Britannica* (Macropaedia) 6:328a, on the importance of spoken declarations as instruments of policy.

to suggest that Peter (as the only one of the "pillars" on hand) took the practical decision to relate the Gospel of Luke to the Gospel of Matthew in a series of lectures in the Christian assembly in order to demonstrate the truth and accuracy of Luke's Gospel. That the Gospel of Mark is the transcript of these discourses, the character of which we must now examine,[17] is the thesis that will be developed in the next chapter.

---

[17]That these ideas are no mere flight of fancy, or the figment of pious imagination, is proved by the fact that quite independently Professor Martin Hengel has come to the conclusion that the Gospel of Mark was originally delivered in the Christian assembly probably in Rome in a series of five dramatic "acts" and that the authority of Peter lies behind Mark's Gospel; cf. "Probleme des Markusevangeliums," in *Das Evangelium und die Evangelien*, ed. P. Stuhlmacher (Tübingen, 1983) 233-34, 255. The "discourse structure" of Mark had also been previously noted by B. Standaert, *Évangile selon Marc, Composition et Genre littéraire* (Nijmegen, 1974).

4

The Composition of the Gospel of Mark

1. The Historical Facts and Their Critical Support

One of the most important things about the five ancient accounts of the composition of Mark (see pt. two, ch. 4, §4, table) is that although they all differ marginally in the amount of detail they provide, they in no way contradict one another but in actual fact give one another effective support. In the most ancient text to discuss expressly the order of composition of the four gospels (Eusebius, EH VI.14), Clement of Alexandria is quoted as stating that the Gospel of Mark came after the two gospels with genealogies, and that it resulted from διδασκαλίας, that is, public discourses or lectures given by Peter himself to a Roman audience, which, as Clement informs us in his *Comm. on 1 Pet* 5:12-13, contained a number of "Caesar's knights." Now we know from Philippians 1:13 that Paul's captivity for Christ was "known in the whole Praetorium," and from Philippians 4:22 that "the saints . . . in the household of Caesar" also sent their greetings through him to the Philippians. It is also a fact that one of the middle grades of officer in the Praetorium was the class of the *equites,* knights; and it seems that these were the persons named by Clement of Alexandria as part of Peter's audience.[1] Clement also added elsewhere (EH VI.14) that the large audience begged Mark to write down what Peter had said, and that Mark, after some persuasion, yielded to their request. Clement concluded his account by relating that when Peter got to hear of their success, he made no effort either to forbid or to promote its circulation. Furthermore Clement of Alexandria's account (EH VI.14) is also compatible with what Papias's Presbyter related about the function of Mark in the composition of the Gospel (EH III.39.14-16). For Mark is here and everywhere else described as the ἑρμηνευτής, the "recorder" or the "agent" of Peter, a term that signifies one who faithfully repeats the mes-

---

[1]See pt. 2, ch. 3, §5, for further detail. Of course, the Praetorium was distinct from Caesar's household.

sage imparted to him without altering it or warping it in any way.[2] Thus
Papias and Clement, and the other ancient witnesses, understood Mark's
function to have been simply that of reporting Peter's words with total accuracy. That is to say, the tradition is quite clear that Mark was not the
author of the Gospel but simply the agent of its publication, because all his
material came from Peter's memories of what Jesus had said and done, and
because what he did was to retrieve faithfully what Peter had spoken on
certain special occasions. And these data are compatible with Clement's
note that Peter exerted no pressure either to forbid or to promote the record,
by which he meant that the pressure to put down in writing and to publish
Peter's lectures only came from the audience *after* their delivery, and not
from any previous initiative on the part of Peter or Mark (cf. EH VI.14).
The external evidence seems therefore conclusive that neither Peter nor
Mark had any previous intention of writing a book or a gospel to compete
with the Gospels of Matthew and Luke. These are the basic historical facts
around which all the internal evidence will be found to fit exactly (see pt.
one, chs. 5-8).

The objective literary characteristics of Mark give indirect support to the
above conclusions. For the Gospel of Mark does not conform to the pattern
of contemporary "bios" literature in the way that Luke certainly does;[3]
for, as Papias's wrote (quoting the Presbyter), "Mark did not make a συνταξις" (Eusebius EH III.39.15). Mark lacks the normal proem of this
type of literature that first places the heroic figure onto the stage of the
world, in a birth narrative; and it also lacks the normal peroration, for at
its conclusion it stops short at Mark 16:8, exactly at the moment when one
would expect to learn the sequel to the hero's life and death, that is, to learn
of his exaltation, or vindication, or apotheosis, or resurrection.[4] The lit-

---

[2]See pt. 2, ch. 4, §7(c). The term ἑρμηνευτής is usually rendered as "interpreter,"
which is correct, provided it is understood as doing no more than "record" without gloss;
that is why it has been rendered here simply as "recorder." Jerome uses it as the equivalent
of "amanuensis" (*Ep.* 120). As regards the "limited purpose" of Mark, see pt. 1, ch. 6,
§§1, 8. For the Petrine background of Mark, see pt. 1, ch. 6, §6.

[3]Cf. P. L. Shuler, *A Genre for the Gospels* (Philadelphia: Fortress, 1982) 2-57. On the
other hand, Norman Perrin could write: "The Gospel of Mark is the prototype which the
other (synoptics) follow," in *What is Redaction Criticism?* (S.P.C.K., 1970) 75.

[4]See pt. 1, ch. 6, §7 for Riley's explanation of the last twelve verses of Mark, in which
he acknowledges his indebtedness to the careful researches of W. R. Farmer (*The Last Twelve
Verses of Mark* [CUP, 1974]), who has shown that the authentic manuscript tradition is
almost evenly divided between those manuscripts that have them and those that do not, and
who has tentatively suggested an explanation of their presence that would make them non-
Markan. However, we prefer, with Riley, to recognize them as the work of Mark himself,

erary plan of Mark, if one can call it one, is its continuous paratactical narrative of events; and insofar as the author has a real plan peculiar to himself it would seem to be his alternate following of Matthew and Luke when he is not in agreement with the order of both. (But see §4 below for Mark's themes.)

Why then does Mark not follow the current literary conventions regarding historial and biographical writing, although the vindication of Jesus is the sole theme of the Gospel? There must be a solid reason somewhere. It could not have been for nothing that Mark followed first the one Gospel and then the other, and then both together, and then omitted matter from one or the other, or from both, for example, the Great Sermon.[5] One good reason could be that the author, or narrator, behind Mark, was not aiming at replacing or even really adding to the other two Gospels to any significant extent. On the contrary, the fact that over ninety per cent of Mark comes from Matthew and/or Luke could imply that his objective must have been in some sense to compare the two Gospels with each other.

The following characteristics of Mark suggest that this was indeed the author's intention:

(1) He ignores the nativity and the resurrection narratives, which he could not have done if he had been writing a book for his contemporaries.[6]

(2) It is striking that Mark begins at the point where Luke first becomes parallel with Matthew, namely, at Luke 3:1, and ends at the point where Luke is again about to diverge from Matthew at Luke 24:12 (= Mark 16:8).

(3) He omits Luke's Central Section (9:52-18:14) entirely. He has no real parallels with this section; for though he is aware of its existence,[7] his only parallels are with Matthew in passages where Matthew and Luke are parallel outside the Central Section (Mark/Q overlap). He has sensed that the Central Section is a special literary creation of Luke.

---

which he added in the light of his knowledge of Matthew and Luke when he formally published his Gospel after Peter's death. This seems to be the best way of reconciling all the data in view of the fact that these verses are almost entirely a conflation of the resurrection stories of Matthew and Luke. Thus the Gospel of Mark would have come into circulation in two stages, the first being in Peter's lifetime when his lectures were circulated informally without the twelve-verse ending; and the second when Mark decided after Peter's death to publish it himself with the ending that he constructed to mitigate the abrupt conclusion at verse 8.

[5]See Riley, above, pt. 1, ch. 2, §7.

[6]Cf. Shuler, *A Genre for the Gospels*, 54-56.

[7]The narrator of Mark shows this by his omissions, e.g., the precise way in which he omits the great sermon and also Luke's Central Section, cf. J. B. Orchard, MLM, passim.

(4) Mark accepts all Luke's changes of Matthew's order of pericopes between Matthew 4:23-14:1, save for two minor exceptions, which are
also clarifications (cf. OSFGG §§38, 99, 55, 58).

(5) He restores certain pericopes to Matthew's order after Luke has moved
them to his Central Section, for example, the Lawyer's Question
(OSFGG §209).

(6) He follows Luke in abbreviating Matthew's long discourses, but unlike
Luke he does not put the material elsewhere (for he has no central sec-
tion), apart from one or two sayings, for example, Mark 11:25-26 (cf.
OSFGG §92, 183, 314, 307-313).

(7) He takes pains to smoothe out seeming contradictions between Matthew and Luke (cf. the Entrance into Jericho, OSFGG §282; the Entrance into Jerusalem, §290-295).

(8) He makes some rather simple attempts to conflate Matthew with Luke
(cf. Mark 2:21; 6:14, OSFGG §§53, 158).

Since both critical and historical evidence support Mark being third in
order of composition, the only satisfactory explanation of these peculiar
literary maneuvers is to see that Mark is purposefully and precisely linking
up together his predecessors, Matthew and Luke. And in order to make
good sense of this procedure it has to be seen as done for the purpose of
making some judgment and proclamation regarding their relationship.

2. The Preparation of Peter's Lectures

a. The "Zigzag" Phenomenon in the Gospel of Mark

The way in which Peter decided to act was in conformity with the currently popular practice in Rome, namely, to give a course of public lectures.[8] We must assume that the lectures were to be given in the atrium of
some large private house and quite possibly during the weekly Christian
assembly. His plan was to take the roll of Luke and compare it with the
roll of Matthew in the light of his own eyewitness recollections of the ministry of Jesus, beginning with John, whose disciple he had been, and ending with the discovery of the empty tomb. His personal memories of this
ministry were indelibly engraved on his mind, and in one sense he had no
need of any book as a memory-aid, especially as he himself was probably
one of the principal influences upon the composition of the Gospel of Matthew nearly twenty years before.[9] Nevertheless, for the task he had set for

---

[8]See H. I. Marrou, "History of Education," *Encyclopaedia Britannica* (Macropaedia),
6:328a.

[9]This is a possible conclusion to be drawn from the fact that Mark on the whole prefers
the wording of Matthew to that of Luke in the triple-tradition passages.

himself he needed the two rolls, and the aid of his spiritual son and secretary Mark, to prepare for the occasion. Among the duties of Mark would
have been that of making sure that Peter's eye fell on the points at which
he was to change over from one roll to the other.[10] Our Gospel of Mark is
the result of their combined effort, Peter's disciple Mark being at his side
as he delivered the lectures, and also being the person responsible for seeing
that a true record should be kept of what Peter had said. We can also correctly infer that whereas when Peter had the roll of Luke in his hands he
naturally tended to follow the order of Luke; when he put down Luke and
took up the roll of Matthew he naturally tended to follow the order of Matthew. At this point we may remind ourselves of a discovery of Riley's that
shows us that we are on the right track (see pt. one, ch. 2, §6 above).

It is this: that as the speaker or narrator of Mark makes his way down
through the story of the public ministry of Jesus he steadily unrolls each
Gospel in turn; and though he frequently switches from the one to the other
he never winds either roll backwards. That is to say, that despite the different order of pericopes in Matthew and Luke he never goes back to some
passage that he has previously passed over in either roll, but always goes
steadily forward alternately through each. That is why, for instance, Mark
does not retell the Centurion's Slave pericope (Mt 8:5-13) for Peter has
moved on to Luke 6:20, which corresponds to Matthew 12:15, though the
roll of Matthew was still open at 4:25. For Peter noted that Matthew 12:15-
21 was curiously reminiscent of Matthew 4:25; so instead of continuing
with Luke 6:20, he passes over all of Luke 6:20–8:3 and continues with
Matthew 12:22ff. until he reaches Matthew 13:1 (= Lk 8:4).[11]

b. The Detail of the Construction of the Gospel of Mark

What then would the preparation of these lectures have involved? For
us this question means: how would Peter, the speaker or narrator behind
the text of Mark, have set about constructing the lectures his disciple Mark
would later reproduce in written form?[12] We must all the time remember
that Peter, that is, the speaker, knew the Gospel of Matthew practically by
heart for the reasons we have noted above. And as soon as he first read the

---

[10]See J. J. Griesbach, *Synoptic and Text-critical Studies 1776-1976* (CUP, 1979) 113.

[11]But of course when Luke was constructing his own Gospel with the aid of the roll of
Matthew (before Mark was thought of), he did indeed go backwards and forwards in Matthew as often as he desired, e.g., after following Matthew down to 12:33 he goes back to
Mt 8:23-27. But Mark always followed Luke in the Triple Tradition passages, with two
small exceptions already noted.

[12]Except, of course, for Mk 16:9-20.

roll of Luke he must have recognized the extent of its dependence on the Gospel of Matthew, and therefore framed his lectures accordingly. Thus the analysis of Mark in relation to Luke-with-Matthew will show us the steps the speaker took to organize his material. As we shall see, he did not accomplish his task in one lecture but took no less than five, each of which would have lasted from twenty-five to forty minutes (Mk 1:2–3:21; 3:22–6:13; 6:14–10:1; 10:2–13:37; 14:1–16:8).

The easiest way to understand the process of construction is to follow his working according to the chart to be found in the first volume of this trilogy.[13] In this chart Luke is in the middle column and the connecting lines show where Luke has changed the order of Matthew and how Mark has usually followed his changes. From the start the speaker determined to confine himself to those pericopes where Matthew and Luke have for the most part common material and are generally in parallel,[14] that is, between Matthew 3:1 (= Lk 3:1) and Matthew 28:10 (= Lk 24:12). Thus Mark omitted the birth and resurrection narratives, the whole of Luke's Central Section, and both the great sermons; but he also adopted Luke's summary version of (a) Matthew's Missionary Discourse (Lk 9:3-5 = Mk 6:8-11), (b) Matthew's discourse on community (Lk 9:46-48 = Mk 9:33-37), (c) Matthew's parable discourse, with some Markan additions (Lk 8:4-18 = Mk 4:1-34), (d) Matthew's main eschatological discourse (Lk 21:1-36 = Mk 13:1-37) (see OSFGG §§124, 183, 100-107, 307-13, 320). On the whole, Peter included only personal memories in the form of χρεῖαι and ἀπομνημονεύματα, all stories at the telling of which he was present; but he also omitted Lukan glosses and Lukan reconstructions (cf. MLM, 114). However, he decided to include not only the events that Luke had taken from Matthew but also certain events that he thought Luke should not have omitted from Matthew (e.g., Mt 14:23-15:39); he also added two or three minor stories of his own which are not recorded by the others (e.g., Mk 7:31-37). Mark also sometimes restores Matthean stories that Luke regarded as duplicates, when the latter inserts a similar story in his Central Section (e.g., the Fig-Tree Parable, Mk 11:20-27 = Mt 21:19-22 = Lk 13:1-6; cf. OSFGG §§237, 295). He also felt free to add little asides from time to time (e.g., Mk 7:19). It would therefore be necessary for him to go through the roll of Matthew as well as the roll of Luke in advance, in order

[13]See J. B. Orchard, MLM; the substance of this chart is to be found in the "List of Pericopes with Gospel Parallels" in the same author's *Synopsis of the Four Gospels in Greek* (Edinburgh: T. & T. Clark/Macon GA: Mercer University Press, 1983).

[14]Note that Luke's Central Section is excluded from this comparison. From now onwards our explanation is best followed in Orchard's *Synopsis*.

to mark up carefully not only what he was going to include but also what he was going to omit, and also the exact point where he was going to switch from one roll or the other. This was a straightforward editorial process.

3. The Delivery of Peter's Lectures

The following is a tentative reconstruction of the way in which Mark was composed. In the situation in which Peter was going to give his talks, he would have been assisted by some secretaries and other members of his entourage. And since a roll needs to be held in both hands at once, the right hand unrolling, and the left hand rolling up again, the speaker would need to have at least one secretary at hand to pass him the roll in the first place and then to take it back and hand him the other whenever he decided to switch. The audience would of course have observed Mark handing the rolls to Peter and receiving them back from him, and so could naturally have asked him later on for the spoken text. Meanwhile, assuming that there were shorthand writers present, probably two in number, they would have been seated near at hand taking down the lecture.[15]

The theme of the *first lecture* was the proclamation of Jesus' message in Galilee. The speaker began at Luke 3:1 (= Mt 3:1) and after a little confusion and unsureness (Mk 1:2-13) followed carefully to Luke 6:20 omitting, however, Luke 3:7-9 (= Mt 3:7-10) also omitting Lk 3:10-14, 19-20 (a Lukan editorial addition to Matthew), also 3:23-38 and 4:15-30, the Nazareth visit, as he prefers Matthew's version, but adding his 1:16-20, parallel to Matthew 4:18-22 (which Luke omitted in favor of his 5:1-11, which Mark omits). The speaker then followed the order of Luke faithfully down to Luke 6:20, paralleling on the way Matthew 4:23-25, though he preferred Matthew's order of units in the latter verses, namely, at Mark 3:7-19. We note that the speaker felt free marginally to harmonize Luke with Matthew, to omit Lukan glosses and to prefer Matthew's wording to Luke's at certain points. He reveals himself as fully conversant with both Gospels. He has now arrived at Luke 6:20 (= Mk 3:19). At this decisive moment in the Galilean ministry, he decided to pause, perhaps ending with Mark 3:19 or 3:20-21, thus sounding the keynote for the second lecture, the theme of which was the opposition to Jesus. This was a convenient place to stop, since Luke had already gone ahead with his incorporation of Matthean material down to Matthew 12:15-21, a passage reminiscent of Matthew 4:25, at which point the roll of Matthew was still open.

---

[15]A sculpture, depicting this sort of situation, dating probably from 2nd cent., and found on a funeral sarcophagus at Ostia, is reproduced in E. G. Turner, *Greek Papyri* (Oxford: Clarendon, 1980) plate VI.

For the *second lecture* —the development of the opposition to Jesus—
the rolls have been turned forward, bypassing both the great sermons and
all of Luke 6:20–8:3. Thus the speaker now turns to Matthew, taking into
account that Luke had already reached Matthew 12:15-21, and opens with
3:22-30 which now parallels Matthew 12:22-30, and continued with 3:31-
35, which parallels Matthew 12:46-50, thus following Matthew until he
reached the Parables at Matthew 13:1, which enabled him to return to Luke
8:4-18 = Mark 4:1-25.[16] At this point Peter added his own unique Parable
of the Seed Growing Secretly, and then went back to the order of Matthew
for the Mustard Seed and Jesus' Use of Parables (Mk 3:30-34 = Mt 12:31-
33). From this point onwards, the speaker followed Luke down to Luke
9:6 (= Mk 6:12-13). We note again that he continued to go forward in
each roll, and never back, despite the variations in the order of Matthew
and Luke. The lecture ended at a natural break, when the rolls of Matthew
and Luke are about to become parallel again (after Mk 6:13).

The theme of the *third lecture* is that of preparing the Twelve for the
passion of Jesus; it opens with the story of Herod's sinister interest in Jesus
(Lk 9:7-9 = Mt 14:1-2 = Mk 6:14-16), which fills in the gap between the
Sending Out of the Twelve at Luke 9:6 and their return at Luke 9:10, though
Luke omitted Matthew's account of the martyrdom of the Baptist (but
compare Lk 3:19-20). However, Peter thought this ought to have figured
in Luke's account (seeing that it is in Matthew) and he decided to restore
it at Mark 6:17-29, at the same time considerably amplifying the details of
Matthew 14:3-11. The speaker retold the Feeding of the Five Thousand,
following Luke and Matthew, but when he came to Luke's Great Omission
he decided to restore it fully to his own narrative, Mark 6:45–8:21 (= Mt
14:22–16:12). (Luke had in fact tucked away a few verses of it, namely
Mt 16:1-4, 5-12, into his Central Section at Lk 12:4-16, and 12:1.) Peter,
however, could not at this point resist an impulse to introduce a healing
story of his own, namely, Mark 8:22-26. He then followed Luke and Matthew together down to the Discourse on Community, Matthew 18:1-5 (=Lk
9:45-48 = Mk 9:33-37), except that where Luke has omitted Jesus' rebuke of Peter, he has restored it—though he did not restore Matthew's
Temple Tax anecdote (17:24-27) which Luke has omitted, because it too
did not concern his Roman audience. Peter also decided to retain Luke's
Widow's Mite unit, as being of interest to his Gentile audience. At this
point Mark inserts a saying of Jesus about Salt, which made a suitable conclusion to his summary of Matthew's Discourse on Community and con-

---

[16]We may note that on the way Mark takes over and enlarges Luke's summary of various
Matthean Sayings, i.e., Lk 4:16-18 = Mk 4:21-25.

cludes this section with his departure from Galilee, Luke 9:51 = Matthew 19:1-2 = Mark 10:1.

The *fourth lecture* details the various confrontations of Jesus with his enemies on the way to Jerusalem and in the Holy City itself. So Peter (Mark), having decided to omit the whole of Luke's Central Section, began by restoring Matthew's Teaching about Divorce pericope (19:3-12), omitted by Luke seemingly because it was an example of rabbinic exegesis unfamiliar to the Greeks (but cf. Lk 16:18). But when Luke rejoined Matthew at Luke 18:15ff., Peter (Mark) went steadily through Luke's roll. As Matthew lacks it, so Peter too omits Luke 19:1-10, 11-28 (Jesus and Zacchaeus, and the Parable of the Mnas). He also omitted Jesus weeping over Jerusalem (Lk 19:41-44) and rearranged the order of Matthew 21:12-22 = Mark 11:12-26. He omitted Matthew's Parable of the Marriage Feast, perhaps because Luke has a similar story in his Central Section at Luke 14:15-24. He also restored Matthew 22:34-40 with his own special version of the Lawyers's Question, 12:28-34, which Luke had transferred to his Central Section to provide an introduction to his Good Samaritan Parable. Further on, at Luke 20:45-47, Peter (Mark) took over the substance of Luke's abbreviated and truncated version of Matthew 23:1-36 (Condemnation of the Scribes and Pharisees) at Mark 12:38-40, with the difference that he omitted all the sayings that Luke had transferred to his Central Section (11:38-52).

Peter (Mark) has now moved on to the Eschatological Discourse (Mk 13:1-37 = Lk 21:5-33 = Mt 24:1–25:46). He followed Luke through this discourse, but brought back Matthew 24:23-28, which Luke had transferred to his Central Section, at Luke 17:23-24. Ignoring the rest of Matthew's Discourse, he complemented Luke's partial summary of Matthew with his Mark 13:33-37. Though Luke adds two verses of explanation of Jesus' movements, our speaker ended his lecture with the above short summary.

The *fifth lecture* was exclusively devoted to the passion narrative and closely followed both Luke and Matthew. The Markan narrator (Peter) restored the Anointing in Bethany, omitted by Luke, whose anointing story is at Luke 7:36-50. He preferred Matthew's arrangement of several pericopes where Luke has changed his order, but the detail need not detain us here. The significant thing is that Peter ended his account at Mark 16:8 at the exact point where Matthew and Luke are about to commence their respective and entirely different accounts of the resurrection appearances of Jesus. This sudden ending, when related to Matthew and Luke, cannot be fortuitous, but is surely calculated even in its abruptness. The speaker stopped where his own personal eyewitness of the events of Jesus' earthly life ended, which was also the point at which the other two evangelists had decided to introduce their independent resurrection stories. Peter's witness to the life of Jesus in his mortal flesh was now complete. This was all that Paul needed; he did not need to ask for Peter's witness to the Risen Christ (cf. 1 Cor 15:5), as the Lord had also blessed him with similar and perhaps even greater visions (cf. 1 Cor 15). Peter had now completed in a concise, restrained, and workmanlike manner the task that Paul and Luke had invited him to undertake, by witnessing to the substantial harmony and accuracy of Luke with Matthew over the total period of his own personal earthly contact with Jesus.

One last point: the abrupt ending of Mark at 16:8 is a telling sign that the narrative of Mark did not originate as a book; it came into existence in a more dynamic and practical way (see §5, below).

4. The Audience for Peter's Lectures

We have seen above (pt. 2, ch. 3, §5) that Clement of Alexandria in his commentary on 1 Pet 5:12-13 noted that Peter's lectures were given *coram quibusdam Caesareanis equitibus,* ''in the presence of some of Caesar's knights.'' We have seen that this must refer to a class of officer in the Praetorium known as the *equites,* ''knights''; and we are therefore entitled to link them with Paul's reference to his captivity for Christ's sake being ''known in the whole Praetorium [πραιτώριον] and to all the others'' (Phil 1:13).[17] Although the knights were not the highest category of officer, they were men in mid-career, and obviously Paul had made converts among them. The fact that these knights were drawn to attend Peter's lectures is a proof of the importance of the occasion, for they were the elite of the imperial army. Their presence is also another link between Peter and Paul.

Another and lower category of imperial servant may also have attended these lectures. In the same letter Paul sends the greetings of a number of members of Caesar's household, of ''all the saints of . . . Caesar's house'' (Phil 4:22).[18]

We should therefore have a right to expect that many friends and converts of Paul would be among Peter's audience. For this reason it would have been natural for them to have been given advance notice of Peter's intention to speak and for suitable arrangements to be made for such a dis-

---

[17]BAG (at πραιτώριον) admits that if Philippians was written from Rome (as seems reasonably certain), it must refer to the Praetorian guard.

[18]According to the contemporary usage these persons were not members of the Emperor's family or relationship, but servants at his court. In early imperial times they were ordinarily slaves or freedmen, cf. BAG at Καῖσαρ.

tinguished audience. And last but not least, since we know that Mark was able to retrieve the actual text without difficulty, this would argue that there must have been shorthand writers present to record them. This need not surprise us since the shorthand recording of public statements of senators and prominent officials was a commonplace of first-century Rome; indeed, it had been a recognized practice ever since the time of Cicero a hundred years earlier.[19] So it does not require any stretch of imagination to see that the provision of shorthand writers for such an occasion as this would have been taken care of by Peter's assistants. At any rate, Clement of Alexandria (EH VI.14) makes it clear that Mark was able to come by a verbatim report of what Peter had said (a tradition confirmed by Papias, Eusebius, EH III.39.15-16), since Mark was able to supply the text on request. Furthermore, the Gospel of Mark is in no way the smooth product of a skilled author seated at his desk, but has all the vividness, the inconsistencies, and the peculiar turns of speech, that one finds in actual transcripts of live speeches, for example, sudden breaks, asides, anacolutha, and so forth.[20] It was surely such peculiarities of direct, and unedited, speech that aroused the early criticisms of Mark's Gospel which the presbyter of Papias was at pains to excuse (cf. my comments on EH III.39.15-16 in pt. 2, ch. 4, §7c, above).

With Paul still living in his own hired lodgings under house arrest, probably with a praetorian soldier to guard him,[21] awaiting the result of his appeal to Caesar, and with Peter taking all this trouble to support the gospel written by Luke for the furtherance of the mission to which Paul had been called, there is no need for surprise that Peter's lectures aroused great en-

---

[19]Cf. H. I. Marrou, *A History of Education in Antiquity* (London, 1936) 312: "Some kind of shorthand was already in existence, going back perhaps to the 4th century B.C., but it did not really appear in all its fullness until Cicero's time. . . . Under the Empire two closely related systems of shorthand were being used together, one in Greek, the other in Latin." Of course, one has no right to expect that the external evidence would bother to mention the presence of the shorthand writers; for they were, like secretaries, part of normal everyday life for public figures in Rome and elsewhere; and Peter and Paul were, for the Christians, just such figures. Paul certainly dictated his letters and judging by their impetuosity his secretaries had need of shorthand skills! Whenever occasion demanded their presence could be taken for granted. On the further matter of note taking as the preliminary to formal composition, see esp. George Kennedy, "Classics and the Gospels," in *The Relationships among the Gospels,* ed. William O. Walker, Jr. (San Antonio TX: Trinity University Press, 1978) 125-92.

[20]For anacolutha, see e.g. Mk 2:21—τὸ καινὸν τοῦ παλαιοῦ ; Mk 6:16—ὃν ἐγὼ ἀπεκεφάλισα Ἰωάννην. For asides, cf. Mk 7:19—καθαρίζων πάντα τὰ βρώματα; Mk 11:14—καὶ ἤκουον οἱ μαθηταὶ αὐτοῦ.

[21]It would seem likely that Paul's guards were praetorian soldiers, cf. Bruce, *Acts,* 476.

thusiasm, and prompted some of his audience to demand copies of them without delay.[22] Paul and his assistants could now boast that "the salvation given to the Gentiles" (Ac 28:28) had got its own special document to proclaim it—a document partly independent of, partly parallel to, and partly dependent upon, the Gospel of Matthew, the gospel of the original church of Jerusalem.[23]

And Mark's edition of Peter's words was now the tangible record of that achievement. No wonder that church tradition was to insert the Gospel of Mark between the Gospels of Matthew and Luke as a reminder that it was the work of Mark recording the oral recommendation of Peter that had made it possible for Luke's Gospel to be accepted on equal terms with Matthew's in the Christian world without danger of further controversy (cf. 2 Pet 1:1).

5. The Publication of the Gospel of Mark

The subsequent history of Mark's Gospel is soon told. Peter took no particular interest in its recovery, for it was perhaps for him little more than a device of his secretary Mark, in response to popular request, to satisfy his hearers. As long as Peter was alive, it seems to have circulated privately; but after his martyrdom, Mark himself seems to have published it, doubtless as an act of *pietas* to the memory of his old master.[24] In doing so, it seems that he added the last twelve verses to make a more fitting and rounded conclusion to Peter's witness to the life and death of Jesus.[25] According to an old tradition Mark took it with him when he went to Alexandria.[26] At least until the end of the second century it remained very much in the shadow of the Gospel of Matthew.[27] But by the time of Augustine of Hippo it had come to be viewed by him at least as the document that unified the Matthean conception of Jesus the Messiah King with the Lukan and Pauline one of Jesus as the High Priest and Savior of the world, though the significance of the peculiar circumstances of its origin appear to have been entirely forgotten in the intervening centuries.[28]

---

[22]See Eusebius, EH VI.14, and comment above, pt. 2, ch. 4, §4.

[23]See J. Dupont, "La Conclusion des Actes et son rapport à l'ensemble de l'ouvrage de Luc," in *Les Actes des Apôtres: Traditions, rédaction, théologie,* ed. J. Kremer (Leuven, 1979).

[24]See the anti-Marcionite prologue to Mark above, pt. 2, ch. 2, §10c.

[25]See n. 4 above.

[26]See Eusebius, EH II.16.

[27]Cf. E. Massaux, *Influence de l'Évangile de Saint Matthieu sur la litterature chrétienne avant S. Irénée* (Louvain, 1950) 647-54.

[28]Cf. Augustine, *De Consensu Evangelistarum,* IV.10.

Recapitulation and Conclusion

The aim of part three has been to show that, on the basis of the Two-Gospel Hypothesis, it is possible to discover a credible *Sitz im Leben* for the Gospel of Matthew as soon as we anchor it in the period 30-44. But if the Gospel is dated post-70, then the problem of its relationships to the other Gospels becomes insoluble. For by putting Matthew into a post-70 historical context, various anomalies arise which defy satisfactory solution. On the other hand, by accepting the priority of Matthew and by putting all three Synoptics well before 70, we escape the great stumbling block of the old "Griesbach Hypothesis," which was to find adequate reasons for Mark being third and for Mark's "zigzag" phenomenon; and we now have clear and cogent reasons for everything. Above all, the particular version of the 2GH that has just been expounded has enabled us to see that the Synoptics are in fact real-life responses to real-life situations and that they are in no way the product of a scholar's "internal-critical laboratory" out of touch with the real world. The Synoptic Gospels can in this context be seen to be the reactions of the church's leaders to the successive phases through which the pre-70 church is known to have passed—crises which can actually be pinpointed.

The first crisis was the need for the church of Jerusalem, the church of the twelve apostles, to assert its separate identity over against the Jewish synagogue; and the Gospel of Matthew is in fact the document justifying the existence of the Christian community as a body founded by Jesus Christ and distinguished from Judaism by its confession of Him as the Messiah and the Son of God. This was the document that piloted the church through the first years of its life until the moment was ripe for the Gospel of Luke.

The next crisis was the one that originated over the clash between the Circumcision party and Paul; it was a painful struggle for the recognition of "the freedom of the Gentiles" from the legal prescriptions of the Mosaic Law. However, as early as 45/46, before he began his first missionary journey, Paul had been instructed by a revelation to lay his Gospel before Peter and the other "pillars" in Jerusalem (Gal 2:2); he did so, and thereby secured their full support for his future mission. This understanding stood him in good stead when the controversy reached its height at the Council of Jerusalem in 49; and, as we know, the Council came down on the side of Paul. Nevertheless, the question, though settled in principle, still simmered in the church and continued to simmer even as late as Paul's Roman captivity (cf. Rom 15:21; Phil 3:2ff.). After some ten years of the most intense evangelistic effort, Paul believed that the position of the Gentiles in the church had grown to such proportions that a further demarche was necessary. Some time before the completion of Paul's third missionary journey, Luke tells us (Ac 19:21) that Paul had already "resolved in the Spirit" to visit Rome after once more going up to Jerusalem. For it would seem that a great project had begun to shape itself in his mind (see above, pt. 3, ch. 3, §3), and he took two preliminary steps towards its fulfilment: he wrote his Letter to the Romans, probably from Corinth, to prepare them for his visit; and he brought Luke along with him from Macedonia not just to be his personal physician, but primarily to research and to write a re-statement of the Gospel of Matthew in terms appreciable by the Greeks (Ac 20:4-5). Paul's ultimate aim was to secure universal approval for Luke-Acts as a symbol of the Gentiles' acquisition of full equality of citizenship in the church (Eph 2:19-22; Rom 15:15-16; 2 Pet 1:1). Those ten years of trial and test had convinced Paul that his policy was the right one and he now wanted universal recognition for his views, in order finally to vanquish the Judaizing party. He must have been greatly disappointed at the cautious and qualified reception that he met with from James and the elders of the Jerusalem church (cf. Ac 21:17-26), and he must then have realized that the original mother church was no longer capable of taking the lead and was in fact no longer the center of progress. If the Jerusalemites would not help, perhaps the Romans would be more accommodating; and it was God's providence and not Paul's own timing that eventually brought him there some five years or so after his letter to the Christians of the capital city.

In this way it happened that Paul's achievement on behalf of the Gentiles received its full recognition when the Roman Christian assembly, who had listened to Peter's lectures comparing and relating the Gospel of Luke with the Gospel of Matthew, proceeded to give enthusiastic welcome to the version of those lectures prepared by Peter's disciple Mark. For they were seen to be the authentic reminiscences of Peter subsequently safely gathered into book form by Mark himself, who then gave them to those who asked for them (cf. EH VI.14.6-7). The final vindication of Paul's lifework thus took place at Rome after he had been all but totally rejected at Jerusalem. But the special reason why Mark's Gospel came into existence (that is, through Peter's support of the work of his brother Paul and his zeal for the unity of the church) was soon forgotten in the general satisfaction given by the Gospel of Luke to the Gentile churches. The event of the creation of Mark thus passed off without any more fuss and without being further recorded in the annals of the time beyond the fact that the

Roman church at a very early date inserted Mark between Matthew and Luke as a mute but significant demonstration of the part played by these lectures in preserving the unity of the gospel message and in paving the way for the publication of Luke's Gospel.

The Synoptic Gospels are the symbols of the successful and final resolution of the great Circumcision question by the joint action of Peter and Paul, with the aid of Mark and Luke. Alternatively, one may say that they represent the thesis, antithesis, and the synthesis of that same question. And here lies the true reason why there are just *three* Synoptic Gospels!

Epilogue

The joint authors of this volume did not become acquainted with each other until after they had independently arrived at the same main conclusion, that is to say, at the Two-Gospel Hypothesis. It is true that there are minor discrepancies embedded in their respective conclusions, chiefly because the internal evidence by its very nature can never be as specific as the external; but such discrepancies do not weaken their case. On the contrary, they may be regarded as a sign of the independence and integrity of their respective presentations. Nevertheless, the convergence of the results of the respective disciplines employed is so striking that they regard it as imperative for all students of the Gospels to rethink the entire system of synoptic relationships in the light of their researches. Their master idea should be especially pleasing to all systematic theologians because of its simplicity, namely, that the struggle of the Christian church to burst out of its Jewish mold and to root itself in the alien Greco-Roman culture is symbolized in the twin Gospels of Matthew and Luke, with Mark as the link between them. The minds of Peter and Paul meet and agree through the media provided by their disciples Mark and Luke, while the Gospel of John will later rest firmly on the framework provided by all three. And this master idea is seen to coordinate, to illuminate, and to satisfy all the data—historical, theological, literary, and social—and to resolve adequately all the problems immanent in the historical and the critical evidence.

A nation's history is necessarily writ large in its literature. It is the same with the Christian church, the people of God. The church's history too is recorded clearly step-by-step in its literature, and the observant eye can perceive it to be the product of its historical development and of the various crises through which it has passed. Just as Justin's *Dialogue* and Irenaeus's *Treatise against the Heresies* are to be seen as the church's reaction in the second century to the threat posed by the Gnostics and the Marcionites, so in the middle of the first century the Gospels of Matthew, Luke, and Mark are to be seen as the church's successive reactions to the Circumcision question.

The Gospel of Matthew is the product of the earliest determination of the primitive church to preserve the teaching of its Founder and to justify its separation from the Old Israel. On the other hand, the Gospel of Luke is to be seen as the product of the crisis caused by the emergence of the

Gentile churches alongside, and indeed out of, the Primitive Jewish church; and they were churches that needed to develop their own interpretation of the mission as a sign and a proof of their full and equal status. And the vital need to fuse together these two cultural traditions, and the Gospels that symbolized them, into an unbreakable unity, led to the Gospel of Mark as the bridge between them, and as the enabling document for Luke's Gospel to take its place as the second authentic witness to Jesus in the churches of Peter and Paul.

Bibliography

Aland, K. *Synopsis Quattuor Evangeliorum*. Stuttgart: Deutsche Bibelstiftung, [1]1963, [10]1978.

Aland, K., et al. *The Greek New Testament*. Stuttgart: UBS, [3]1975.

Albright, W. F., and C. S. Mann. *Matthew*. Anchor Bible 26. New York: Doubleday & Company, 1971.

Allen, W. C. *The Gospel according to St. Matthew*. ICC. 1907.

Augustine, Sancti Aurelii Augustini. *De Consensu Evangelistarum*. Ed. Weinrich. Libri Quattuor. CSEL. 1904.

Bacon, B. W. "The Anti-Marcionite Prologue to John." JBL (1930): 43-54.

Bardy, B. G. "Cérinthe." *Rev. Bib.* (1921): 343-73.

_____ , ed. *Eusèbe de Césarée, Histoire Ecclésiastique*. Sources chrétiennes. Four volumes. Paris, 1952-1960. 19bis, 41, 55, 73.

_____ . "Muratori." DBS. 1399-1408.

Bareille, G. "Cérinthe." DTC. 2151-55.

Barnes, Timothy D. *Constantine and Eusebius*. Cambridge MA: Harvard University Press, 1981.

Barrett, C. K. *Luke the Historian*. London: Epworth, 1961.

Baus, Karl. *From the Apostolic Community to Constantine*. Volume 1 of *History of the Church*. Ed. H. Jedin. London, 1980.

Beare, F. W. Review of W. R. Farmer's *The Synoptic Problem*. JBL 84 (1965): 295-97.

Bellinzoni, A. J. *The Sayings of Jesus in the Writings of Justin Martyr*. Leiden: Brill, 1967.

_____ , ed. *The Two-Source Hypothesis: A Critical Appraisal*. Macon GA: Mercer University Press, 1985.

Benoit, P. "The Ascension." In *Jesus and the Gospel*. Volume 1. London, 1973. (Reprinted in English from *Synoptische Studien*. Munich, 1954.)

_____ . "The Death of Judas." In *Jesus and the Gospel*. Volume 1. London, 1973.

Benoit, P., and M.-E. Boismard. *Synopse des Quatre Évangiles*. Two volumes. Paris, 1972.

Bleek, F. J. *Einleitung in das Neue Testament*. 1869. ET: *Introduction to the New Testament*. Two volumes. Edinburgh, 1876.

Bligh, John E. "The Prologue of Papias." *Theological Studies* 13 (1952): 234-40.

Bludau, A. "Die ersten Gegner der Johannesschriften." *Bib. Studien* 22/1,2 (1925) 1-230.

Boismard, M.-E. "The Two-Source Theory at an Impasse." NTS 26 (1980): 1-17.

Brown, R. E. *The Critical Meaning of the Bible.* New York, 1981.

Bruce, F. F. *The Acts of the Apostles.* Second edition. London, 1952.

——————. *Commentary on Galatians.* Exeter, 1982.

de Bruyne, Dom D. "Les plus anciens prologues latins des évangiles." *Rev. Ben.* 40 (1928): 193-214.

——————. "Prologues bibliques d'origine marcionite." *Rev. Ben.* (1907): 1-16.

Bultmann, Rudolf. *Die Geschichte der synoptischen Tradition.* 1921, ²1931. ET: *The History of the Synoptic Tradition.* Oxford, 1963.

Butler, B. C. *The Originality of St. Matthew.* Cambridge, 1951.

Cadbury, H. J. "Four Features of Lukan Style." In *Studies in Luke-Acts.* Ed. L. E. Keck and J. L. Martyn. London, 1966.

von Campenhausen, H. *The Formation of the Christian Bible.* London, 1972. ET of *Die Entstehung der christlicher Bibel.* Tübingen, 1968.

Chapman, J. *John the Presbyter.* Oxford, 1911.

——————. *Matthew, Mark, and Luke.* Ed. J. M. T. Barton. London, 1937.

——————. *Notes on the Early History of the Vulgate Gospels.* Oxford, 1908.

——————. "St. Irenaeus and the Dates of the Gospels." JTS 6 (1904-1905): 563-69.

——————. "St. Paul and the Revelation to St. Peter." *Rev. Ben.* 29 (1912): 133-47.

Conzelmann, H. *The Theology of St. Luke.* London, 1960.

Cope, O. Lamar. *Matthew: A Scribe Trained for the Kingdom of Heaven.* CBQ Monograph Series 5. Washington DC, 1976.

Corley, Bruce, ed. *Colloquy on New Testament Studies: A Time for Reappraisal and Fresh Approaches.* Macon GA: Mercer University Press, 1983.

Cranfield, C. E. B. *Romans.* Two volumes. Edinburgh, 1979.

Creed, J. M. *St. Luke.* London, 1930.

Denzinger-Schönmetzer. *Enchiridion Symbolorum Definitionum et Declarationum de rebus fidei et morum.* Freiburg: Herder, 1963.

Dibelius, Martin. *Die Formgeschichte des Evangeliums.* 1919, ²1933, ³1959. ET: *From Tradition to Gospel.* London, 1971.

Didier, M., ed. *L'Évangile selon Matthieu: Rédaction et Théologie.* Gembloux, 1972.

Dodd, C. H. "The Fall of Jerusalem and the 'Abomination of Desolation'." JRS 37 (1947): 47-54.

——————. *The Apostolic Preaching and its Developments.* London, 1936.

——————. *Historical Tradition in the Fourth Gospel.* Cambridge, 1963.

Donovan, J. *The Logia in Ancient and Recent Literature*. Cambridge: Heffer, 1924.

Drury, J. *Tradition and Design in Luke's Gospel*. London, 1976.

Dungan, D. L. *The Sayings of Jesus in the Churches of Paul*. Philadelphia: Fortress, 1971.

Dupont, J. "La Conclusion des Actes et son rapport a l'ensemble de l'ouvrage de Luc." Pages 359-404 in *Les Actes des Apôtres, tradition, rédaction, théologie*. Ed. J. Kremer. Leuven, 1979.

_____ . *The Sources of Acts*. London, 1964.

Edmundson, G. *The Church in Rome in the First Century*. London, 1913.

Eusebius, Pamphili. See below under Lawlor and Oulton.

Evans, C. F. "The Central Section of St. Luke's Gospel." Pages 37-53 in *Studies in the Gospels*. Ed. D. E. Nineham. Oxford, 1955.

Farmer, William R. *Jesus and the Gospel: Tradition, Scripture, and the Canon*. Philadelphia: Fortress Press, 1982.

_____ . *The Last Twelve Verses of Mark*. Cambridge, 1974.

_____ , ed. *New Synoptic Studies: The Cambridge Gospel Conference and Beyond*. Macon GA: Mercer University Press, 1983.

_____ . *The Synoptic Problem: A Critical Analysis*. London/New York: Macmillan, 1964; reprinted with corrections, 1976.

Farmer, William R., and Denis Farkasfalvy. *The Formation of the New Testament Canon: an Ecumenical Approach*. New York, 1983.

Farrer, Austin. "On Dispensing with Q." Pages 55-86 in *Studies in the Gospels*. Oxford, 1955.

_____ . *St. Matthew and St. Mark*. Ed. D. E. Nineham. London: Westminster Press, 1954.

Fitzmyer, J. A. *The Gospel of St. Luke*. Two volumes. New York, 1980-1985.

_____ . "The Priority of Mark and the 'Q' Source in Luke." Pages 3-40 in *To Advance the Gospel: New Testament Studies*. New York: Crossroads, 1981.

Frye, R. Mushat. "The Synoptic Problem and Analogies in Other Literatures." Pages 261-302 in *Relationships among the Gospels*. San Antonio TX: Trinity University Press, 1978.

Gamba, G. G. "La Testimonianza di S. Ireneo in Adv. Haer. III, 1, 1, e la Data di Composizione dei Quattro Vangeli Canonici." *Salesianum* 39 (1977): 545-85.

Gerhardsson, B. *Memory and Manuscript*. Uppsala, 1961.

_____ . *The Origins of the Gospel Tradition*. London: SCM Press, 1979.

Gnilka, J. *Der Philipperbrief*. Freiburg: Herder, 1980.

Goulder, M. D. *Midrash and Lection in Matthew*. London: S.P.C.K., 1974.

_____ . "On Putting Q to the Test." NTS (1978): 219-34.

Grant, Robert. "The Oldest Gospel Prologues." *Anglican Theological Review* 23 (1941): 236-43.

Grant, Robert M. *Eusebius as Church Historian*. Oxford, 1980.

Griesbach, J. J. *Commentatio*. In Orchard and Longstaff, see below.

Gundry, R. H. "The Language Milieu of First Century Palestine." JBL 83 (1964): 404ff.

——————— . *Matthew: A Commentary on His Literary and Theological Art*. Grand Rapids MI: Eerdmans, 1982.

——————— . *The Use of the Old Testament in St. Matthew's Gospel*. Suppl. Nov. *Test*. 18. Leiden: Brill, 1967.

Gutwenger, E. "The Anti-Marcionite Prologues." TS 7 (1946): 393-409.

Haenchen, E. *The Acts of the Apostles*. Oxford: Blackwell, 1971.

Hall, Stuart G. "Aloger." TRE. Berlin/New York, 1981–.

Harnack, A. "Die ältesten Evangelien prologe und die Bildung des NTs." SPAW. Phil. Hist. 24 (1928): 322-41.

Harvey, W. W. *Sancti Irenaei ep. Lugdunensis libros quinque adversus haereses*. Two volumes. Cambridge, 1857.

Hawkins, Sir John. *Horae Synopticae*. Oxford, 1909.

Heard, R. G. "The Old Latin Gospel Prologue." JTS n.s. 6 (1956): 1-16.

Hemer, C. J. "Luke the Historian." BJRL 60 (1977-78): 28-51.

Hengel, M. *Acts and the History of Earliest Christianity*. Philadelphia: Fortress Press, 1980.

——————— . "Probleme des Markusevangeliums." Pages 221-65 in *Das Evangelium und die Evangelien*. Tübingen, 1983.

Hennecke, E. *New Testament Apocrypha*. Two volumes. London: SCM Press, 1963, 1965.

Holtzmann, H. J. *Die synoptischen Evangelien*. Leipzig, 1863.

Houlden, J. L. "The Purpose of Luke." JSNT 21 (1984): 53-65.

Howard, W. F. "The Anti-Marcionite Prologues." *Expo. Times*. 47 (1935/1936): 53.

Huck, A. *Synopse der drei ersten Evangelien*. Ed. H. Greeven. Tübingen, ¹1892, ³1906, ⁶1922, ¹³1982.

Jedin, H., ed. *History of the Church*. Ten volumes. London, 1981-1985.

Jeremias, J. *Jerusalem in the Time of Jesus*. London, 1969.

Josephus, Flavius. *Works*. Eight volumes. Loeb Classical Library. London, 1926-1937.

Jourjon, M. "Papias." DBS (1960): 1104-1109.

Justin Martyr. *S. Iustini Opera*. Second edition. Ed. I. C. T. Otto. Jena, 1847.

Kaye, B. N. "To the Romans and Others." *Nov. Test*. 18/1 (1976): 37-77.

Kilpatrick, G. D. *The Origins of the Gospel according to St. Matthew*. Oxford, 1946.

Kingsbury, J. D. *Matthew: Structure, Christology, Kingdom*. London, 1976.

Körtner, Ulrich H. J. *Papias von Hierapolis*. Göttingen, 1983.

Kümmel, W. G. *Introduction to the New Testament*. London: SCM Press, 1965.

_____ . *The New Testament: A History of the Investigation of Its Problems*. Trans. S. McLean Gilmour and Howard C. Kee. Nashville TN: Abingdon Press, 1972/London: SCM Press, 1973.

Kürzinger, J. "Das Papiaszeugnis und die Erstgestalt des Matthäus Evangeliums." *Bib. Zeitschr.* n.f. (1960): 19-38

_____ . *Papias von Hierapolis und die Evangelien des N.T.* Regensburg, 1983.

Lampe, G. W. H. *A Patristic Greek Lexicon*. Oxford, 1961.

Lagrange, M. J. *Évangile selon Saint Matthieu*. Third edition. Paris, 1928.

_____ . *Histoire ancienne du Canon du Nouveau Testament*. Part one. Paris, 1933.

_____ . "Les prologues prétendus marcionites." *Rev. Ben.* 35 (1925): 161-73.

_____ . Review of de Bruyne's article on the Latin prologues. *Rev. Ben.* 40 (1928): 194-214.

Lawlor, H. J., and J. E. L. Oulton. *Eusebius, Bishop of Caesarea, Ecclesiastical History and Martyrs of Palestine*. Volume 1: translation; volume 2: introduction, notes, and index. London: S.P.C.K., 1927-1928; reprinted 1954.

Léon-Dufour, X. "Redaktionsgeschichte of Matthew and Literary Criticism." Pages 9-35 in volume 1 of *Jesus and Man's Hope*. Pittsburgh, 1970/1971.

Lightfoot, R. H. *History and Interpretation in the Gospels*. London, 1935.

Lindsay, R. L. *A Hebrew Translation of the Gospel of Mark*. Jerusalem, n.d. (1971?).

Lohmeyer, E. *Das Evangelium des Matthäus*. Ed. W. Schmauch. Göttingen, 1967.

Lonergan, B. *Method in Theology*. London, 1972.

Longstaff, T. R. W. *Evidence of Conflation in Mark: A Study in the Synoptic Problem*. SBL Dissertation Series 28. Missoula MT: Scholars Press, 1977.

Maddox, R. *The Purpose of Luke-Acts*. Edinburgh, 1982.

Mann, C. S. *Mark*. Anchor Bible 27. New York: Doubleday & Company, 1986.

Marrou, H. I. "History of Education." *Encyclopaedia Britannica*. Macropaedia Edition. 6:328a.

_____ . *A History of Education in Antiquity*. London, 1936.

Marshall, I. Howard. *The Gospel of St. Luke*. Exeter, 1978.

Martin, Ralph. *Mark, Evangelist and Theologian*. Grand Rapids MI: Zondervan, 1973.

_____ . *Philippians*. Tyndale New Testament Commentaries. Grand Rapids MI: Eerdmans, 1983.

Massaux, E. *Influence de l'Évangile de Saint Matthieu sur la littérature chrétienne avant S. Irénée*. Louvain, 1950.

Merkel. *Die Pluralität der Evangelien*. Bern, 1978.

Metzger, B. N. *The Text of the New Testament*. Oxford, 1968, ²1973.

Meyer, B. F. *The Aims of Jesus*. London, 1979.

Mosshammer, A. A. *The Chronology of Eusebius and Greek Chronological Tradition*. Lewisburg PA: Bucknell University Press, 1979.

Moule, C. F. D. *The Birth of the New Testament*. Second edition. London, 1981.

Munck, Johannes. *The Acts of the Apostles*. Revised by W. F. Albright and C. S. Mann. Anchor Bible 31. New York: Doubleday & Company, 1967.

Mussies, Gerard. "Greek as the Vehicle of Early Christianity." NTS 29/3 (1983): 356-69.

Mussner, F. "The Historical Jesus and the Christ of Faith." In *Dogmatic v. Biblical Theology*. Ed. H. Vorgrimler. London, 1964. ET of *Exégèse und Dogmatik*. Mainz, 1962.

Neirynck, F. *Duality in Mark*. Leuven, 1972.

————— . *Minor Agreements of Matthew and Luke against Mark*. Leuven, 1974.

Nineham, D. E. *Saint Mark*. London: Penguin Books, 1963.

————— , ed. *Studies in the Gospels*. Oxford, 1955.

Orchard, J. B., gen. ed. *A Catholic Commentary on Holy Scripture*. London, 1953.

————— . "The 'Common Step' Phenomenon in the Synoptic Pericopes." Pages 393-407 in *New Gospel Studies: The Cambridge Gospel Conference and Beyond*. Ed. William R. Farmer. Macon GA: Mercer University Press, 1983.

————— . "Ellipsis and Parenthesis in Gal 2:1-10 and 2 Thess 2:1-12." In *Paul de Tarse: Apôtre de notre temps*. Rome, 1979.

————— . "The Ellipsis between Gal 2:3 and 2:4." *Biblica* 54 (1973): 469-81.

————— . "J. A. T. Robinson and the Synoptic Problem." NTS 22 (1976): 346-52.

————— . *Matthew, Luke, and Mark*. Greater Manchester: Koinonia Press, 1976.

————— . "Once Again, the Ellipsis between Gal 2:3 and 2:4." *Biblica* 57 (1976): 254-55.

————— . "The Problem of Acts and Galatians." CBQ (1945): 377-97.

————— . "Some Guidelines for the Interpretation of Eusebius's Hist. Eccl. III 34-39." Pages 393-403 in volume 2 of *The New Testament Age: Essays in Honor of Bo Reicke*. Two volumes. Ed. William C. Weinrich. Macon GA: Mercer University Press, 1984.

————— . *Synopsis of the Four Gospels Arranged according to the Two-Gospel Hypothesis*. Macon GA: Mercer University Press/Edinburgh: T. & T. Clark, 1982.

————— . *Synopsis of the Four Gospels in Greek*. Edinburgh: T. & T. Clark/Macon GA: Mercer University Press, 1983.

————— . "Thessalonians and the Synoptic Gospels." *Biblica* 19 (1938): 19-42.

Orchard, J. B., and T. R. W. Longstaff, eds. *J. J. Griesbach: Synoptic and Textcritical Studies, 1776-1976.* Cambridge, 1979.

Owen, Henry. *Observations on the Four Gospels.* London, 1764.

Peabody, David. "Augustine and 'the Augustinian Hypothesis'." Pages 37-64 in *New Synoptic Studies: The Cambridge Gospel Conference and Beyond.* Ed. William R. Farmer. Macon GA: Mercer University Press, 1983.

_____ . *Mark as Composer.* Macon GA: Mercer University Press, 1987.

Perrin, N. *What Is Redaction Criticism?* London: S.P.C.K., 1970.

des Places, E. *Eusèbe de Césarée commentateur.* Paris, 1982.

Powell, Enoch. "The Archaeology of Matthew." Chapter 18 in *Wrestling with the Angel.* London: Sheldon Press, 1977.

Quasten, J. *Patrology.* Three volumes. Utrecht-Antwerp: Speculum, 1966.

Rawlinson, A. E. J. *St. Mark.* London, 1925.

Regul, J. *Die Antimarcionitischen Evangelienprologe.* Vetus Latina Series. Freiburg: Herder, 1969.

Reicke, Bo. *The New Testament Era.* London: A. & C. Black, 1974.

_____ . "Synoptic Prophecies on the Destruction of Jerusalem." Pages 121-34 in *Studies in N.T. and Early Christian Literature: Essays in Honor of Allen P. Wikgren.* Ed. D. W. Aune. *Nov. Test. Suppl.* 33. Leiden: Brill, 1972.

Riesner, Rainer. *Jesus als Lehrer.* Tübingen, 1981.

Rigaux, B. *Épitres aux Thessaloniciens.* Paris, 1956.

Rist, J. M. *On the Independence of Matthew and Mark.* Cambridge, 1978.

Robinson, John A. T. *Redating the New Testament.* London, 1975.

Rordorf, W., and A. Tuilier. *La Doctrine des Apôtres (Didache).* Sources Chrétiennes 248. Paris, 1978.

Sanders, E. P. *The Tendencies of Synoptic Criticism.* Cambridge, 1969.

Schneemelcher, W. "Canon Muratori." TRE. 1976–.

Sherwin-White, A. N. *Roman Society and Roman Law in the New Testament.* Oxford, 1963.

Shuler, P. *A Genre for the Gospels.* Philadelphia: Fortress Press, 1982.

Siegert, Folker. "Unbeachtete Papiaszitate bei Armenischen Schriftstellern." NTS 27: 605-14.

Standaert, B. *Évangile selon Marc. Composition et Genre littéraire.* Nijmegen, 1974.

Stendahl, Krister. "Commentary on Matthew." Section 673c in *Peake's Commentary.* Sixth edition. London, 1962.

Stoldt, H.-H. *History and Criticism of the Markan Hypothesis.* Macon GA: Mercer University Press/Edinburgh: T. & T. Clark, 1982.

Streeter, B. H. *The Four Gospels.* London, 1924.

Stuhlmacher, Peter, ed. *Das Evangelium und die Evangelien.* Tübingen, 1983.

Sundberg, Albert C., Jr. "Canon Muratori: A Fourth Century List." HTR 66 (1973): 1-41.

Sutcliffe, E. F. "The Replies of the Biblical Commission." Sections 47-53 in *A Catholic Commentary on Holy Scripture*. Edinburgh, 1953.

Styler, G. M. Excursus 4, pages 285-316, in C. F. D. Moule's *The Birth of the New Testament*. London, ²1981.

Tarazi, P. N. *I Thessalonians*. New York, 1982.

Taylor, R. O. P. *The Groundwork of the Gospels*. Oxford, 1946.

Taylor, Vincent. *The Formation of the Gospel Tradition*. London, 1933.

——————. *The Gospel according to St. Mark*. London, 1963.

Tillard, J. M. R. *The Bishop of Rome*. London: S.P.C.K., 1983.

Trocmé, E. *Formation of the Gospel according to Mark*. London, 1963.

Tuckett, C. M. "On the Relationship between Mt and Mk." NTS 30: 130-42.

——————. *The Revival of the Griesbach Hypothesis*. Cambridge, 1983.

——————, ed. *Synoptic Studies: The Ampleforth Conferences of 1982/3*. JSNTS Suppl. Series 7. Sheffield: JSOT Press, 1984.

Turner, C. H. "Commentary on the Gospel of St. Mark." In Bishop Gore's *A New Commentary on Holy Scripture*. London, 1928.

Turner, E. G. *Greek Papyri: An Introduction*. Revised edition. Oxford, 1980.

Tyson, J. B. "Parallelism in the Synoptic Gospels." NTS (April 1976): 276-308.

van Unnik, W. C. "Luke's Second Book and the Rules of Hellenistic Historiography." Pages 37-60 in *Les Acts des Apôtres: Tradition, rédaction, théologie*. Ed. J. Kremer. Leuven, 1979.

Walker, W. O., Jr., ed. *The Relationships among the Gospels*. San Antonio TX: Trinity University Press, 1978.

Williamson, G. *Eusebius: History of the Church*. London: Penguin Classics, 1967.

Wordsworth, J., and H. J. White. *Novum Testamentum DNJC. Latine secundum editionem S. Hieronymi*. Three volumes. Oxford, 1889-1954.

Yarbrough, D. M. "The Date of Papias for Reassessment." *Journal of the Evangelical Theological Society* 26/2 (1983): 181-91.

Indexes

Index of Subjects

(See also the analytical table of contents.)

Index of Ancient Authors and Churchmen

Index of Modern Authors

(See also the bibliography, 281-88.)

Index of Place Names

Index of Scripture References

(Only passages quoted in full are included.)
(See also the analytical table of contents.)